THE SINGLE REALITY

THE
SINGLE REALITY

Preston Harold
Author of *The Shining Stranger*

Winifred Babcock
Author of *The Palestinian Mystery Play*

Introduction and Summary by Oliver L. Reiser
Preface for the Physical Scientist by Robert M. L. Baker, Jr.

A HAROLD INSTITUTE BOOK

DISTRIBUTED BY DODD, MEAD & COMPANY

NEW YORK

DODD, MEAD & COMPANY, New York and Toronto, distributes the books of
Preston Harold to the trade. Bookstores may order from:

Dodd, Mead & Co., Inc.
79 Madison Avenue
New York, New York 10016

Individuals may order Harold's books from HAROLD INSTITUTE if local bookstores do not stock them. Send order and check to:

Harold Institute
P. O. Box 11024
Winston-Salem, North Carolina 27106

The following Harold books are available:

THE SHINING STRANGER by Preston Harold, Introduction by Gerald Heard
  Hardcover: $7.50 plus 50¢ mailing charges
  Paperback: $1.95 plus 50¢ mailing charges

A SYNOPSIS OF THE SHINING STRANGER by Winifred Babcock
  Pamphlet — 40 pages. Single copy: $1.00 postpaid
                       Four or more copies: 50¢ each postpaid

THE SINGLE REALITY by Preston Harold and Winifred Babcock
  Introduction and Summary by Oliver L. Reiser
  Preface for the Physical Scientist by Robert M. L. Baker, Jr.
  Hardcover: $7.95 plus 50¢ mailing charges

THE PALESTINIAN MYSTERY PLAY by Winifred Babcock*
  Introduction by Oliver L. Reiser
  Preface by Robert M. L. Baker, Jr.
  Paperback: $2.95 plus 50¢ mailing charges

*THE PALESTINIAN MYSTERY PLAY also appears as Book I of THE SINGLE
REALITY

ISBN 0-396-06206-7
Library of Congress Catalog Card Number: 71-121985
Printed in the United States of America
by Vail-Ballou Press, Inc., Binghamton, N.Y.

Contents

PREFACE FOR
THE PHYSICAL SCIENTIST

by Robert M. L. Baker, Jr.

This treatise is not a textbook for the nuclear physicist—it does, however, introduce us to a philosophy of science that is couched in terms that are familiar to the layman. The translation of hard science, expressed explicitly and succinctly in mathematical terms, into pseudoscientific yet familiar terms, is always fraught with difficulties, and when this situation is combined with the development of a new scientific philosophy the difficulties are compounded. But are these difficulties important? I think not. The physicist can find ample opportunity to nit-pick, but if he understands the physical processes described in this work well enough to criticize, then perhaps he is seeking the wrong areas of the book from which to draw new information. The appropriate audience would be those who find sentences such as in the following quotations either illuminating or appealing:

> Gravity is the "socializing" force for the Cosmos, which creates cities of light—our solar system and galactic systems. But measure the distance between "dancing twin stars" and you will find that they are not "cheek to cheek." The dancing is much more modern—there is sufficient distance between them so that each star can "do its own thing."

If such phraseology disturbs you, then proceed with caution through the text.

Having dispensed with these preliminaries and sufficiently admonished the strict scientists, let us turn to one of the central themes of the book—the physical interpretation of the philosophy of "Harold." Allow me to again quote a passage from the text and then elaborate on its meaning to me—an important meaning in my view.

> This measure of progress cannot be undone, any more than the measure of entropy can be decreased. The measure of progress (syntropy) can only increase, in a universe now able to support life, toward the

3

optimum state which will allow for the everlasting operation of the system in a way that it can support life more abundantly.

Essentially, I view the philosophy of "Harold" as a description of the gradual evolution of the Universe from its absolutely inanimate physical conception to its absolutely animate biological conclusion. As the measure of physical disorder, entropy, inexorably increases, so also the measure of biological orderliness and sophistication ("syntropy") increases. The physical universe subsides in relevance while the "life" aspects of the Cosmos abound ever more fully, finally becoming the exclusive characterization of the Universe. The fascination of this process lies in the fact that the "life" aspects of the Universe must rely upon purely physical processes for their support and development. This suggests that this physical-principle cradle of "life" (i.e., the laws governing physical processes) may itself exhibit characteristics that are ordinarily attributed exclusively to life forms, e.g., love, hate, affection, etc. It is a bit far out, but some rather convincing arguments are included in this book.

I cannot say that I embrace some of the concepts in particle physics, such as those which lead to the steady-state energy creation process in our Sun. On the other hand, the sign/symbol particles seem to be an interesting concept—but here the particle physicist must not be too demanding for a mathematically elegant and rigorous theory. Basically what one will receive is a taste of something new. Although the ultimate or fundamental particle (possibly the neutrino) is indivisible, the Harold theory, as translated and related in beautiful language by Winifred Babcock, suggests that it can exhibit an internal "structure." This structure can be characterized by a sign symbology, e.g., $(+ - + - +)$, that does not really imply $(-)$ or $(+)$ "particles" but rather indicates the concept of identification and/or "strength" or "value" of a particular particle. Based upon such a symbology a number of theories can be developed—some seem reasonable, others seem not to conform totally to our current understanding of the physical world.

One of the difficulties faced by the physical scientist who reads this book is the reference to new particles, forces, fields, etc., that bear rather exotic names, such as Psychon, Logon, and Q-force. A glossary aids in comprehending these terms, but basically it should be recognized that one never truly "understands" a concept as described by a given vocabulary, one only becomes so familiar with the concept and its descriptions that a feeling of understanding manifests itself. Consider the concept of gravity. Most people (not necessarily scientists) would indicate that they

4

"understand" gravity, but do we really know in detail why our furniture and ourselves are pulled tightly down to the floor of our office? Thus the scientist-reader should remain open-minded and search patiently for a familiarity with the nomenclature involved in Winifred Babcock's exposition of Preston Harold's philosophy of science. In my view, if the book succeeds in arousing the curiosity of only a small number of serious students of philosophy, it will have been a success.

Robert M. L. Baker, Jr.

* * * * *

Dr. Baker is a thirty-eight year old scientist who received his B.A. with highest honors in Physics and Mathematics at UCLA in 1954 and was elected to Phi Beta Kappa. In 1956 he was granted an M.A. in Physics and was the recipient of the UCLA Physics Prize. In 1958 Mr. Baker received a Ph.D. in Engineering, which was the first of its kind to be granted in the nation with a specialty in Astronautics.

With respect to his academic background, Dr. Baker was on the faculty of the Department of Astronomy at UCLA from 1959 to 1963. Since that time he has been on the faculty of the Department of Engineering at UCLA, where he currently offers courses in astronautics, fluid mechanics, and structural mechanics. He is a trustee of West Coast University.

Dr. Baker is an internationally recognized expert in various fields of science and engineering. He was a research contributor to the development of preliminary orbit determination procedures utilizing radar data, astrodynamic constants, near free-molecular flow drag—all utilized in the nation's space programs. He has also developed unique theories in the area of hydrofoil marine-craft design.

In private industry Dr. Baker has initiated, supervised, and conducted research programs in astronautics, physics, fluid mechanics, mathematics, and computer program design. He has contributed to problem definition and analysis of scientific and engineering problems in both industrial and military projects.

Dr. Baker has been the editor of the *Journal of the Astronautical Sciences* since 1963. He was the joint editor of the *Proceedings* of the 1961 International Astronautical Federation Congress and the senior author of the first textbook on astrodynamics: *An Introduction to Astrodynamics*, published in 1960. Dr. Baker is the author of four books and over seventy technical papers.

5

INTRODUCTION

by Oliver L. Reiser

By this time it is abundantly clear that Preston Harold's relentless efforts at synthesis represent his impressive contribution to the reconciliation and integration of scientific and religious motivations, attitudes, and achievements. His deep and sustained research toward this end is one of the great monuments to the spirit of man. The earlier book, *The Shining Stranger*, in its published form, did not develop at any length the "cross-action" hypothesis, for the reasons given by Winifred Babcock in her Prologue. Accordingly, while there have been numerous reactions to *The Shining Stranger*, the response to the concepts presented in *The Single Reality* is yet to come. It will be of special interest to observe the responses of the scientists to Harold's unique and mind-stretching synthesis. A verdict relative to its merits as a comprehensive philosophy of science must await the study and assimilation of its doctrines.

With the publication of *The Single Reality*, Harold's philosophy as a systematic whole is now before us. In the two volumes just referred to, it is available in the author's own words. In addition, the components of this synthesis have been set forth and at times interpreted by Winifred Babcock as she recalls as best she can the contents of documents that no longer are available. It is now the obligation of scholars in all disciplines and areas of endeavor to study this material and evaluate it for whatever they judge it may be worth.

The first book has already made its way into the world. But what will be the fate of the even more controversial book, *The Single Reality*? We must await the verdict, whatever it may be. The jury is not even "out," since the evidence only now is "in."

My response to the challenge of this unique and novel philosophy of religion and science is that—beyond all doubt—it is worthy of concentrated and prolonged study. This clearly does not mean that the reader must agree with all, or even most, of what is set forth. For, as Gerald

9

Heard has pointed out, one must only believe that it has sufficient merit to warrant publication and serious study. The validity of that judgment, I take it, is beyond question.

As he proceeds, the reader will notice that, here and there, the terminology of Mrs. Babcock's interpretations is couched in the language of *Cosmic Humanism*. This is an expression of Mrs. Babcock's desire to link up with other similar integrative efforts in the field of contemporary thought. Of course, this concern also harmonizes with Preston Harold's desire for a spiritual unity of mankind based on firm scientific foundations.

As part of the strategy for gaining a "fair trial" for our absent and unknown author, I now beg leave to offer several suggestions to the reader.

In the first place, it is to be hoped that the reader will make a deliberate effort to divest himself of his preconceptions—or at least keep them in the background—while he studies this work *in its own terms and on its own merits*. This desideratum is important because of the highly original and unorthodox nature of Harold's ideas. Among such preconceptions (prejudices) is the notion, widely held by scientists and philosophers, that one simply must not be guilty of the fallacy of anthropomorphism— the "pathetic fallacy," as G. E. Moore termed it—that is, the projection of human traits, such as "feelings" and "ideas," into the phenomena of objective nature. For example, in Mrs. Babcock's exposition (Book II, Section III), Harold is presented as affirming that "There is no way to describe a neutrino except in terms of 'love'. . . ." To the positivists, this language is anathema. But, in defense of such language usage, it must be remembered that Harold's philosophy posits that the universe is a living system with a flow of energy that courses through it (the Q-force) much as blood does through the living body.

Whether this combination of words is legitimate depends on one's philosophy. Such eminent scientists and philosophers as Alfred North Whitehead and Henri Bergson have advanced similar views and adopted analogous language. And Fechner's panpsychistic notions still have followers and advocates among reputable thinkers.

In the case of Harold, the justification for this "anthropomorphism" is provided in the hypothesis of cross-action. In Chapter 9 of *The Shining Stranger* (especially Section III), Harold finds his justification for this in the "cross-action" between the two forces of electricity and magnetism. Harold intimates that Jesus realized something of the nature of electromagnetic phenomena and "left as His symbol the cross, the configuration that revealed the electromagnetic fields of space." This sentence is of key significance in the understanding of Harold's philosophy.

If the reader becomes a bit squeamish about the eerie audacity of Harold's thinking, perhaps it may reassure him to be reminded of the following episode. The story as told by Freeman Dyson[1] is as follows:

> A few months ago, Werner Heisenberg and Wolfgang Pauli believed that they had made an essential step forward in the direction of a theory of elementary particles. Pauli happened to be passing through New York, and he was prevailed upon to give a lecture explaining the new ideas to an audience which included Niels Bohr. Pauli spoke for an hour, and then there was a general discussion during which he was criticized rather sharply by the younger generation. Finally, Bohr was called on to make a speech summing up the argument. "We are all agreed," he said, "that your theory is crazy. The question which divides us is whether it is crazy enough to have a chance of being correct. My own feeling is that it is not crazy enough."

Now my question: If "sober" physical scientists feel the need for "crazy" ideas, why should our modern philosophers be so far behind? And why not let *The Shining Stranger* show the "way," if it can?

My second suggestion also relates to attitude. The point is made quite clear by Mrs. Babcock: Harold's ideas are not to be taken as the "gospel truth" of a "new revelation," aspiring to the eventual status of a new orthodoxy. Harold's philosophy is capable of further developments, and finality is not claimed or expected. For Mrs. Babcock, some of the new applications will come in the field of an emerging Cosmic Humanism, and she has provided an example of this, as will appear in a moment. My own loyalty to Harold's hypotheses is sufficiently elastic to allow for further extrapolations, one of which will be linked to Mrs. Babcock's proposal just referred to. This fact, that Harold's "system" is capable of novel applications, is what makes it possible for Mrs. Babcock and myself—and others are invited to join in—to work out ideas like the following interpretation.

The extrapolation just mentioned is the development of the concept of the "Helium-Psychosphere" as a proliferation of Harold's synthesis. In a forthcoming book the suggestion will be developed at some length that the helium layer surrounding the earth and other celestial bodies (a diagram of this is presented in *Cosmic Humanism*, page 434) can and does serve as a Psi-field or Psychosphere for the emerging "World Sensorium," *so that human consciousness is a product of a bipolar interaction or circuitry—a kind of celestial cybernetic feedback—between man's nervous system and the pulsing Psi-field or plasma.* This, incidentally, is another example of the "divine materialism" of the Play.

1. See page 351 for references.

Strange to say, I have recently discovered that Mr. A. A. Cochran has advanced a theory which, in part, overlaps my own picture of the man-Cosmos resonance.[2] Mr. Cochran has put forth the view that the elements hydrogen and oxygen have *life* and *mind* properties (for reasons that he states in his articles), so that quantum mechanics may contain the solution to the time-honored "mind-body problem" that has plagued philosophy, religion, and science since the time of Pythagoras, Plato, St. Paul, and others.

On discovering this parallelism in our thinking, I inquired of Mr. Cochran whether helium at low temperature (supercooled) can be a superdispersive plasma; whether the helium shell that surrounds the earth could satisfy the conditions for a superfluid, such as helium II, in a space environment? If the answer is "yes" to both questions, this would make possible the "psychon" phenomenon that Mrs. Babcock mentions, as well as the simultaneous transmission of longitudinal and transverse wave trains; not to mention other remarkable interactions that we need for the Sensorium "syntropy" and "resonance." Specifically, the question is this: Can the helium layer around the earth (helium II, if it is a superfluid) serve as a plasma medium and thus provide a circumglobal Psychosphere, somewhat comparable to the "pulsing ionosphere" of Mr. Sleeper (see *C. H.*, pp. 571-573), only higher up in the "heavens" and with more remarkable properties than the ionosphere?

The reply from Mr. Cochran was comforting. He states that he knows of no empirical evidence against my hypothesis, and indeed he has made some suggestions that will be helpful in the further development of this conception. The full story will be told in a subsequent volume, now in preparation.

But Mrs. Babcock's restless and inquiring mind seized upon this as possibly related to Harold's "cross-action" formula. Let me quote from her recent letter:

> I was thrilled to learn that helium has such strange properties when supercooled, especially the properties of life and consciousness. I always wondered why Harold stopped his "construction" of elements at helium, and I suppose because once such properties are exhibited under any conditions, the condition for life is there. He says that all elements are constructed of various arrangements of four types of "cores"—the four types of decay indicating this.
>
> Could it be that mental energy *acts upon helium to supercool it?* And if helium II can be associated with longitudinal and transverse wave propagations together, isn't this the beginning of "cross-action"?
>
> It is all so intriguing. It is as though the secret of everything is hanging

on these ideas like a drop of water about to fall, but they don't cohere sufficiently to drop in one's mind in a conveyable way.

The observant reader will notice the similarity of this statement with the corresponding paragraphs in Mrs. Babcock's *If Thine Eye Be Single*, Book II, Section IX. Since the interconnections between the latter paragraphs and the present text paragraphs are important and the latter so beautifully expressed, I quote the passage:

> Oliver Reiser seeks the Psi-belt that surrounds the planet and provides a psychosphere for the Celestial Child. We suggest that the logos of the planet is where we find the logos of the cell—in the nucleus. In the case of earth, this would be in its liquid core. Here, there may well be a fluid with the properties of a superdispersive medium wherein new types of field influences occur. As the neutrinos move readily through the earth, so thought waves may also. Their approach to our planetary center may create the wave patterns that spread outward involving all the layers of the earth's cover, finishing in the outermost reach of earth's magnetic field into a Psi-belt of thought.
>
> In the interior of the planet, the effect of the Q-force is reduced to virtually nothing; here, magnetic energy and its force or guidelines predominate. The mental wave trains that are propagated in this subfield may set in motion the plasma of neutrino energy at rest, which permeates our environment, providing the oscillating source that causes mental light to arise in the outermost magnetic field—or even the gravitational field that the Q-force determines. The psychosphere of the planet would then be a pattern that follows the structure of the Cosmon. Recent Mariner missions to Mars appear to indicate that the earth may be unique among the planets, both in its magnetic field and in the presence of life. In consequence, it may well be that the two are related in some fashion.[3]

This is well stated, and I cannot improve upon Mrs. Babcock's paraphrase of my thoughts. I trust that Preston Harold, wherever he is, is saying the same thing. Meantime, I would add the following as a postscript—and here I am employing some of the language of Dane Rudhyar: "Before his birth the human embryo swims in the intra-uterine amniotic sac which is his closed sea environment; and after birth he finds himself being incited by and growing into a circumglobal environment—the 'auric plasma'—which eventually will create the 'soul field' of mankind" (from a personal communication).

It is precisely because any ingenious student can indulge in similar thought experiments that Harold's synthesis generates excitement about the new findings of the "knowledge explosion" in all areas of science and religion and the arts. This is why Harold's "unfinished symphony" is captivating. If such imaginative proliferations were to be interdicted, then I, for one, would be compelled to leave the Play and the theater with: "Thank you, but this is not for me!" But such a catastrophic denouement is not in the script. *The Palestinian Mystery Play* is still open-ended. Let us see what happens.

But first, because there will be many references to Cosmic Humanism as the Play unfolds, a word about what Cosmic Humanism is will clarify the concept for the reader.

Cosmic Humanism is the name we give to man's ongoing search for truth. By the word *Cosmic* we indicate immediately that our search for truth must range from nuclear physics to biochemistry, involving all the natural sciences. By the word *Humanism* we indicate that we must also search for truth through the whole range of life sciences, history, psychology, the arts, and the religious expressions of mankind.

In the sense that man's hunger for truth is fundamentally a religious motivation and that essentially his religion is a synthesis of man's beliefs as tested in experience, Cosmic Humanism takes its place as the coming religion of humankind. As a world-view it is committed to the task of synthesizing all that mankind discovers about himself and nature in the hope of producing a secure and universal community of belief, because it is based upon firm scientific foundations *and* a more complete understanding of all that man has experienced in dealing with his own psyche. Community of belief in fundamental principles neither necessitates nor invites uniformity at the expense of individuality and diversity in the cultural forms and structures of society.

Cosmic Humanism seeks to provide the framework within which scientific investigation of nature and the psyche of man can proceed in harmony with religious expression to lead man nearer to an understanding of his own being and of his Cosmic environment.

There is presently at hand sufficient evidence to allow us to transcend both the nihilism of materialistic philosophy and the fragmented exclusiveness of the world's authoritarian religions. From the higher plateau of consciousness man has already reached, new vistas, scientific and psychological, open up. This panorama now invites us to affirm:

1) the ability of the evolving universe to support life unendingly;
2) the uniqueness of man in the biological kingdom; the spiritual unity of mankind; man's ability to surmount problems;
3) the ongoing life of the individual, through the process of purposeful evolution to grow into a complete consciousness—evolution's goal.

The search for synthesis must be inward into the psyche of man, and outward—from elementary particles to the furthest reaches of Cosmic space that technology and the mind of Homo sapiens can reach. Action on the social scene will reflect what man believes about himself, the universe, and his place in it. An enhanced and ennobled image of man will lead to an age of peace on earth, respect for every human being, and the development of a society conducive to the development of the human potential. A cosmology that affirms the creative principle inherent in universal operation will lead to a release of the creative capacities in man.

Toward this end, Cosmic Humanism focuses on the following interrelated areas and objectives:

(a) the study of the methods and the goals for the conscious control of human evolution: biological, psychological, spiritual;

(b) the formulation of subjective plans for "consciousness expansion" toward inner freedom and authority;

(c) the discovery of the laws of harmonic union to interrelate man and the Cosmos and provide a basis for communication between human beings and intelligent creatures in other, extraterrestrial systems;

(d) the development of programing for a global communications satellite system (Project Prometheus-Krishna) as part of the maturation of the emerging planetary civilization.

These objectives call for the *integration of all human knowledge* for the purpose of learning how to convert the "power of resonant thought" into vehicle and guiding field for the embryogenesis of the Noosphere (World Sensorium).

Of highest priority and first step toward educational television by global communication satellites is the establishment of workshops for the training in techniques for teaching by television—a crash program of war on ignorance, illiteracy, disease, poverty and hunger, prejudices, overpopulation, environmental pollution, and crime and delinquency. World-level wisdom is the goal of Cosmic Humanism.

And, now, as the dramatist-producer puts it: *Let the Play begin!*

*　*　*　*　*

Oliver L. Reiser has published numerous books on his "philosophical journey" which culminates momentarily in *Cosmic Humanism*. Albert Einstein, referring to *World Philosophy: A Search for Synthesis*, comments that Reiser "has overcome, without sacrificing his intellectual integrity, the paralyzing relativism that so many clear thinkers of our times feel themselves forced to accept." John Dewey described Reiser's earlier *Philosophy and the Concepts of Modern Science* as "comprehensive and vital." The *Annals of the American Academy* refers to this book as "the most promising guide out of our present world of chaos and confusion."

The *Journal of Philosophy* reviewed *New Earth and New Humanity* as presenting "ideas needed for the creation of a better world." *Fortune* summarized that "an extraordinary work, *The Integration of Human Knowledge*, . . . is an impressive internally consistent work." And *Time* Magazine called Reiser's *The Promise of Scientific Humanism* "lucid, ambitious, and profound."

Dr. Reiser was formerly chairman of the Philosophy Department of the University of Pittsburgh. Upon the occasion of his becoming Professor Emeritus, the A. W. Mellon Educational and Charitable Trust awarded him a fellowship for his next major undertaking, the research and writing of a book entitled *Magnetic Moments in Human History*.

Dr. Reiser is presently chairman of The Committee for Cosmic Humanism.

BOOK ONE

THE
PALESTINIAN MYSTERY PLAY

by Winifred Babcock

ACT ONE

Setting the Stage for *The Shining Stranger*

Prologue

Preston Harold is a pen name. No one connected with publishing the Harold papers knows who or what the author was. We were informed that he is deceased, and we are confident that his identity can never be made known. Extraordinary precautions were taken to insure this. In accordance with the unknown author's instructions, all copies of his manuscripts have been destroyed in order to maintain his anonymity.

The new answer to the mystery of man, the mystery of Jesus, presented in *The Palestinian Mystery Play* is drawn from *The Shining Stranger*, by Preston Harold, with introduction by Gerald Heard,[4] and from Harold's hypothesis, *On the Nature of Universal Cross-Action*, which is being published as a part of this book, *The Single Reality*.

Although Gerald Heard sponsored *The Shining Stranger*, he did not commit himself to Harold's hypothesis regarding universal cross-action. Nor did he reject it. He did not feel himself sufficiently competent in physics to evaluate this work. Therefore, it was determined to publish it separately.

Harold's hypothesis was originally intended to be included with *The Shining Stranger*, and the whole volume was to be given the title *The Single Reality*, using the pen name of Mason M. Taylor for the unknown author. Difficulties arose. The book was too long, even after many passages that we felt to be essential to understanding the material were omitted. A few copies of the chapter dealing with the hypothesis on universal cross-action were printed and privately circulated to see what the reaction would be. It became apparent that both works would suffer if they were combined, and we concluded that they should be handled separately. A new pen name for the author was chosen, and the title for the first volume of his work was changed from *The Single Reality* to *The Shining Stranger*.

Much material was cut to reduce the original manuscript to manageable size. More was deleted when the two works were separated. I regretted the omission of a single sentence. As I typed and retyped the manuscript, certain passages to be struck impressed me deeply. I have drawn upon my memory to reconstitute them as best I can. It is difficult to separate what I remember of Harold's own words and my interpolations and interpretations. Because of this, we are coauthors of *The Single Reality*, which is more or less a paraphrasing of his published and unpublished work, except for Book III, *On the Nature of Universal Cross-Action*, in which the author speaks for himself, detailing his hypothesis.

Part of my job was to check the 1,241 references Harold gave to document his statements in *The Shining Stranger*. As Henry Miller commented, "the author's erudition is formidable. But anyone eager to get his 'message' will be able to read between the lines. . . ."[5]

I have read the lines many times and have also tried to read between the lines to capture the essence of the monumental synthesis Harold drew, bringing into harmonious relationship the religions of the world, the sciences, and psychology, the arts, and economy of humankind.

On the Nature of Universal Cross-Action is a hypothesis dealing with the constitution of elementary particles and the way energy communicates its forces. The hypothesis is a synthesis of astronomy and nuclear physics that provides a comprehensive theory of the living universe in which the wave-particle theory of light (a synthesis of the opposing theories) operates. The five major cosmogonies are synthesized and transcended to produce a cosmology that lifts science from the *cul de sac* of nihilism and affirms the never-ending ability of the Cosmos to engender and support life.

There is nothing mystical about Harold's work, but he left no mathematical formulas. This has been of great concern because physicists speak and listen only in mathematical terms. Mathematics is a shorthand, a concise method of presenting concepts that have the quality of encouraging the flow of logical thought. But words also have this quality, and they have the advantage of being understood by the mathematically uninitiated. Words, too, pose exquisite equations, as poetry does. I am neither physicist nor mathematician, but I fell in love with the subject as I read the books Harold draws upon. They made me so anxious to know more about every branch of physics that I can express my feelings only in the words of Oscar Wilde: "The anxiety is unbearable, and I hope it lasts forever."[6] Then a line from Harold's material, now lost in its original form, came to mind—anxiety attenuates and is recast as *interest*. He was referring to the evolution of consciousness as a process through which the destructive potential in life is reorganized in time and converts to something of value.

Regardless of the response accorded Harold's work by the scientific world, I believe it has great value because of his ability to create interest in science, and his approach to it helps to bridge the "two cultures" that now stand divided.

Of equal importance is Harold's synthesis of religions, which provides a basis for true reconciliation and unity among them—although the integrity and individual approach of each is supported. He centers attention upon Judaism and Christianity, seeing the reconciliation of these Western religions as the necessary prelude to a harmonious relationship between the religions of the world.

Harold uses the King James Authorized Version of The Holy Bible, and James Moffatt's new translation of The Bible. At no time did he mention The Apocryphal New Testament, but I do, calling upon the Gospel of Thomas as Jesus' childhood is discussed.

I might say here that although Harold's view of Jesus is anything but traditional, he followed the tradition of capitalizing pronouns referring to Jesus. He also did this in referring to each of the world's great religious figures. My preference is to use lower case for pronouns referring to Jesus and other such figures. I trust that this will not detract from the text, since when quoting Harold I follow his practice of capitalizing pronouns.

I would like to say also that there are sections where one "blanket" reference is given at the beginning, since so many quotations are made that to list them individually would prove distracting to the reader. There are other passages where no reference is given, because references would detract from the dramatic effect I hope to create. In these cases placement of the text indicates that the passage is drawn from *The Shining Stranger*, which in *The Palestinian Mystery Play* takes the role of *The Stranger*.

Questions and comments from the "audience" are enclosed in quotation marks to indicate dialogue, and the spacing indicates "who" is speaking. Having called attention to these liberties I have taken, I will return to Harold.

To Harold, depth and growth psychology, operating in complementary fashion with a philosophy as expansive and penetrating as Oliver Reiser's, will provide the framework within which scientific investigation and religious expression can proceed in harmony to lead man nearer to the truth of his own being and that of his universal environment. Harold's ideas of depth and growth psychology will be dealt with in another book, *The Inner Messiah*, to be published soon.

Cosmic Humanism by Oliver L. Reiser[7] was not published during Harold's lifetime. But knowing the work of both authors as well as I do, I feel confident that had Harold lived to read this book and Dr. Reiser's subsequent writings, he would have been as appreciative of Dr. Reiser's work as Dr. Reiser has been of his. I am grateful to Dr. Reiser for his Introduction and Summary. I am indebted to him also for the title, "The Palestinian Mystery Play," which he suggested that I write with a view to incorporating it as a chapter in his forthcoming *Magnetic Moments in Human History*. But the Play grew to book length in itself, and so it is being published separately.

In my contribution to *The Single Reality*, I have tried tentatively to unite the thought of Reiser and Harold, because each man's philosophy is Cosmic in dimension and to me many of their ideas are complementary. I would like to point out, however, that it is not necessary to accept Harold's philosophy as a prerequisite to subscribing to Cosmic Humanism, which is on the forefront of time and stands in its own right as a philosophy seeking new dimensions to accommodate the evolving consciousness of mankind.

I must also point out that Harold did not once use the word *humanism*. He may have refrained because the word is associated with atheism and "heartless" scientism, to which he, most certainly, did not subscribe. But today there are religious humanists who seek only to transcend outgrown theologies, as Harold did. And in Cosmic Humanism I see a modern translation of "God is love." I have associated Harold's work with religious humanism. But like Reiser's, it, too, stands in its own right as a philosophy that adds dimension to science and religion.

I am also deeply grateful to Dr. Robert M. L. Baker, Jr., for writing the Preface for the Physical Scientist and for the suggestions he has given me to improve my part of this book. To have a physicist of his reputation and qualifications lend support to Harold's work and mine is indeed heartening and gratifying.

And I would like to thank Dr. Beatrice Bruteau, to whom I am indebted for the word *Logon* used in Book II, and Mrs. Daniel Ziegler II, for the helpful suggestions they made and the work they did on the manuscript and proofs in the process of producing this book.

Harold cast his work into anonymity. He was committed to the concept that truth must and will make its own way in this world. If the unknown author's thought touches upon truth, it will elicit response.

There have been many guesses as to who Harold might be. None strikes us as being plausible. Many questions have been asked—but nothing that Gerald Heard, Michael Barrie, or I could reveal in the way of small details would throw any actual light upon the mystery. Therefore, we have determined to say no more than is said here.

There is another reason for our silence. We do not know who the author was, but anyone presenting himself as the author would have to know the many details we will not reveal. The story of our part in the publication of Harold's work is written and will be held in the files of Harold Institute. We believe in the integrity of the author, and in the sincerity of his desire to remain anonymous. We also believe that he is deceased. Our knowledge makes it impossible for anyone but the author to claim the work.

Who and what was Harold? This question must remain. The kind of person he was shows in his work. In a letter to me, Professor Aarne Siirala of Waterloo Lutheran Seminary wrote, "*The Shining Stranger* is really fascinating. The more I read it, the more I am convinced of its impact. The inner coherence of Harold's thoughts is really fantastic. There is something in the spirit and in the personality of the unknown writer which is exceptionally humble, pure and clear, something which touches the reader deeply. Behind the book must be an extraordinary and solid person."

In the opening pages of *The Shining Stranger*, Harold tells us only this, "The new answer to the mystery of Jesus offered in this study has not been received through mystic revelation. It has presented itself of its own accord as into one fold were gathered as many of Jesus' words and as much of fact and philosophy as the limited mental capacity of one man could assimilate and express in a limited number of words. Many of these words are quoted. . . ." His book is dedicated to those he quotes.

The only statement Harold made about his scientific work was appended as an epilogue to "On the Nature of Universal Cross-Action" when it was first printed. It seems fitting now to use his statement in this Prologue, so that the reader may know in the beginning all there is to be known about the anonymous author. His statement is as follows:

The author of the hypothesis, "On the Nature of Universal Cross-Action," while studying the life and work of James Clerk-Maxwell, became intrigued by Maxwell's preoccupation with the New Testament and his efforts to interpret it. Suddenly, he felt that the bond between the great scientist and the Nazarene might be meaningful in a way not generally recognized, for both men had attempted to reveal the nature of *light*, and Clerk-Maxwell's brilliant intuitions might have stemmed, unbeknownst to him, from his mental immersion in the words and drama of Jesus.

Thus, there began a search of the Gospels from which Clerk-Maxwell drew his inspiration—indirectly, no doubt—and a search of the Old Testament, upon which Jesus drew heavily, to see if there could be found simple principles from which a theory of light might be drawn. The author did and did not find what he was looking for. The principles were there, as unobtrusive as electrons hidden in space, but from them a new and different theory—complementary, not contradictory—must be constructed.

In a climate so inhospitable to religion, however, to present this work giving credit to Jesus, author of the principles upon which it rested, was to foredoom it. Would any scientist so much as read the work, in Jesus' name?

As this question was being pondered, another question arose. If the hypothesis to be drawn from Jesus' principles provides a new interpretation of many of the phenomena with which scientists contend, and does not contradict the data they have gathered, although it leads beyond current concepts, might not the rest of the "fruit" of this tree be good? A fresh look at the whole of Jesus' work might reveal other principles in other disciplines. Most important, one might find the principles upon which a new interpretation of His mission could rest, thereby restoring faith in His integrity and giving *new meaning* to His message.

The larger work was begun, and the conviction grew that the hypothesis, "On the Nature of Universal Cross-Action," could not be presented apart from Jesus, the author of its principles, and that it must be stated first in terms any interested layman or student could understand.

My effort has been to present both the scholarly book, *The Shining Stranger*, and Harold's scientific theories, to the layman.

And now, because "the play's the thing,"[8] let us get on with it.

SCENE I

The Premise

The beginning of the Palestinian mystery play is lost in the dawn of the day man was cast from the womb of nature into a state of consciousness unlike that of any other living thing. He comprehended *life*, and himself as a creator who must be identified with the Cosmic creative cause, which he named "God." God-consciousness, Cosmic-consciousness, indeed, Cosmic Humanism, began in the coming of mankind's self-consciousness.

Ever more sophisticated conceptions of God followed man's changing conceptions of himself and nature. These realizations were passed from generation to generation by words, spoken, then written. Each sacred writ tells essentially the same story of God/Man.

A new organization of energy, and therefore a new *evolutionary force*, entered to shape this planet's history with the advent of mankind, because in him word power, *a new type of energy*, was initiated. The effect of word power upon the inorganic and organic realms is unknown because this power involves a synthesis of measurable physical energy (sound waves) and the unmeasurable, perhaps unknowable, human energy that man calls mental.

The advent of word power marked a magnetic moment in planetary history that makes all others pale in comparison. In this moment a creature broke out of the vicious circle of the animal world in which every member is an offensive and/or defensive *biological weapon*. Man is not. The breakthrough came *after* man had relinquished claws and fighting canine teeth. Naked of weapon, without cloak, he stood upright upon the earth, let his gaze travel to the stars—and beyond—seeking his ancestral home. He sought also the meaning of his consciousness that lifted him from the ground of Cosmic dust, and then from "all fours," causing him to evolve into an expression of life that cannot be completely identified with other living forms and their evolution.

26

Although from the beginning man knew himself to be a part of nature, he knew that his species stands apart from nature because he is vested with God-consciousness and word power, and this would be true wherever "man" appears in the universe. He knew that God is all of nature, yet God must stand apart from nature in man's mind because God is the creative force, the reality, the mind of the Cosmos that expresses itself to the fullest only in humankind.

What we know of evolution reveals man's kindredship with all living creatures. Yet he remains a greater mystery than he was before the work of Darwin and others appeared upon the scene. Man's evolutionary path, his behavior, his physical differences, his emotional responses, the dizzying rate of change to which he adapts—and which he expresses in the development of his consciousness, in his work, in his art—shows him to be so different from anything else he has known that he cannot be explained as the culminating product emerging from the material environment of which he is, undoubtedly, also a product. When all that is different about humankind is posed against the undeniable facts of biological evolution in the natural world, can we say that man is a product of lower life forms, or must we say that he is *chalice and residual expression of the creative force, the reality, of which the Cosmos is made?*—a parallel development in the animal kingdom, destined from the beginning cell of his life to have dominion over it.

But he will not realize this *dominion* until he understands the meaning of the word, which is: *supreme authority*—and until he understands that the supreme authority in life is *love and understanding*. He will not gain dominion by attempting to "lord it over" nature and all other creatures, acting the arrogant master and despoiler. He will realize his dominion when he realizes the power and glory of knowledge and love and expresses goodwill toward man and nature.

In *The Palestinian Mystery Play*, this is the case we will present: nature is the *devolution* of Parent Cosmic Energy, physical and mental, which preserved unique power and glory in one expression of itself, vesting this power and glory in humankind, when it had spent itself of all but one measure of its absolute and original power. Creation is entrusted to the operation of perfect natural law, which eternally renews and restores to perfect balance and satisfying likeness all that is essential to life, insuring its evolvement into an optimum state of change and being.

The verdict is left to you—the jury of readers.

The Beginning

God-consciousness opened man's eyes to behold the world in the allegorical human being named Adam-Eve with whom the Palestinian mystery play begins. Mankind spoke. The Cosmos changed. What man said altered the pattern that Cosmic energy took on in response to this altogether new stimulus arising from Planet Earth. Devolution ceased. The evolution of human consciousness began.

Such magnetic moments may have occurred elsewhere in the universe before or after. But the stars themselves felt the impact of earth man's first, "Hello, your name is—what?" This sound rang with a resonance no other sound could have. It was the Cosmic Voice, given into individual, independent expression. The word-maker had been led through nature's channels. Faith in the incipient God-power within him had led him to disarm his body. His sense of kindredship with the light in the skies above had raised him from the ground to stand upright. Love for life, for himself and his kind, led him into and out of the jungle mind, made him long for something else—something better.

Mankind was a being so different from all he beheld that he felt a sense of exile from nature. How different is he? In these ways, and more:

He is the only creature that possesses the gift of speech which he can use, because he alone has a chin.

He is the only true biped.

He is the most "naked" of all creatures that roam the face of the earth.

He lives the longest period of any creature in the helplessness of infancy and childhood—making the greatest demand upon his parents throughout life.

He (male and female) expresses sexual desire year around—not periodically, as other creatures do.

He is generally left- or right-handed—"asymmetrical" as opposed to the symmetry generally expressed in nature, which is ambidextrous. He is the only creature with a true thumb, making of his hand the world's most marvelous tool.

He is the only creature that sheds real tears and laughs real laughter. He is the only creature that "plays" his life long.

He is not a biological weapon—all other creatures are to greater or lesser degree "physical weapons" for offense and/or defense by virtue of their bodies or behavior, or both.

He possesses the greatest brain on earth and has unmatched capacity to learn, to imagine, and to create.

So endowed with "difference" is man that he is both the most helpless and the most powerful creature on earth.

Grounded in fear, yet driven by courage—an alien who was yet perfectly at home in earth through which his body had evolved from one-cell creature onward—man's consciousness called out to and from his very being, "O God, I am—what?" The question has not yet been answered. But mankind has never ceased to ask it.

As the Palestinian mystery play moved on from Adam-Eve to other sets of characters, the sounding of one note repeated itself. Whenever man tried to answer the question of his being, the Cosmic Voice *within him* answered, "I, One, am the Lord, *your* God." At intervals, prophets speaking in the name of "I, the Lord, God," promise that One will come who will reveal the meaning of that recurring answer; and this One will reveal in his person the power, glory, grace of God, Cosmos. The coming of this One will mark the entrance of God-Incarnate into the affairs of man to take over their management and usher in the golden age, bringing perfect justice and harmony on earth. This One will be the *Messiah*. He will be born into the House of David. This and many other prophecies concerning the Coming One were spoken through the voices of the prophets of Israel.

Not only in Palestine, but throughout the earth, the promise of an Avatar, or a Messiah called by many names, to usher in the golden age and reveal to man the true nature of his being, came in answer to his question, "Who and what am I?" As civilizations rose and fell, as leaders strode across the stage and into the wings of time, this promise as answer took on many meanings. By whatever name this One was called, the word meant "Son of God, or Deity incarnate, bearer of Cosmic truth." That which began as an idea of *God involved in human life* became so objectified that God was set apart from man's own being. Mankind in all cultures awaited the advent of God/Man—Messiah. Through Him, and only through Him, could the human problem be resolved. Through Him, freedom and the salvation of man's degenerating society would come.

In Palestine, Israel in bondage to Rome awaited the Coming One, in their urgency looking to Him for deliverance. And in Rome, seers were foretelling the coming of a succession of gods, leading to the renovation of the world. At that time, mankind on Planet Earth awaited and sought supranatural intervention and the advent of One or a series of Messiahs to save the human race from *itself*.

SCENE III

Jesus of Nazareth Takes the Stage

Into this waiting age, in Palestine, crossroads of the civilized world, Jesus was born. Little is known of his childhood. If the apocryphal Gospel of Thomas can be believed, the boy had extraordinary psychic power and exercised it in a way that must have made him the terror of his companions, his family, his village.[9] But the Gospel of St. Luke also tells us that by the time Jesus was twelve years old the brilliance of his mind astounded the astute scholars of Judaism.[10]

The Gospel of Thomas reports that Jesus refused to learn his "letters." He would not allow his teachers to discuss the "beta" (two) until they could explain to his satisfaction the meaning of the "alpha" (one). *One* is the number upon which arithmetic (through which mathematics is given practical meaning) rests. *One* is the number upon which each individual, the whole of the universe, the concept of God, of reality, rests.

The meaning of *one*, the principle upon which it operates, appears in Thomas's Gospel to be the dominating thought in the mind of the boy Jesus. As he explains the "alpha" to his teacher, Jesus' word-picture calls up a vision of the principles of geometry, a vision of the propagation of light, expressed as only an artist can express such as this. Artist I. Rice Pereira says:

> Unity (one) can be grasped only from a synthesis of a manifold. . . . This constitutes a unity of the *two*: the *senses* and the *intellect*. . . . *A third principle* stands outside of the two—the horizontal plane of the senses and the vertical plane of the intellect. . . . The third principle stands outside in order to unify the whole.

And then she explains:

> When the horizontal and vertical planes come into a balanced relationship, the third principle—the illuminative principle—transverses the whole

content. Thus the fourth principle comes into "Being." *The fourth is the form-giving principle* by means of which a structure of Reality is made manifest on the world-plane. The fourth principle is "Being." It brings into Reality the Formal structure of the content of the Whole. It contains the cosmic reason.[11]

Now, listen to the boy Jesus, according to the Gospel of Thomas, as Zacchaeus, the teacher, tells him all the letters from "Alpha even to Omega, clearly, with much questioning":

> But Jesus looked upon Zacchaeus the teacher and saith unto him: Thou knowest not the Alpha according to its nature, how canst thou teach others the Beta? thou hypocrite, first, if thou knowest it, teach the Alpha, and then will we believe thee concerning the Beta. Then began he to confound the mouth of the teacher concerning the first letter, and he could not prevail to answer him. And in the hearing of many, the young child saith to Zacchaeus: Hear, O teacher, the ordinance of the first letter and pay heed to this, how that it hath [what follows is really unintelligible in this and in all the parallel texts; a literal version would run somewhat thus: how that it hath lines, and a middle mark, which thou seest, common to both, going apart; coming together, raised up on high, dancing (a corrupt word), of three signs, like in kind (a corrupt word), balanced, equal in measure] thou hast the rules of the Alpha.[12]

Words of a difficult and precocious child? Or of a born mathematical genius? "Lines and a middle mark common to both"—this can call up only the vision of the bisected diameter of the whole, the *cross encircled.* "Lines going apart, coming together, raised up on high, dancing"—was the child envisioning the opposing frequencies of a light-wave group? "Three signs, like in kind, balanced, equal in measure"—was he describing the equal charges of *positive* and *negative* energy that accompany each other in nature to produce the third sign, *neutral,* which brings balance, wholeness, unity, *one?* How near to truth is the "literal version" that Montague Rhodes James gives us! These words are not unintelligible in the twentieth century—they are an astounding, although poetic, description of reality, as scientists perceive it.

From birth, this strange and brilliant child, Jesus, had been thought by his parents, and no doubt an inner circle, to be the long-awaited Messiah. He was born to Mary, a virgin, and was adopted by Joseph of the House of David. By design or through force of circumstance, Mary and Joseph fulfilled prophecies concerning the Coming One. For example, they took the child into and out of Egypt. When Jesus was twelve years old, the curtain dropped, and it did not rise again on the Palestinian mystery play until he began his ministry at about thirty years of age.

Legend tells us that Joseph of Arimathea, Jesus' uncle, took the boy to Glastonbury in England. If we give credit to the Gospel of Thomas and its reports of Jesus' extraordinary demonstrations of psychic power in childhood, these exhibitions in addition to his refusal to learn from his teachers provide reason for Jesus to be taken away from his home. Tensions must have mounted as his strange power and behavior caused consternation. If Joseph took Jesus to Glastonbury, he took him into the heart of the ancient history of his day—perhaps into the history of lost Atlantis—and certainly into the midst of teachers who understood his unusual psychic powers and could develop them to the fullest.

In Glastonbury, Jesus may have learned of the many phenomena arising from expression of psychic energy and how to employ it, utilizing its range from minimum to maximum degree. Because he was possessed of such large measure of psychic power, he could have come to understand it as few have before or since. According to the legend, Jesus came as a boy, stayed long enough to build a church, and left.

There is much to indicate that Jesus spent at least a part of the lost years in the community of the Essenes. Much has been revealed in the Dead Sea Scrolls to show the beliefs and practices of this group. Their influence upon Jesus, however it came about, is evident in his teaching. The Essenes must have played a major role in shaping his thought. How long he tarried among them is an open question. Today, we can also see the image of the great religions of Asia, as well as the traditions of Judaism, indelibly imprinted upon the body of Jesus' doctrine. A few examples that do not purport to be conclusive, but present likenesses, are:

Hinduism, with its emphasis on truth's outworking through karma, which is described in Jesus' words that pertain to sowing and reaping and to the measure a person has meted out being meted out to him.

Buddhism, with its insistence that apart from oneself there is no light, no Buddha—and Jesus' words that turn man to seek the kingdom of God within himself.

Zen, with its emphasis upon the "here-now" of the "pure land" and the inward working that brings one to perfection through practice of the commonplace in humble joy—and Jesus' statements indicating that the reign of God is in the midst of man, and in the midst of society, here *now*, working to insure that the humble in heart will inherit the earth, that the pure in heart will know God.

Taoism, with its dedication to nature, its worship in natural surroundings—and Jesus' like pattern, teaching by the seashore, turning men to consider the lilies of the field, the sparrows.

Space does not permit giving examples of the likenesses between the Chinese religions and Jesus' teaching, other than to say that the situations of change are held to be primary in life in the *I Ching*[13]—and this precept is echoed in Jesus' words that indicate all things are made anew.

Nor does space permit a discussion of the likenesses between Jesus' teachings and those of the Greek philosophers. But in the Gospels there are indications that Jesus was an educated man.

Here, the curtain must rise on that brief moment in time when Jesus played the starring role in the Palestinian mystery play. The strange child, grown into an even stranger man, described by Ernest Renan as the summit of human greatness,[14] the strongest individual force ever to come upon the earth, takes the stage.

This was a magnetic moment in the history of humankind. The words Jesus spoke reverberate today. They do not resonate with the theology that has been preached in his name. But they resonate with nature's voice ever more strongly as man begins to understand what the universal energy is "saying" as it speaks through him and through every manifestation in the Cosmos, from elementary particle to distant quasar. Everything seems to be "dancing lines" of energy expressing in wavelike motion.

The scene opens as John the Baptist, also strongly influenced by the Essene community, baptized Jesus. Then Jesus suffered the "temptation" in the wilderness, described as Satan's prompting him to use his power to rule the world. *This was what large numbers of people expected Messiah to do, thereby bringing on the Golden Age.* Jesus refused to respond to the tempting.

The ministry of the man of Nazareth then begins. As Jesus made his way through Palestine, he invited twelve men to work with him. Each responded almost spontaneously. There was a disciple known only as the "beloved." Today, he is called John. Gospel records say that the others were not a part of the learned world of Judaism. Jesus taught them in private, entrusting to them explanations of his meaning that could not be preached to the crowds that began to follow him. These disciples shared with Jesus a number of strange experiences—visionary, miraculous but elusive in nature.

Jesus taught the crowds also, using the words that are gathered in the

Sermon on the Mount—honesty, charity, love of neighbor is its theme. And he brought about many healings. As he came to the attention of the Judaic authorities, they questioned him closely. He challenged many of time's accretions to Mosaic Law, but he upheld the Ten Commandments, and spoke with an authority that astonished the people. He exhibited wisdom so profound that his questioners were unable to contend with him. He became *the personification of the "being question"*—Who and what am I?

From this scene onward, the Palestinian mystery play revolves around the question, "Who and what was Jesus?" Was he the long-awaited Judaic Messiah who for some reason refused to fulfill the role as he was expected to fulfill it—and was in turn refused by Judaism? Was Jesus, as Christianity came to assert, nothing less than God incarnate, playing the role of man, His creature—tasting the bitterest cup He could drink in order to bring Himself to forgive man's sin? Or was Jesus a man so deluded that he believed God, Cosmic Cause, had delivered into his hands all of humanity to judge and sentence to life or death, to heaven or hell, because he would make restitution for their sins by dying on the Cross? Or are none of these interpretations correct, so that the real mission and meaning of Jesus is not as yet understood?

As Jesus leaves the stage, the mystery that will dominate the next scene is set. He is thought to have died on the Cross—and he was buried in a tomb from which his body had disappeared on the morning of the third day. His followers insisted that he had then reappeared to them for a time, telling them again that *Son of man*, the title by which he called himself, would come back within the lifetime of the "beloved disciple." He had told his interrogators that they would *all* see the *Son of man* descending in glory upon the clouds of heaven. He had instructed his disciples to go forth and preach his gospel to the world; he had said that his Church was to be built upon the disciple Peter, "the rock." The Resurrection drama lasted forty days as the curtain slowly fell on fading scenes of Jesus' life on earth.

St. Paul Steps into the Starring Role

As the curtain rises on the "Acts" of Jesus' small band of followers, the Apostle Paul shares and then begins to dominate in the establishment of early Christian doctrine. It is a time of waiting for Jesus' return.

As the years passed and he failed to reappear, the *mainstay* of this new religion—indeed, the only ground it had or has to stand upon—appeared. The Gospels. The mystery of how, when, by whom they were written has not yet been resolved. But they "spoke again" with the authority, the profundity, the simplicity of Jesus. Because of them, Christianity could live on after the original band was gone.

It is hard to imagine a more improbable happening than Christianity's survival. The irrational and paradoxical turns the religion took during the course of its evolution match the irrational and paradoxical turns man took in his evolutionary journey. Christianity, as the world has known it, is based upon St. Paul's interpretation of the man he had never met; but Jesus' words evoked in him such resounding echoes of truth that his faith only grew stronger as time passed and the promise of the return of Son of man failed to materialize. The healing ministry of the disciples waned, Jesus did not come back, but the Christian community only grew stronger, despite persecution by the Jewish hierarchy and the later persecution by the Romans. Its greatest growth took place long after time had made it impossible for Son of man to return as promised during the lifetime of Jesus' contemporaries. The pivotal point upon which Christianity began was utterly shattered. Yet, the growth of the religion became synonymous with the growth of Western civilization.

As the structure of Christian theology was elaborated, the Church was built not upon the doctrine of Peter, "the rock," as given in the Gospels, but upon the doctrine of Paul—the man that Saul of Tarsus became after the blinding brilliance of Jesus overcame him on the road to Damascus. Christianity is not the Religion of Jesus. It is the Religion of Paul, who drew his ethic of love from Jesus, the ethic the Church fails all too often to practice.

More than a computer would be needed to calculate the good versus the evil done in the name of Jesus by Pauline Christianity. This must be measured against the good versus the evil done by mankind to mankind before Jesus or Paul appeared on the scene. This must be measured against the projection of what type of society would have evolved had Jesus and Paul not undertaken their missions from which Christianity was derived.

The more powerful the Christian Church became, the more foreign it became to Jesus' teaching and to Paul's—the less it practiced what they preached. At the same time, around and within it such an edifice of magnificent ritual, sublime art, music, architecture, and literature was built that:

> I, still drawn to the faith of my youth
> Loving its beauty while doubting its truth,
> Wonder if beauty is not truer than truth.[15]

Strange, because for centuries the depravity of man was the Christian theme. This depravity was exemplified most surely in the treatment the Church accorded those who challenged its power—and, once power had turned the table, in the unconscionable persecution of the Jews that culminated in Nazism's brief triumph, which sickened the world. Not until 1968 were the Jewish people living today "exonerated" of guilt for the Crucifixion of Jesus. Those who have stood in the shoes of the "big fisherman" seem to have forgotten that Peter thrice denied knowing Jesus and that there is nothing in the Gospels or in the Epistles of Peter or Paul that calls for the subtle or overt destruction of the Jews.

Around the planet, Christianity spread its message: Jesus was the only incarnation of God this world has known. Salvation is possible only through acknowledging him as Saviour. He will return and this will mark the end of the world, the beginning of heaven and hell, between which mankind will be divided as Jesus judges each person who has or will ever live. Not even theologians will talk about the "meat" of the Christian message today—but there it is. It is incredible that intelligent people could have spent their lives defending and elaborating this theology. But they did.

Paradoxically, through the efforts of the clergy, who were honest and ardent truth seekers in every sense of the word, *the base of education was broadened* until this became a major function of the Christian

37

Church in all of its denominations and remains the shining light of its accomplishment today. Galileo, Copernicus, Kepler, Newton, and others too numerous to name worked out the problems of Christian theology that were posed by their findings as carefully as they worked out the mathematics of their discoveries.

Did these people, and millions of other human beings through the centuries who must be counted as intelligent, really believe in Christian theology? Or did they pay lip service only, as they nevertheless *responded to the Christian symbols that evoked action below the conscious level because these symbols correspond with psychic and natural truth* even though the theology of Christianity taken literally does not?

Ignoring the irrational, the unbelievable, the unintelligible, the great majority of the Western world must have practiced a "wordless" faith in God and man, in the Cosmos itself, calling themselves Christians because the symbols and rituals of the Church evoked a certainty within them, and the words of the Nazarene that filtered through the trappings struck the chord of resounding truth.

Christianity must coat its "theological pills" with the ethic of honesty and love—the practice of which was demanded by both Paul and Jesus. The difference between the doctrines of these two men is not one of ethics. It is much deeper seated. It is a question of the *psychology of man*—the answer to the question, "Who and what am I?"

> Paul answered, "You are not your own, you were bought for a price." By Jesus.[16]
> Jesus answered, "Ye are the salt of the earth, ye are the light of the world . . ." and even the least of you are brother-beings to me, the *same* that I profess myself to be, the Son of God, the Father. Scripture cannot be broken, "I said, Ye are gods . . ."—"Ye shall know the truth, and the truth shall make ye free."[17]

How could two answers be more contradictory? Traditionally, Christianity has spoken only out of the Pauline side of its mouth when it answers the being question. But Jesus has a spokesman of his own.

The Bible Begins Prompting the Actors

With the advent of the printing press, the Bible became available in the Christian world. This did not happen until the contents of it had been fixed for so many centuries that any tampering with it then or now could be only ridiculous. For the first time since Jesus had the starring role, *multitudes of people could come into direct contact with him through the Gospels.* This "second coming," however, bid fair to herald the "end of the world" for Christianity.

No sooner had the *words of Jesus* in the Holy Writ begun prompting the actors in the Palestinian mystery play than Christianity began to come apart at the seams. That is, theology did. People began interpreting the "word" for themselves. New denominations of Christianity arose. There were many alterations to the orthodox theme. Even so, by the time the curtain was raised on the midnineteenth-century scene, the audience simply "filed out" mentally whenever a theologian rose to speak his piece. Soon they were leaving literally, and in droves by the time the midtwentieth-century began its act.

Belief in the orthodox doctrine of the Christian churches failed so rapidly that even the "believers" were unaware that they no longer really accepted the dogma. But the stage was still full of the cast that played the role of followers. They clung to their parts, even after heaven knows how many theologians themselves ceased to believe in the Apostles' Creed, which they nevertheless dutifully recited.

From the nineteenth century onward, Christian theology became, in large part, an apology for what it had been—and a suitable whipping boy was found. The whipping boy was none other than the Holy Bible itself—especially the four Gospels. Scholars set out to show that the Gospels and the strange story they told—replete with accounts of miracles that science scoffed at—were not altogether true. Indeed, they were just about altogether false. Words such as *kerygma*, which refers to the content of the "early Christian message," were developed to give the appearance of technical competence and authority to the process of "Jesus Research" and "Form Criticism." If you do not believe that this is all that Christian scholars and theologians will talk about or teach today, try them and see for yourself.

Any passage that was found to be embarrassing to Christianity could be "read out of the record" on the ground of "misguided" kerygma, or it was found to be spurious for some other reason, or it was an interpolation of a dissenting group, or it was found to be at odds with the prevailing attitudes and practices of the day, or the passage was omitted in the most reliable Gospel, or it was contradicted in another. The Gospel of St. John came under such heavy attack that some scholars rose to defend it—scholarly works repudiated each other. Some researchers took refuge in the Old Testament legends, coming to their defense, showing that they are based upon historical fact. Others saw them as a "biased" history of the Israelites. In sum, a case was made for and against the authenticity and reliability of every part of the Bible, each of the Gospels, and every account of Jesus' works and words.

As we observe the twentieth-century scene, it is played against a backdrop of the shreds and tatters of the Gospels. Jesus is bypassed—his meaning is a question that is brushed under the rug. No one will discuss it. Some theologians flog the dead horse of their orthodox doctrine as though it can be brought to life if they abuse and disclaim it sufficiently. Others act as though belief in it can be renewed and sustained if they ignore it and devote themselves to belated good works on the social scene, involving Christianity so deeply in the problems of the day that the world will forget all that is implicit in its creed.

The simple fact of the matter is that *Jesus and the Gospels are indivisible*. There is no other record of him. In disclaiming the truth of this record, Christians themselves have sawed off the limb upon which they must sit; they have undermined the only ground upon which they can stand; they have made suspect *their only reason for being*.

No amount of research will erase the compelling fact that the four Gospels cannot be rewritten; they will confront Christianity as long as it exists. The story of the man who took the stage so many centuries ago cannot be retold, and it cannot be untold. When it is told, it evokes a response that cannot be explained in rational terms. It goes too deep. It stirs something in the depths of man that he is just now beginning to be aware of: an authority within himself that *matches the certainty* with which the Palestinian asserted himself to be uniquely the Son of the Creator of the Cosmos, of the universal energy that expresses throughout, but expresses itself to the fullest only in the mind of man.

The integrity of Jesus depends upon the integrity of the Gospels. There is no Jesus other than the Jesus of this record, and certainly there is no reason for Christianity to continue to exist if the sacred writ it is founded upon is invalid. It cannot survive on a diet of "Form Criticism" and "Jesus Research." Nor can it survive if it must depend upon the notion that "God on high" somehow pushed the pen of the men who wrote the Bible so that it was supranaturally created. Christianity must pin its hopes upon finding answers other than these as to how the miracle that the Bible is, came to be wrought. And miracle the Bible continues to be. Whatever is said about it, it continues to prompt men to action and to higher levels of consciousness. Is it not a living edition of Homo sapiens himself?

Miracle of the Twentieth Century—The Return of Palestine to the Children of Israel

The stage upon which the Palestinian mystery play takes place has many sets. The actors become audience for each other. As Christianity waxed, Judaism did not wane. It persisted, although driven from set to set, and sometimes underground to find a place to continue its part in the drama. In the twentieth century, no less a miracle than many reported in the Old Testament occurred when the governments of the Christian world brought their power to bear and returned Palestine to the Children of Israel.

The fact remains that if the Judaic interpretation of Jesus and his meaning—that he was not the Messiah, not God incarnate—is right, then the Christian interpretation of him is wrong, and vice versa. The beliefs of the Judaic and Christian communities remain in complete opposition, each a denial of the other. In view of this, there is no greater mystery than the return of the remnant of Israel to its homeland, its ancient prophecy that heralds the Golden Age fulfilled for it by the action of the Christian world.

But by the time the miracle of Palestine-regained occurred, Christian theology was so well watered that tolerance prevailed. And the Christian community *had been forced back into its antecedent Judaic belief*— there is one God who will someday reveal Himself to man. Christianity had become and continues to be more Judaic than Christian. The meaning of Jesus was the thorn in its side—still is.

As though this mystery play were not contrary enough, by the time Palestine was returned to the Jewish people, ancient prophecy fulfilled, the Jewish people, too, began to file out of the audience as their orthodox theologians spoke. Their age-old Messianic tradition bids fair to join Jesus, under the rug, where it is brushed. Few Jewish people will discuss it.

Judaic rituals are observed, lip service is paid. There remains, of course, the hard core of the committed, just as there is in Christendom. But among the educated, commitment wanes.

Meanwhile, on the Palestinian set itself, Islam contends with the miracle the Christian world wrought in returning Israel to the Holy Land and the ensuing displacement of the Arabic population. The Islamic community takes small comfort in the knowledge that Judaism is the mother lode from which this religion, as well as Christianity, was drawn.

Islam is an offshoot of a Christianity that had grown intolerable to some of its adherents centuries ago. They, nevertheless, revere Jesus as a prophet of the same God who made his *final and complete revelation* through the prophet Mohammed. Islam reads its lines from the Koran.

Israel has done a miraculous job in Palestine, both in turning it from desert to garden spot and in protecting its position there. The surrounding Islamic countries have not and no doubt cannot come to terms with the situation until their displaced peoples are reestablished and their own situations are somehow made more viable. But beneath and overhanging the apparent causes, economic and otherwise, that lead to unceasing strife, are the reverberations of a holy war. So deep are the scars, so fresh are the wounds, that it may well be that only a true reconciliation between the contending religions can pave the way for peace on the social scene.

The world, however, is no longer listening to the religionists fretting in the wings. Some time ago, as among educated people the world over belief in the orthodox doctrines of *every* religion began to wither, Science stepped into the starring role.

Science Upstages Religion

THREE SONS OF ISRAEL—MARX, FREUD, EINSTEIN— SPEAK THEIR PIECES

Science is involved in the Palestinian mystery play because much in the development of Science was brought about by people whose Judaic and Christian backgrounds often played a part in the shaping of their thought and scientific research.

By the nineteenth century, a *community of belief* such as the world had never before known began to develop in Science—belief in its methods, findings, theories. Scientists were bound in fellowship more real than any other that mankind has experienced. Community of belief allows Science to speak with authority. But until recent decades what Science said was as far from the true nature of energy and the universe as religions were far from the true nature of God, and as nineteenth-century capitalism was far from the practice of an ethical economy.

What capitalist could look back into the practices of early industrialism and wish to perpetuate the abuses that were the accepted norm of Marx's day? Who could tolerate nineteenth-century economic practices or theological demands? Karl Marx repudiated Religion and addressed himself to correcting economic injustice. He became the "high priest of atheism," and declared himself the infallible prophet of history.

Is a man an atheist when he rejects the theology of the nineteenth century—Judaic or Christian? Shortly before his death Marx said, "I am not a Marxist."[18]

Perhaps Marx's deepest meaning was, "I am not an atheist." He must have come to understand that each person comes in the end to believe in something, however hard he tries to sift his existence into "nothing." And "nothing" is itself another name for God, if "nothing" is what a man believes in. At the end, Marx came to grips with human nature—

economic and religious. Hence, he repudiated his "infallible" doctrine before he died.

God is a condition of man's being—the condition of his necessity *to believe* as a prerequisite to sanity and action. When belief in one set of propositions fails, belief in another must take its place. Karl Marx became the Messiah, and Marxism became a religion that took the place of declining orthodoxies for many people the world over. These actors read their lines from the *Manifesto*. And this religion, too, is akin to Christianity (therefore to Judaism), in that as Khrushchev put it, "We have taken many of the precepts of Jesus."[19]

Marxism and communism are not synonymous. The first is a "religion." The second is an economic and political system that is simply a monolithic corporation and a paternalistic, completely authoritarian government engineered by Lenin.

As Marxism waxed and orthodox religions waned, our mystery play took another paradoxical turn. *Marxism saved the life of the system it had set out to destroy.* Marxism became the catalyst which so speeded the evolution of industrialism into modern capitalism with its more ethical practices that the economy of the Western world escaped the inevitable doom that its nineteenth-century portrait portended. Capitalism lived to become the most viable system on the economic scene, because it rapidly opened itself to the most beneficial of the socialistic practices. Its evolution in this regard continues. The essential principles of capitalism are contained within the evolutionary process, however, so that incentive is sustained.

Again, paradoxically, as communism waxed, Marxism, as a religion, waned. It became apparent within a few decades that Marxism could never be a "substitute religion" which would satisfy men's souls or forever insure that their material needs would be met. By the midtwentieth century, in order for communism to sustain itself, it had to begin to admit into its operation the capitalistic practice that human nature demands—the profit incentive. Slowly, very slowly, communism begins to evolve.

It would take more than a computer to calculate the good and the evil done in the name of Marx. Whatever the score, as a religion, Marxism declined as rapidly as it arose, sharing the fate of traditional religions. And, paradoxically, Science, which had appeared to be the infallible "religion," found itself in the same boat.

Judaism lives in a state of crisis. In the twentieth century, Christianity found itself in acute crisis. Then the Religion of Science—belief in Science as savior, hope of the world, bearer of the golden age—found itself in a state of crisis. Science had proliferated into more sects and denominations than religions could claim. Each had become so exclusive that *communication* in the "grand fellowship" began to falter and then to fail. Laymen had long since given up attempts to hold "dialogues" with the scientific world, which is now a veritable Tower of Babel; and the "confounding" of its tongues continues as ever more obscure words are coined to convey what seems to be a convoy of answers, but turns out to be a convoy of questions.

Onto the scientific set exact and inexact sciences had crowded. Sigmund Freud had seen this place as the "promised land" for psychology. But Freudian psychology, brought to stand examination in the light that psychology itself had cast upon the dark inner world of man, was found to be "sicker" than the sick religions it had tried to displace. Psychology was upon us—more threatening and demanding and degrading than "Jehovah" in his worst fit of temper or pique. And the cry went up, "O God, save us, but don't shut up sex in Pandora's box again."

Then a funny thing happened. Physics woke up one night and found Psychology in its bed. Carl Jung and Wolfgang Pauli turned Physics and Psychology to face the microscopic and macroscopic problems of inner space and outer space as parallel problems, which could well have parallel answers, laws, processes.[20] The idea was stated, but never precised. Physics and Psychology remain strange bedfellows, puritanical in their approach to each other, the union unconsummated.

But more than a cacophony of disciplines, each whirling in a *cul de sac* of its own making (as were the religious sects of the world), toppled the high and mighty structure outgrown from nineteenth-century Science. Another son of Israel, Albert Einstein, who had shifted his attention from Judaism to exploring the mysteries of nature, spoke up. His concepts and a resulting equation, simple and profound, shook the stars. The universe felt the impact of $E = mc^2$.

How far into space have the energy patterns spread that were born of that convulsive moment when Enrico Fermi could say that this equation stated workable truth? From this moment onward, Science became a more "absolute terror" than God had ever been. For Science had brought down upon our heads the "day of judgment"—*the day when judgment must take over from power* to solve the problems of the world. This was a magnetic moment in the history of man. An understatement. There are no words to describe the import of this moment. It may mark the beginning of our utter destruction. Or it may have been a signal to the Cosmos,

"Earth is ready to peck out of its shell. Our embryonic and fetal days are over. Our soma cells have taken their places in organs, tissue, muscle, blood, limbs, and brains—in a marvelous number of organizations. Taken together, mankind is a body of consciousness, coming into Cosmic awareness, ready to explore the mansions of this solar system—even others."

The audience is not listening.

For a hundred years, the drums of the Religion of Science have been rolling one note that accompanies every trill of discovery: *Nihilism.* Here is its pitch: Nature's supreme law, the second law of thermodynamics, which has been found to govern every expression of energy— and to be involved even in the expression of the *word*, in communication —says that the universe is dying a heat-death. Every celestial body in the system is dying. The organization of energy which provides the fuel that is consumed to supply the warmth that life needs is being constantly disorganized with subsequent loss of temperature—in every move made, or even if a system is left to itself—and there is no evidence in the purely physical sense that it is being reorganized.

Let us hasten to say that not all scientists hold this view. In fact, more and more of them are now refusing it. But for a long time it held sway. This is the doctrine of an ungodly materialism wherein it is presumed that everything in creation feeds like a parasite upon the stuff of its Cosmic host until the host's energy is consumed and both go down to destruction.

Relatively speaking, not a handful of people on this planet have any idea of what nature's supreme law is or how it works—not even the most highly educated people. But it is the scientists' interpretation of this law that is grinding like the salt mill at the bottom of the ocean of modern knowledge, flavoring the whole of it so that it is no longer potable for man's soul. Artists may not be aware of this law, but they are aware of the despair that flavors life; and they are aware of the repudiation by the young not only of today's value system, but their repudiation of the idea that there can be a valid value system if life, evolution, and the universe are meaningless and purely materialistic.

To the degree that man *believes he is a thing,* product of blind and purposeless nature that *is moving toward senseless oblivion,* be assured that *he will act* according to this belief. Life is bereft of a motivating *principle.*

Space age in a dying universe? So what? An unmotivated audience amuses itself. And "happenings," hapless, light the dark theater like fireflies on a warm June night. The bright promises of Science and technology fall on deaf ears. What *value* can there be in such a system, even if it will

47

take billions of years before its witless course is run? If this is actually the condition of the universe, it holds forth no reason, no promise, to man.

The good and the evil done in the name of Science are difficult to measure. Against its triumphs, we must pose our polluted environment, our scarred and blighted landscape, our souls sucked dry of purpose in being. On the other hand, Science has unquestionably been a blessed benefactor to life, a purifying discipline that has rid us and Religion of many a false and foolish notion. No doubt, in time technology will bring great abundance—affluence everywhere on this planet. This is not enough. Across time come the words of the mysterious Nazarene, "a man's life consisteth not in the abundance of things which he possesseth"—man does not live by bread alone, the body is more than raiment.[21]

The Religion of Science offers no food for the soul. A wave of fear sweeps over the audience as they see so many of the brightest, most dedicated young people of this decade say to Science and to the traditional religions, now making feeble overtures to each other, "A plague on both your houses."

And the Religion of Science is in the same fix as the rest of the religions. No one does much more than pay lip service to the doctrine of *Nihilism* and blind materialism. There is a certainty in man which prohibits faith in "nothing." Science itself numbers among its members countless devoutly religious men, in that they cling to their faith in the Cosmos, God; as they observe its marvelous working and order, the similarity of its underlying patterns of operation, they express or feel confidence in its sanity. Like the theologians, they can neither fully accept nor fully reject their own doctrines. And they share in another dilemma.

Science is as fixed in Messianic expectation as ever Judaism and Christianity were. You do not believe it? Consider that Messiah by any name or definition is a *perfect entity*, superior to the limitations and transitoriness of man and nature—therefore, mystical and not altogether explicable. Now, listen to Gerald Holton speaking of Science's seeking such an entity:

> This entity, superior to all limitations and even above man's thought, is easily recognizable in scientific thought, from the beginning to this day, as the conception—a haunting and apparently irresistible one despite all evidence to the contrary—of the final, single, perfect object of knowledge to which the current state of science is widely thought to lead us, more or less asymptotically, but continually and inexorably. Like the exemplification of this conception outside science—in the Supreme Being,

48

or the millennial utopia—the final state of science is one that is generally agreed cannot be defined with any degree of precision by means of concepts or the use of ordinary language. That would be incompatible with its perfection. It is seen as a conception far beyond those arising directly from an examination of the empirical world. Occasionally a scientist rashly dares to put this dream into words, and then it is likely to emerge that the best he can say is that the goal has already been achieved.[22]

You see? Science, too, must deal with the Messianic claims of its early adherents, and with its persisting Messianic expectation.

Paradox enters the picture. *As the Messianic complex of all religions withers*—and all of them are infected with it to some degree, including the Religion of Marxism and its opponent, the Religion of Democracy—*the Messianic complex of Science blossoms*. This is strange because it was the Messianic-mindedness of traditional religions that led Science to distrust them—their various assertions that (1) the "perfect entity" could be produced only within the vessel of their particular group, (2) the "perfect entity" had been produced by a particular group, (3) this "Messianic dream" was possible of realization.

Science decries the Messianic complex that has haunted the history of mankind's religious expression. "Give us the facts," Science says, "and we will construct valid theories that warrant belief." Well, then, here are the facts: Science is suffering a serious if not critical case of Messianic pretension and delusion. What does Science make of that?

It appears to us that the Messianic complex is a condition common to mankind and every individual is likely to suffer it sooner or later to some degree because it involves the will to power, and the notion that truth can be had by the exertion of the intellect, to the exclusion of intuitive gleanings or certainties based upon feelings and vice versa.

Perhaps this continuously shifting spectrum in which Messianic delusion is bandied between men of intellectual bent and men of intuitive bent—between Science and Religion—can be understood better if we blow up the picture to Cosmic proportions. We will use one of Rudolf Thiel's "Modern Fables of the Stars." He describes a certain pair of stars as cannibals. Here is his description of them:

> The partners whirl around one another in four hours. As a result, both are distorted; they form a kind of double egg, with ends almost touching. The smaller of the two stars has emitted a gaseous appendage that is wrapped around its big partner. But horrible to relate, the big one is sucking the substance out of the little one, as a spider might a fly. The

end, however, will not be fatal, said astronomer Paul Guthnick. Soon the smaller star's turn will come, he maintains, and it will feed on its partner for a few years, until the big one is only a skeleton of its former self. Then the whole procedure will begin over again.[23]

This is a pretty gruesome story—but, then, it depends upon how you look at it. It would make no difference whether we liken the big star or the little star to Religion or Science. Each takes its turn of waxing fat and waning lean—of glutting itself with will to power and claim to all truth, or claim to be the vehicle that has or can absorb and radiate all truth. But as one of them attempts to draw all substance from the other and leave it but an empty shell, it partakes on the one hand of the delusion that bloated and on the other hand of the pretension that collapsed the structure into a body composed of a good deal of degenerate matter.

But, let us look at the fable in another way. It would make no difference whether we called the big star or the little star the intellect versus the intuition. The drama would say that there are times when truth can express itself best in the house of intellect, times when it can express itself best in the house of intuition—but the essential thing is that the cyclic cross-action does not destroy *either house*, it simply allows for resting the forces of each. Since this cycle repeats itself so often, it must be seen as a continuous play between the two forces. The scene begins to look now like the most "Cosmic kiss" the Cosmic Imagination could dream up —no doubt an expression of lust of Cosmic proportions. And it is not to be expected that Science and Religion would be comfortable in such a passionate embrace. But it would be in line with the facts of the case if Science and Religion could see themselves as a "double egg" germinating planetary consciousness and Cosmic awareness in mankind.

Scientists are aware that, in concert with observation, *discovery* depends upon and has come from the *intuitive* promptings and inexplicable flashes of insight, quantum jumps in understanding, that mark the history of mathematics and research in every field. The creative, innovative capacity in man rests upon his intuition, not logic. But intellect and reasoning power must be called upon to precise the ideas that intuition hands to consciousness. They must be stated in workable and transmissible terms, and they must be oriented within the body of human knowledge. The ability of a trained and disciplined mind to receive the ideas *and* to precise them leads to the expression of genius in Science that has sent it soaring at rocket speed. With precious few exceptions, men of genius in Science have been deeply, mystically, religious—some orthodox, some unorthodox. But Science as a body abhors mysticism. It should. Because mysticism as such, mysticism that repudiates intellectual probing and refuses to deal with reason, is not only as sterile as intellectualism that refuses to consider psychic phenomena seriously, but it is apt to be a shady business.

Mysticism does not begin this way, but bereft of the correcting discipline that intellect and reason provide, it degenerates—sometimes into petty swindling, sometimes into a menacing expression of the will to power over others, sometimes into a misguided attempt at self-control, sometimes into a futile effort to escape reality.

When men of intellect, men grounded in reasoning power and logic, refuse to deal with psychic phenomena, a "black market" that deals in intuition appears. Investigation of the "occult" moves underground. Mankind will not have done with the subject. The entertainment industry is quick to capitalize upon the public's fascination. Morsels of fact are elaborated into such farce insofar as truth is concerned that Science is given still another reason to turn its back on the subject of psychic phenomena.

Mankind's fascination continues because intuition and individual experience insist that there is a power that may be projected outward and inward, a power that cannot be explained in physical, sensory terms. And there is a certainty in man that insists that death is not the end of the individual's life.

Today's "occult dramas" are usually set in a pseudoscientific scene. The public forgets that the type of science fiction that keeps "coming true" involves achievement in the realms of physics and chemistry—hard and exact sciences. The directors of the drama do not forget this. Therefore, the modern witches' brew is an array of instruments—tubes, lights, and dials. And there is a morsel of truth in the suggestion that "hard scientists" are investigating psychic phenomena "by night" as they practice their professions "by day" because the prejudicial attitude of the scientific community necessitates their keeping the two areas of research separate if they are to continue to operate within the Establishment.

There are other scientifically trained people, however, who are openly devoting their lives to research in psychic phenomena because they realize that this is the great frontier to be explored, using the methodology of Science insofar as is possible. They realize that until Science comes to grips with the many states of human consciousness, scientists are not dealing with the most compelling question that faces them.

There is no denying the evidence of inexplicable psychic and physical phenomena occurring as a result of hypnosis. But hypnotism, even the word, is shunned by most. We need but one movie (viewed by millions on TV) which solves its mystery by saying that the criminal or victim was hypnotized, to set research in this most important field back another year or two. There is good reason, no doubt, for the public to be wary. This simply emphasizes the need for Science to do full-scale research.

To be in a state of hypnosis is simply to be in a state of trance, which varies in degree from momentary unawareness to deathlike oblivion. It is likely that all states of consciousness are states of trance, because we are seldom if ever completely aware of every stimulus impinging upon us. In the hypnotic state, suggestion is the tool. There are as many degrees of response to suggestion as there are states of trance. All stimuli "suggest" something.

Any tool can be used constructively or destructively. Most tools can be turned into weapons, but most tools serve life well. One of the most valuable tools in nature's chest is—or could be—hypnosis. Every human being should be trained to use this psychic power beneficially for self and others, if called upon. And every human being should be taught how to defend against its misuse. Knowledge of the dynamics of hypnosis and its possibilities should be made common. Only when knowledge is *not* common can it be dangerous. The closely guarded secrets of what we call hypnosis are very probably at the root of all the "mysteries" and "strange cults." Releasing this strange power in the mind of man is a goal that could not, and cannot, be reached until and unless ethics keep apace.

Today, there is extraordinary interest on the part of the public in the occult, the metaphysical, the parapsychological. Such interest is likely to increase—leading to a discipline that may be called "paraphysics"—because scientific knowledge has led to such refinement of physical energy that research, in order to strike a new vein of knowledge, may well lead into areas that are paraphysical and metaphysical. Materialism has reached the end of its rope only to discover that it is still but a short way up the "mountain of mystery" that life and universal energy present. Knowledge has reached what may be called the "para-meta" plateau, and this is the *natural consequence of scientists' accomplishments*.

The questions have become "para-meta"—exploration of space, for example, demands extraterrestrial geography. And the scientific study of human consciousness demands that physics join with metaphysics to discover, for example, the effect of *sound* upon consciousness and flesh, the effect of consciousness upon the body, and the effect of word power, suggestion, upon mind and body because sound and mind are involved and therefore involve physics and metaphysics. Does the brain become a superconductor of Cosmic mental energy that recharges the mind when a person is in that blessed state of *trance* called meditation? Krishnamurti describes it beautifully:

> Meditation is a never-ending movement. You can never say that you are meditating or set aside a period for meditation. It isn't at your command. Its benediction doesn't come to you because you lead a systematized life, or follow a particular routine and morality. It comes only when your heart is really open. Not opened by the key of thought, not made safe by the intellect. But when it is as open as the skies without a cloud, then it comes without your knowing, without your invitation. But you can never guard it, keep it, worship it. If you try, it will never come back again: do what you will, it will avoid you. Because in meditation, you are not important, you have no place in it, and the beauty of it is not you, but in itself. And to this you can add nothing. Don't look out of the window hoping to catch it unawares, or sit in a darkened room waiting for it: it comes only when you are not there at all, and its bliss has no continuity.[24]

We cannot call for a moment of meditation—it will not come. So, give attention, please!

Something has been happening on every set that crowds the stage. For a number of years, the wise men of the East have been returning, quietly bearing their gifts to the Western world.

The Light of Asia Is Again Shed
upon the Western Scene

Asiatic religions are marching in force across the Western scene, and throngs are going forth to greet them. Gurus are in demand. As the various Oriental doctrines are taught, those who have ears to hear, eyes to see, are beginning to understand that every great religion in the world speaks the same truth and presents itself as representation of the being-truth of man. The wisdom of Asia is feeding the starving soul of Western man. The advent of these religions has turned *The Palestinian Mystery Play* into "theater in the round." Religion is observed from its every point of view—its "sets" girdle the planet.

But as the Asiatic religions wax in the West, they wane in the East, where Science and technology are being imbibed as rapidly and happily as the wine of Eastern religions is being imbibed in our sphere. All over Asia, among the educated, faith in traditional religions with their prohibitions and restrictive customs is declining. Need we say that large numbers of the populace are paying dutiful lip service and are cherishing the beauty that is attendant upon the rituals and festivals? This is true. Loyalty remains—conviction does not.

Just as a mother cannot hold in bondage the healthy adult, so the old orthodoxies—be they of Religion, of Science, or political in nature—cannot hold in bondage a consciousness that has outgrown them. But we can see, now that the play is "theater in the round," that the *church* of every religion in the world plays the mother role for mankind. Through the ages, religions have borne the legends, symbols, and sacred writings that provide the material from which humanity freely fashions its own body of philosophy in secret. Churches meet the need of the "children" of this world. They feed the emotional hunger of man and cushion his irrationality with their own irrationality. More effectively than any other organ in society, the churches teach ethics and divert man from criminal

54

expression, allowing him to wear a hair shirt if he must or to love life and serve his fellowmen. Be this mother lode as full of frailty as the human mother, she is better than none. Man's churches must be supported.[25]

Man, the individual, returns to his "mother faith" for sustenance and comfort in times of tribulation and crisis. This regression into childlike faith sustains him. The person who has no grounding in a mother faith, be the faith pantheistic, deistic, theistic, is indeed in jeopardy when inner or outer threats beset him. Because for many, if not for all, *faith is the condition on which sanity itself rests* as time bears life's inevitable stress into the here-now state of being, whatever it is. And faith, whatever it is in, is all that man has to fall back, move forward, or mark time on.

Man has outgrown the orthodoxies of the past—even of recent decades —but he has not outgrown his need for Religion, his compulsion to act out whatever he believes, and in one way or another to support the doctrine that "mothered" him or his kind.

As the whole scene is viewed, the power of the word becomes evident. Centuries of preaching the brotherhood of man are bearing fruit in a society that demands that this doctrine be practiced in spirit and in truth. True brotherhood goes far beyond according equal dignity to each sex, age, and race. It demands harmony between the religions, between the sciences and religions, between the governments of man.

A true community of belief that will lead to unified purpose and constructive action on every front is the need of this age. Community of belief neither requires nor permits the sacrifice of individuality. Each discipline, faith, race, and sex is required only to express in its own way the fundamental principles that apply to all, just as scientists the world over utilize the same mathematical principles.

There can be no real community of belief until there is a unifying concept as regards the nature of man and the Cosmos—a concept with which all the actors and the audience can identify. Today, each religion or ideology that has a place on the world stage tacitly repudiates all of the others because, despite their toleration, each is exclusive and each is awaiting, seeking, serving, or acting the part of its own version of Messiah that in the end tolerates no other version.

Everywhere, people are seeking the meaning that underlies the external structures—the meaning of Religion *and* Science in the history of man. Is not the propagation of Science as great a mystery as the propagation of Religion in the history of humankind? Mankind is seeking a faith of *Cosmic dimension*. And the *audience insists upon becoming a part of the play*.

The scene shifts. The stage is wherever the action is—in the pit, on the balcony, in the boxes, or in any "cornered space" in this "theater in the round."

Now an unknown voice begins to speak through a book he left behind when the end of his life ended the Palestinian mystery play for him. Who or what this author was can never be known. Those who published his manuscript do not know his identity. His "script," *The Shining Stranger*, must speak for itself.

The title is taken from a line, "*truth* is often a shining stranger. . ."[26] —it refers to no person. The pen name of the author, Preston Harold, expresses in part what this author felt to be the truth of mankind—truth so beautifully spoken by Lord Byron in *Childe Harold's Pilgrimage*:

> . . . there is that within me which shall tire
> Torture and Time, and breathe when I expire;
> Something unearthly, which they deem not of.[27]

Preston Harold offers answers that the world has never heard before to the many questions raised by the Palestinian mystery play and its evolution into the "science fiction" of our day, which says God is dead and the Holy Ghost, the Cosmos, is dying.

Since audience participation is now the thing, let us hear in Act Two what *The Shining Stranger* has to say. We will ring down the curtain on Act One with Harold's premise:

> Stating a valid, rational, ethical, and soul-satisfying religious concept is the problem that confronts humankind with each enlargement of the boundaries of consciousness. Whatever else may appear on the surface to be engaging the efforts and attention of Homo sapiens, religion is the fundamental problem he deals with, for at base it concerns the problem of himself, the question of "Who and what am I?" . . . Such a religious concept must be psychologically based. Only then can it be universally valid.

This transition from theology to psychology, in understanding the meaning of Religion in man's history, can come simply as "each man takes a new view of his own religion."[28]

ACT TWO

The Shining Stranger Speaks

A New Answer to the Question of Jesus' Messiahship

Jesus appeared on the scene when the whole world was waiting for an external or supranatural force, personified in the person of a Messiah, to intervene in the affairs of man and accomplish for him all that he is potentially capable of accomplishing. History and the evolution of consciousness were marking time. Jesus *reversed* the force of Messianic expectation by assuming the role of Messiah and at the same time repudiating it. *The Shining Stranger* says:

> Jesus, Himself, so thoroughly undermined the prevailing Messianic concept, left the question of it and His relationship to it so entangled in contradiction, so twisted and bent in every direction, that the controversy He began could not be closed, the question could not be answered, the battle He started could not cease, until the last fragment of any Messianic image was gone and His own Messianic image, become in time a hated object of odium, had been pounded into dust.[29]

Therefore, Preston Harold concludes: *Jesus was not, and did not believe Himself to be, the long-awaited Judaic Messiah. His mission was to* destroy *the Messianic tradition of his day and* supplant it *with the idea of God indwelling every person, each expressed as God-son, Logos, Christ—or chalice of the life and unique power of universal parent being.* This is, indeed, a strong statement. But Harold develops a strong and solid basis for it, drawing upon Jesus' own words and actions. The case for this conclusion is presented in Chapter 2 of *The Shining Stranger*, and is elaborated in each succeeding chapter as the various aspects of Jesus' life and work are discussed. Each reader must draw his own conclusion as to the validity of this interpretation of Jesus' Messianic mission. To Harold, it is inescapable, because it rests upon Jesus' statements as given in the Gospels—not upon St. Paul's interpretation of the man he had never met.

The Stranger says that Jesus counted on the stubborn integrity of his people to continue their refusal of him as Messiah, thereby keeping the question open until his actual meaning came to be understood. And this was his meaning: *Jesus saw that each person speaks of himself only in the name of God, which is "One, I." Speaking in this name, Jesus deliberately made Himself* a symbol *of the God-Son in man, showing how God-consciousness operates in an unknown psychological realm within each person. This realm He called the "Kingdom of God, or Heaven." He said, it is "within you." Today, psychologists call this realm the* unconscious *and acknowledge the reality of its existence.*

Jesus understood that truth flows with equal force in the *unconscious* of every person and is accessible when one seeks it in his inner kingdom. He knew how to reach this psychological realm and let its truth express through his voice and guide his drama. He realized that *truth alone reigns and governs,* freeing the individual from error.

But, more important, he understood that as truth comes into conscious expression among mankind, *Messiah comes into human expression,* bringing ever closer the golden age destined to manifest itself as truth takes over from error.

Jesus showed that neither the Jewish people nor their spiritual leaders will accept the fulfillment of *an externalized Messianic concept.* Consciously or unconsciously they know that all that Messiah represents cannot be vested in the frailty of Homo sapiens.[30] But *mankind* bears this seed, this promise, within him. Homo sapiens must, like Israel, bear this promise until the end of his days. It cannot be realized until a more mature expression of mankind comes into being through the evolution of consciousness, which must extend to include all of humanity. Man is still a childlike expression of what he is destined to be.

Jesus knew that many men before him had tried, but failed, to reverse Messianic expectation and turn mankind to look to itself, each seeking within himself for truth and working to establish an ethical society. Jesus turned the spotlight of history on the problem and its answer by dramatizing and symbolizing the Messianic complex and its psychological implications within the most intense expression of the complex in the world —in the midst of the Jewish people in Palestine. He knew what he was doing and was solely responsible for his death. *The Stranger* is saying that:

(1) The historical stand of the Jewish people has been correct. But he is also saying that Judaism must transcend its traditional Messianic expectation and *internalize* the concept. Only the concept of the coming of truth, full consciousness, and complete empathy to every individual—

which will in time insure the coming of the golden age—can contain the fullness of the promise that man has borne since the dawn of consciousness, symbolized in Adam-Eve. In accepting the concept of the *Inner* Messiah, Israel does not repudiate its historical role. Instead, it repudiates once and for all the political threat that realization of its externalized Messianic ideal inevitably and tacitly poses.

(2) St. Paul's concept of *saving grace coming to man* as the spirit of Jesus, *the Christ spirit*, entering into his consciousness is correct. Correct, because this spirit embodies full consciousness of oneself as Son of God, child of Cosmic mind and energy; this spirit expresses complete empathy with and love for all living things, seeing itself as brother to each human being; it is dedicated to seeking truth, acting honestly, accepting in "blind" faith if need be that man cannot be separated from the love of God or the life of the Cosmos, and this is "saving grace." But *The Stranger* is also saying that Christianity must accept Jesus' own evaluation of himself: a brother-being to the least person ever born, the same as he, without reservation, so that Jesus cannot be the "only Son of God," the only means of mankind's redemption. Christianity does not repudiate its historical role in *recognizing the whole story of the Son of man to be a symbolic representation of psychological factors and processes.* Instead, it repudiates once and for all the psychological threat that Jesus is when he is held to be purchaser, ransomer, judge, master over life and death, heaven or hell, for every person born on earth.

The meeting ground for Judaism and Christianity is: Judeo-Christian Depth Psychology. The Inner Messiah is ever coming to consciousness, but truth is also ever present in the "midst" of the individual, in his unknown psychological realm, the *unconscious*. The Messiah (Christ) symbolizes the inner psychic Authority which governs the life of the individual. This is the Authority-Ego which Jesus symbolized and spoke of in the name of *Son of man*.

In Jesus' dramatic revelation of the psyche, Israel represents the world of consciousness made up of a multitude of selves, past and present, so that in the realm of consciousness man has no "one ego" as such. He has an "ego-group."

From this ego-group are drawn the "elect of consciousness"—symbolized by the disciples—who respond to the invitation to do truth's work in consciousness. These are the "superego-group" and they act as liaison between consciousness and the *unconscious*, between Authority-Ego and its ego-group. This superego-group is not censuring and ascetic, harsh. It expresses in every degree love of life and man. Nor is it perfect. It demonstrates every *human* trait.

Conscience is symbolized by John the Baptist.

St. Paul and the figures that enter the drama in the New Testament symbolize the change that occurs in the world of consciousness after it has an encounter with its Authority-Ego, the Inner Messiah, Christ consciousness.

The dynamic processes of the psyche are revealed in the Bible when it is seen to be a symbolic revelation of the development of consciousness in man. The role of the Authority-Ego, Son of man, is detailed in the Gospels.

It is appropriate here to let another voice, from *Equals One*, the journal of Auroville, speak, because his words describe so well the "secret programming" in the psyche of each person that leads to fulfillment of the Messianic dream in the whole body of Mankind:

> Everything which has been promised in the old religions about the "second coming," about the "last avatar," the "twilight of the Gods," the "New Jerusalem"—this society would be able to manifest beyond our wildest dreams, because behind these dreams is a hidden truth, a secret programming in the human being which guides him through his evolution—the shadow of the light which the society of the future projected into our past. It was these dreams which slowly constituted the soul of mankind even before mankind had a bodily form. All our past has been only the foetal life of the society of the future, and each human being carries in himself this child of light, this secret programming, this dream. . . . We learn it gradually, and we have all eternity in which to prepare ourselves for those vast and intimate meetings of the future where we can exchange our whole fullness of being, of being human, with the whole fullness of being of everyone else.[31]

We will bring this scene to a close by giving you the A B C D of Jesus' message. It is:

TREMENDUM

History had arrived at the dividing point in calendar time, but only one person was aware of this. Standing at the crossroads of earth, he heard the converging tongues of humankind beseeching High Heaven as with one voice to fulfill man's ancient dream:

> "Oh, Holy One, come! Bring on the reign of God! Establish God's kingdom in this sorry world and right its wrongs! Save us!"

Then he spoke words that divided the calendar into before (B.C.) and after (A.D.) they were said. Here, in substance, is his message:

The reign of God is not coming as you expect it to come. No one will be able to say, "Here it is," or, "There it is." Behold, I say unto you, the reign of God is now in your midst. The kingdom of God is *within you.*

The Holy One is not coming as you expect him to come. In the kingdom within yourself you will find the Anointed One, God-Son, who speaks only in the name of God. And the name of God is *"One, I."* You see, "I" is God's *name* by which you call yourself. "I" is God's *name* by which I call myself. Although each of us is unique as an "only one," the name of God which we all bear, "I," binds us in the sameness of brotherhood.

Each of us has this One same measure of God's Parent Being within us, the same measure as I profess for myself. Even the lowliest or most despicable person, man or woman, has *it*. This One-God-measure is leader, teacher, Lord of each one's being, the Self of selves within him, upon whom the government of his life rests.

I will speak of this *One Self* of selves in each of us as *Son of man.* Listen well. When I speak of Son of man I speak of that of God which is within you and *is you*—of that of God which is within me and *is me*—of that within humankind which is divine, divinely guided, divinely human, divinely certain of everlasting life and love, purpose and satisfaction in being—of that which is full of power, glory, grace, and reality.

Son of man is that which is *tremendum* in each of us who was, or is ever to be, born: B.C. or A.D.

This is the A B C D of Jesus' message.

*   *   *   *   *

One moment, please! There's a question from the audience. The young lady in the first row—your name?

> "My name is Eve. Why *Son* of man, if
> woman, too, has *it*? Why not *Child* of man?"

This question is answered in Section XIII of Book II of *The Single Reality*, the Book titled, *If Thine Eye Be Single*. But we may deal with it briefly here.

In life's beginning, only femaleness was present. This is to say, the first

62

living cells that divided to become two must be seen as "daughter cells." In time, these cells began to reproduce through means of a process that is today called parthenogenesis, which typically involves the development of eggs from virgin females without fertilization by spermatozoa. When parthenogenesis is accomplished in laboratory experiments, only female offspring are produced.

We do not know how long in life's history femaleness reproduced only itself. Or what happened in the cross-action of the nuclei of female cells that produced the first male. We do know today that *all* mammalian embryos are anatomically female during the early stages of fetal life. Therefore, each of us *begins in femaleness*—just as life began.

A new generation entered into life with the advent of maleness. Each of us, regardless of our gender, is a part of maleness because our bodies are sexually conceived by means of spermatozoa fertilizing ova.

In order to correspond to biological fact, the creation story would have to tell of femaleness preceding maleness, of Adam's being drawn from Eve, if Adam is seen simply as a male. But the story says: "In the day that God created man, in the likeness of God made he him; Male and female created he them; and blessed them, and called their name Adam, in the day when they were created." (Gen. 5:1-2).

From the beginning, mankind was Adam-Eve, a correspondence to the hydrogen molecule in which two whole ones share a field. What the creation story tells us is that *Eve is of the new generation drawn from maleness*—Woman is as Adam, constituted as is Man.

Adam, in the beginning, must be seen as representation of a "body of consciousness" that expresses its own physical body to which it is mated until death. Inherent in both the consciousness and the physical body is maleness and femaleness, regardless of sex—as was the case with Adam. Mankind, maleness, able to produce male or female offspring, is life's triumphant generation. Since all of us are of that generation, we are "brother-beings."

And Son energy, the Son-Self of God within us, is the Authority we possess which is *tremendum*—is that of which Jesus spoke when he spoke of Son of man.

The razor's edge, which each of us must walk, begins as the power and glory of this Authority, the Inner Messiah, stirs in our depths and, to greater or lesser degree, enters into our conscious expression. Let us turn attention now to this aspect of mankind.

The Threat and the Blessing of
Messianic Pretension and Messianic Delusion

As we return to *The Shining Stranger*, we find that the theme of the Messianic dream, the "secret programming" of the Inner Messiah which each person carries within himself, threads its course throughout the book.

The Messianic complex has been the "secret programmer" of history, individual and social. Its effect can be devastating, leading to insane and criminal expression which can be as far-reaching as Hitler's. But the effect of the Messianic compulsion that arises in the individual can also lead him to be society's great benefactor. Dr. Abraham Maslow says that all really serious men are Messianic, having no interest in anything but their mission.[32] Such men are the "growing tip" of the human species and are responsible for the evolution of its consciousness as well as its social systems.

Jesus saw that because each person carries the Messianic promise within himself, each is subject to Messianic pretension and delusion. He realized that only when the Messianic complex is understood is its social and psychological threat mitigated; and through such understanding, the constructive potential inherent in the ideal is released.

The Messianic complex expresses itself in two ways:

(1) As the will to power, exerted to deliver the world from what the self-styled Messiah sees to be evil, or to save man from himself, in one way or another reserving power to the few, the sufferer himself becoming master. Such will to power leads to Messianic pretension and the delusion that the pretender has been strangely and uniquely selected by Providence to fill the role.

(2) As the need to express the truth one has grasped, in the firm conviction that he alone possesses it and can save the world through somehow forcing attention upon it, even if this requires his own martyrdom.

64

This leads to Messianic delusion, and the sufferer's self-sought persecution. In one way or another, he demands his own crucifixion and gives his life for the message he would convey.

As a rule, both aspects of the Messianic complex are expressed simultaneously, one or the other predominating to greater or lesser degree. Each aspect is a perversion of truth. Each person is uniquely endowed to exert his power to deliver the world from evil; but this power does not extend beyond the Lilliputian ability to secure one cord upon the Gulliver of society; and that one cord binds the person's own measure of evil. Each person must also express the truth as he sees it; but the only thing unique about the truth he possesses is his mode of expressing it; and no one person can express the whole of truth; insanity overtakes him to the degree that he attempts to do this.

Jesus understood and revealed in his drama every facet of the Messianic complex. *The Stranger* says that Jesus could not have done so unless he had suffered it himself, because from birth the belief that he was Messiah had been implanted in his mind by his parents and the small group who shared their conviction.[33]

But Jesus' failure to respond to Satan's "tempting," and Jesus' consistent repudiation of the prevailing concepts of what Messiah was to be, what he was to do, indicate that as the forces of the Messianic complex culminated in him, he recognized its insanity and recovered from it before he began his ministry. In this ministry, he "ransomed the righteous"—because *expression of the Messianic complex always begins in righteousness.*

History is full of noble reformers, truth bearers, world savers, whose righteousness and search for truth leads them to their own destruction or the destruction of their sanity and then to devastating acts upon themselves or in society. Jesus relieved the righteous of the necessity to play the Messianic role because it was finished in his person—its self-sought martyrdom revealed. He broke the mold in which the ancient Messianic expression, as the will to power in this world, could be cast. And he fashioned the "mold of righteousness" to take the shape of: servant to one's fellowman and truth, commitment to the ethic of love, empathy (compassion), and honesty. He emphasized that the Messianic man must see himself to be no more, no less, endowed with truth and power than the lowliest of his fellowmen.

Jesus saw that sooner or later each person must struggle with the Messianic complex because sooner or later each person becomes aware of and must struggle with the promptings of the power vested in him. Until mankind realizes that the God-Son is born in every babe, that each is endowed with one full, equal measure of truth and power—and that each is governed and guided by his own Inner Messiah who "programs" his life through time, so that his evolution into wholeness and glory is assured—man and society will suffer the ravages of the Messianic complex.

When the realization comes that each is One, Son, equally endowed, a person is reborn in consciousness. The need to "save the world" has left him and he "labors humbly in Truth's vineyard, awaiting the grace of nature, knowing that life has given itself, its voice, to man and for man."[34] Love of life, joy in living in ways both great and small, becomes *pure* worship, unsullied by false piety and the vicariousness that an externalized Messianic concept demands. The wisdom of Zen is expressed here. And a person needs a teacher because, as *The Stranger* says, "a man must grasp the Christ (truth) in another, and realize the Christ to be in all men, before he can realize the truth of its being in himself and sustain this realization in sanity."[35] Each must choose his own teacher, who expresses truth in his person and leads his pupil into its paths. Teacher, servant of truth, is what Jesus stated himself to be. This is what he saw every person to be who worships in spirit and in truth.

Every great religious figure in history is such a teacher. The day of the fulfillment of the prophecy of Micah draws nearer. The world begins to recognize the *underlying psychological truth* that gives rise to religious expression in every tongue, however the *name* of God or teacher be called. Hear the words of Micah:

> For all people will walk every one in the name of his God, and we will walk in the name of the Lord our God for ever and ever.[36]

This, our generation, needs a new name for God, a new name for Teacher. We understand better the magnificence of the Cosmos and of universal energy in its least and most far-flung expression. Should our new name for God be: Cosmos? And we understand better that the great Teacher must be above all a very *human* being, artist of life in his love for its every expression. Should our new name for Teacher be: Humanism? *Cosmic Humanism*, the name, the new name, for emergent Religion?

The Stranger does not offer this name for the unifying concept of God and man that Harold's book invites. Preston Harold had left the play before Oliver Reiser's book came upon the scene. Reiser's work is not mentioned by him, but the attitude and approach of the two authors is compatible. *The Stranger* speaks of *Christian Realism*,[37] and we must hear his answer to other facets of the Palestinian mystery play in order to understand what he meant by this term.

66

The Sacred Books of Each Religion
Are the True Historical Messiahs

The Stranger says that "although Jesus, Himself, was not historical Messiah, through His work the Bible, itself historical Judaic Messiah, came into the world, its content delivered by the pen of the Jewish race. . . . The Bible is not the unquestionable word of God; it is the now unshakable work of men giving expression to consciousness of God in their being. . . . It is the Bible of human consciousness. . . ."[38]

The Stranger is saying that the Bible fulfills the Judaic promise to bring the truth of man into expression in this world—and this truth itself is the governing factor. Through the Bible, Judaic Messianic expectation has been fulfilled. In it, Christian Messianic expectation vested in the second coming of Jesus has been fulfilled; because through the Gospels Jesus returned to the domain of men, speaking with the same authority that marked his ministry, and this happened during the lifetime of the "beloved" disciple.

But what of the Messianic expectations of the rest of the world? *The Stranger* says that truth speaks the same words in every tongue. Therefore, each great religion must rightfully treasure its own Objectified Messiah, its Sacred Book, through which truth is brought to man's consciousness in every generation. Jesus recognized this, and in the formulating of his doctrine drew upon the treasured writings of all mankind. But he could not mention them by name. Why?

Jesus realized that each religious figure who preceded him and each that followed must himself become the being-symbol of the individual's psyche in order to convey psychological truth. The being-symbol must represent the Authority-Ego in the individual's *own world of consciousness*. Therefore, such a symbol could speak only *of himself* and *to his own people*. In order to be a true symbol of the Authority-Ego in each person, Jesus could address himself only to Israel, his own "ego-group."

Each such symbol must speak in the name of "I" if he would speak in the name of *One*, God, Cosmos.

Therefore, in *The Stranger*'s view, as each person takes a new view of his own faith, he will find the symbols that match the structure of personality which are found in the Judeo-Christian tradition; and he will find the revelation of essentially the same dynamic psychic processes that Harold describes, following the course of *Son of man* in the Gospels.

Christian Realism will lead Christianity to realize that it cannot explain away the Gospels. If they were written in the way that scholars now propose—many years after Jesus' death, dependent upon the failing memories of old men, the accounts changed or slanted, so that the real message of Jesus breaks through only here and there almost in spite of, rather than because of, the men who recorded his story—then Christianity is founded upon a mythical character.

The Stranger says that the Gospels were not tampered with. But how accurate can the Gospels be? In ordinary course, much of what Jesus said could not have been remembered, even as it was spoken. Harold could not accept the view that God pushed the pen of the authors any more surely than God pushes the pen of every person who writes a word on any subject. *The Stranger* deals only with that which is natural, not supranatural. Every interpretation is based upon, measured against, evidence within the realm of demonstrable phenomena.

Harold saw that the only known way in which the Gospels could convey the very words of Jesus, giving real substance to the record upon which Christianity rests, is by Jesus' use of hypnotism, through which he could be assured that his disciples would *remember* what he told them to record and would follow his instructions regarding the bringing forth of the Gospels.

Jesus using hypnotism? Hypnotism!

Withhold judgment, please. Do not turn away from the word *hypnosis*. Read Harold's handling of the subject in *The Shining Stranger*. More will be said about it later in our Play.

The important point we would make here—the point we hope you will remember—is: Harold believed that Jesus understood psychic power and its use to as great a degree as Homo sapiens can, although Jesus himself said that others would perform greater works than he did. At the level of Jesus' understanding, and the consequent way he exercised psychic power, his use of the hypnotic means cannot be thought of in the way we, with our limited understanding, usually think of the practice. Jesus' practice, his understanding, so far transcends this that Harold

68

used the word *hypnotism* only because there is no other word that provides as good a frame of reference within which to explore and examine the many mysterious workings of man's mental, psychic, and physical energy.

As for these strange workings, here we will say only that it is a well-known fact that a person in trance can remember what he is told to remember; and he will follow the suggestions or commands given, long after he has wakened. He may not know why he feels compelled to act as he has been instructed to act—regardless of how irrational his behavior seems to himself or others—but he will perform as told to perform unless the instructions are contrary to his very basic commitments.

The disciples themselves may not have understood their own behavior in the "birthing" of Jesus' record. The veil that was drawn to shroud this nativity—the disappearance of the original "Q" source and the "M" and "L" elaborations, the tolerance, each for the other's version of what happened—was a part of the plan Jesus made to insure his return through the advent of these documents, and, at the same time, *to lay down the pattern of how the words of truth that issue from a person's Authority-Ego are conveyed into his conscious domain.* Here is the pattern:

Jesus, symbol of Authority-Ego, wrote nothing. The disciples, symbol of the superego that bridges the conscious and *unconscious* domains, conveyed Jesus' words and drama to the world. We see that the Authority-Ego does not communicate directly. Because the message must be conveyed through the superego, which is involved with conscious knowledge and fantasy to some degree, at best there will be a modicum of interpolation, distortion, and adulteration of the message that is conveyed. Remember this as you ponder the messages of prophets and oracles, modern or ancient, wondering how accurate they may be. Through Jesus' use of posthypnotic recall, this threat to his message was reduced to an absolute minimum—another reason for utilizing this means—and the psychic pattern of how the words of the God-Son in man come into expression was laid down.

The amount of information that can be apprehended by Homo sapiens' consciousness is limited. When man questions beyond his ability to understand the answer, or when he questions in terms too broad, or when the question itself is composed of error, the answer must be given in parable, allegory, metaphor, or symbolic form. And the answer must be given in the terms in which the question was posed, just as an algebraic problem must be worked utilizing the given set of symbols.

The Stranger says that Jesus chose for disciples men who were neither intellectuals nor mystics. He committed them to the one task of conveying his message as the "spirit" (psychic power) brought remembrance. Harold points out that Jesus, too, must speak through his own superego as he went into trance and let "I" reveal itself through his voice. The message he gave the world is eternally fresh in meaning because Jesus was committed in consciousness to the natural in life and to the discipline of mathematics. His parables follow nature's path and the channels of everyday living, or they are given in the language of arithmetic, which everyone can understand.

The most important thing Jesus had to do was to insure that in the Gospels he would be presented as a true symbol of the Authority-Ego in man, with its Christ-consciousness. Here, we must face the question of why the Gospels are so contradictory. They differ even in the matter of the length of Jesus' ministry.

In Harold's view, *Jesus saw to it that the Gospels would contradict each other in many ways, on many levels, in order to symbolize the psychic truth that the coming of Son-consciousness into a person's conscious mind cannot be forced into a chronological pattern applicable to everyone. Nor can the operation of Son-consciousness be formalized into a given pattern. It comes and goes in different ways, at different times, and stays for different durations in those who express it. But, sooner or later, it comes to everyone.*

Jesus did not attempt to convey the whole of truth. He called upon the Scriptures, and he called upon the psychic power of other men to help him. He told his disciples that the *holy spirit would bring remembrance* of all he had said to them.[39] Here, he clearly indicated his use of the means of posthypnotic recall.

In Jesus' day, psychic power was called "spirit." Hypnotism is exertion of psychic power. Harold believed that Jesus understood this power as few have before or since and that he demonstrated and revealed its every aspect. An enlightened world must examine this extraordinary power that, when understood, could be the greatest of blessings. Coming onto the scene is a generation that is not afraid of the idea of psychic power and demands to know more about it. But even to them hypnotism is apt to be a distasteful subject—we need a new name for it.

Whatever we may think of hypnosis, *the idea that Jesus employed the natural power of posthypnotic response to suggestion to insure that his message be given as he wished to give it is a completely new answer to the mystery of the Gospels.*

It is also an answer that undoes a century of "Form Criticism" and

"Jesus Research." This ragged rug is pulled out from under a Christianity that is largely an apology for Jesus, because Christians can no longer really believe the Pauline interpretation of him. Young and old are understandably disenchanted with traditional theology, Judaic and Christian. Western religion literally finds itself between the devil and the deep blue sea.

On the one hand, there are the fundamentalists, who cling to the image of God and the Bible that is dead or dying in our time—wrathful Jehovah, heaven and hell, the devil tempting humankind, angels dictating every word of the Holy Writ.

On the other hand, there are the sophisticated scholars, who have researched the Bible to death, pronouncing the Gospels to be an unreliable record of Jesus. They seem to forget that there is *no other record*. If the Gospels are not a valid account of Jesus, there is no *reason* for Christianity to continue to exist; it must follow that Christianity is founded upon no more than a literary character drawn from conglomerate and contradictory views. Theologians, take note: Christianity is drowning in the morass that "Form Criticism" and "Jesus Research" has made of the Gospels.

We have said this before. But it is worth repeating. Jesus and the Gospels are indivisible—the one as valid as the other, the one as easily explained away as the other.

There is an answer that transcends the dilemma, an answer that confounds the "devil" and escapes the "deeps." Harold gave it.

The Gospels truly bring Jesus to life when we view them as the product of man's ability to remember correctly what he is told to remember in trance. The integrity of the disciples in relating Jesus' drama as they participated in it and as each was told to convey it is established. It also becomes clear that any valid interpretation of Jesus must be based upon his *own words* as given in the Gospels—not upon St. Paul's interpretation of him. *The Stranger* takes its stand upon Jesus' words.

Jesus spoke strange words, which did not appear to be fulfilled. He said to his questioners that they would *all* see the Son of man descending upon the clouds of heaven.[40] To the early Christians, this event would herald the end of the world.

How does *The Stranger* handle this predicament that beset Christianity from its beginning? We shall deal with this in Scene IV.

Return of the Son of Man
Is a Subjective Reality Fulfilled at Death—
A Part of Jesus' Doctrine of Reincarnation

Son of man means simply *man*. It is the name Jesus used to identify himself as *symbol* of the psychic factor that Harold calls the Authority-Ego, God-Son in the unconscious psychic realm, whose return heralds the end of the world. When will this happen?

The end of this world comes for each individual at death.

Jesus' words say that this psychic factor, Son of man, Self-of-selves, full of glory, grace, and reality—this Self-knowing—descends upon the "clouds of heaven," *which means the clouds of inner space*, reuniting with its ego-group or world of consciousness at death. Then, on another plane of being, and in the womb, the "secret programming" of one's life that will bring him to fruition in evolution's process, whatever the hue that lifetime takes, continues.

The term *unconscious* is an unfortunate choice for the innermost depths and outermost reaches of the human psyche. This realm is unknown, but it is not unknowing. Because Jesus knew how to set his consciousness aside and let universal truth speak from the depths of his psyche, he could reveal man's nature and the psychic operations that take place in the inner kingdom. The "clouds of heaven" indicate the subjective nature of Jesus' words. *By pointing out the subjective nature of the end of the world, Harold resolves the apparent contradiction between what Jesus said and his failure to return as expected. The psychic factor, Son of man, returns at death.*

Only a few face death with open eyes or are able to indicate what happens. When Stephen, the first Christian martyr, was dying, he opened his eyes and cried out, "Look, I see the heavens opened, and the Son of man standing on the right hand of God." In April, 1967, when Aaron

72

Mitchell was executed in San Quentin Prison, as he was dying he screamed, "I'm Jesus Christ." Jesus said that the least person on earth must be seen to be the *same as himself*. Harold believed that this realization comes at death, although few are able to communicate it.

In *The Stranger*'s view, Jesus deliberately prohibited any description of his physical appearance being recorded in the Gospels. He did this in order that he might become a symbol of the Self of any person, and his entire drama might become a pattern of the psychological operation within the unknown inner kingdom.

If Son of man comes at death to gather his world of consciousness into the inner fold, what then? What of heaven and hell?

Jesus promised neither. Indeed, he said that *heaven* and earth would pass away.[41] Jesus promised eternal *life* and said that God *had* committed mankind to this: ". . . the Father raises the dead and makes them live. . . ." —"Ye must be born again."[42] This, clearly, simply, is the doctrine of reincarnation.

Centuries ago the doctrine of reincarnation was edited out of Christian theology. But the Gospels permit no editing. Throughout, they proclaim everlasting life—to be realized step by step as the childlike expression of man, that Homo sapiens is, matures in consciousness. Life cannot become eternal until mankind through learning develops incorruptible consciousness that will lead to his generating incorruptible flesh. Then the pendulum between life and death will move evenly with no loss of consciousness —death will be in life as sleeping and waking are in life. Heaven, the *unconscious*, will have passed away, because its truth will have come into conscious expression. Earth, the body, *passes away while it is in its living state*, as its cells divide, replenish, and renew it.

Homo sapiens' limited consciousness cannot envision a future state of being that will correspond altogether with the reality of it. Even the "earth" of this generation of man, his flesh, will have passed away as his ever-enlarging consciousness constructs a new temple of being to house itself in a body that will constantly be made anew.

We are just beginning to learn how completely consciousness controls the flesh. It was Jesus' understanding of this and his understanding of the involvement of psychic energy in normal perception, that led to his demonstrations which seem miraculous. These will be discussed later. It is enough to say here that man cannot answer the being-question until he comprehends the limits of his natural powers and understands death as a part of the process of his ongoing life until evolution reaches its goal: life everlasting.

Jesus said that each person "hath one" that judges him—God does not judge man.[43] The Son-Self in man judges his own world of selves, carrying on in the inner kingdom all he has known of love, truth, joy—returning to life that part of himself which he has found wanting, to experience good and evil in order that he may become conscious of life as it operates in truth and reality. And with each rebirth, a person brings into life a measure of himself that has yet to experience life. In his inner kingdom, the living images of all he has loved continue as a part of his very own being and eternal life. The understanding he has gained can never be lost. As he moves through his many lives, his evil attenuates and is recast, turning in the end to laughter or humor (ask a psychologist what laughter is "made of").

The Stranger says:

> Just as the child cannot love beyond the limitations imposed by his immaturity, so Homo sapiens cannot love beyond loving another *as himself*. As the beloved's image becomes a part of himself in being, the beloved's essence is experienced, but not possessed. Like a child, Homo sapiens enfolds the promise of knowing a different kind of love as he reaches maturity. With whom will he know it, share it? With the incomparable of himself made of *all* he has known of love. Nothing other can satisfy him eternally and be perfectly at home in his own world and being. This is not to suggest that the hope of reunion with others is false. It is to suggest that each becomes an eternal and essential part of another who has loved him, and he will recognize himself in that person; just as another he has loved becomes an eternal part of himself, and will recognize himself as an essential part of one's own love. One *keeps* one's loves. As to that which he loses, in Shakespeare's words, "Nothing of him that doth fade, but doth suffer a sea-change into something rich and strange." Beyond this, the "dimensions of heaven" cannot be mapped. . . . Man's first creative act is to fashion from his life experience a complementary-being: a personality he truly loves, born of and incorporating all he has loved. . . . Man is to possess a new *sense* of being: a companion-sense in life born of love itself. . . . Today, man senses his "I-being"—in some tomorrow he will sense "us-being" when the love he has known in life twice glorifies him.[44]

Son of man is "I-being" which *perfectly understands the frailty of its conscious soul,* and comes at death *to gather its ego-group in loving embrace, as a "bridegroom" comes to his bride.*

Jesus does not qualify the nature of this coming—whatever the hue of one's life, Son of man gathers the soul in loving compassion. There need be no fear of death itself. (And when man understands that nature has provided him the means of perfect anesthesia through exercise of auto-hypnosis—about which more will be said later—there need be no fear of the pain that may be attendant upon dying.) Death brings one's very own beloved Self of selves.

The uncertainty of the hour of one's death matches the uncertainty of the hour of the returning Son of man, as Jesus described it.[45] He said that the many who would come in his name were not to be believed, and left no indication that he as person would ever return in recognizable form.[46] But he had to describe the psychic dynamic of death: self-union with one's own Divine Absence, which is ever present on the other side of the mask he wears as he plays his role.

The Western world seems ready to accept the principle of rebirth, reincarnation. It corresponds with man's sense of justice and fits into the pattern of the evolution of consciousness. Much fantasy attaches to the idea, and this will continue until the study of man's consciousness throws more light upon the subject. Mankind may have *fetal knowledge* of reincarnation, which gives rise to his feeling of the certainty of life. This knowledge may be accessible—the facts of life might be gleaned—if man will seek first the kingdom within as he seeks the truth of his being. Hypnosis presents itself. In trance, a person can be regressed in time, perhaps into the womb. But, in Harold's view, not beyond. He believed that we should explore only within the discernible limits, from conception to death; and not for the purpose of seeking knowledge of our pasts, but for the purpose of understanding, and gaining guidance for the future.

Reincarnation confronts man with the necessity to make *this world* a better place to live in if he hopes to come into a "better hereafter." Jesus' concern was with this world, and his teaching leads men toward establishing an ethical society in which mankind may have life and have it abundantly. This is his own statement as to why he was doing what he did.

The Miracles Are Demonstrations of Psychic Power

The play of energy in man's inner space accounts for the miracles, and Harold relates that play to hypnosis. That stumbling block of a word again!

Harold chose to use the word *hypnotism* because all too many scientists refuse to admit that any form of ESP or psi-power exists. What else but the exercise of psychic power accounts for hypnotic phenomena? The most skeptical scientist cannot deny that an unknown range of hypnotic states can be produced, and the phenomena occurring in such states can be repeated. In discussing the data of hypnosis, Willis W. Harman says:[47]

> Of all those phenomena whose existence is widely recognized by scientists (whether or not they are felt to be understood), among the most fraught with significance and implication are those associated with hypnosis. The basic facts are generally known, but we have hesitated to draw the conclusions to which they point. A recent inventory of scientific findings about human behavior (Berelson & Steiner, 1964, pp. 121–123) lists a number of established findings regarding hypnosis, including the following:
> Hypnotism works: that is, there is no question today that hypnotism can induce all of the following "unnatural" states:
> 1. anesthesia and analgesia, local or general
> 2. positive and negative hallucinations
> 3. regression to an earlier age
> 4. unusual muscular strength, rigidity, resistance to fatigue
> 5. organic effects, normally outside voluntary control. . . .
> For example, a hypnotized subject may be induced to perceive an imaginary kitten placed in her lap. She experiences stroking the kitten and hearing it purr; the senses of sight, touch, and hearing seem to corroborate the hypnotist's suggestion. Yet this is a "positive hallucination." There is no kitty there.

Other examples are familiar. A subject accepts the suggestion that a person sitting in a particular chair really is not there; he perceives an empty chair. . . . Blisters and burned spots can be produced by hypnotic suggestion. . . . By changing the way in which [an] individual perceived the world his depth perception, time perception, movement perception, color perception, and so on, major behavior changes, as well as mental states ranging from psychoticlike to euphoric and mystical, were produced.

In combining the study of all paranormal phenomena into the study of the hypnotic state, Harold brings his reader into immediate contact with undeniable reality and provides a framework within which the miracles can be studied.

In the hypnotic state, the effects that Harman lists as well as many others—some strange indeed—can be produced, so that the range of possibilities is extremely wide. In Harold's view, the range of the hypnotic state is also wider than it is usually considered to be. The hypnotic state is simply a state of trance, which can be anything from a momentary lapse of awareness, or "shift" of consciousness, to deathlike coma. The dynamics of inducing trance or the hypnotic state are outlined as Harold begins his discussion of the miracles. Although he does not necessarily rule out all other explanations, he shows that *all the miracles can be seen to be demonstrations within the known limits of hypnotic phenomena*, so that all of them fall within the realm of natural happenings.

The Stranger urges that research by medical men and psychologists be broadened, and that everything that is known about hypnosis be made common knowledge. Throughout history the power to employ hypnosis has been used—and often abused by design or through ignorance of its effects. It is a natural power which mankind must understand because man is subject to its use and misuse from birth to death. Harman puts it well:

> Now what are the conditions essential to the production of hypnotic phenomena? In their barest simplicity, they are (1) a source of suggestion and (2) the willingness, at a deep level in the personality, to accept suggestion from that source. But surely these conditions are met in our infancy and early childhood. . . . The inference is as obvious as it is startling: *We are all hypnotized from infancy.*

Today, it is thought that a person under the hypnotic control of another cannot be made to do anything that is actually against his will or contrary to his desires. But we do not know for sure. We do know that when a person does respond by accepting suggestion, he is expressing *his own will* and willingness to cooperate at the deep levels of his being.

It is difficult, if not impossible, to hypnotize an *unwilling* subject—although not necessarily an unaware subject.

Scientists must determine whether a person can be made to act against his own will in the hypnotic state. If so, young people must be taught the dynamics of hypnosis—how to recognize hypnotic tactics and defend against them. Power of any sort may be constructively used, or it may be misused. The more subtle the power, the more susceptible it is to misuse and also *the greater is its potential to produce beneficial effects.*

Because we know that the person who responds to suggestion is expressing his own will and willingness to cooperate, it must follow that Jesus' disciples were not "used" or "misused" or "controlled" by him. They were his willing co-workers in his mission to reveal the nature of man and the power with which he is endowed.

Harold says that Jesus showed the effects that can be produced through exercise of psychic power in man—*its ability to delude as well as to illuminate*—and he demonstrated the release of the body's own healing power in hypnotic trance.[48]

Harold designated the hypnotic state as any state in which the person is not normally alert and concentrating *intellectually* upon whatever he is doing. Trance may be self-induced, induced by another, or it may come spontaneously. In certain trance states, if not in all such states, something other than normal consciousness takes over—and miraculous feats, physical and otherwise, may be accomplished without apparent effort.

The whole story of hypnosis is a story of miracles and failure to perform miracles—of use and misuse, of possibilities so wide that *all* mysterious phenomena can be related to it or produced through use of it. It is necessary that man understand the power of hypnosis because it is *a part of his natural endowment.* He may use this power beneficially or to the detriment of himself and others. This is why, according to *The Stranger*, Jesus showed in his works and described as best he could in the language of his day the dynamics of this power. Man cannot understand himself until he understands it; he cannot reach his full potential and a new plateau of freedom until he knows how to defend against its misuse and use it himself to meet countless needs. For example, he could use it to produce anesthesia, without use of drugs, which in cases of long illness often lead to traumatic side effects; he could use it to easily "program" his mind with data he needs to remember.

But again and again, Harold stresses the point that Jesus made in his every demonstration of psychic power: it is not itself a "cure" for anything, not a panacea on which man may depend for the working of "miracles" to meet his needs. With every use of this power, there is that within man (his own Authority-Ego) which demands that *he take a corresponding step in exhibiting conscious control of himself.* He can accomplish this only as his consciousness of truth and reality also widens. He must understand that something he is expressing in his conscious or subconscious mind, in his behavior or emotional responses, has led him into his predicament or created his need in the first instance.

It is appropriate to say here that Harold believed the necessity for further research in hypnosis and psychic phenomena should in no way lessen or diminish further research in regular medical practice such as surgery and the development of beneficial drugs. Mankind should utilize all the blessings and knowledge that medicine has put within reach.

It remains true, however, that the advances medicine has made have served inevitably to deepen man's understanding that mind and body are inseparable. To an ever-enlarging degree it is apparent that the mind and emotions control the flesh and the health of the human being. *The Stranger* says that medical men are becoming ever more aware that restoring health and prolonging life is not in itself enough. The physician must restore meaning to the life of the patient:

> The sickness besetting man's soul cannot be healed by medical science or by hypnotherapy—this illness is caused by loss of religion, which gives rise to a decline in one's sense of purpose and meaning in life, and to unspoken despair. . . . To the twentieth century, Jesus' words still say: "If thou canst believe, all things are possible to him that believeth . . ." And like the father of the tormented child, this century cries out and says with tears: "Lord, I believe; help thou mine unbelief." Today, as always, "mine unbelief" is the sickness that must first be healed.

Harold said that as the biblical miracles are considered, a person should not dwell upon how much he knows that makes it impossible for them to be true. He should think about how little he knows to make it possible for him to understand them and *describe* them in the scientific terms he now demands. A miracle cannot be *willed*, and belief, doubting not, is the most difficult of all psychological states to induce when a person is in dire distress—it is doubtful if anyone could muster sufficient faith unless he could lose his conscious fear in a blessed state of trance.

To those who could receive it, Jesus imparted his own faith. But he pointed to an easier way than seeking a miracle for a person to meet his every need, saying that we must seek first the inner kingdom of God and his righteousness. Today, we seek this inner realm, but we call this the practice of depth psychology.

The Stranger says that in today's world it would be a miracle if anyone could fulfill the conditions Jesus outlined. Yet miraculous faith healings take place. Katherine Kuhlman, for example, somehow helps many in her audiences to release fear and accept the healing evoked by the "holy spirit of God"—the spiritual or psychic energy with which man is endowed—as she stands, a shining example of faith, before thousands of people to whom she imparts it in varying degree.

But for all too many, fear of derision, or knowledge of the "impossibility" of the situation, prevent expression of faith. The medical fraternity could create the climate in which it would not be so difficult to release fear and to put aside the intellectual knowledge that stifles hope. They could send teams to study the great faith healers living today to try to determine the psychic principle that is being employed, no doubt with many variations.

We, the audience, must insist that such a mysterious and uneducated "medic" as Arigo of Brazil be studied while he is living and practicing medicine so successfully—at the same time defying much that today is standard medical practice. He employs both surgery and drugs but ignores antiseptic measures. He uses no narcotic anesthesia, but his patients feel no pain. He "closes" incisions with his hands—not stitches —and they remain closed and heal. Some medical men are courageous enough to undertake serious study of such healers. Dr. Andrija Puharich is one who has made trips to Brazil to study Arigo and film his work.[49] Arigo must induce trance rapidly and unobtrusively to produce anesthesia in his patients as he operates so swiftly, using a small unsterile knife. No infection follows. Long ago in India, Dr. James Esdaile, learned surgeon, used hypnosis to induce anesthesia and performed hundreds of major operations with very little postoperative infection. Edgar Cayce went into deep trance before taking his journeys into the bodies of faraway patients to diagnose and prescribe treatment—these were psychic probes that caused no pain.

Well, let us look now at Jesus, the healer. He said that others would do greater deeds than he did—thereby ruling out the idea that God worked through him in a supranatural way.

Harold points out that the type of illnesses Jesus cured are limited and that he told people their own faith, belief, *expectation* had made them whole. He did not effect a healing every time he attempted to cure, or else he did not attempt all the cases he was expected to cure. In his home territory where he was known as the son of the carpenter and was without prestige, he could not perform many miracles of healing. The dynamics he used follow the well-established pattern of releasing the body's healing power in hypnotic trance, wherein the prestige of the operator plays an important role and the patient's own expectations and wishes (conscious or subconscious) determine his response to suggestion.

We must remember that the operator's beliefs, prejudices, expectations also play an important role and that the ability to induce trance or to go into trance state varies widely. But there is more than this involved. Some *principle* is being touched upon, and we must discover it. What was the secret of Jesus' success?

Harold saw that something must break the grip of fear before healing power can be released. Trance, however light and fleeting, provides a moment's mental or physical anesthesia, so that *anesthesia itself* might be the healing secret. He saw also that the patient must somehow be "shocked" into making his response, but the shock must not be too traumatic if it is to be fully effective. There are many kinds of anesthesia, beginning with words of reassurance. There are many kinds of shock, beginning with surprising words or unexpected authoritative commands. Harold believed the principle involved a play between anesthesia and shock which in itself can produce anesthesia.

Consider for a moment that spontaneous remission of the most hopeless cases of cancer is the great mystery researchers face. Might some type of shock be involved?

"Is there a doctor in the house? If so, will he come to the stage and tell us if research is being done in shock therapy for treatment of cancer? Has anyone tried electric anesthesia, which produces both unconsciousness and what might be called total physical shock? Might sleep treatment hold promise?"

"Will a psychologist step forward and tell us whether hypnotists are attempting to discover in Mesmer's records what *principle* he employed, although he may not have understood himself what he was doing?

Could he have been so successful because he reinforced verbal suggestion with physical touch, or motions that directed attention upon the ailing part of the body?"

"I'm wondering about some sort of shock therapy for mentally retarded children—to wake them up—somehow they seem to be in a sort of sleep. There are so many who have no discernible brain damage. Could a retarded child be hypnotized?"

Let us have order, please! The best we can do to answer your questions is to look again at Jesus' method of healing. *The Stranger* suggests that Jesus went quickly into trance himself, leading his patients into the hypnotic state so swiftly that the observers were unaware of what was actually happening. Inducing the desired state of trance is not easily done.

Harold says, "To go into trance, a person must have *faith in the operator*. Consciousness of man's fallibility and knowledge of the operator limit this faith. . . ." And insofar as expectation or faith that a healing will take place is concerned, reason and intellectual conditioning limit faith. "Thus, the limits of faith that it is possible to possess *in reality* limit the effectiveness of hypnotherapy, which may, *theoretically*, be without limit in its application, but in reality is limited because reason limits faith. As one reviews the healings of Jesus when the patient was there and conscious, one sees a pattern of:

Rapid induction into trance.
Authoritative command or surprising word to produce a degree of shock, coupled with a physical factor, such as touch or stretching forth the hand, *to reinforce and direct verbal suggestion*. Therapy is administered by an operator devoid of ego-group in play [the Authority-Ego, the Christ-factor, is the only psychic factor in Jesus that is active in the process]; the patient is given over to the forces within him; faith is the determining factor. . . .

. . . The image Jesus formed and projected was the Christ of God in man which makes him whole and perfect. . . . Through this symbol, Jesus healed: . . . the symbol of Self as 'Divine Child'. . . . His secret appears to rest in knowing that only the Christ which is in man can perform the miracle of a true and lasting healing. . . . Jesus warned that the approach is broad, but the way is narrow. Each may have a secret 'loop hole' through which he enters the state of sleep or trance—both conditions could be differing degrees of anesthesia which permits the self-healing power to operate. . . ."

Again and again, Harold stresses that the problem is to discover the principle Jesus employed—*the call he made on a person's consciousness and unconscious forces, because the process involves a change in both these dimensions of one's being.* It is to be hoped that aversion to the word *hypnotism* will not prevent a careful study of that principle as *The Stranger* details it.

This is especially important in those cases when Jesus' patients did not come into immediate contact with him. Three such healings are reported. In these cases *The Stranger* says that Jesus demonstrated extrasensory perception and showed that telepathic communication can be directed through a medium to heal a patient who is not present.

As for raising the dead—raising the *dead*! Doctors do it today, sometimes using means that might well kill the living. And today, with all their instruments, it is a pressing medical problem to determine when death begins and when it is complete. Jesus showed that death *begins* in the deathlike sleep of plenary trance—"our friend, Lazarus, sleepeth"— and he showed that man can be returned to life from this state, in which the body does not deteriorate. The "dead and buried" have been raised from such trance. The mother of General Robert E. Lee is one example. What principle is involved—why do some respond and others not?

The Stranger points to Scriptures which indicate that "in the last extremity of life, in death-trance, the ego-group of the patient will respond only if the physical measure applied to the body is reduced in traumatic impact to a *whisper* as the force penetrates the inward psychic reaches. . . . Tyrrell describes the painful reemergence of a man from the hinterlands of life. . . . Jesus demonstrated that even from the extremity of death it is possible to return a man's ego-group to its conscious existence, but death processes were not arrested by Him when a person was beyond the prime of life or when the body was not in good condition. . . . Of the many called, few indeed respond. Perhaps in death one knows himself and is unwilling to return *to the condition of amnesia man calls consciousness.*"

In the "illusory miracles," such as Jesus' walking across the water, he demonstrated that a person in trance will see and hear what the operator tells him to see and hear. The vision will be *real* to him, *but the miracle happens only to the percipient.* Strange, is it not, that the Gospel of St. Mark, which is considered to be the remembrances of Peter, does not report that Peter walked forth to meet Jesus.

In almost every case of visionary, illusory experience with Jesus there is difference in the way the episode is reported. Each account is subjective, given as that particular disciple experienced it. And there is evidence that everything was suddenly normal as the disciples were returned to their normal states of consciousness at a touch, by a word. Again, the pattern is that of being brought quickly out of trance.

Harold believed that Jesus created these symbolic dramas to reveal the psychological operation in the universe behind men's eyes. And that Jesus deliberately set up in the Gospels the contradictory reports so that these episodes must be questioned and studied until time revealed them to be demonstrations of the phenomena that can be produced while a subject is in trance. *But each demonstration also enfolded the pattern of some type of psychic operation. The Stranger* says:

> In the illusory miracles, Jesus created the symbolic dramas that portray man's experiencing the ultimate aspect of his being. These dramas are redrawn, or are seen piecemeal, in the descriptions many men give when commanding truth is aroused within them or when the intellect, like Peter, is sinking in the deeps of the mind. The illusory miracles portray psychic action in valid terms, and they give an insight larger than is possible in any attempt to describe what happens to the terrified visionary. If a man can grasp the Christ, as symbolized by Jesus, he will be able to withstand the psychic travail. When one is in the midst of the purgatorial ordeal, he cannot be helped by metaphysical dissertations and systems—a more "present help," a more human understanding, is required to meet his need: he must have something to turn to, a mental image of the Christ, a *symbol* of the grace of God in man, which will take him in hand, to which he may cling as a child. . . . Turning to prayer or to a religious symbol to still the inner tempest is likely only if one has had religious training as a child and prayer is a ritual with him. If, habitually, he turns away from violence, when he must suffer inner violence habit itself will stay the mind and hand from abuse of self or another.

Harold says that in the drama of the Transfiguration, Jesus indicated that at the height of realization "one is illuminated in his being and undergoes a metamorphosis which puts upon him the shining raiment of love." But as this happens, "the body and emotions he is 'roped to' will, like the disciples, be 'sore afraid.'" But if man has grasped the God-Son within himself, "this One will lead him up to the heights and safely down again—will warn him that the full meaning of this vision cannot be realized in life or so long as one is in this world, but he must none the less bear witness to it. The miracles upon the waters show that if a man is aware of the Christ in being, he may call upon this One to still the tempest in his mind, and that as he ventures out alone to meet truth upon the deeps, this One will stretch forth a hand to save him as he sinks."

The Christ in being—this One that *The Stranger* speaks of—is a person's own Authority-Ego, God-Son within him, to be seen as the *same* as Jesus portrayed in playing the role of *Son of man*.

"Lead us not into temptation . . ."

The Stranger says, "To know truth forever *tempts* the intellect; to know God or holiness forever *tempts* the intuition. Jesus saw that man's consciousness of God is revelation of God-being within him, saw that it is truth incarnate in him that *poses always the temptation to grasp and know it*, leading the mind to higher consciousness until fear engulfs. Jesus understood that such power as truth engenders must be shared to be had or tolerated in sanity. He saw that because each man is independent in his being, he will come to realize his independent existence and must struggle with this madness until he can grasp truth larger than his solitariness: the Fatherhood of God insuring the brotherhood of man, the Christ within himself as his indestructible bond with the whole of life insuring his communication and communion with each other human being, making him a free agent in a social whole wherein every person on earth has the *same* endowment of power, glory, and truth at his disposal when his conscious and *unconscious* domains are summed—the Beatitudes project this summation."

The Beatitudes are the "Blessed are the . . ." series that begin the Sermon on the Mount (Matt. 5:1-12), and *The Stranger* says that this discourse is itself a miracle because of the effect of Jesus' words upon succeeding generations. And in what Harold calls the "social miracles," Jesus showed that the power of suggestion moves groups of people to action and that man responds to truth when it is presented to him with shocking clarity:

> When Jesus entranced His audiences, He gave them the suggestion of sharing their hidden reserves of food, their hidden reserves of mercy, their hidden reserves of conviviality—and He gave them the suggestions

85

recorded in the Sermon on the Mount. The twentieth century, however, confronts a stark horror that is no less a miracle for its hue: Adolf Hitler entranced his audiences and loosed their "legion" along with his own upon a world that realizes it was somehow party to his acts. The drama of Legion shows the destructive potential arising from mass susceptibility which makes it possible to transfer manic Messianic impulses from one man to a large group.

In this drama, a maniac is asked to name his demon, and it calls itself "Legion," saying, "there is a host of us." Whereupon, Jesus casts Legion into a herd of swine that rush to their destruction in the sea. What does this strange demonstration teach?

The lessons to be learned from each miracle (and parable) are manifold. Harold says that the maniac, so the story goes, was chained but could not be kept bound. "Legion" represents a pattern of numerous repressed, subliminal fears bursting loose—a phobia that could not be defined or "named" because it consisted of a lifetime's accumulation of destructive emotions and "silent" small terrors which had grown into a powerful force that must by its very nature be sent somewhere. *The Stranger* says, "Jesus had revealed in a parable that a psychic force of destructive potential (an evil spirit) cannot be destroyed merely by driving it out of consciousness (repressing it) because it will return, its force increased, and devastate the 'house' from whence it came. In this parable and in the drama of Legion one may observe that as repressions are reversed and re-presented to consciousness, if they are not reconciled within it by a widened understanding they gather into a host of nameless, unrecognized fears, a mass that can no longer be dealt with one by one for they have lost their identity. The Authority-Ego must then present them to the world of self by casting their destructive force onto the cellular level, as symbolized by the swine. When transferred to or cast upon the animal flesh in which man is clothed, Legion drives it to panic and self-destruction. Thereby, Legion expends itself and the Authority-Ego wipes out an expression in flesh that can no longer contain its accumulation of unidentified fear. When Legion's tensions and conflicts cross over into the cellular realm, they give rise to a death-dealing disease which moves at panic's pace. . . . In society, man has had experience of one man, or one act, stemming the tide of panic—and certain individuals appear to be immune to panic's lure. Although man does not know how it is achieved, he does know that there is no panic-paced disease in which spontaneous remission has not taken place."

Each of us must contend with our own Legion—the accumulated fears and destructive emotions, the tensions and hatreds we have repressed. Since "panic-paced" and death-dealing diseases occur even in infancy, we must project that Legion may be carried over from a past life. Or it may accumulate into a host of prenatal or birth fears that destroy the chances of the individual to fulfill his life's promise. We know little or nothing of prenatal psychic influences.

The vast majority of us suffer the violence of Legion in our own flesh before our Legion becomes a host. Much of Legion is dispatched in small detachments that kick up no more than a common cold. We must remember, however, that fear is contagious. But so is laughter. And so are tears. So are a number of illnesses. Harold would say that you must remember to have your medical vaccinations because together with the physical protection they afford they also reduce the host of your Legion of fear, your concern that you might contract the disease.

The drama of Legion tells us that as we undergo life's physical, emotional, and mental stresses, a host of repressed fear is accumulated on the subliminal level. And it will be expressed in terms of mental illness if it reaches intolerable strength—else, it will be transferred to the cellular level, causing death-dealing disease. Since Legion must be expressed, we must learn to deal with it day by day so that it cannot mount its force, and is disposed of as nontraumatically as are the body's wastes. When we understand how to deal with our Legion, we will understand how to maintain our health.

Society must deal with its corporate Legion. *The Stranger* says, "Jesus saw that man may change only himself—that each man 'hath one' [his own Authority-Ego] which judges him and deals with his own evil and will in time save his own world. Society's salvation must follow. Society's Legion must be bound as the Lilliputians bound Gulliver. If a man can secure one cord upon it, he will find satisfaction: he may secure a cord upon it as he secures a cord upon his own. The man who thinks he can change society is expressing to some degree Messianic delusion. In the drama of Legion, Jesus showed that the attempt to rid man of evil in one grand play that changes society's dealing with him results in destruction of the masses. His whole ministry points to the realization that society cannot be delivered of its ancient evils within the life-span of any one man—not even upon the advent of a Messiah—for He tells of the struggles men will have to endure in society before the final struggle is met, and He indicates that this struggle will be met upon the psychic plane."

The Stranger is not saying that we should not try to right social wrongs—or that they cannot be righted. To the contrary. But progress in this direction *begins* with the individual's own behavior; and social problems must be handled one by one before they grow into an unidentifiable host that cannot be dealt with save in one grand play that defeats the purpose because of the traumatic effects it produces upon those who are "innocent" of the dilemma.

But here we are not dealing with social problems. We are dealing with psychic energy. The *unconscious* is the seat of the psychic power. Harold says that Jesus exercised His psychic power to show the real limits of this mysterious force in man, "so that any strange phenomenon that cannot be reconciled within the framework drawn by his deeds must be regarded with suspicion. . . . Jesus appears to have seen that the psychic power is deeply involved in awareness, perception, the process of learning, and artistic expression, so that to show its inward play upon man, and Himself to express the true limit of its power within and without oneself, was His mission. As teacher, He was artist and He used His psychic power to teach and demonstrate His lessons. In the lesson of the loaves . . ."

Here, we come to what Harold calls the "fantastic" miracles, which he believed were demonstrations of an operator's ability to obliterate the ability of his small audience to perceive what is happening. Perception is distorted. The opposite of hallucination occurs. "Hallucinatory blindness and deafness" is induced. A fantastic answer? Any good hypnotist with subjects in trance can produce this effect. And after a subject has been hypnotized to the desired state of trance, the operator can induce trance almost instantaneously by employing some unobtrusive signal.

The Stranger deals with the miracles *as they are reported*. The reports of the feeding of the multitudes do *not* say that Jesus commanded the few loaves and fishes to grow and that before the eyes of the people they grew as he broke them, nor that as the food was taken from the baskets more food appeared. The reports give only the beginning and the end of the drama. Because they tell nothing of what actually happened, Harold concluded that Jesus commanded his disciples in trance state to see everything *but where the food came from*. Expectancy played a role: "Jesus had the disciples arrange the people in groups. Each one was thus 'fixed' in the expectation of eating. Then He took what He had, gave thanks, broke the food into pieces and placed it before the crowd. The suggestion of sharing and eating, implemented by His own decisive action, must have spread with the lightning of telepathy throughout the crowd, for the simple story then ends, 'So the people ate and were satisfied.' . . . This event appears to be a spontaneous mass reaction to suggestion. . . ."

The disciples did not see that a perfectly natural thing was happening. People brought out their own hidden reserves of food, ate, and shared. The "miracle of the loaves" taught the lesson that the hidden reserves in man are sufficient to provide for life however hopeless the scene may appear.

Harold says that Jesus may have used this opportunity to teach another lesson: "a fantastic demonstration involving objective matter to a degree entirely beyond the creditable is not what it appears to be—through hypnosis, hallucination or hallucinatory-blindness has been induced. . . . Jesus said that faith as a grain of mustard seed could move a mountain, could uproot and transplant a tree in the sea. But *He made no such demonstration.* . . . In Jesus' words, a mustard seed is *as the realm of God*—this seed, less than any on earth, grows larger than any plant. Therefore, faith 'as a mustard seed' indicates *faith larger than is possible to Homo sapiens' consciousness* which cannot enfold the whole realm of God. . . . One might say, in truth, all things are possible, but the attempt to exercise faith that is potentially as great as the mustard seed Jesus described often flowers into fantastic hallucination, and what actually may be achieved through hypnosis is limited because there is a limit to the faith man can express, doubting not in his heart that what he asks will be done."

But Harold points out that Jesus said greater works would be done than he did, and that there are many demonstrations which have no explanation other than mental or psychic power affecting material substances. Nevertheless, of all psychic phenomena, psychokinesis (objects set in motion, affected, or produced through unseen means) is "least understood and is most likely to lead to self-deception and trickery if one embraces the concept too hastily."

There is one area, however, in which we *are* sure that an "unseen" force affects an object. That force is a person's own psychic energy; that object is his own flesh. We may also be reasonably sure that certain altered states of consciousness allow for *paranormal perception* giving the gifted subject commanding insight on the physical as well as the intellectual level. We know now that everything is surrounded by, permeated with, indeed, *is*, an energy field. We may expect to refine our sight or instruments—our receptors—to receive stimuli and information at levels undreamed of in Jesus' day, making possible and probable greater deeds than he performed. We know now that somehow the

Cosmic Mind generates from the ethereal "nothing" of these interpenetrating energy fields all the solid stuff there is.

We know today that mental or psychic energy can affect a growing plant. But Harold believed that the drama of Jesus' withering the fig tree was created to demonstrate posthypnotic response to suggestion—since one report says the tree withered instantly and another says it was seen to be withered next morning. The disciple who saw it withered next morning was responding to suggestion posthypnotically. But the episode was used to teach a deeper lesson: the power to produce an effect through the manipulation of an effigy. The drama also indicated that "the odious and irrational in life is best destroyed through a withering process that is initiated when one destroys a symbol representing whatever he would have done with."

This particular "miracle" embarrasses Christianity. It was not the time for the tree to bear its figs. Could God-Incarnate, Saviour of the world, essence of love itself, petulantly destroy a tree because it was growing normally?

The Stranger says, "An intricate message must be enfolded in this drama and it must hinge upon what the tree and its fruit represent. Jesus made a tree the symbol of Himself, calling Himself the vine. Thus, the withering of it becomes the withering of something to do with Himself. The incident takes place the morning after His entrance into Jerusalem, just before He is to provoke His own destruction in terms of an *effigy* of Judaic Messiah, on the cross. . . ." If the fig tree represented Jesus cast in the traditional Messianic role, which he sought to destroy, reversing the force of it by internalizing the concept, then his words, "may no one ever eat fruit from you after this," fall into place as the meaning behind this episode which *has* done so much to wither the concept of Jesus as God become flesh, to the exclusion of all other human beings. Now, listen to *The Stranger*:

> . . . the withering of the fig tree teaches that art is making an effigy of oneself to destroy through it the irrational or odious in life—to destroy it not explosively, but surely. At the same time the artist makes of his work a symbol to convey as large a measure of truth as he can. Thus, every artist is both destructive and creative. And every man is artist: of his life he creates both an effigy he would destroy and a symbol of truth he would express. As artist, Jesus was both destructive and creative—He destroyed the ancient Messianic mold and created the concept of the Christ in every man. Even the least bears this glory—is human, is divine. . . .

This "theater" of miracles has become as crowded as a ball park. Let the audience take a seventh-inning mental stretch. Then we will get on with a discussion of ESP.

S T R E T C H

"I'd like a bottle of beer and two hot dogs—lots of mustard."

"Where do you think you are?—in a ball park? Well, so we are. Hey you, with the beer! Over here, please."

> Jesus was called glutton and drunkard. He did not deny that He ate and drank as He chose—He stated that wisdom vindicates ascetic or non-ascetic practices: "For John the Baptist has come, eating no bread and drinking no wine, and you say, 'he has a devil'; the Son of man has come eating and drinking, and you say, 'Here is a glutton and a drunkard, a friend of taxgatherers and sinners!' Nevertheless, Wisdom is vindicated by all her children." Jesus provided wine at the wedding in Cana. Does His mysterious refusal of wine at the last supper provide the basis for a doctrine of abstinence—if so, making of Jesus a man reformed at the door of death? The teaching and practice of Jesus, however, do not invite to drunkenness or gluttony. He teaches that there is nothing in life that cannot be used to further its joy and abundance when man has learned to control himself. . . . He saw that men must grasp the art of play: "To what then shall I compare the men of this generation? What are they like? Like children sitting in the marketplace and calling to one another, 'We piped to you and you would not dance. . . .'"

"Another beer, and a hot dog for *The Stranger*."

"Is it true that laughter is made of every nastiness you can think of—aggression, sadism, and so on—like the psychologists say?"

"That's the way they've analyzed it. But what people will laugh at changes—almost from year to year."

> Jesus did not laugh—did not smile so far as the record is concerned. . . . Jesus knew "what was in man." Thus, He would have known what prompts laughter, and the mystery of why He did not laugh is resolved. . . .

"He means that as symbol of a person's own Authority-Ego, Jesus could not represent it truly if it expressed hostility for its own world of consciousness, even through laughter, or humorously."

> Although Jesus did not laugh, He offered that which has come to be identified with humor: salt. . . . "Salt is good. . . . Let there be 'salt between you' . . ." but let there be also humanity between men, for what good the salt if it has lost its savor? Jesus calls God love and good; He calls salt good; it must follow that aggression gentled through humor constitutes an essential ingredient of love, and that hostility will in time lose itself in laughter. . . . Jesus said, "everyone shall be salted with fire, and every sacrifice shall be salted with salt." These words give promise that man shall become immune to that which corrupts and that humor is playing a redeeming role in life. Jesus could not laugh; He could not risk that a fragment of the profound paradoxes He posed would be taken in jest. But the art of life—seen as an appreciative awareness and participation in it—was practiced by Him. . . . His was a total empathy, a compassionate rendering, an exquisite edition of the art of life.

"We seem to have a genius for making a lousy mess of life—those of us under and over thirty. What did *The Graduate* say?—emotional maturity in the average person arrives at about age twenty-nine and lasts for an hour or so?"[50]

"Like fools we rush in, and then where angels tread, we peter out. . . ."

> If one calls his brother "fool," he has taken the first small step in judging life that leads to a

season in hell, to the rise of unconscionable fear
that engenders madness, else to judgment that
reborns his consciousness in the fire of pain that
is the blinding-seeing action. . . .

"The blinding-seeing action? What do you mean?"

In the agony that blinds one to the leprous in
himself and all others, a new face is born upon
him and upon each of his fellowmen—his every
contact with humanity is healed, his sanity or
inner world is saved.

"You mean he becomes blind to evil?"

"He means that we must not judge the world in terms of good and
evil—drawing lines. But what does the blinded man *see* that heals
his contacts? What does he understand?"

He has understood, finally, that the *human*, the
commonplace, is divine, that man can be neither
good nor evil—he can be sane or insane, and
sanity is more precious than life itself. In the
act of judgment, he grasps the grace of God,
understands it to be: *sanity*. He becomes a disciple of the Authority within him that revealed
unto him the hypocritical self-righteousness of
anyone who judges any other man, the world,
life, as evil. The act of judgment humbles him,
not before the world, but in his own heart.

"Who is the 'Authority' that judges him?"

Not Jesus, but a man's own "divine absence" is
his judge. Jesus says, "He that rejecteth me, and
receiveth not my words, hath one that judgeth
him: the word that I have spoken, the same shall
judge him. . . ." The Word, "I," the Logos in
man, is a definite sounding in an authoritative
voice that is one's own—and yet is apart from
any of one's selves. . . . It does not come from
consciousness, nor superego, nor ego-group—
these are in the sinking boat engulfed in fear—
nor does it lodge in consciousness, and thus it

cannot be captured in the personality world. One who has heard it knows it to be *sane*, to be the grace of God, given a man—his own of it—it is the "I" of himself lifted up, drawing his ego-group together into a communicable sanity in the ranks of Homo sapiens. . . . And afterwards, it is blessed to be an ordinary soul.

"Are you speaking of that old saw the preachers play upon—the 'fall' that is prompted by intellectual pride?"

Each man's experiencing of his own soul as he ventures upon the deeps of his being, each man's suffering the temptation of the intellect to explore the heights and depths of good and evil, leads to psychic travail that varies in degree from nebulous, mongering anxiety to the horrifying prospect of beholding madness in himself. No description of what happens can meet with general acceptance because the pattern of response to psychological stress and the symbols employed to describe it will vary.

"Could you suggest some of the forms it takes?"

The drama may not play itself out to any reportable conclusion; it may reach its end in agonizingly slow motion; it may be so confused one cannot remember it; it may happen spontaneously in a flash of realization that brings one through it with a sort of baptismal "gasp"—or it may come through the plodding of conscience in seemingly unrewarding labor, or through the wrestling of an intellect that will not "let go" until the "angel blesses." Conrad Aiken chose the word *Gehenna* to title his short piece, which describes the disintegration, the granularization, of one's soul as it struggles in the watery depths. . . .

"Gehenna—I associate that word with hell or *fire*—is hell the *watery depths?*"

94

In the world of spiritual perception, away from "solid land," the illusory miracles take place. In this world man becomes more than he was as he falls from the heights, sinks toward the abyss of madness, and through this ordeal grasps the hand of truth. The illusory miracles *show* the coming or awakening of the grace of God in man—this is the mystery, permeating every great religion, which cannot be explained. . . . A man with re-born consciousness turns again to the church. The petty, conditional requirements of dogma are passed over. . . . He simply knows himself to be involved in consciousness with the church and comes to it of his own accord—that which was irrational in it has somehow withered before his eyes—for through the ages it has borne the *symbology* that came to him as the grace of God in the midst of his private hell. . . .

"God! The idea of returning to the Church—dreary Sunday."

"He doesn't mean you have to go to Church. He means that you have to see the Church in its historical perspective—not bedamn it."

Jesus observed the Sabbath, but He disengaged the ritual day from its all-engulfing regulations, stating that the Sabbath is made for man . . . it is to be rewarding, rehabilitating—not monotonous —it is a habit man is to keep himself, for it breaks the chain of days however he lives and relieves him of the conscious or unconscious intensity that repetition or monotony mounts.

"What's so bad about intensity?"

Intensity grows as unobtrusively as Samson's hair, and will expend itself in violence. . . . Each person suffers to a greater or lesser degree his own violence be it reasonably or unreasonably aroused.

"Pardon me, I just arrived—can you tell me where *The Palestinian Mystery Play* is playing?"

Jesus sought the open beauty of mountains and sea, the solitude of far places. He came also to the cities, the marketplace, the feasts, and to the temple.

"*The Stranger* means, it is playing wherever you are playing. . . ."

"And what were you saying when I interrupted?"

"We were talking about intensity and self-judgment."

The Son in man is the Self-factor that will lead a person to reap in kind his sin and error. Thus, each punishes himself.

"Then there is no vicarious atonement."

"Vicariousness itself is the sin. If there were vicarious atonement our lives would be meaningless—we would also be living vicariously."

"Is there *no* atonement, no forgiveness?"

Jesus proclaims also that the power to forgive is vested in the Son, the Self-factor, and one's return on the bread he casts upon life's waters is hundred-fold. He saw that in reality a man cannot abuse a brother-being without in the same measure abusing himself; and that he cannot forgive a brother-being without forgiving himself a like measure of the evil he has done. . . .

"Hey! You with the beer—a bottle for the stranger. . . ."

"*The Stranger* has left—he has gone into the theater."

"The beer is for this young man who just joined us."

"My given name is I."

"What a coincidence! So is his, and so is mine."

"Everyone is going into the theater—come on, bring your beer."

"Where is the theater?"

"Right here in the world, where we are. Everyone has a reserved seat, or he wouldn't come in, you know."

"Just sit down."

"What a S T R E T C H that was. . . ."

"Listen, *The Stranger* is speaking."

> The name glorified in the thunderous moment sounding the voice from heaven appears to be "I" or "it"—in effect, "I am it," the Father's name each speaks, a glory now, to be glorified again as love transfigures man. In the Transfiguration, Jesus indicates that at the height of realization when one is illuminated in his being he undergoes a metamorphosis which puts upon him the shining raiment of love. . . .

"What a glorious bright night it is—here, 'by the sea, I and' . . ."

"I . . ."

"And I. I wish I had thought to get a box of popcorn."

"Take this wafer in your cupped hands . . . and place it upon your tongue."

"The body of Jesus?"

"If Jesus were here kneeling at the altar with you, he, too, would cup his hands—he too would take the wafer."

"Don't you see? There is a body of consciousness of which you partake. This is the meaning of the Eucharist."

"If you eat so much as a grain of wheat, you are partaking of the body of God, the flesh of God—there is no other body, no other flesh."

"Jesus made this clear by giving thanks every time he broke a piece of bread or ate a bite of food."

> The flesh any man wears in this world is the flesh of God, is God extended into living matter, and to live man must partake of that which is or has been living. . . . All that is enfolded in the Communion rite Jesus established cannot be elaborated at this point, but it may be pointed out that this rite dramatized the need of man to partake of the flesh and blood of brother-being

97

> to come through this into life, for Jesus stated
> Himself a brother to mankind.

"What does he mean?"

"Hush, I cannot hear. . . ."

> Only, however, as this food is handed him by
> his Authority-Ego, only as he has his being in
> the *unconscious* primarily, is this permissible—
> this is to say, as embryo, fetus, and infant. There-
> after, he must become as a child, must move
> forward from his parasitic state, reaching forth
> his own hand to partake of his share in nature's
> realm. . . .

"Thank you for the wafers and wine. Shall I say grace before
I eat and drink?"

"Only if you give thanks not to Jesus, but with him."

"You do not pray to Jesus. You pray with him—Our Father."

"We should move closer—it's hard to hear on this mountaintop. . . ."

"But we are in our reserved seats!"

"There is always room for you when you are ready to move up
front."

"Or closer to the center of your own being."

"I think we are talking to ourselves."

"Yes."

THE MIRACLE OF PERCEPTION

Harold saw that sensory stimuli alone cannot account for man's ability
to perceive. "No description of events in the brain that is expressed in
purely physical terms explains . . . what it is that bridges the gap between
physical sensation and the perceptions in a man's consciousness." Therefore, he offered a theory that, insofar as his publishers are aware, has
not been offered before, and it throws new light on the subject of extrasensory perception.

To Harold, sensory stimuli and extrasensory stimuli may be likened to two "liquid" strands of energy that meet in space-time and give rise to an "epoxylike" reaction, which in turn gives rise to the "solid" perception and comprehension that we call normal.

If any condition prohibits or diminishes sensory stimuli, the delicate balance is upset. Then abnormal, but not supranatural, perception occurs. Extrasensory stimuli come from the operation of a finer type of energy than the type we acknowledge to be physical. Therefore, they possess different properties and operate upon a different field. Electrical impulses are the most gross expression of universal energy—not the finest. Mental or psychic energy is still Cosmic energy. But it is another kind of expression of the parent energy that composes the Cosmos and all within it.

Harold saw that mental/psychic energy can be understood in terms of physical energy when physical energy itself is understood. This part of his work is discussed in *If Thine Eye Be Single* and *On the Nature of Universal Cross-Action*.

Extrasensory stimuli impinge upon us constantly, and we assimilate much more information than we are consciously aware of—just as we assimilate much more sensory stimuli than we are aware of. And just as in outer space the sun is below the horizon and into tomorrow before we see it setting, so our inner light is always ahead of consciousness's sight.

Jesus appears to have seen that *man's insight* is the greatest miracle nature has wrought. Insight enfolds the past (postcognition) and shows the future possibilities (precognition) inherent in the situation. This allows man to see through the whole arrangement and to perceive what he must do. Insight allows man to pose himself a problem and solve it. The more "abstract" the problem he poses, the closer the answer touches upon underlying reality.

The problem confronting Jesus was how to conclude his drama in such a way that:

1) He would be a true symbol of *light*.
2) He would be a true symbol of a person's Authority-Ego.
3) He would fulfill prophecy regarding Messiah, thereby sealing his claim to the role that would be finished and destroyed in his person.
4) *And* in solving his problem he must act with *the integrity* that marked his course from beginning to end.

99

The Stranger's Solution to the Mystery of the Resurrection

The Palestinian mystery play has revolved for the past two thousand years around the Death and Resurrection of Jesus. There has been much speculation about what really happened, including the suggestion that the Crucifixion drama was nothing more than a "plot" through which it could be made to appear that Jesus had died and come back to life in order to gain support for his Messiahship. Such an idea, of course, destroys the integrity of Jesus and those who supposedly plotted with him in the scheme that failed because he died later of the spear wound and was secretly buried. No kind words about Jesus would, in such circumstances, erase the implication that his whole ministry and message was involved in a grand hoax that did not come off.

Harold did not believe that there was a "plot." To begin with, the prophecy that Messiah must fulfill was not a demand that the body of the One to come must be roused from death and resume its normal functions. The prophecy said that the body, the flesh, of this One would not *suffer decay in the grave*. The necessity, then, was to demonstrate control of the flesh by psychic power exercised in the death process in such a way that desiccation of the flesh would not occur.

Harold believed that the legends of Moses' and Elijah's strange *disappearance* indicated to Jesus that the utmost exertion of psychic power to bring about a psychosomatic reaction would induce an "internal cremation," which would cause his body to "vanish" into a handful of dust. We know that organic changes can be effected under hypnosis and that extraordinary physical reactions have been demonstrated. The question becomes—to what degree can exertion of psychic power affect the flesh?

The Stranger offers the conjecture that as Jesus passed from life into the state of death, he uttered the cry (of certain pitch) that would initiate posthypnotic organic response to autosuggestion made in advance, *causing a rapid disintegration of his flesh into dust—the end nature slowly accomplishes.* Jesus, as symbol of Adam, man, become fully conscious of himself as offspring of Cosmic Parent-Being, must like Adam return to dust. God-consciousness had said to Adam, "dust thou art, and unto dust shalt thou return."[51]

Harold points out that Jesus spoke of casting fire on "earth" and of a strange "baptism" he must undergo; and of the tension he must suffer until this be accomplished. Casting fire on earth—the "earth" of his own flesh? Baptismal—in that he could not test his conviction that through exercise of psychic power he could quickly reduce his body to earth, dust? What could "casting fire" mean?

As illumination comes, many men describe it as an inward conflagration. Richard Maurice Bucke described the moment as coming when he was in a quiet and passive state (which means that he was in a degree of trance). Without warning, he felt as though he were enveloped in a flame-colored cloud and thought of fire, but realized that the flame was within. Understanding came as in a flash of lightning.[52] Such illumination may be an expression in smallest degree of the inward flame that in *the greatest degree of its expression* can effect "internal cremation."

In order to fulfill Messianic prophecy, Jesus must accomplish something else. He must die quickly enough that not a bone of him would be broken. Harold believed Jesus knew that fear can *kill quickly* by bringing on a state that today physicians would call "shock." This type of shock often causes death when the physical injuries a person has sustained would not. The blood separates into a colorless serum and a heavy mass.

The Stranger says Jesus knew how to open the door of his inner realm and let a host of fear—his Legion—cast itself upon his body, knowing that it would rush him to death, just as the Legion cast into the swine caused them to rush to destruction. In the cry, "My God, my God, why hast thou forsaken me,"[53] Jesus indicated that he let fear flood his body on the Cross, and death came quickly. The record says that when the spear struck, blood and "water" (serum) came from Jesus' side.[54] Today, we can see that fear, bringing on the state of shock, was the killer. In his medical ministry, Jesus had shown over and over that fear tends to kill and faith tends to restore to health. Almost always, he began his healings with, "fear not," and ended with, "your faith has made you whole."

Jesus' cry, "My God, my God, why hast thou forsaken me," also showed the pattern of the culmination of the Messianic complex: unconscionable fear overcomes the sufferer at the height of his realization. Jesus on the Cross, "King of the Jews" written above his head, was the *effigy* of Messianic delusion which, at the end, he had let be created of himself in order to lead the ancient Messianic tradition to destruction in his person.

But neither fear nor the necessity to reveal the pattern of Messianic delusion had the last word on the Cross. As the ordeal was finished, Jesus—magnificent human being that he was—said, "Father, into thy hands I commend my spirit." Faith triumphed. And Jesus' spirit—his psychic energy—began accomplishing its task of reducing his body to dust.

We have said before that in his interpretation of Jesus, Harold calls upon only natural phenomena, which are demonstrable and are supported by a body of evidence. Harold acknowledged that in suggesting disposal of Jesus' body through "internal cremation," he had departed from this ground. He offered this solution only as a conjecture, and pointed out that there are other answers which fit into the pattern of posthypnotic response to suggestion. Jesus could have roused himself from deathlike trance. But if he did, the Gospel records clearly show that *he did not appear in the flesh to his followers.* Therefore, Harold concludes that Jesus then acted to fulfill prophecy by disposing of his body in a way that it *would not see decay in the grave,* which was the requirement, and true to his word gave his life to seal his mission.

The Stranger shows that *by Jesus' own words, his Resurrection was not to be literal. He said that the world would see him no more—thereby indicating that he would not again appear in the flesh in normal ways.*

Having said that the world would see him no more, Jesus then described to his disciples the visionary nature of his reappearance to them. He speaks of appearing *only* to those who possess his commands and love him. He says that on that day he will be living in *another realm,* "in my Father." But he will also be living in his disciples' inner realms, as they will live on in his. The image and knowledge, each of the other, is a living reality in the ongoing world of each.[55]

The very end of the Gospel of St. Mark, which is acknowledged to be the earliest one and is considered to be the "bone structure" of Jesus' record, is lost. There is very little in it about the Resurrection. But *all* the reports we do have in this and other Gospels clearly imply that Jesus' appearances to his disciples after the Crucifixion were visionary. The reports indicate that these visions merged quickly into the reality that attaches to hallucinations. But *The Stranger* says that regardless of the reality these experiences assumed, once the vision appeared, in each case it is clearly indicated that the encounters were abnormal, first and last. In the visionary encounters, the words, Jesus *had* spoken, the commands he *had* given, came to those who possessed them already, because they had been implanted in their minds previously.[56]

It was necessary for Jesus to conclude his drama by disposing of his body and not appearing in the flesh in order to complete his revelation of the power of psychic energy over the body and to show the psychic dynamics of contact with the dead in a valid way. Jesus must show that after death a person can return to those left behind only in a subjective way, as the still living image of the dead one in their minds rises to their consciousness and communicates with them as realistically as though the dead one himself were there. He must show that the dead live on as an integral part of the life of each person who has known them. This is true also of those who are or have become literary figures, as Jesus is today, and as Moses and Elijah were in Jesus' day.

The Gospel records show that Jesus made no secret of implanting in his disciples' minds the *suggestion* that they would see him on the third day after his death. The Resurrection drama shows the pattern of post-hypnotic response to suggestion.

Indeed, Jesus' whole drama is a revelation of the operation of psychic energy in man. It is a revelation of man's natural power designed to show the valid limits of its expression as well as the *delusions that can be engendered when this power is not understood.* Jesus set up the contradictions in the reports of the miracles that would force examination of them until their true nature was comprehended. There were no words then to describe the mysterious phenomena of hypnosis—the "mysteries" that had held mankind in bondage to superstition and fear, inviting the practice of dark magic.

Jesus explained as clearly as it was possible then to explain in words that after his death he could show himself *as he was in life* only in the *minds* of living men who knew him and in whom he had implanted the suggestion that they would see him; or that his presence could be felt as any man was transformed in the mind of the beholder into Jesus' essence-in-being as the stranger's face took on the compassionate look that Jesus must have worn, vesting his eyes with the *look of the Christ,* which can rise to the eyes of any person.

In the Resurrection drama, Jesus showed that there are two ways in which communication between the dead and the living can take place. First, actual information (verbalized) which comes from the dead has been implanted in the minds of those who received it while the dead one was still living. The recipient is not always aware of the knowledge. It may have been received by telepathy and stored in the subconscious without making appearance in consciousness, so it appears to be new information. The "materializations" accompanying such revelations are hallucinations which are so easy to induce that the person experiencing them does not realize this and has no idea that he has been led into trance state. In this state, a person's own extrasensory perception is heightened. *The hallucinations seem so real because ESP is an essential part of normal perception.* Psychic, sensory, and mental force is needed to "compose" whatever scene we ever see, or whatever sound we ever hear, and the power to hallucinate is involved in everything we perceive.

Jesus also showed that the dead who are living on another plane—in the realm of their *unconscious*—can communicate with the living, but only through or upon this plane of being in the living person. Contact is on the *unconscious* level. At this level, communication is so complete, so full of meaning, that it cannot be verbalized and conveyed as information in the ordinary sense of the word. What comes is understanding, perfect in its wholeness, enveloping the total being of the recipient. The totality of the experience so energizes him that his reaction is physical, emotional, mental. It is a reaction such as a *dream* can produce when it brings one out of sleep and into a waking vision. Communication with the dead is structured through a dream or dreamlike state. It is impossible to describe the *synthesis* of all that has been imparted. After Jesus' death, the disciples must have experienced such total communication with his still living psyche. In the Gospel of St. Luke (24:45), it is described as Jesus' *"opening their understanding"* that they might understand the Scriptures.

Contact with the still-living dead, which comes as communication on the *unconscious* level, may also take the form of inclination to do something that leads one into a situation so poetic or so meaningful that it brings to consciousness a message that is real. The message is real because what is *felt* in the dramatic moment is consistent with the totality of the experience the two people have had together and with all that such experience could project. This, too, is more than can be put into words. The experience is completely subjective and therefore is not susceptible of proof or verifiable demonstration.

The dead cannot explain in words that the living can understand what it is like to be on the other side of the veil. Communication can take the form only of a feeling of assurance that life and love continue.

The Resurrection drama shows that communication with the living dead is a *direct* one-to-one correspondence between those involved. Such correspondence neither requires nor permits the intervention of mediums on either side of the veil. All a medium can do is read what has been implanted in the mind of another. Feelings of guilt, remorse, ambivalence, may call up images and remembrances from the subconscious, and these may haunt one's dreams. But this, too, is self-contained communication— not real contact.

Jesus' words say that actual communication comes only as love calls and love answers. If love is real, honest, it will lead the communicants to release each other and be content with remembrance and the promise of a tomorrow. If love is not real, honest, neither will the communication be real, although communication with self-contained knowledge may go on for as long as a person wishes to indulge it. And because man's power to hallucinate is real, he may conjure up as often as he will materializations born of his own imagination.

Jesus did not mislead anyone. Mankind is prone, even determined, to mislead itself. The visionary appearances of Jesus had greater impact because his body was not in his tomb. Only the linen cloth in which he had been wrapped was there—shielding a handful of dust?

Jesus made it clear that the coming of the *Son of man*, which *all* who were present with him or living in his time would see, is an *inward* event that must take place for each individual at his death. But we cannot escape the fact that Jesus also implied that *he* would come back. We do not need to try to escape this implication.

The Stranger says Jesus *did* come back into the world, and within the lifetime of the beloved disciple. But he came back in precisely the same way as he had told the world that each one of us comes back: the Father raises the dead and makes them live, *ye must be born again*. In an hour his disciples expected not, in a way unrecognizable even to himself, Jesus was born again and died again—soon, *The Stranger* says.[57] Why? Because Jesus did not need to live long. His empathy for life in Homo sapiens' generation was complete, and he was ready to enter life in a more mature species. Perhaps in another of the Father's many mansions?

There is one more mystery connected with the Crucifixion and Resurrection drama—a mystery that haunts the conscience of Christianity. Judas, the betrayer. Christianity hangs itself in making Judas the culprit who must bear the blame for Jesus' death. One wonders how many more years will pass before Judas is officially "exonerated."

Harold shows, using Jesus' own words, that Judas was instructed and commanded to his act by Jesus.[58] And that Judas was his trusted friend, the only one Jesus could count on to perform the awful role that was an absolute necessity to the drama of *light*, which Jesus also symbolized —inner and outer light.

In the drama of light, there must be opposing wave trains of action, operating on different frequencies, which reinforce each other at the central point, thereby *providing a boundary for light's action*. This effect is known as "constructive interference." Judas played the "opposing role," providing "constructive interference."

The Judas role was also necessary to show that in accordance with the operation of nature's supreme law, the second law of thermodynamics, a measure of energy (heat) is *lost* as each cycle of action completes itself. Jesus speaks of having to lose *one*. New energy must be supplied if the action is to continue—St. Paul fills this role.

And, in order to fulfill Messianic prophecy, the potter's field must be purchased. Judas purchased it.

And, if Jesus' revelation of the culmination of the Messianic complex was to be complete, he must show that the "betrayed" *arranges for his own betrayal—insists upon it*.

Jesus did not misuse Judas. Each of his disciples was committed to giving his life if need be to help him in his work. Judas understood, but dimly, the nature of the role he must play. When the time came, he faltered—but did not fail. He somehow understood that truth, guiding the drama from the *unconscious* realm, insisted upon fulfillment of the awful role because through the Jesus–Judas drama the mystery of good and evil *that act together* is highlighted.

When he had finished his mission, Judas committed an act that he was not commanded to by Jesus, although Jesus had forewarned him of the horror that would overtake him. Judas did a very *human* thing. Unable to live with his agony, he killed himself.

And so, as happens in the drama of light's propagation, the opposing wave trains "cancel out" in phase—together.

But before we move on to a discussion of good and evil, we must say a word to those who may resent or be disturbed by Harold's putting the spotlight on Jesus' words, which clearly state that his Resurrection would not occur in the literal sense, but it would occur as a psychic—a spiritual —event *to those who loved him and possessed his commands*.

We would say that spiritual, psychic happenings are *real*. Unless we can accept this simple fact, there is no ground upon which religion of any sort can stand—no footing for psychology, no explanation of a reborn consciousness, or for psychosomatic phenomena that confront physicians every day. Jesus' Resurrection is no less real for its being visionary experience and communication with his still living being on the *unconscious* level from whence dreams bring their strange cargo of truths.

Today, when numbers of those who appear to be "clinically dead" have been returned to life, what meaning does a resurrection of Jesus in the flesh have? We cannot concede that our modern resurrected people were actually dead—the actually dead do not come alive again in the same flesh. If Jesus returned in the body that suffered on the Cross, then he did not actually die on the Cross.

Therefore, there is but one reality upon which the Resurrection of Jesus can rest—a psychic event, *real*, and so seminal in meaning for those who experienced it that the truth Jesus revealed in these few days rings through the centuries with the only promise regarding the hereafter that he ever made: each life is everlasting, our own inner world without end. Amen.

And when, in time, through the many lives we live, our consciousness becomes complete and incorruptible, this consciousness will express flesh that is complete and incorruptible—a body that death no longer need divest us of.

SCENE VII

The Mystery of Good and Evil

"Before you get going again, may I ask if it would be evil for me to bring sex into the dialogue?"

"Who considered it a sin in the first place?"

> *St. Paul, not Jesus*, beclouded the subject of sex with sin, or saw it as immoral, an evil of the flesh that man must contend with.

Suppose we let Harold speak directly to the question.[59] He says, "When one gathers Jesus' words on the subject of sex, he sees that Jesus expressed a very different attitude toward sexuality from that expressed by St. Paul. In answer to the Pharisee's question of divorce, He refers to Scripture that attests to the need, right, and desirability of male and female to engage in sexual union. . . . Because God, Love, joins them, male and female are not to be put asunder—thus, in Jesus' view it is not an 'excellent thing to have no intercourse with a woman,'" as St. Paul puts it, consenting to marriage only because "there is so much immorality, that every man had better have a wife of his own and every woman a husband of her own."

Jesus said to his questioner, "Have ye not read, that he which made them at the beginning made them male and female, and said, for this cause shall a man leave father and mother, and shall cleave to his wife: and they twain shall be one flesh?" Here, he turns us to think upon the beginning of man and woman, their innate equality, their needs as individuals and in their male and female roles. *The Stranger* says:

> . . . each person is as Adam: a body of consciousness through which is expressed a body of his own that he takes to wife, for Adam is joined to his *own flesh* in Eve. Thus man cannot separate himself from the desire for a body, or from the desires of his body, on the assumption that life

can be divorced from physical manifestation and the need of male and female in Homo sapiens generation to express their sexuality. But Jesus' listeners did not grasp the poetry of the Adam-Eve legend: humankind wedded each to himself in the beginning, and then each sex to the other. Nor would they accept His presentation of the equality of the sexes, so they replied, "Better not marry at all!" Jesus answers this plaint, "True, but this truth is not practicable for everyone, it is only for those who have the gift." These words do not prohibit the indulgence of sexual desire. To the contrary, they are utterly permissive. But they are also practical, for few have the gift to live and love freely. Jesus then lifts the discussion to another level: continence. He says that men are born eunuch, are made eunuch, or make eunuch of themselves for the sake of the realm of heaven, which is to say, in response to inner need. Such continence is to be practiced only if practicable.

Jesus saw that man's nature is changing. In time he will not need the bonds marriage imposes to make him behave responsibly toward the other sex and the children that derive from the union. He saw also that the inner worlds of two people cannot be fused to become "one world," so that any consorting with another in thought or deed adulterates one's inner world in the sense that it brings to bear upon self-union. Harold says:

> Homo sapiens therefore represents an adulterous generation, and is dissatisfied because the Self of himself for which each person searches cannot be found in another, nor in the personality one exposes, nor in the frailty he knows his consciousness to be. Nor can the longing for this Self-absence be mitigated more than temporarily by loving or lusty union with another.

Jesus did not say that divorce should be prohibited—he pointed out that Moses had given a "bill of divorcement" upon which mankind could call, but he indicated that it was not equitable and did not touch upon the reality of the situation. Harold says:

> In Jesus' encounter with the Samarian woman at the well, He shows that in Homo sapiens' inner world he can never be divorced from any part of his experience with another, for He numbers the men she has known, indicating that the image of every person with whom one has become one flesh lives with him as consort in his kingdom within. In the psychic sense, then, divorce is an illusion. And one cannot be divorced by law from whatever problem it is within himself that causes his marriage to become mean bondage or contributes to its failure. Jesus' emphasis on words must lead one to strive to master the problem with the person he has wed in his vow before God and man, for this vow

broken divorces him from his word as his bond, creating in his human power a dichotomy he must live with.

Here, we may pause to consider the nature of the marriage vow imposed upon so many well-meaning souls. To put it mildly, it does not reflect the teaching of Jesus. To tell the truth, it ought to be against the law.

"What God hath joined together . . ."—consider what "God" means, as described by Jesus. God is spirit, good, love. Spirit means psychic energy, operating above and below consciousness or on another frequency that cannot always be described in rational terms. Good is that which brings true satisfaction, "salt," humor, empathy for the other. And love must engender delight in life, though with it comes the *agonia*— the pain of loving, which is also the measure of its joy.

As long as any one or all of these measures are binding, a union is a union. But when any one or all of them cease to function, there is, actually, no union to be "put asunder." A state of unhappy legal bondage exists.

As long as God binds a union, the partners cherish and support each other. When God ceases to bind the union, the marriage vows cannot in truth be kept. As for "forsaking all others," how many can escape adultery? Harold says, "Jesus named adultery for what it is—lust. 'I tell you, anyone who even looks with lust at a woman has committed adultery with her already in his heart.'" And what is sauce for the gander is also sauce for the goose.

Marriage vows predestine the partners to break their word, to greater or lesser degree. And each time one's *word* is broken, having been solemnly given, confidence in himself decreases—although he may not be aware of this or admit it.

Marriage begins whenever God brings two people into union. Marriage vows should reflect this union and commit the partners only to act responsibly and equitably toward each other and their children, whatever the course their lives take thereafter. No vow should be taken, "until death do us part"—because life can also engender a parting of the ways that may well be for the good of all concerned.

Jesus saw the necessity, the practicality, of making marriage a legal estate that tends to enforce responsible action upon the participants. He recognized also that there are intolerable marriages, so that society needs a bill of divorcement to dissolve these. But in his day, and in our day, neither the marriage vows nor the bills of divorcement reflect the true nature and need of mankind. Harold says:

Jesus commanded humankind to love one another in every sense of the word, for love joined them in the beginning in sexual union and this He pointed out. He saw bondage of any sort, however, to be hateful—be it bondage to lust's insatiable appetite, or bondage to ignorance, or to illness, or to a religious priesthood's sometimes greedy and sometimes ridiculous demands. Jesus spoke truth to free man—not to bind him to social laws that fail to reflect the truth of his nature and of the situation with which they attempt to deal. He spoke truth to free man from his own self-deceptions that lead him to circumvent social law even as he transgresses psychic law, for these transgressions take a heavier toll of him. He spoke truth to free mankind of degrading traditions that cripple the soul of male or female.

Sexual expression in itself is not the sin—degrading oneself or another is. This is the point Jesus makes whenever sexual intercourse of any sort, inside or outside the bonds of marriage, enters the picture. Harold says, "He neither condemns nor condones the rescued adulteress: 'Neither do I condemn thee: go, and sin no more.' Nor does He scorn the sinning woman, bathing His feet with her tears. He says that one who has much love will be forgiven much, and one who has not much to be forgiven, has not much love."

Let those of us who have much to be forgiven thank God, thank love for its forgiving nature. And let us remember that sexual intercourse is the means through which life's new and triumphant generation has been brought forth. So, with love, and with Jesus, we give it our blessing.

We may digress here to say that although life is now sexually based, Harold accepted the virgin birth of Jesus, and many others in human history. He pointed out that parthenogenesis (development of embryo from unfertilized egg) may possibly be accomplished unconsciously—just as false pregnancy is a psychosomatic phenomenon. Although so far scientists have produced in their laboratories only female offspring via parthenogenesis, at some point nature must have produced the first male cell through some type of cross-action between female cells. In rare cases, the primordial pattern repeats itself and a male child is produced through unconsciously accomplished parthenogenesis.[60] A man (or woman) born of a virgin may be thought of as clothed in the flesh of "primordial maleness."

Remember, please, that Adam and Eve are of the same generation— man and woman of "one flesh" vested with Son-consciousness. Therefore, we cannot see the one as good (positive) and the other as evil (negative)—if we hold the idea that the "negative" label is derogatory.

Actually, as we shall see, expression of the negative is as essential to life as expression of the positive—good and evil must operate together in the natural realm.

* * * * *

The secret of good and evil—as Harold saw it and believed that Jesus saw it—is: in its *maximum* expression, good turns into evil; in its *minimum* expression, evil turns into good.

Good and evil act in concert—always. God (good) and the serpent (evil) in Eden "program" the course of man. The Jesus–Judas drama lays down this pattern. Good (positive energy) and evil (negative energy) operate harmoniously throughout nature—the one is as necessary to the other as the electron is to the proton.

Good's expression gives rise to *constructive potential*—but life can no more tolerate the maximum expression of constructive potential than the body can tolerate the uncontrolled construction of cells that cancer generates.

Evil's expression gives rise to *destructive potential*—it is the disorganizing force. If it were not for the operation of a disorganizing force, life and creation could be "finished" or completed. Because of the operation of the destructive potential, hand in glove with the constructive potential, life cannot be finished, and creation cannot be completed. Therefore, life is everlasting and creation continues *ad infinitum*.

Evolution is the process of disorganizing and reorganizing the potentials of good and evil until the *optimum* expression of each potential is reached. All things work together for the good—so we are told. Nature is such a constructor! Such an organizer! Will good totally overcome us? Take heart. Jesus says, "Sufficient unto the day is the evil thereof" (Matt. 6:34).

As most scientists interpret nature's supreme law—the second law of thermodynamics—nature is not busily constructing and organizing. To the contrary. This law is interpreted to mean that fuel to heat the universe is constantly being disorganized, and there is nothing to indicate that it is being organized anew. There is an always increasing measure of the random element, and this measure is called entropy. The increase of entropy leads to the decrease of temperature. Hence, these scientists predict the "heat death" of the universe. Harold disagreed. He insisted that entropy must be treated as a *signed number*, and that the apparent effect is always balanced by a like measure of opposite effect, which is unapparent, so that disorganization and organization are maintained in desirable balance as reorganization continues.

To say that nature's supreme law has but one meaning or aspect, destructive in nature and promise, is to say that evil (negative potential) can operate apart from good (positive potential) of a constructive nature and promise. It is also to say that the *absolute* can be expressed and that the *absolute state* can be achieved. Nothing in empirical data or observation supports this conclusion.

At the maximum, both good and evil attempt to express absolute power. But *expression of the absolute* was finished in life and in the universe in the devolution of God that *was*, which coincides with the beginning of evolution. The absolute state changed from "expression" into a state of "being." God is. The Cosmos is. Within this being, absolute expression of any sort is prohibited by the operation of the supreme law, which takes its toll of every expression of power, and tithes the energy, banking it in space, providing a reserve for tomorrow.

We must understand that, because the absolute cannot be expressed, *every* act in nature, and by man, involves the expression of good and evil. Positive and negative potentials are inherent in it; constructive and destructive potential is spent; and the results of the act will involve some measure of both forces.

Man and nature are being "delivered" from evil's destructive power by expending and experiencing it. Through this process evil's potential is reorganized and constantly reduced. In time, and through experience, man must so attenuate his ability to do evil that its residual expression turns it into good.

We must understand that to attempt to separate completely good and evil in life and to express evil so absolutely as to have done with it or rid the world of it in one grand play is to do such evil deeds as only *insanity* can engender. When man attempts to overresist or to overdo good or evil, he runs into trouble. He deludes himself if he thinks he does only good—or evil. A measure of each will be operative, just as in the atom the proton and electron are both involved in the play.

Whenever we attempt to express maximum good, good turns into evil, as it inevitably does when man attempts to "play God," or be "the absolute" in any endeavor. Who can call himself good? Jesus said, "Why callest thou me good? There is none good but one, that is, God. . . ."[61] God, the positive and absolute existence of space, the Cosmos, remains; but the play of energy has been given over to nature (mammon) and man in which good and evil are met.

Life is "weighted" toward the positive, the constructive. We see this in the mass of the proton versus the exquisite wisp of energy that the electron is. But we must remember that the proton can express in negative terms, as antiproton; and the electron can express in positive terms, as positron. *The Stranger* says:

> The fruit of the tree of life that would give man imperishable flesh could not be partaken of, after knowledge of good and evil had been incorporated in his consciousness and being, until life had taught him the secret of these opposing forces and had attenuated through many generations the *virulence of both.* . . . Up through the strange, twisted tree of knowledge that turns good to evil, and evil to good, man must grow, led by the spirit of attraction first to the one idea and then to the other, to become neither good nor evil, but divinely human—as love is.[62]

"Tell us, *why* must sin enter life—and how original is it?"

Each person is initially endowed with one full measure of the absolute power of God that *was.* Each one's measure of good and evil (or constructive and destructive potential) is no more, no less, than any other's. Sin enters life because the potential for evil-doing is inherent in total power, in God-power, with which man is endowed.

"Original sin" can come to rest only upon the doorstep of the "Absolute Parent Energy and Mind," which endowed man with its power as it cast its substance into its creation. Man can sin against himself or fellowman—but he cannot sin against God. The idea of sinning against God is, indeed, a foolish notion. As man shares in God-power, total, he must share also in the "sin" that is inherent even in the minimum and divided measure of such power that a person represents, a God-given measure of it. *Self*-judgment has been given into each one expression of this power. God cannot be sinned against, and God does not judge. Man can be sinned against, and each man judges himself—although he may not be aware of this.

Each of us lives only once in the body we inhabit. No one owns "for keeps" the flesh his consciousness generates. This material body is a temple of God's *pure evil*, or matter, because *evil* is the symbolic word for matter. Upon this body made of God's flesh the destructive expressions in life are cast. Thereby, man's evil is expiated in the destruction of the "flesh of God," which his own body *is.*

In each lifetime, man earns at least a modicum of understanding, which is the currency he needs to purchase, from the Cosmic store, matter of his very own—a body he can keep when he has learned how not to corrupt it and how not to corrupt the society of man and nature in which life has its being. Death must be built into life until man's understanding is complete.

"Scripture says that the sins of the father are visited upon the child. If God is father, then God's sin must be visited upon us?"

"Blasphemy! Isn't it?"

"An illogical conclusion, logically arrived at, I would say! Or vice versa."

As we share in the glory, grace, and reality of life, we must also share in its sin.

Judas symbolizes the sin that each man brings to life and knows not what it is. Its wage is death. But through paying this wage, man's evil is redeemed.

The "Judas-sin" represents something a person has done for which he has been unable to forgive himself in a past life. Or, it is knowledge that he cannot bear to live with forever, and as the sin is committed, it is repressed. It enters the newborn world of consciousness unknown, even to itself. It is derelict, nameless, and an outcast in the world of the ego-group. Only through death can this knowledge be buried in the "potter's field" of our personal worlds, which each of us purchases with blood money, as Judas did. What is deposited there is not remembered. Death, then namelessness in life, and then death again stand between us and that which we would cast out of our lives. Just as in the "potter's field" time turns derelict substance into pure matter, so in the "potter's field" of consciousness our evil is recast and purified.

As this nameless evil is abstracted from consciousness through the death process and is cast into the "psychic random element" under the control of good's "adverse chance," our psychic energy suffers a measure of disorganization and the potential for evil-doing is lessened. In the lessening of evil's potential for destructive action, there is an automatic shift in balance between man's forces. This produces an increase in his potential for constructive action in relation to the prior arrangement of his powers. Destructive potential can culminate only as it moves "hand in hand" with a like measure of constructive potential. In the outer world, in our age, the possibilities inherent in atomic power represent this psychic parallel.

The force of good (positive) and of evil (negative) energy is expended in every act, and in every act psychic energy is disorganized and recast into a measure of psychic force that is beyond either good or evil. We call this psychic force *empathy*. It is the measure of our humanity, the mark of the divine in man.

The Diminishing Role of Sin and the Growing Role of Empathy

Empathy expresses the constructive potential born of understanding. Empathy derives from knowing in our very depths the whole measure (the good and the evil) of the situation that confronts us and the feelings of all involved. Empathy prevents a person's doing unto another what he would not have done to himself, because the empathetic soul suffers in his own being the pain that comes to another and the pain that he beholds. As empathy increases, evil-doing decreases. As we undergo the various experiences in the many lives we lead, the measure of our empathy—our *understanding*—constantly increases, so that the measure of empathy at work in society constantly increases. And empathy demands progress in the expression of humanity between individuals in society. Progress in mankind's expression of humanity between men is moral progress. Ideas of morality change from generation to generation—but the expression of true humanity between men and in society remains the basic measure of morality in any time or clime.

In the psychic realm, evil is organized as *raw lust,* and each person is endowed with one full measure of it. As this "fuel" is consumed, it produces as side product (and often as end product) the "psychic heat" of greed, covetousness, anger, and untempered fear that leads to abusive behavior in one way or another. But, as lust is expressed, its forces are disorganized, its powers are weakened. At "lowered temperature" and in attenuated form, lust's expression transmutes into the expression of humor, wit, laughter, ingenuity, idea, desire for life and love—into all that makes life worth living.

The decrease of lust spells the increase of compassion—of empathy. Empathy does not lead to the death of desire or the cessation of passion. To the contrary, the empathetic condition so enormously enhances life that the measure of a person's empathy is the measure of his capacity to enjoy it.

Harold was among the first to say that the constantly increasing empathy in the psychic realm parallels in the material realm the operation of nature's supreme law, through which there is a constant increase of entropy.[63]

Just as disorganization of lust in the psychic realm leads to organization of empathy (the constructive psychic potential), so in nature the organization of energy into usable fuel keeps pace with the disorganization of the fuel that is consumed. Harold outlined the dynamics of this process in his hypothesis, *On the Nature of Universal Cross-Action.* In his view, a perfect but ever-changing balance is maintained through the process of evolution in the physical and psychical realms that leads toward expression of the optimum rate of change and changing arrangement of opposite forces to allow for the constant renewal of all that is needed to sustain life and the desire for it.

Harold saw that nature's supreme law operates throughout creation. It is involved in the operation of good and evil, in the operation of the psychic and physical realms. He believed Jesus realized that *one law* reigns supreme in the Cosmos and in the life of man. Jesus called its operation the "reign of God." He could not have understood this law as it is understood today, in terms of the second law of thermodynamics. But he could have *realized intuitively* its meaning in terms of the operation of nature, as this truth came to him from his *unconscious* store. Truth cannot be described in the same words from generation to generation because language is constantly created. But truth does speak the same meaning throughout time, because truth's meaning does not change.

In Jesus' day, men had realized that the supreme law involves constant disorganization, and this was expressed as the epitome of man's wisdom in the concept that "this, too, shall pass away." The expected end of the world and of life as man had known it was tantamount then to today's expectation of the heat death of the universe and the end of life within it.

Jesus could have realized then, as a person may today, that the other side of the operation of this same law insures life, although this cannot be readily perceived. Until man understands that life is everlasting, he will not begin to live *in truth.* To learn to live *in truth* is what man must do before a more mature expression of life can come into being. Jesus could have realized then, as a person may today, that evil is the *symbolic word* that denotes the material realm expressed as matter organized to provide the necessary fuel for life.

The Stranger says that Jesus gave the answer to the meaning of nature's supreme law (and the source from which he had drawn it) in the Sermon on the Mount when he said, "Seek ye first the kingdom of God [within you], and his righteousness; and all these things shall be added unto you. Take, therefore, no thought for the morrow: for the morrow shall take thought for the things of itself. Sufficient unto the day is the evil thereof."[64] He is saying that knowledge drawn from the kingdom within, the *unconscious*, will provide the knowledge man requires to answer his every need; and the universe operates in time in such manner that there will always be sufficient matter organized as fuel and sufficient psychic energy organized as desire to support life abundantly; and despite the fact that all things pass away, all things are made anew; and "Let there be light" is a command that denotes its constant creation.

When man understands that his own and every other life is everlasting and that each one bears an equal measure of life's evil which must be expended in order that the destructive potential be attenuated, Jesus' words that follow take on new meaning. He says, "Judge not, that ye be not judged. For with what judgment ye judge, ye shall be judged: and with what measure ye mete, it shall be measured to you again."[65]

How shall we judge the evil-doing—the sometimes unconscionable expressions of it—that marks the course of human history? Ignorance leads to evil-doing—ignorance of what the other is suffering, until we have suffered it ourselves. But we must know also that only *insanity* is capable of expressing unconscionable evil; and insanity can take the form of insensate sanity, or what appears to be "cold sanity." We must realize that in the end the expression of evil depletes the evil reserves of the whole species. Why? Empathy brings home the pain of evil-doing to every man who becomes aware of it; he experiences the evil of it himself, and has done with a measure of his own raw lust. Human society cannot arrest the increase of empathy. Ever larger numbers of people are, therefore, experiencing the evil that is being done and are ready to have done with it. Whoever has borne to the grave an unconscionable load of evil, has borne it for humankind, because humanity will not be able to re-express it again, *precisely*.

A person cannot keep his sanity if he commits unconscionable evil. Such a "load of evil" was placed upon Judas that he could not sustain it in sanity. He becomes *symbol* of evil's end result: it is cast into the "potter's field" of consciousness and destroys itself as a force capable of expressing evil again. Jesus did not command Judas to kill himself, but he knew that Judas would not be able to live with himself after the betrayal because of the love between them. Jesus said, "Greater love hath no man than this, that a man lay down his life for his friends. Ye are my friends, if ye do whatsoever I command you."[66] Judas betrayed Jesus, as Jesus had commanded him to do. As Judas betrayed him, Jesus called him *friend*.

No one man can reveal the whole of truth. Jesus understood this, and Judas must have understood that his help was necessary to Jesus to dramatize the story of light in the physical realm, as well as the pattern of the end of sin and evil-doing.

In sharing the responsibility, the privilege, of bringing truth to the consciousness of mankind, Jesus showed that he was the very opposite of a self-deluded Messiah who must be all, reveal all, and thereby corner the power, glory, and grace of life. But he saw his revelation as a necessary step in the development of the consciousness of his own people and the consciousness of the Greco-Roman world in which the seed of Science was trying to flower.

There is no way to explain the persistence of Jesus' message—seemingly so contradictory, and so distorted at the hands of theologians—except to conclude that he evokes devotion in the minds of intelligent men because his drama rings with the sound of truth on every level —material and psychic. Theology cannot destroy the true symbol Jesus made of himself and of every actor who takes a role in the Palestinian mystery play. *True symbols evoke unconscious response and work at subconscious levels to release understanding, regardless of what the superstructures of consciousness and the churches might be saying.*

As we reach today's scene, we cannot tell whether Judaism and Christianity will walk through the door *The Stranger* opens and into a rebirth that will insure the vitality of the Western religions in tomorrow's world. But it is evident that in the developing planetary civilization, Western man cannot present himself as committed to either orthodox Judaic theology or orthodox Christian theology much longer. This is good. Either they will evolve into "temples of understanding" that transcend their exclusiveness and limitations—inviting Islam to follow suit—or these kindred religions will wither. Arnold Toynbee observed that *practice unsupported by belief is a wasting asset.* Western man no longer believes in these theologies.

In Christendom, a growing number of fundamentalists are turning to *new revelations* of Jesus that come through modern mediums or by means of automatic writing.[67] Because such revelations differ in part from the Gospels, and include so much information about the "holy family" as well as people extraneous to the story, they create what may be called a "mystic brand of Form Criticism and Jesus Research." The trouble is, these new revelations differ widely from each other—the question remains of what version of Jesus' story to accept. How do we appraise these new revelations?

Jesus said, "Many shall come in my name, saying, I am Christ; and shall deceive many."[68] But he also said, "For whosoever shall give you a cup of water to drink in my name, because ye belong to Christ, verily I say unto you, he shall not lose his reward."[69] The new revelations are not to be decried—they slake the thirst of those who can neither believe nor relinquish traditional views. But neither can they be accepted as the "Gospel truth."

Granted that it is possible to question the *unconscious* and receive from it true answers, we must still acknowledge that the replies must be given in parable, metaphor, symbolical and allegorical ways—or be rendered too vague for real comprehension—when the questioner is unable to understand the nature of what he has asked or the answer that truth would give. We must also acknowledge that a person's superego transmits the message, clothing it with his own choice of words and coloring it with his consciousness and commitments. Therefore, a person cannot speak in the name of another to the exclusion of himself.

We must conclude that each person who speaks in the name of Jesus is offering simply his own understanding of him, drawn from the heights and depths of his psyche and knowledge.

Harold did not profess to have received any sort of psychic revelation. He speaks neither in his own name, nor in Jesus' name. He speaks in "the name of the Gospels," because he realized that the Gospels must and would remain authoritative insofar as Jesus is concerned. And Harold offers his work only as *his own understanding of the Jesus of the Gospels*, showing how they can be seen to be Jesus' message as he wished to leave it—free of "information" that would becloud the precise symbol he wished to create, and "information" that would serve only to help perpetuate the concepts he strove to transcend and reverse.

Although modern psychic revelations are not without value, they cannot support the sagging Judeo-Christian religions. The Bible cannot be rewritten. This is the record the Western world must contend with. And its popularity, even as a literary masterpiece, is rapidly dwindling.[70]

Harold contends with the *record*, the Bible. Through the pen of this unknown author, the Scriptures and the Jesus of the Gospels have been brought to life in the twentieth century. Following the path that Harold's pen traced, let us now observe Jesus and the Scriptures on the sets where the worldly philosophers and Science hold sway.

ACT THREE

Truth Is the Shining Stranger Mankind Seeks

Science Needs Religion

There is a growing suspicion—and here it is: however far afield traditional Religion may have gone, the general insights into man and nature it
provides are in closer touch with reality than those Science is offering.

Because Preston Harold's devotion to Science equaled his devotion to
Religion, he strove to unite these two forces—not for the sake of Religion so much as for the sake of Science and mankind. He saw that today
the world is desperately in need of a reinterpretation of natural laws and
phenomena. Irrational and nihilistic scientific doctrines are misleading
man; scientists are unintentionally devastating man's faith in himself and
in the universe. Because scientists tend to demean life, their promises are
arid. But *Science remains the last best hope* in man's search for truth.
Dr. Robert M. L. Baker, Jr., defines Science as: "The systematization of
knowledge and quest for truth, including ever more general laws, as
motivated by curiosity."

Science is the quest for truth, and its influence staggers the imagination.
This is why a more penetrating and comprehensive view of the findings
of Science—a view that generates a new philosophy of Science, a new
cosmology, a new view of man—is the crying need of the world.

But first, let us take a look at the irrationality of the scientific view
of man and the universe that holds sway today—the view that is under-
mining meaning and purpose in life.

Science poses itself as man's best hope and salvation. But hope and
salvation become meaningless *in principle*, the possibility that there is salvation or reason for hope is repudiated, when many scientists state that
the universe is dying.

Science preaches and attempts to practice the highest ethic, demanding
to share its knowledge freely. It commands the whole of society to do

likewise. Then it announces that behavior is so conditioned that there is little if any choice in the matter of a person's belief and behavior.

Scientists demand that war cease in the name of human morality and the preciousness of human life. Yet, scientists proclaim that man is no more than the product of a blind and purposeless nature in which such moral attitudes can neither exist nor be commanded. In nature, creatures must kill and be killed; might is right, whether it be the might of the parasite or the lion; the crippled or helpless must be abandoned, devil take the hindmost.

If man and a cabbage are siblings of insensate energy, scientists might as well call upon vegetation to stop rotting as to call upon man to stop polluting his environment. Either man is a superior and special product of Cosmic mind and energy, or it is ridiculous to demand more of mankind than animalistic behavior.

In short, nihilistic Science renders itself and all attempts at social progress inane. If in principle there is no purpose, no meaning, no rewarding goal toward which evolution progresses in individual and in universal terms, then Science has no meaning, and it matters not whether man's flame of consciousness, caught in an insensate universe, is snuffed out.

The nihilistic view is irrational, because it does not conform to the data Science has amassed. The facts keep pointing to the conclusion that although man inhabits a natural body, he is altogether different from every other expression in nature—and the formulation of Science and technology is itself the best proof of this view. The facts also keep pointing to the conclusion that scientists scarcely know more about the universe than a fetus knows about the world; life in the womb may be coming to an end, but it is coming to a beginning in a wider sphere of being. The facts also keep pointing to the conclusion that the real nature of energy is not yet understood; it is too early in the day of knowledge to rule out the probability that there is a converse process that balances the disorganization of energy.

Science is irrational because the great majority of scientists feel within themselves that the marvel of the Cosmos is not the product of blind forces moving toward senseless, lifeless motion—and neither is man. The deeper they delve, the greater their reverence for the order they behold, the greater the mystery of "energy," the more similarity they find between the underlying patterns of organic and inorganic expressions of energy, and the more evident it becomes that man must and will express God-consciousness, even though he refuses outgrown theologies. Scientists who should be leading the world into a new religious concept of

Cosmic dimension too often pay lip service to nihilistic doctrines they do not really believe but are too cautious to repudiate. These doctrines create the "mental smog" that hangs heavy, heavy over the head of man, although he may not be aware of the source of it.

Scientists, like theologians, have become so doctrinaire, so exclusive, that those who seek to know the truth of inner space and psychic energy as well as the truth of outer space and physical energy, must seek elsewhere. For the most part, parapsychology and metaphysics are shunned.

The whole picture is confounded. There is a loss of understanding of causality in the various disciplines. The world that Science studies is bound up by cause-and-effect relationships with the world in which Religion has meaning because, as Einstein realized, the observer is a part of the observation. This takes us back to an early battle between Science and Religion—the question of whether the earth revolves around the sun or vice versa. The real question was not so much whether the earth is the center of the universe as whether Cosmic (God's) attention is centered upon man. Religion insisted that man is central to the issue, whatever the issue may be. Now Science admits that this is true. As we understand the structure of the universe today, the center of it has no real meaning; but recognizing the role of the observer in making observations does have meaning. Genesis says that the observer's role, Adam's role, is the central role in the process of observation and "naming" or *understanding* the forces of nature over which he is to gain dominion. Therefore, each man is *a* center of Cosmic concern. *The Stranger* says, "If man is the most highly developed form of life, the only speaking creature in the universe, then in the most profound sense of the word, the earth is the 'center' of it."[71] Certainly, earth is *a* "brain child" of the Cosmos, such as Reiser envisions our planet to be.

It is time for Science to take a deeper look into religious expression.

Is there an ancient and *intuitive* understanding of DNA–RNA, which takes the shape of a coil, a double helix, a spiral, and is today known to be the "very stuff" of life? Genesis says that the "play of energy" that leads to the expression of life is "serpent"—a coiling action—involving an "intertwining" code script (the tree of knowledge of good and evil and the tree of life), so that *a double helix and spiraling form is basic in energy's expression.*

If scientists will look again at the legend of Adam, Eve, Cain, and Abel, they will see that it describes in a *poetic way* the operation of nature's supreme law with astonishing accuracy. It tells us that as the energy source (Adam-Eve) goes to *work*, heat is a "by-product" of what is produced (Cain slays Abel in the heat of anger). In this operation, a measure of energy (Abel) is lost, "buried" in the "field" of matter. And the organization of the energy involved changes in a way that increases the "random element" (Cain wandering in the wilderness). The legend tells us that in time, source energy (Adam-Eve) is reorganized in such way that replacement energy is introduced into the system to allow it to continue its operation (Seth comes as "replacement seed" and through him manifest energy continues to be organized, disorganized, and re-organized). The legend indicates that there is a centering of energy or power in *one* "atom of action" (Seth). This one "quantum of energy" produced by parent source plays the commanding role in its house. But we may also see that the "random element" (Cain) plays a constructive role in producing the ongoing manifestations of energy because his force is reorganized. The "wave trains" (progeny) emanating from this opposing frequency (Cain) cross-act (intermarry or "constructively interfere") with the "wave trains" (progeny) emanating from the *one* that is playing the commanding role (Seth) to provide the ongoing propagation of Israel, the "wave group" that brings "light" (Jesus) into expression.

Harold believed that the laws and findings of the sciences are simply *developments in the expression of truth* that has been intuitively grasped and poetically stated in the great religions. He believed that as Jesus studied the Scriptures he saw in them the same thing he, Harold, saw in them and also in the records of Jesus' drama: these writings embody a symbolical representation of the underlying laws functioning throughout nature.

Harold saw that with each enlargement of the boundaries of consciousness, man's ability to *describe* his realizations of the reality that underlies appearances and the principles that operate throughout nature has become more precise because of the development of more exact language and better mathematics. But reality itself does not change. Progress in describing reality equals progress in mathematics, which gives a precise and unambiguous description such as words and early symbols could not convey.

Harold was the first to measure Jesus' description of the realm of God and its working (and what is this realm and reign, if not the Cosmos and energy operating within it?) against the description of nature's supreme law and the basic laws of physics. He showed that, in every particular, Jesus' poetic words and the symbols he used are harmonious, congruent in every way, with the scientists' understanding of the "reign" of the second law of thermodynamics in the physical realm; and with the principle of indeterminacy, and the principle of detailed balancing; and with the concept of field energy, with the Lorentz-Fitzgerald contraction, with light quanta and other paradoxical mysteries of physics too numerous to name.[72] Here are three examples:

(1) About two thousand years after Jesus, scientists discovered that nature's supreme law gives rise to a *measurable property*, and to the concept of *chance* versus *adverse chance* (or probability that the law might fail). The measurable property is involved with the action of energy throughout the universe, and is so vast in its reach and implications that man cannot yet comprehend its actual meaning. *Adverse chance*, on the other hand, is *so small* that if it were written out in decimal notation the number of significant figures would be *so large* that (as Eddington puts it) all the books in the world could not hold it. Jesus described Cosmic operation in terms of the kingdom and reign of God. He likened the operation of the "system" to a seed, which involves the action of energy, and said that "this measure" or seed is *smaller than any on earth* and grows to be *larger than any plant*. Therefore, the "measure" of the fundamental aspects of the "reign of God" (or nature's supreme law operating throughout the universe, the kingdom of God) is not readily conceivable in ordinary "earthly" terms.

(2) Think of all the discussion today about the curvature of space. In the play of physical energy there are no absolutely straight lines; think of all we know about the many *interpenetrating fields of energy* in which *particlelike motions* occur; think of the energy flowing through space. Is there a better description of this Cosmic structure and play of energy than to say, as Jesus did of the kingdom and reign of God, that it is like a *net cast into the sea* that holds *fish* ("particlelike motions") of all sorts? Today we know the limitations of Euclidean geometry, which in Jesus' day described reality in terms that might be likened to a net stretched taut, upon which perfect spheres were balanced. But, Jesus himself, whether in childhood or in manhood, must have had a vision of energy's "dancing" lines, flowing apart, coming together, bisecting, in a flow or curving motion, as do the lines of a net in the sea.

(3) What is the actual wealth that a particle of energy represents really like? Jesus said that it is like treasure buried in a field. Scientists cannot give you a better answer today, but they would point out something that Jesus also pointed out in parable so long ago. *You cannot at the same time "possess" both the particle and its place of being.* To do so, you would have to determine both its position and its velocity, and

these measurements cannot be obtained with complete certainty simultaneously. In Jesus' explanation, once you know that the "treasure" is buried in the field, you must be off to purchase the field. Therefore, you do not simultaneously and with certainty possess both the treasure and its place of being. The position and velocity of the treasure and of yourself are involved. The treasure is always elusive. You find the perfect "pearl of high price," but you must then be off to "sell all you have" to purchase it. Again, you do not simultaneously and with certainty possess both the treasure and its place of being. The treasure is never exactly pinpointed.

Jesus presented himself as *symbol of light, insisting that he must be understood in terms of one, only*. All that man knows about light and its actions tells him that there is a centering of energy, light, or power in *one measure* (the quantum), and a transferring of energy from the unapparent underlying source of it into light wave groups, or quanta, which somehow are enfolded by and then are subject to release by atomic matter with which they interact. Jesus' words and drama symbolize the whole complicated and paradoxical story of the quantum and light wave group so correctly that it is astounding. Consider now that if he were accurately to symbolize light and its propagation, his "story" as given in the Gospels must be as seemingly contradictory, paradoxical, and strange as is the "story" of light's functioning in the physical world. If the Gospels were not contradictory, paradoxical—strangely so—they would not conform to the "story" of light, in the inner and outer worlds, which is what Jesus' revelation is all about. To Harold, this was why Jesus, through use of posthypnotic response and recall, saw to it that his record was given as he wished it given regardless of the controversy such conflicting reports must engender.

That Jesus' story and utterances could have so perfectly threaded the course of modern physics by "accident" would call for "fortuitous chance" beyond anyone's ability to calculate. It is to be expected that scientists are reluctant to relate Jesus' message to nature's underlying operations and laws. But strange, is it not, that orthodox Christians who believe that Jesus was the only incarnation of God to come upon the earth appear unable to believe that *God in the flesh* could have an understanding of the all-pervading operation of the second law of thermodynamics. Or that He (as God) might devote Himself to describing the working of this law in the only way it might come in time to be understood—in poetic, symbolic words which, Jesus said, described the reign of *the* law that could not fail and the working of energy within God's kingdom, the Cosmos. Would not God in the flesh of one man understand also the secret of light's propagation?

Whatever orthodox theologians may think of Harold's interpretation of Jesus and his mission, it is to be hoped that they will recognize the value of the parallels drawn between Jesus' strange words and the laws of modern physics in Chapters Six through Nine of *The Shining Stranger*. It is also to be hoped that they will use these parallels to show that, however one regards the Nazarene, *he was in touch with reality in all its depths, that what he said is more relevant and meaningful in today's world than it could possibly have been to his own generation.*

What is the answer to the mystery of Jesus' poetic description of these complex laws and the phenomena that confront physicists? Reason would have us conclude that the underlying patterns in nature are similar and that there are *parallels of operation in the physical and psychical realms*. Therefore, anyone who could draw upon his *unconscious* to reveal the dynamics of man's inward kingdom would in the same "telling" reveal the dynamics of Cosmic operation. *The Stranger* says:

> It is not essential to concede that Jesus understood physical phenomena and mathematics as such—it is necessary only to concede that truth pre-exists and inescapably imposes the path to be followed, and that the *unconscious* in man has direct access to truth, and that Jesus knew how to tap this fount within himself, letting it express through him and direct his drama.[73]

Jesus was not the only man to draw upon the fount of truth that flows in the depths of man and to then utilize the symbols that arise as guiding images to lead him to a deeper understanding of nature's operations.

Many scientists have acknowledged the "kingdom within" to be the source from which their discoveries were drawn. Here, briefly, is the story of a great scientist who also saw energy "dancing" with his inner eye. Dr. Ira Progoff tells about August Kekulé in *Depth Psychology and Modern Man*. Kekulé's discoveries were of greatest importance for the development of both applied and theoretical organic chemistry. In 1890 he gave a speech in which Progoff says he described "some of the intimate experiences that led him to his discoveries; and these are of very great significance for our understanding of the depth processes that operate in the psyche of the creative scientist." Kekulé said:

> It is said that a genius recognizes truth without knowing the evidence for it. I do not doubt that even in ancient times this kind of thinking occurred. Would Pythagoras have offered up a hecatomb if he had recognized his famous theorem only after finding a way to prove it?

Progoff comments, "New insights do not depend on the outward observations, measurements, and analyses of the subject matter. The crucial step in gaining the new knowledge comes from within, and its validity may be perceived, or at least *felt*, before it can be outwardly proved." Kekulé said that while on a bus ride across London:

> I fell into a reverie, and lo, the atoms were gamboling before my eyes! Whenever, hitherto, these diminutive beings had appeared to me, they had always been in motion; but up to that time I had never been able to discern the nature of their motion. Now, however, I saw how, frequently, two smaller atoms united to form a pair; how a larger one embraced the two smaller ones; how still larger ones kept hold of three or even four of the smaller; whilst the whole kept whirling in a giddy dance. . . . This was the origin of the "Structural Theory."

Progoff says, "He tells us that in times past he had permitted himself to fall into a reverie in order to 'see' the inner workings of the atom before his mind's eye," and he realized that he "must move deeper into the subliminal levels of his psyche than he had done in previous reveries," if he were to see these workings in the detail that his scientific knowledge required. It was after this that his second great discovery, the benzene-ring theory, was made. He was dozing before the fire:

> Again the atoms were gamboling before my eyes. . . . My mental eye, rendered more acute by repeated visions of this kind, could now distinguish larger structures of manifold conformation; long rows, sometimes more closely fitted together all twining and twisting in snake-like motion. But look! What was that? One of the snakes had seized hold of its own tail and the form whirled mockingly before my eyes. As if by a flash of lightning I awoke; and this time also I spent the rest of the night in working out the consequences of the hypothesis. . . . Let us learn to dream, gentlemen, then perhaps we shall learn the truth.[74]

Here, we see that the ancient religious symbol of the serpent appeared again in the mind of a perceptive man who then precised its meaning in the modern language of chemistry and mathematics.

Before Kekulé's time, before Jesus' time, many drew forth truth from the kingdom within and expressed it in the language and symbols of the day with such perfect and poetic precision that the sacred books of all religions become a mother lode upon which Science can draw. And Science is in desperate need of something to draw upon.

Science now confronts an impasse as formidable as theology's, because it has come face to face with that which is as inexplicable as the Holy Ghost—the real nature of energy. Splitting energy into elementary particles to penetrate deeper into the make-up of the "stuff" leads to an impasse, because there is nothing small enough to penetrate the least active of the elementary particles, the neutrinos. There are two types of neutrinos, which are identical except that they have opposite spin. The one is not the antiparticle of the other, for each has its own antiparticle. Both are stable. They are produced in the decay of larger particles, but they themselves do not decay. A Science committed to the theory of the "heat death" of the universe sees them as the "ashes" of energy. They permeate our environment just about as consistently as does space itself.

To Preston Harold, they were the veritable "stuff" of the universe— the Adam and Eve of energy, the alpha and omega of it, which means that through these particles all is created anew. He saw them as nature's building blocks or "tiniest pair of hands." They provide the basis for a new definition of God, which is implicit in Harold's writings, but it was put into words by Frederic Lassiter:

> God is an irreducible number of indestructible elementary particles, being everywhere present, out of which everything is made.

In order for this definition to conform completely to Harold's concepts, it would be necessary to substitute *neutrinos* for *elementary particles*. *Everything made* must include the creation of space, derived from a particular expression of this energy, and it would be necessary to add that God is all that these indestructible particles are *not*, which means energy too finely drawn to be considered in terms of a material particle, however minute, to which we give the name of mental energy, but derived from the same source of Cosmic energy from which the particles were drawn. This mental energy was called the Word in Jesus' revelation. It is called the Cosmic Imagination by Oliver Reiser.

Science keeps coming face to face with Jesus' poetic words. If what a person says keeps coming true, there is good reason to believe that he knows what he is talking about.

We are on the verge of catching up with Jesus' view of evolution. Evolution is involved in his doctrine because he presented mankind as child. This must mean that man is growing, changing, evolving into what he is going to become. Jesus also insisted that mankind is *more* than the rest of nature's expressions, and that this has been true since the beginning. Therefore, Harold presented man as a *parallel* development in nature, to a degree self-conscious and, therefore, God-conscious from amoebic state onward, guided by an inner force or light that took man into and out of nature's stymied forms and led him to the pinnacle of its development. Now, hear this:

In March of 1969, Dr. Louis S. B. Leakey discussed his finds that once again scramble the pieces of the puzzle of man's evolution: "Recently unearthed fossil bones indicate that both a very early man and a very early gorilla coexisted in Africa 20 million years ago. . . . Even then, both man and gorilla were advancing along different and separate evolutionary paths. . . . Man descended along with the apes, not from them." Dr. Leakey also observed that we must either change the definition of man as "toolmaker" or invite the chimpanzees to send a representative to the United Nations, because "toolmaker" is no longer a valid definition for man—chimpanzees fashion primitive tools, and teach their young to use them.[75]

Noting that chimpanzees, man's closest "relatives," do not *speak* and cannot be taught even to try to speak (although they communicate primitive messages "intelligently" via sound waves), Harold had long since changed the definition of man. *The Stranger* says, "All in creation is alive, and may be seen as the 'flesh' of the living God to be used with intelligence and compassion. But the mind that thinks to speak is abstracted from all living material except man. Man did not inherit the power of the word from the animal kingdom; speech was initiated in him. . . . Is possession of this power synonymous with possession of life itself, *in reality*, as opposed to being living material to some degree conscious as is a proton or a gorilla? The opening verses of the Gospel of St. John define life and God in terms of the *word*: the word was God, in the word 'was life; and the life was the light of men.' By this definition, *life* can be ascribed only to man."[76] Life can be defined only in terms of man, and man can be defined only in terms of the power of the word—speech, reading, writing. It is very probable that scientists will create living material in their test tubes; but it is very improbable that they will ever create *life*. All that there is of *life* was created in the beginning, and is evolving in a parallel process with universal evolution.

A Science that seeks to understand the secret of life as opposed to the mechanisms by which living material comes into being and operates must seek first the "kingdom" within man, because herein it finds the only contact there is with the reality that *was* in the beginning of the evolutionary process and the reality that *now* underlies appearances.

Mental and mathematical concepts, such as the neutrinos are, have brought Science to a new level of understanding. Now, a "quantum jump" is called for. Science will be able to make it when scientists realize that *man is the book* in which the secrets of the Cosmos are written. This means that the anthropomorphic view must be taken, and completely taken. In the past, the anthropomorphic approach has singled out the male in his prime as conveyor of nature's whole pattern. What about the "little ones" and the very ancient? What is the meaning of woman enfolded in man's being? Does not this make mankind an expression that is *parallel to the neutrinos*—divided into like but opposite particles that are equal in every way except in the direction of "spin"? How much of this neutral energy, and in what arrangement, does it take to express a male or positive charge, or a female or negative charge?—the proton, or electron?

Many scientists have seen that Science will come to terms with the anthropomorphic view. Teilhard de Chardin was one of them. Such a view leads to the "Divine Materialism" that Harold ascribed to Jesus.[77] Only by taking a completely anthropomorphic view can we see the earth as a planetary body with a World Sensorium that communicates with itself and with the Cosmos as it responds to and resonates with the divine Cosmic Imagination. The earth becomes as one person (Adam-Eve), the Cosmos becomes as God, in the same one-to-one correspondence as Genesis portrays between God and man and as Jesus said existed between each human being and God.

True scientists grow humble, meek of heart, when they confront their own ignorance as opposed to the majesty and mystery of the Cosmos. Who, then, shall inherit the earth? Coming generations who will be guided by the methodology and ethics of Science, when it has opened itself to the study of God-consciousness in man and man's psychic powers.

Otto Rank saw that the will to immortality is the strongest force operating in humankind.[78] Jesus' doctrine is the doctrine of everlasting life. Did he see as Rank did that *immortality is mankind's goal* and that *because of this* man's evolving consciousness will achieve it? But first, man must determine what kind of society he really wants and what it is that brings real satisfaction in life.

Human Nature Dictates the Course
Economy and Government Follow

For several centuries past, the crusade toward human dignity and free-dom has been led by those who spend their lives on the political scene, wrangling with the problems of the day. Harold calls them "political saints" and says that there are more than can be counted in each country, in each period of history. Because of them, the world stands on the brink of hope.

Many will shudder, many will applaud when they read the name of Karl Marx in the category of political saints, which includes such men as Thomas Jefferson and Abraham Lincoln. But the capitalism that Marx experienced and repudiated along with all its trappings was a disgrace to humanity—it was doomed to change or die, once the force of Marx's pen had been turned against it. It changed and is still changing. It would be difficult to determine how much humanity owes this man, despite the evil that has been done in his name. Capitalistic countries are most in his debt. He forced them into a more ethical practice—made capi-talism a more ethical system, if ethical is to be measured in terms of *actual* ownership by the greatest number of people of the means of pro-duction and the goods produced.

Much poverty remains in capitalistic countries, but people also have much control over their lives. This does not mean that the poor should count their blessings; it means that the system in which they live has not yet completely corrected itself, but that it is capable of doing so and at a rapid pace. Communism, too, changes. But not so rapidly. The cross-fertilization continues and works to the advantage of all.

But what both the capitalistic and the communistic worlds are coming to see is that the trouble in this planetary society is not traceable to economic malpractices so much as it is traceable to what may be called malpractice of religious concepts—especially the religious ideal of the brotherhood of man. This ideal receives little more than lip service in both worlds.

The validity of the brotherhood of man must rest upon the principle of the Fatherhood of God and the unique endowment of each person, which elevates him to a very special place in nature and puts each human being into one-to-one correspondence with each other human being. This principle makes each person worthy of every consideration that would be shown to one who is considered to be the summit of human greatness. Unless man is born of One Parent Energy (God), and unless he is uniquely endowed, "brotherhood" extends throughout nature, giving society the right and reason to treat the brothers as they treat any beast of burden, barnyard fowl, or insect.

Neither atheism nor a pantheism that denies the uniqueness of man can support the ideal of the brotherhood of man, which commands for the lowliest equal dignity, opportunity, and the other rights and blessings humanity aspires to. A society that disavows Religion, God, limits itself to the law and society of the jungle in which *fear keeps constant company with beauty*. Or the society may pattern itself after the barnyard or the antheap. But it has built into it limiting ideas that prohibit its evolution into a society that is better than any nature has produced, including those societies that man has brought forth thus far.

The cardinal error of Marx was to repudiate God. He should rather have repudiated the oppressive and irrational theology of his day, thus leaving the door open for an evolution of man's understanding of God-consciousness in himself, which is as much a part of him as self-consciousness is and commands him to exercise *freedom and responsibility*. In time, the communistic world will correct this error.

In the capitalistic world, failure to practice the doctrine of Jesus, which insists upon the preciousness of each human life, the equal potential of every person, is at the root of our troubles. In truth, we have failed to educate "even the least of these, my brethren"—in spirit, we have failed to appreciate the richness of their contribution to the cultural life of the nation, failed to accord them justice, opportunity, dignity, and brotherly love. Paternalism is intolerable. The religions of the West have been saying this (although failing to comprehend the message) for as long as they have told the story of the paternalistic state of mankind in Eden, which God (Cosmic mind) *set the stage to destroy* in order that mankind might come into his own and live—and from which God drove mankind when they rose to the "bait" and acted in accordance with human nature. The legend says that man will not acquit himself in a responsible way when he is locked in paternalistic bondage. Freedom evokes responsibility.

The discrimination that is at the root of all discrimination is inequality between the sexes and discrimination against the female, which reduces her to the status of chattel. The first equality was, and must again be, mankind equal to *itself*. Eve was not a female person. Vinciata (Joseph Wallace King) has painted a true portrait of Adam's "rib"—a feminine being with no navel. Eve, actually, is the feminine aspect of the consciousness of each person. Neither Eve nor Adam considered separately represents Homo sapiens in the legend.

As men degrade the women of their race, they are degrading the *race* and themselves—socially, mentally, emotionally—because they are degrading the feminine aspect of their psyche. The same is true as regards women degrading their men. But more often in human history the reverse has been true—and continues to be true. Woman has been treated as a *thing* in too many societies, and she has, therefore, too often allowed herself to be used as such. As a person possesses a thing, it possesses him, and so the sexes have tended to entrap each other.[79]

The Stranger says that the Genesis legend reveals the primordial misuse of the human being that is at the root of all misuse of people. It is misuse of man by his *brother-being*: Cain's murder of Abel, and man's enslavement of mankind that threads through the ensuing story.[80] This points to the fact that a people must first misuse *its own kind* before other peoples can misuse them. Each sex must first misuse itself before the opposite sex can misuse it.

Harold says that mankind must first become equal to itself, woman equal to man, before there can be equality among all peoples.

Today, mankind faces the necessity of coming to grips with the truth presented by Jesus and echoed in the words of Walt Whitman, "Whoever degrades another degrades me, and whatever is done or said returns at last to me."[81] The society of the future will shape itself upon this precept, because this is the truth of human nature, and human nature itself will dictate the course society must follow. Social organization is the "tool" that mankind is now shaping. It is a tool that must be fashioned to serve him as he serves life well, and also serves himself.

Law is actually the most powerful and constructive implement that man has fashioned. *Government under law was the promised land toward which Moses led Israel.* But, like any tool, law must be cleansed of time's accretions; it must be made workable. If it is to meet with the need and nature of man, it must evolve apace with the evolution of his consciousness. And so must the economic system man operates. Jesus recognized both necessities.

Jesus concerned himself with life in this world. His parables present a pattern of economic practice which shows that the course man's nature leads him to follow traces the same path, whatever the name he gives the operation or the political superstructure. Economic history has followed the pattern these parables present, as Harold shows in Chapter Seventeen of *The Shining Stranger*. Jesus did not name his economic doctrine, but the principles he stated must be identified with those associated with capitalism. Jesus' economic principles are both ethical and dynamic, geared to producing abundance—not merely to meeting need.

Technology promises abundance, whether the technology is developed by capitalistic or communistic societies. But Harold saw that men deceive themselves when they believe that affluence or economic development by itself has or will determine the history-making process by which any "ism" will be settled. Human nature demands *more*. This is what Jesus understood. He saw that although man seeks always to profit himself, the psychological rewards and costs outweigh the material rewards and costs. Jesus synthesized his economic doctrine: "For what shall it profit a man, if he shall gain the whole world, and lose his own soul?"[82]

Affluence in itself does not rob a man of his soul, but any system that makes him first of all a creature of the State, its chattel, does rob him of it. Harold believed that Jesus espoused the profit system upon which capitalism depends because he saw that "*each person is his own first capital-good. He must realize a profit upon this capital: himself, his life,* rather than working for his keep as does slave or animal. One lends himself to his job, may invest himself as heavily as he will in his work, must insist upon a premium for his efforts, and this in addition to the return of his capital: himself as a free agent. His demanding a return on money, capital investment, allows him to insist upon a wage or interest that will constitute a profit on his labor. His money represents his or another's labor—as he invests it, he must demand both interest and the return of his capital if he is to demand a premium for his efforts and freedom for himself. . . . In simple truth, *man cannot escape capitalism for he, himself, is capital-good,*"[83] and therefore to take a dispirited view of private enterprise and the capitalistic system is to take a dispirited view of man.

The Stranger says that opportunity, as opposed to enslavement or coercion, creation in addition to mere labor, and *a society structured to meet the needs of those who for any reason cannot or will not respond to opportunity* will meet the nature and need of man. There will always be those who cannot or will not compete, but for the vast majority, a chance to work and to create will elicit their efforts. Harold saw that "opportunity involves a chance to compete, and a certain degree of competition appears to be a necessary ingredient to insure real achievement, as well as to give the bread by which man lives a satisfactory taste."[84] Now listen to this:

> A study of suicides in both literate and non-literate societies shows that societies with a high suicide rate appear to be characterized by a placid, cooperative and uncompetitive style of life.
>
> Professor Stuart Palmer, a University of New Hampshire sociologist, conducted the study. He also observes that these societies do not stress individualism, but are community-oriented instead. He finds that those societies with a low suicide rate stress moderate competition and individualism. . . .[85]

Acquiring a "Group-ego" will never satisfy man's need to seek and follow his own Authority-Ego, the Divine Absence of himself. Eden-like provision for man's every need only drives him to desperation, saps his will to live and meet the challenges of life. But in today's world, these challenges must be tempered, or otherwise they would be overwhelming.

We do not have to resort to *either* capitalism *or* communism. There are wider possibilities. Society may take the shape of organization that provides for the needs of the human race, every member to be held precious, and also provides for the opportunity to compete, create, and turn a profit on one's life whether the profit be measured in psychological or material gain.

Marx did not believe a real and honest profit was to be made. He saw profit only as money squeezed from the laborer who can produce in a day more than it takes to provide his keep—and in Marx's day, the laborer was paid no more than enough to keep him. Marx also believed that the "correct" price of a product was its calculable labor value. Harold took another view of pricing and profit. *The Stranger* says:

> . . . from the day Homo sapiens began his operation of the market, each thing he could produce and sell could rightly be sold for more than the amount of calculable labor the article represents; and real profit is to be realized as accrued labor-value gives rise to improved tools and methods which allow for more to be produced in less time and with less work. . . . an incalculable amount goes to the consumer as gift from the past, even as a calculable amount is charged as profit.[86]

Matter is not "dead stuff"—even an elementary particle is "conscious" of its like and opposite kind of charge. And the things that man makes of this "living material" incorporate something of the life of the one who shapes them.

Jesus appreciated the living quality of things, and he realized that things possess a person in the spirit in which he possesses them. *The Stranger* says, "One might say that Jesus was 'housed' in His robe—and that the difference between the tortoise who wears his home and a person in his home is only one of degree. A man's home reflects his being, his possessions reveal him, and if there is nothing he can in truth call his own he cannot in truth call his soul his own, for his soul must have a *housing*. . . . Jesus' doctrine comes to rest in the concept that man cannot view mammon supinely nor use mammon dishonestly and reap a profit on his life. He damns the damnable with candor, and commands man to pluck out, to cast off, the offensive in himself. He teaches that when a man is honest and friendly in his dealings with and usage of mammon, things, the material realm, mammon serves him well. . . ."[87]

Man cannot serve mammon, because mammon is here to serve man. Jesus saw that as man uses mammon, he serves life, and as man serves life, he serves *God*.

Listen now to *The Stranger*: "Human frailty and human nature bring to bear upon the practice of any system. But as Frederic Bastiat saw in 1848, the danger is that men will pay too much attention to the imperfections of the profit system and will sacrifice their freedom to dictatorial authoritarianism, or what he saw to be the evil of socialism, in its stead. In the words of Heilbroner:

> He began a book entitled *Economic Harmonies* in which he was to show that the apparent disorder of the world was a disorder of the surface only; that underneath, the impetus of a thousand different self-seeking agents became transmuted in the market place into a higher social good. . . .

Jesus calls mammon 'unrighteous' but He, too, appears to have seen that self-serving becomes transmuted in the market place for He says, 'Make to yourselves friends of the mammon of unrighteousness. . . .' This is to say, know the working of nature's physical realm and of the mundane economic world. The temporal, which is mammon, *serves life*. . . . That which is unrighteous in life's operation, mammon, gives way in time to the righteous, to the truth in being which calls man to self-service in the most enlightened sense of the word, that his life may be of profit to himself *in reality, which means that it must also be of profit to his fellowman*."[88]

Harold believed that the market system, operating at some level in terms of private enterprise, will persist in the society mankind evolves because people enjoy buying and selling and turning a profit. And in the new market that leisure will open, enjoyment will tend to be reinitiated into work. But there is another and more important reason that led Harold to this belief. This is the place of the market system, the profit system, in the evolution of life and society from amoeba to Homo sapiens. *The Stranger* says:

> Man brought forth this system himself. It is unprecedented in the animal world and therefore in line with the whole development of the cell of life that became Homo sapiens. It is the newest economic system under the sun, and as with any powerful new idea or tool, it must be tempered and disciplined before the real profit in it is to be fully realized. Underlying the profit system, upon which capitalism depends, is a principle which in the view of this study led Jesus to espouse it: He saw that the capitalistic system cannot in truth profit itself by malpractice, and thus it tends toward the ethical in its best self-interest and must come in the end to measure its worth in moral and aesthetic as well as material terms.[89]

This is the lesson the capitalistic world is learning today.

In commanding man to render unto Caesar that which is Caesar's, Jesus commanded mankind to recognize the need for government and to support it. In these poetic words, he also indicates that a people who will not support a government that operates apart from Religion will not render unto God his due—which is cooperation with their fellowman. *The Stranger* says:

> Government is communal business that must accrue a profit and invest capital to expand its services to include all of its people and improve their lot. . . . In any type society the world has ever known, however, there is a degree of uncertainty as to whether the needs of the populace will be met. . . . As men deal with the uncertainty problem, the mathematical theory of communication could teach a valuable lesson; the uncertainty that arises from *freedom of choice* is desirable uncertainty— which is to say, to put security, stability, certainty above all else is to trade precious freedom for a myth because actual security does not exist and cannot be guaranteed.[90]

Pause to consider again the message from Eden.

The Eden legend tells us that neither affluence nor security—not even the *assurance of survival*—could satisfy the questing consciousness of man. His primordial instinct, the most compelling one, is to know the secrets of life. He must know enough to provide him with what might be called the first freedom—the freedom of choice. He must exercise this freedom, even if he brings evil upon himself in doing so, because freedom is the most precious of life's attributes.

But freedom of choice is a limited freedom, because human beings cannot realize their potentialities except through the means that organized society provides. The paramountcy of the individual is limited by the need of maintaining and improving social organization. Organization is a tool, nothing more. And civilization progresses as the tools man devises are improved. Jesus understood that truth would prevail, and in the long run only the Religion and only the social organization that meets with the truth of man's nature and need will prevail, because it will command humanity's wholehearted support without coercion.

This optimum society will evolve as empathy evolves, commanding a response that is both unconsciously tempered and in accord with the reality of the situation. Only through empathy is it possible to step into another's shoes without displacing him, or foisting oneself upon him, or losing one's own precious identity. Empathy not only makes this possible, it makes it mandatory. In empathy—loving oneself and loving one's neighbor as he loves himself—rests the hope of the world, in which all are now neighbors. Jesus' great command shows that man can love his neighbor only to the degree that he loves himself, and *as* he loves himself. This poses as the first necessity, in establishing a desirable society, the restoration of self-love and self-respect in each sex and in all of the races of man.

The curtain is more than halfway drawn over the twentieth-century scene as it holds the stage in *The Palestinian Mystery Play*. Power no longer rides supreme. Arms are self-defeating, contradictory in their might. The great powers are as Goliaths posed against many Davids who have for weapon but a pebble. *The Stranger* says:

> Man's helplessness at the height of his power presents the concept that truth when fully stated must conclude in contradictory truths of equal magnitude—in a bifurcation, a forking outward from the penultimate point of truth so that the end of it cannot be reached save as point that opens itself to question, requiring judgment in order to settle the issue or to act upon either the one or the other premise it projects. Thus, no one *final* or *absolute* statement of objective truth can be made. Law may be seen as a penultimate point of objective truth that opens itself to question requiring that judgment be exercised. Today's truth or contradiction in magnitude, seen as man's power versus man's helpless-

ness, comes to rest upon the question of whether he will accept law as the means of governing and settling disputes. . . . When ancestral creature picked up a stick to use for weapon and bequeathed to man his sword, he did his being-duty: only by fashioning a weapon could he survive, rise above the animal kingdom, and be different from it by refusing to evolve into, or in himself *be*, a physical weapon as all other creatures are to greater or lesser degree. Because their swords are built into them their threat to each other persists generation after generation so that fear and enmity are reborn in each species and between neighboring species. Man alone can lay down or pick up his sword. Man can be friend or foe, can love his neighbor as himself. . . .

This civilization may be destroyed in one last conflagration. But twentieth-century man may not destroy his civilization. Enough men may come to see that no "tree" can produce its fruit before, in the natural course of events, the tree is ready to bear it; they may come to see that "rear guard" action allows for retreat instead of chaotic rout as humanity withdraws from its old positions; they may see that opposition is as necessary to effect real progress as antithesis is to effect synthesis. Enough men may come to see that man's consciousness is fluid, and thus he cannot, will not, move against the natural law that water seeks its own level. Empathy, and lack of empathy, divides men into classes, endeavors, and attitudes that support their need to avoid or to join in, to know or not to know, to oppose or to assist. But empathy itself is a gathering force. It will not forever divide. . . .[91]

Willis W. Harman observes that there is mounting evidence to say that we have undersold man, underestimated his possibilities, and misunderstood what is needed for him to make the transition that these times demand. The evidence indicates that—let Harman say it:

> . . . the most profound revolution of the educational system would not be the cybernation of knowledge transmission, but the infusion of an exalted image of what man can be and the cultivation of an enhanced self-image in each individual child. . . . The solution to the alienation and widespread disaffection in our society is not alone in vast social programs, but will come about through widespread adoption of a new image of our fellow man and our relationship to him. . . . The most pervasive illness of our nation is loss of the guiding vision, and the cure is to be found in a nobler image of man and of a society in which his growth may be better nurtured.[92]

This enhanced self-image, this exalted image of man and his relationship to his fellowman, is what *The Stranger* proffers, bringing to this century the guiding vision of the Judeo-Christian tradition in new and meaningful terms—in the terms *of depth and growth psychology*, and a revival of the pioneering spirit of the West as men explore the unknown frontier of human consciousness and its development.

Harold could not have said it better than Harman—this nobler vision of man is the cure, more surely than vast social programs. It is essential if action on the social scene is to be sustained and efficacious. But Harold would have added to Harman's insights that there must also be the infusion of an exalted and affirmative image of the universe, because observations and empirical data do not warrant the nihilistic view that Science nurtures—and disaffection will persist for as long as such a view is held.

For example, Gerald Feinberg says, "I, therefore, think it time that scientists made it clear to others that the hypothesis of God is unnecessary within the scientific picture of the world. Those men who wish to retain their belief in God must recognize that none of the wide variety of phenomena revealed by the senses gives any support to their belief."[93]

We see here that scientists are willing to let everything in the universe evolve *but man's concept of God*. Religionists do not insist that Science be forever saddled with its outgrown conceptions. It has been nearly a century since the theology that views God as the bearded one in the sky collapsed. Today, God means the Cosmos and the energy operating within it in its every form. The concept of God cannot be less than Cosmic, universal, the whole situation and condition that scientists are dealing with.

To say that a hypothesis of God is unnecessary within the scientific picture is equivalent to saying that Science needs no cosmogony, no life sciences, no theory of light, space, particles, and that this condition of consciousness in an environment that communicates itself to our senses has no meaning. If so, there are no "long-range goals." Science cannot escape including in its picture a hypothesis of God, because the way Science views the universe *is* its hypothesis of God.

To say that the phenomena revealed by the *senses* fail to support belief is irrelevant. We do not taste, smell, touch, hear, or see a thought or self-consciousness that asks, "Who and what am I?" The phenomena revealed by exercise of mental energy do support the belief that understanding the universe and our part in it is primary. This is no more, no less, than an ongoing search for God. How exquisitely our senses support the belief that we are immersed in a *Supreme Reality* that expresses itself in countless ways—*and this reality is God*. Taste a loaf of bread, and you are tasting God. Feel the warmth of the sun, you are feeling God. See or hear what you will, you are seeing and hearing God.

The simple fact is that Religion and Science share the search for reality in all its depths, and the meaning inherent in man's ability to perceive it, even to the slightest degree. Therefore, they share the need for a new hypothesis of God, Cosmic Reality, and of man, the comprehender.

Today, forecasting the "shape" of society in the future has become a new science. The October 1968 and April 1969 issues of *The Futurist* carry articles by Burnham Beckwith, Robert Theobald, and others, discussing the changes that technology will bring.[94] Theobald is perceptive enough to see that a study of cybernetics demonstrates that technology will command of mankind the same ethical responses that Religion demands of humankind—in human terms: honesty, responsibility, love, and humility. Theobald says, "Cybernetics confirms religion as do the insights of those at the leading edge of almost all disciplines." Technology (mammon), too, serves God. Man is not to serve technology—it must serve him, his uniqueness in nature and as individual.

Remember this: Jesus did not decry nor despise mammon. He called mammon *unrighteous*, but he said that man was to *use mammon*—and he also said, "make to yourselves friends of the mammon of unrighteousness."[95] Why did he call mammon unrighteous?

Jesus saw that God and mammon form the "polarity" of Cosmic life. God—the remaining One, the WHOLE that is greater than the sum of its parts, is *righteous*. God, the righteous, is as nature's laws are: steadfast, unchanging, timeless. Mammon, the unrighteous, is as nature's energy is: volatile, constantly changing, and involved with time's action. Man is not to "serve" the energy; the energy is to serve him. Man is not to "serve" natural law; natural law is given to serve him. Natural law and the energy that operates according to its principles *cannot be separated*. To attempt to separate them into "two masters" is to try to separate God and nature or mind and matter. God and mammon are met in LIFE. Man is to serve life—his own, and all other. The question becomes, how best to serve life?

Theobald answers, "A single cultural norm is not necessary in the world of the future, rather we can expect great diversity. This point must be heavily stressed; it is one that Beckwith misses completely. He assumes a continuing process of homogenization of cultures despite the fact that the new dominant trend is toward the uniqueness of the individual and the diversity of cultures."

J. Blanton Belk, speaking of the future in *Pace Magazine*, says that the youth who participate in the "Up With People Sing Outs" are opening our eyes:

They will help us understand that the new order will come neither from technology nor politics nor even diplomacy, but much more from man himself, from a radical and permanent change in our way of thinking and our way of living.[96]

The views offered by *The Stranger* agree with this. But Harold did not decry technology. He saw it as the blessing that it is and will be. He saw also, however, that in man's understanding of himself and his natural powers rests even greater promise. As Religion evolves, "psychic technology" will also develop, bringing greater freedom *and* responsibility, because with each use of psi-power, man's conscious command of himself must be enlarged if the effect is to be lasting and beneficial.

Where Does Real Synthesis Find a Place to Lay Its Head?

1) Son of man has no place to lay his head. Why?
2) How could Jesus have understood so much if he were not in some way a "special" introduction into the human race? Was he the only man to realize truth in such depth and magnitude?

To these questions, *The Stranger* answers as follows:

1) Jesus' doctrine was not his alone. It represented a *synthesis* of the religious beliefs, thought, and knowledge of his day. Living at the crossroads of civilization, he had access to worldwide views and beliefs, even if he never ventured out of Palestine. Synthesis, such as his teaching is, evokes the synergistic force that is somehow greater than the force of its component functions, of any one or all of them taken separately. It is for this reason that real synthesis can find no place to lay its head. A new structure large enough to house synergistic synthesis must evolve—and this is an ongoing process.

2) Every human being who ever lived has the same capacity to realize truth in all its depths as Jesus had. But not every person knows how to tap this fount within himself and let the truth express itself through his voice and deeds. Many men before Jesus knew how to tap this fount —did, indeed, tap it to as great a degree as he did. But with each synthesis that brings together the sum of knowledge and experience, the view is of wider dimension, because the knowledge and experience to be incorporated is of wider dimension. And the vehicles of language and mathematics that convey the realizations are more precise, enabling wider meaning to be conveyed.

Jesus knew that synthesis would follow upon synthesis in time to come —each surpassing the other and yet not invalidating it. He said that other men would do greater deeds than he did. He knew that *a planetary con-*

cept of God and man would in time take over from the fragmented and divided religions. This would be the day when *the unity of God-consciousness in mankind would be recognized to be the basic factor to be considered in seeking truth.*

In order to reveal the dynamics of the psyche and its development, making himself a symbol of the Authority in man, Jesus could not state himself to be a "synthesizer," nor allow the symbol of Son of man to become involved with the personalities and lives of those from whom he drew, because in truth Son of man means the SELF, which is one, unique, only, in each human being.

But Jesus revealed that he strove for synthesis when he said that the day would come when all people would realize that worship of God, or expression of God-consciousness, would be valid only as it was done *in spirit and in truth* (John 4:24). This means: in a synthesis of intuition and intellect, in a synthesis of man's knowledge of the inner and outer realms of being, in a synthesis of world-wide religious expression and that intellectual accomplishment which we today call the sciences.

Harold takes such a giant step toward accomplishing this synthesis that *The Shining Stranger* may be considered to be *A New Testament for Our Times.*

The old concepts of God are dead or dying. They were slain by Science and Marxism, by the secular philosophers and the radical theologians. But Godless existentialism, scientific or otherwise, is now being hissed off the stage by a generation that somehow understands, even if it cannot yet articulate its belief, that there is within each person "something unearthly" which he must communicate to every soul on this planet, and to the stars. There is an Authority within him that prohibits his being a mere creature, or creature of anyone who has ever lived, or creature of any State. This generation says, "Love!"

And *The Stranger* replies, "Love forever remains the most daring answer to universal mystery. . . . Love is the answer to the mystery of nature, of life, of God, that Jesus gave."[97]

If Western religions are going to have a place in the *Synthesis of God-consciousness* that tomorrow's Religion must be, they must transcend their Messianic claims and expectations by *internalizing* the Messianic ideal and developing it along psychological lines. The sacred writings of each of the religions must be studied anew in the light of modern knowledge, which keeps catching up with the legendary truth of the Scriptures, and with Jesus' poetic words, and with the first and most piercing insight of Mohammed:

Read! For thy Lord is most beneficent
Who hath taught the use of the pen;
Hath taught man that which he knew not.[98]

Nothing in nature knew the "use of the pen," nothing in nature could teach it to man. Only "thy Lord," the Authority within him, vesting him with God-power and God-consciousness, could accomplish this.

If this generation would seek a frame of reference within which it may measure its grasp of the inward Authority in man and come to understand its psychic functions, it may study the words and lives of the great religious figures in human history. Each is a prototype, each confirms the other, each insists that holiness is to be identified with the divinely human, each says man is uniquely an expression of the Divine Mind through which the Cosmos took form.

Today, if the Gospels are studied in the light of modern knowledge, Jesus' *own words* show that—well, let *The Stranger* say it:

> Jesus presented Himself *as* Messiah must present himself to fulfill the role as it was described in Scriptures, the frame in which and against which Messiah could be measured. He chose this way to show the "truth of truth": it finishes itself always in cross-action which demands a change-over and reconciles opposites by reflecting the confronting image as likeness. Likeness is all that can be perceived.
>
> In finishing the Judaic Messianic role by playing it to its bitter end, He broke the mold and any like unto it. Judaic-Messiah came into the world in the Bible, made manifold in the one volume encompassing the expression of Homo sapiens' consciousness. Until Judaism reborn in Christianity had been presented to the East, to which Jesus acknowledged His debt in His birth legend, mankind could not be relieved of false Messianic expectation by coming to see that the same truth is expressed in every religion. . . .
>
> Truth—what is truth? Each man who seeks life's profound mystery long enough, diligently enough, comes finally to say, "I am truth." . . . Jesus' teaching leads man to grasp truth, the Christ-being, in another and in all others, for until a man has done so he cannot sustain in sanity the knowledge of the Christ-being within himself as he becomes aware of its truth and power.
>
> This need to see Christ-being in another can be met only by preserving the religions that enfold symbols of God incarnate in man. Jesus recognized the need to preserve the mother-church even as the tissue of the new religious idea is given shape and form. . . .
>
> What is God? Jesus said: God is *love*. Love is the mystery that gives meaning to life, *the force of attraction that binds in imperishable union*

all in creation from the "least" particle, the neutrino, to the universe it-self, and every precious relationship within it. . . . Jesus said: God is *spirit.* Spirit is unmanifest, save as the unmeasurable energy of mind, and of space itself. Jesus said: God is the *word.* The power of the word, of speech, is now expressed by man, although he cannot define it, or discern its dynamics, or calculate its limits.

Jesus taught that in the power of the word rests the creative principle which insures the enlightenment of man, and the becoming of the universe to express the ideal in being and change that sustains life and satisfaction in life.

He taught that God, "The Absolute," gave itself into nature and man, thereby destroying "The Absolute" in life's operation wherein power is shared with man and expressed in the working of perfect natural law through which truth reigns and governs.

Jesus taught that through the working of natural law, God works. He showed and taught, however, that within natural law the "miraculous" is possible—as is evidenced in phenomena arising from hypnosis, *and* in the miracles wrought when man seeks truth, applies knowledge in the natural realm, and operates the ethic of love and honesty in dealing with mammon.

Jesus taught that truth and God-power are perfectly divided, perfectly stated, in "one," each as "I," and in the principle *one* enfolds: *one* is absolute unto itself only, is indestructible, inexhaustible. God is One-Parent-Being with life in itself which cannot be *objectified,* save as the universe and all within it, because this One-Parent-Being is *subjectified* in man, Son, who thereby has everlasting life in himself and in whom is reserved one power no other creature expresses: word-power.

It is the Father-Son relationship between God and man that brings love to life, brings moments of joy complete, brings moments of peace that passeth understanding, brings quiet confidence in the grace of nature and of God.[99]

Jesus saw that the seed of God that man bears within him will come to flower if man but sleeps and rises—but just as nature brings with each cycle a fruition that must be harvested and resown to produce greater abundance, so in the many lives man lives he harvests the understanding that has come to him. Thy Lord, seed of God man bears within him, "will not suffer thy foot to be moved. . . . The Lord shall preserve thee from all evil: he shall preserve thy soul. The Lord shall preserve thy going out and thy coming in from this time forth, and even for ever-more."[100] You will not lose what you have gained in understanding. You and nature will be preserved from the *absolute* or "all evil." Your soul is made of all you have known of love and satisfaction, and from life to life it is preserved in the kingdom within. Your life is eternal, ever-lasting; even though you "go out," you "come in" again. The more you mature in consciousness the more evenly this transition occurs, until it becomes in time like breathing. Self-union, whole-being associated with whole-being, consciousness that resonates perfectly with the Cosmic con-sciousness of God, will someday express itself in humankind, who will have then conquered death.

"Come now, let us reason together, saith the Lord . . ."—and this is what Harold says to the religions, to the sciences, and to the contesting political ideologies.[101] The *Synthesis* that will command man's faith, the Religion of tomorrow, must encompass all knowledge and experience. Only then can the continuous cross-action between intellect and intui-tion, between desire and practicality, work through the evolutionary process to make society anew, and proffer a faith that warrants belief because it accords with all that man knows of reality. Such a faith will invite its own further development. When the principles of such a faith are stated, *practice supported by belief* will bring on action that is real —action that will give our "planetary being" a unified human soul as well as a "world brain" that will lead mankind toward self-government under law, evolving always to meet society's needs. *The Shining Stranger* proffers the unifying principles upon which such a faith may base itself.

How can this "Celestial Child" be other than schizophrenic if a part of its mind is consumed with fear that it is a dying body in a dying host? Some millions of years are but as a watch in the night to Planet Earth. Its *human mind* can leap ahead in time and experience the condition of cold, senseless chaos.

How can this "Celestial Child" pull its wits together if half its brain thinks that it is no more than an animal, and the other half thinks it is God? Who will tell it that it is neither—it is divine material made human and habitable for life? What can life mean to it if with half its thinking it sees its own particular life of no more value than an insect's, here today, forever gone tomorrow—and with the other half of thinking it concludes that it is to live forever in heaven or hell, or in an endless chain of death and birth which leads to nothing? Why should it try to correct its ways if there is no purpose, no goal, no becoming in its journey through the sunlit days and starry evenings? Can you imagine the terror of a living child, ready for birth, encased in the womb of a dead or dying body?

Today, our "Celestial Child," Planet Earth, is encased in the sac of the body of belief which is dead or dying—and yet envelops the globe.

Someone must perform a Caesarean that will give the *individual and the universe* a living principle from which to draw the breath of life. Harold has done this. *The Shining Stranger* speaks to the principle of life vested in the individual, giving every life purpose and meaning. But *The Stranger* cannot speak to the principle of the living universe because this part of Harold's work was not included in that book. We will deal with it in *If Thine Eye Be Single.*

Here, we must admit that the final answer to the Palestinian mystery play cannot, of course, be given. *The attempt to give a final answer has been the trouble in the past.*

Christianity insisted that St. Paul had given the final answer. *The Stranger* says that St. Paul gave the best answer that could be given according to the light of his day, and he dealt magnificently with his own generation—better than could the "children of light," the disciples. But it would take time to reveal the real meaning of Jesus—and time is revealing it. Messianic expectation, Judaic or Christian or Islamic, can be realized only in a subjective way: looking for an objectified Messiah is like looking for a final answer or final truth. There *is no finality in truth —and this is why life and the universe are everlasting.*

Harold accomplished such a monumental synthesis that there is no place for it to lay its head—not in any one or all of the religions combined, not in any of today's temples of the various sciences and psychologies, not in the confines of any ideology. If it could fit into any of these places neatly, it would not be real synthesis. And it is.

Oliver Reiser has also accomplished real synthesis in his philosophy of Cosmic Humanism. The reach and scope of his work is such that there is no specific structure to contain it. Therefore, it may well become the framework with sufficient dimension to shelter the emergent planetary concept of man, as well as God-consciousness now expressing itself in terms of Cosmic consciousness.

Bringing together Harold's and Reiser's syntheses produces greater synthesis than either author has produced alone. Reiser could bring to this union something that Harold did not. That is, the name to house tomorrow's living principle, which is what Religion is: Cosmic Humanism.

Again, it must be pointed out that Harold did not once use the word *humanism.* He may have refrained from doing so because humanism is associated with atheism or "heartless" scientism by so many people. Today, there are religious and nonreligiously oriented humanists. It is fitting to associate Harold's work with Cosmic Humanism only if we see that in this name we have a modern translation of "God is love."

Cosmos = God
Humanism = Love

Love is made of understanding. Therefore, it must embrace all knowledge and experience.

Cosmic Humanism, which actually began with God-consciousness coming into expression in man, must continue to be what it has always been: an ongoing synthesis of the light of humankind—man and the planet operating as symbiotic bodies within the universe, guided in their development toward an optimum state of being by the mind and eye of God.

Epilogue

After this day, July 20, 1969, can man express less than Cosmic consciousness? Can he express less than his divine humanity as he treats with his fellowman? Men walked upon the moon, all the while conversing with men upon the earth, and the world watched.

But something more than this happened. Something far more important. Planet Earth, our Celestial Child, thought its *first coherent thought*. Simultaneously, and all over the globe, millions of its mental cells—human minds—had but one concern, one desire. *One image only was acting upon this concerted consciousness*. The World Sensorium must have sent into the universe wave-trains of mental energy that may fall upon some distant receptor and shape the words which in any tongue speak the message the planet transmitted in full force: God give victory to our astronauts and bring them safely home.

One will, *one* wish, *one* exultation cohered the minds of people the world over, and therefore the mind of this earth. All that divides us was forgotten—must it be again remembered?—in those magnificent hours when for the first time in human history so many *simultaneously sent forth goodwill toward man*. Toward *man*, who in some dim past had emerged a creature from sea deeps, now to keep his first rendezvous with life's rich promise: "dust thou art and unto dust shalt thou return"—to stand upon a sea of glittering moon dust and speak to the universe in the name of humankind.

The earth was hushed and holy—wholly involved in the dream and in the *reality* of its fulfillment.

More than a new age was born in this magnetic moment—a moment that must resonate with that long-ago magnetic moment when the first aquatic creature "walked" of its own accord from water to explore dry land. A new consciousness stirred in the unified mind of *humankind*.

Empathy, global, drew the viewers and the actors into harmonious union as they shared the anxiety and experienced the triumph our species had worked from its beginning to achieve. Where do we begin giving praise? Who lit the first fire, shaped the first wheel?

Our generation is the first to reap a space harvest. And ours is the first generation to hear Planet Earth cease for a moment to babble fretfully. It spoke as with one voice: "I am the body that has borne man, dreamer of Cosmic dreams, doer of Cosmic deeds, and never more human, more divine, than in this moment of power and glory when his heart is humble, when awe falls like dew upon his mind."

While *Apollo XI* was visiting the moon, was not earth actually broadcasting its first comprehensible message into space? This, because, for the first time in history, there may have been sufficient mental energy perfectly focused and intensely concentrated to resonate as one voice sending a powerful and clarion call of goodwill toward the stars.

We do not know whether there are ears elsewhere to hear. Never mind, Humankind gets the message: man will occupy new spheres—new spheres of consciousness, and new spheres in the universe. And, if we are alone in the Cosmos, *The Stranger* says:

> . . . in some very distant tomorrow, man's destiny may be to "Be fruitful, and multiply, and replenish" the "many mansions" to be found in space. . . .
>
> As to the question of how to live in this world or in the universe, it is not possible to present a new answer that will surpass the highest and most practical ethic of Homo sapiens—his consciousness cannot rise above the ethic of love, enfolded in the Golden Rule which is given in all of the world's great religions. Although this, man's light, may be as little as the firefly casts, nevertheless, it is to be regarded as India's great poet, Rabindranath Tagore, regarded the firefly's: his light may be tiny, but it is not small, for it is akin to all the light in the universe. Someday, Homo sapiens may bring light to mansions far flung in space—for:
>
> Neither do men light a candle, and put it under a bushel, but on a candlestick; and it giveth light unto all that are in the house.[102]

We may yet catch a ray from the reflector man put upon the moon—the first candle he has set to light our solar house.

On earth, we see in the morning newspapers that as always people are saying yes and no to everything that pertains to the space program. Many insist that tax money would have been better spent salving our social wounds. An Indian tribe protested, saying that to them the moon is sacred, and now it has been defiled. But even while clucking concern, something in the heart of every man is saying, "Still higher, ever upward —Excelsior!" It is as though the earth itself knows that on this, the day of man's visit to the moon, the mind of humankind struck the lost chord, and the voice of the planet soared into the night.

"A U M . . . heaven . . ."

On the jacket of the record, *The Moody Blues in Search of the Lost Chord*, we read, "The most important word of power in the Hindu scriptures is the word *OM*, which pronounced A U M means 'God,' 'All,' 'Being,' 'The answer' . . ."[103] Did you, by chance, listen to Mike Pinder's song, *OM*, as Eagle sat on the moon?

Have you seen the special issue of *Pace Magazine*, devoted to space, and come upon the picture of Dr. Viktor Frankl, mountain climbing, commenting, "Man goes beyond necessities to the very limits of possibilities because he wonders where those limits lie. And behold, they don't lie anywhere because like the horizon, they expand with every step he takes toward them."[104] In the same issue, Igor Sikorsky, speaking of the possibilities of space travel, made a daring remark, "I venture to make the totally heretical statement—from the standpoint of modern science —that the velocity of light is not the limit of velocity. Much greater velocities can exist in the universe even though we have never observed them and cannot imagine them."[105] Well, Preston Harold ventured to say the same thing. He described this "Q-force" in *On the Nature of Universal Cross-Action* and saw that it must exist and will be used to trace a royal road to the stars.

Man has increased the speed at which his vehicles can travel until now the sound barrier has been broken. As he thinks of venturing far into space, even the speed of light seems insufficient, if he could actually travel at this rate, as time is measured by our life span. We must break the "light barrier" before travel into distant space becomes practical. Or, we could say that such space travel cannot be accomplished until complete consciousness produces the incorruptible flesh that will permit everlasting life, so that the "time barrier" will be broken. Or can we stretch our minds to think upon the "speed of darkness" as opposed to the "speed of light"? If the Q-force flows through space, as Harold envisions, is it possible to break the "light barrier" and travel at the speed of "dark" energy—a speed at which, in Harold's view, matter takes shape and might hold its form? The question is dizzying, but it must be asked. And among the barriers we must break are mental barriers—those born of Religion and Science. We must seek to achieve everlasting life in robust health, not for the purpose of eternal harp playing, but in order to fulfill our destiny of exploring space—if this be our destiny. We must seek through Science to tap the power of unmanifest energy, the "dark," as well as of manifest energy, the light. Which is to say, scientists must learn how to call upon the manifest *and* the unmanifest power in man and the universe that we call God.

And, now, please turn to Act One, Scene I, "The Premise," upon which this Play takes its stand, leaving the verdict to you, the jury of readers. Will you agree that the "Moon Scene" in the Drama of Man makes our point for us: Humankind is chalice of the power of God, and is destined to have dominion over nature's realm—the dominion that understanding brings—just as Adam was told by the God-consciousness that opened his eyes to behold the world in the beginning of the Palestinian mystery play.

BOOK TWO

IF THINE EYE BE SINGLE

A Presentation of Preston Harold's Theory of
the Living Universe

by Winifred Babcock

There is a pleasure in the pathless woods,
There is a rapture on the lonely shore,
There is society, where none intrudes,
By the deep Sea, and music in its roar:
I love not Man the less, but Nature more,
From these our interviews, in which I steal
From all I may be, or have been before,
To mingle with the Universe, and feel
What I can ne'er express, yet can not all conceal.

CLXXVIII
Canto IV
———*Childe Harold's Pilgrimage,*
by Lord Byron

The diagrams and representations that appear in *If Thine Eye Be Single,* and in Book III, *On the Nature of Universal Cross-Action,* are not depicting real conditions. They must be considered to be simple diagrammatic logic for the purpose of visualizing the concepts and should not be interpreted literally.

A Glossary explaining the terms Harold used and the meaning he gave to certain ordinary words appears in the back of the book.

1. In the beginning God created the heaven and the earth.
2. And the earth was without form, and void; and darkness was upon the face of the deep. And the Spirit of God moved upon the face of the waters.
3. And God said, Let there be light: and there was light.
4. And God saw the light, that it was good: and God divided the light from the darkness.
5. And God called the light Day, and the darkness he called Night. And the evening and the morning were the first day.
6. And God said, Let there be a firmament in the midst of the waters, and let it divide the waters from the waters.
7. And God made the firmament, and divided the waters which were under the firmament from the waters which were above the firmament: and it was so.
8. And God called the firmament Heaven. And the evening and the morning were the second day.
9. And God said, Let the waters under the heaven be gathered together unto one place, and let the dry land appear: and it was so.
10. And God called the dry land Earth; and the gathering together of the waters called he Seas: and God saw that it was good.

(Genesis 1:1-10)

I

If, Therefore, Thine Eye Be Single,
Thy Whole Body Shall Be Full of Light

What do Jesus' strange words mean? "If, therefore, thine eye be single, thy whole body shall be full of light." *Single* is defined: One, only.

Preston Harold narrowed his vision and focused upon One, following the lead of the Nazarene. We can take it only as apocryphal that the boy Jesus intuitively recognized the necessity to understand the *alpha* before discussing the *beta*, which involves organization, the whole business that nature's supreme law is all about. We do know, however, that the man Jesus based his entire message upon the principle involved in the concept of One. He said that One is teacher, leader, parent.

Wherever One led, Harold followed—and with singular vision, saw the whole body of science in a new light.

If the reader is averse to mathematics, let him relax. Harold left no mathematical formulas. To him, the need was for a better understanding of the principles underlying the formulas we have. He believed that deeper insights and a more comprehensive view would lead in due course to the refinement of mathematics needed to express consciousness of wider dimension. Using numbers and the signs to denote positive, negative, and neutral energy, he stated his hypothesis in simple language, addressing himself to the layman first, but also to the scientific community.

Although anyone who can count to ten, and who understands that a negative number multiplied or divided by a negative number produces a positive number, has at his command the mathematics he needs to follow Harold's argument, nevertheless, we must say that Harold's view is *purely mathematical*. He saw that *energy's operation is synonymous with the operation of numbers, of arithmetic, which is the practical expression of mathematics*. This is why mathematics arose in the human mind, why mathematics is the most concise and unambiguous vehicle to describe physical phenomena, why mathematics works.

Mathematics begins with arithmetic—upon which the whole edifice of science stands. The import of the relationship between mathematics and energy has not yet penetrated the depths of the scientific world—or perhaps its pride. Such a realization would require scientists to begin again to ponder the mystery of simple arithmetic. They could not discuss *two* until they understood *the principle* involved in the number *one*, which measures and governs all numbers and entities.

Eddington says that nature's supreme law speaks the "language of arithmetic. It has a measure-number associated with it and so is made quite at home in physics." If this law speaks in arithmetical language, does not the operation of energy which is so involved with the law also speak the language of arithmetic?—and are there not to be measure-numbers associated with its every expression? Eddington further says, "We often think that when we have completed our study of *one* we know all about *two*, because 'two' is 'one and one.' We forget that we have still to make a study of 'and.' Secondary physics is the study of 'and'—that is to say, of organization."[106]

Harold saw that Jesus devoted himself to a study of the *alpha, one.* And that this study is not yet complete. He, therefore, concentrated his study upon One and its principle of operation—seeing it as the reigning principle throughout nature. Because the number is so important we will capitalize it. If the supreme law itself speaks in the language of arithmetic, so, too, "energy" may speak in this language. Therefore, this is the language Harold uses.

Harold saw that Jesus devoted himself also to the study of "and," leaving its symbol (+) forever associated with his name. This symbol *by itself* represents balance and symmetry. Harold saw that mathematics, beginning with arithmetic, operates upon *balance*. One, therefore, must involve a self-balancing operation. And, if mathematics is a description of the operation of universal energy, it is reasonable to accept as a working hypothesis that the Cosmic System is, like One, a self-balancing system. We may view mathematics as the *tool*, and universal energy as the *concept* that this tool "describes." If precisely described, the tool and the concept constitute an *equation*: tool = concept.

One signifies unity. Unity signifies the balanced operation of two complementary factors in dynamic union. It must follow that *One's expression is not absolute*—it is never other than a dual operation in which these factors operate to maintain perfect balance, measure, and wholeness. The principle of One, then, *prohibits expression of the absolute*—and this is why absolute zero, or absolute vacuum, or absolute power cannot be expressed in the material realm.

Complementary factors cannot be analyzed or even described in terms of *sameness* (any more than the complementary bodies of male and female can be described in terms of sameness). Therefore, One must always be dealt with in terms of *signed number*: positive or present One, and negative or absent One. Only the positive or present One can be *apparent*. Nevertheless, the negative or absent One must constantly be reckoned with as an *unapparent* force or operation that brings the whole operation into perfect harmony and balance.

The "*alpha*, or beginning, *set* of One" is: ($+1$ vs -1). This set projects and retrojects the "*omega*, or end, *set*," which means that energy can be dealt with from beginning to end (from neutrino to galaxies of matter and field forces) only in terms of *positive and negative sets of energy*. There can be no purely positive, no purely negative energy. Positive and negative energy must each be *certain arrangements or measures of the neutral energy that composes the alpha set*, ($+1$ vs -1), which gives rise to One, neutral, whole. And if complementary factors cannot be dealt with in terms of *sameness, there can be no purely neutral energy composed of like measures of opposite types of energy. Positive and negative must also denote "more" and "less," involving maximum and minimum expressions and operations acting in conjunction.*

If operation of the *alpha set*, ($+1$ vs -1), provides the guiding principle throughout nature, then the universe and everything within it must *first* be understood in terms of positive, negative, and neutral being or force. *All* phenomena—energy, nuclear binding force, gravity, magnetic fields and forces, electric charge, light, darkness, mass versus energy, space itself (and not what it contains)—should be generally explicable in these terms. And this is the way Harold describes the phenomena.

Now, "if thine eye be single," the key to unlock nature's secrets can be perceived. This is to say, the three "signs" in nature—positive, negative, neutral—must be dealt with *in terms of single units or measures of each type of energy*. Harold saw that there must be degrees of each type of force, which differ in magnitude, and it is this *difference* that gives rise to the forces we call electrical, magnetic, gravitational, and to light versus dark, mass versus energy. This was indeed a profound departure from the norm. But he realized that whatever the degree of energy in expression, the *behavior* would follow the pattern shown in electrically charged particles, wherein like signs repel each other and opposite signs attract. Neutral masses pose attraction for each other—as Newton's universal law of gravity describes—and yet from atoms to galaxies masses remain differentiated. Why? Harold saw that a singular force separates, even as a complex force attracts—but this must be discussed later on.

Dispensing even with numbers for the most part, Harold took the singular approach. He used only the signs that denote the positive (+), the negative (−), and *degrees* (°) of neutral energy, employing several neutral signs such as (+ −) and (o) to indicate units of neutral energy. Please note that a strict distinction is made throughout this presentation and Harold's between the words *degree* and *unit* (or *measure*) when they refer to energy.

The positive sign (+) denotes simply *one unit or one measure* (the minimum expression) of positive energy or value, not positive *charge*, which Harold saw as a gross expression of positive energy. The negative (−) denotes simply *one unit or one measure* (the minimum expression) of negative energy, not negative *charge*. The neutral signs (+ −) and (o) denote simply *one unit or one measure* of neutral energy, not in itself a communicable mass. A degree of neutral energy (°) does not denote mass in measurable terms, but it is nevertheless the *minimum measure* of latent energy.

The problem narrowed to a single question: how does energy communicate? The whole of science is a problem in communication—of being able to read the signals that every type of stimulus represents. To Harold, the question became many-faceted. How much of a given type of energy does it take to communicate a positive or a negative electrical charge—or neutrality, or mass? What does less than that amount communicate? What does more than that amount communicate? Do greater and lesser forces acting in conjunction communicate one harmonious answer—or contradictory messages? Why does communication present a problem—what takes a toll of the information as it is sent and/or received, or even as it is "stored," much as the alchemists stored their knowledge in esoteric language?

The answer must rest in the principle of One, because this principle must guide every iota of energy in the universe, and *its operation as a whole*. For Harold, recognizing this, the Cosmos was indeed a "whole body . . . full of light." What might be called the maximum problem— the meaning of nature's supreme law—answered itself.

The second law of thermodynamics is the *ONE law* that is involved in every expression of energy. This law, bound up in the word *entropy*, must, like One, be interpreted in terms of *signed number*, or the *alpha set*: ($+1$ vs $-1 = 1$).

This law states that entropy (the measure of disorganization, or the random element) constantly increases, even if a system is left to itself. Harold saw that whatever the measure of entropy (disorganization), there is a corresponding measure of negentropy (organization). Entropy is the *apparent* and, therefore, positive measure. Negentropy is for the most part an *unapparent* effect, suggested in the antientropic nature of living organisms, and this, in turn, suggests the nature of the One effect that is achieved through the complementary action that must be measured in terms of syntropy. The One effect is *reorganization.* Syntropy (re-organization) is, therefore, the meaning of the law, indicating a balanced operation *and progress in the direction of reorganization of original energy.*

Progress implies that there is a goal to be reached. Harold saw that the goal could not involve "maximum" reorganization because reorganization can continue endlessly, which edits meaning from the law. It is also counter to the suggestion given us in the antientropic nature of living organisms, which evolve into more complex, intelligent, and free forms culminating in man's life and purpose-seeking mind. The goal, then, is *optimum* syntropy—or a state of being and change in a universe able to support life everlastingly.

Just as the measure of entropy, the apparent effect, cannot be decreased, and only under certain conditions might it be temporarily arrested, so progress in terms of universal evolution cannot be undone. Nor can this progress be arrested. The One law involves original organization, its complete disorganization, and its reorganization in time through the process of change.

The universal system can support life here-now. This measure of progress cannot be undone, any more than the measure of entropy can be decreased. *The measure of progress (syntropy) can only increase, in a universe now able to support life, bringing the Cosmos ever nearer the optimum state that will allow for the everlasting operation of the system in a way that it can support life more abundantly. Evolution has a goal that will be accomplished in affirmative terms.*

Like One, the ONE law is finite and infinitely workable. It is operating here-now in the midst of all nature; and just as One can be infinitely stated, is infinitely stated in the uniqueness of each atom or grain of matter, so the ONE law is infinitely operable, inexhaustible, perfect in its operation.

Jesus symbolized One's operation and *light.* Harold saw that Jesus must represent the *positive* and *present* One—or *apparent* energy. Therefore, he must make the cross (+) his symbol, because this is the symbol that arises in the mind to denote the positive (although the origin of this usage of the symbol for this purpose is lost in history). Jesus must say, "When you have seen me, you have seen the Father."[107] The Father

166

represents *unapparent energy*, which cannot be directly observed. Only the effects it produces can be measured. In order to accord with the findings of science—or what we can perceive of reality in all its depths —Jesus must also say that it is the unapparent or underlying energy source (negative or absent or unobservable One) which actually produces the light and does the work, as physicists have discovered in attempting to penetrate the mystery of light waves and their source. Jesus said that it was the "unapparent" One, "the Father within me who doeth the work."[108]

Jesus insisted that the operation of One is a dual operation, saying that both he and the Father worked and "work unto this hour."[109] Because a dual operation is involved, absolute action, measure, or expression is prohibited. There is nothing absolute about Jesus, nothing absolute that can be said about his record. But there is certainty and authority in his every move, every word. It matches the certainty and authority of scientists when they speak of the *chance* that stands between nature and absolute action in the "other" direction, shifting time's arrow from future to past instead of keeping it pointing from past to future until progress is complete—or, in Jesus' words, until the law is *fulfilled*.

Jesus saw that there was *a* "beginning."[110] God, originally, may be thought of as "total organization." Time began when this body of universal energy completed its utter disorganization or devolution and in this act set in motion the forces that would insure its reorganization in terms of creation and the universe as we can comprehend it. The universe had a "new" beginning, in terms of the beginning of evolution at that point. The opening verses of Genesis pose a marvelous word equation in terms of light (positive) and dark (negative) energy; and in terms of firmament (space), land (mass), waters (field forces and energy). The equation of Genesis, interpreted in these terms, presents a cosmology unlike any past interpretation of the creation story.

As symbol of light, Jesus was positive in his statements, positive in his approach. Harold saw that because light is *apparent* we must regard it as *positive energy*, although it is not positively charged, electrically speaking. Because light exhibits a degree of force, it must have *body* that is totally involved in action, although the measurable mass of the photon is zero. The photon is its own antiparticle. It simply "disappears" or is "stored" as it is stopped, although its quantum of energy remains. Jesus made himself a symbol of this single quantum of light. His approach had to be completely anthropomorphic. There was no other way in which he or any other man could express deep insights into nature

167

until the language of mathematics was sufficiently well developed to describe the phenomena.

Even with the mathematics we have today, scientists are accepting the fact that they explain their deepest insights in anthropomorphic terms—especially when they describe the elementary particles. As Gerald Holton points out, particles "attract and repel," just as people do; they live and decay; signals are accepted or rejected; forces are experienced.[111] A newspaper article describing the "battle plans for an assault on one of the frontiers of science—the forces that bind protons and neutrons in the nucleus of the atom and account for nuclear energy"—goes on to say that when the director of the project at Los Alamos Scientific Laboratory, Dr. Louis Rosen, "speaks of the tiny particles," he speaks of them as "a proud father describes precocious children," and all of the particles he mentions, "receive equal affection."[112]

There is nothing wrong in thinking of the particles as "children of light." As Harold writes about them, they seem to develop personalities of their own. He saw that only mental energy can probe the photon or the neutrinos. And when he got to the problem of how energy communicates, he saw that taking the anthropomorphic view held greatest promise. No person can communicate his entire body of knowledge—completely. Harold found in Jesus' words the clue that led him to see that the same is true of energy.

Jesus called the physical, temporal aspects of nature *mammon*. He called mammon *dishonest*, but he urged mankind to use mammon faithfully, honestly, and insisted that man make a friend of the mammon of unrighteousness.[113] If dishonest mammon is to be so regarded, it must be that mammon *cannot* communicate the actual constitution of itself in terms of positive, negative, and neutral energy. If mammon cannot truthfully communicate its actual constitution, what does it communicate of itself?

Jesus gave what Harold calls "The Law of Communication." In the King James Bible, this is stated, "Let your communication be: Yea, yea; nay, nay: for whatsoever is more than these springeth from evil."[114]

Evil denotes the purely material realm—matter and/or physical energy. The words, "springeth from evil," bring to mind the "quickness" of spontaneous or radioactive decay. The word *yea* denotes the positive; the word *nay* denotes the negative; the whole statement denotes an aggregate of neutral energy, which we know today is the most *penetrating* form of energy (in the sense of nondeviating) as, for example, neutrons are used to penetrate and "split atoms."

Most important, however, Harold saw that Jesus was saying that *communication depends upon a redundancy in expression, and that only a redundancy can communicate.* If this be so, only a redundancy of positive energy can communicate a *positive charge,* and the charged particle must be an aggregate of energy composed of opposite forces in which the positive force predominates; otherwise there would be no binding energy to hold together the like signs necessary to compose a redundancy, and they would repel each other. A proton could not be represented, therefore, by a *p* that is synonymous with a simple $(+)$. Nor could an electron be represented by *e* that is synonymous with a simple $(-)$. In order to communicate mass, a neutral particle could not be represented by *n* synonymous with one simple measure of neutral energy (o).

In order for an electron to possess a redundancy of negative energy that could communicate negative charge *and* to possess sufficient opposite energy value to bind the force into a particle, it must be made of two parts negative value to one part positive value. Harold represents it as: $(- + -)$.

A positive charge must possess a ratio of two parts positive energy to one part negative energy: $(+ - +)$. But the difference in mass between electron and proton indicates that the positive charge is never free in space (as the electron is). Instead, it is "immediately" embedded in matrix energy (slightly negative, as explained on p. 303) which has sufficient neutral energy (a redundancy of it) to communicate mass. In this way, the positive charge is "grounded." The particle must have both a neutral and a positive redundancy. In such case, the positive redundancy takes precedence, so that positive charge is the prime bit of information about itself that this expression of mammon communicates. The proton would have a ratio of 2:1 units of positive versus negative energy; and a ratio also of 2:1 units of neutral versus negative energy. Each redundancy must be communicated. Therefore, the proton communicates both mass and positive charge. (See p. 303.)

The negative charge does not communicate its positive energy. The proton does not communicate its negative energy. What is the nature of the energy that the whole atom, which communicates in terms of a *neutral body,* possesses but does *not* communicate? Harold answers: a single unit of positive energy $(+)$, a quantum of light. Its presence is hidden, its value "silent," because it is associated with a redundancy of neutral energy, which is all that the atom can communicate. What is true of this microscopic bit of mammon, the hydrogen atom, is true of the

169

macroscopic bodies in nature that *communicate* themselves as neutral in their entirety, but are actually "slightly positive" in their constitution.

The single positive "value" or unit of positive energy that *does not communicate*, and cannot be associated with positive charge, is synonymous with Planck's constant, h. This is the regulating, governing factor in the atom which causes it to operate in accordance with "quantum rules" (see Eddington re "seemingly artificial" h rule).[115]

Therefore, we summarize by saying that matter in atomic composition in ground state is *slightly positive in its being* because of the presence of the "silent" photon $(+)$ in its midst, despite the fact that electrically speaking it communicates neutrality. This has far-reaching consequences, as we shall see later on. Right now, we must concern ourselves with the question that was not answered. What is the photon composed of?

We will try to penetrate it with mental energy. Long ago man's mind penetrated matter and he conceived of the atom, which in Jesus' day was thought to be the least and an indivisible unit of matter. The word comes from Greek, and means *indivisible*. In the fifth century B.C., Democritus stated that matter is composed of atoms in motion, and this theory was restated by Lucretius.

But as Jesus' mental energy probed the atom, this iota of mammon, he saw that "the light shineth in darkness; and the darkness comprehended it not."[116] Mammon cannot communicate the photon at the heart of the dark mass of neutral energy that gross matter is—the light that governs the operation of each atom within itself—because being a single value with no redundancy, the photon cannot communicate its presence. Only if the eye be single, can we perceive that the whole body of the atom is lighted by this one lamp.

II

Opposites May Be *Equal to* Each Other, but They Cannot Be the *Same*

Harold hung his hat on a profoundly simple observation. There is no such thing as "opposites" being "equals." But there is such a thing as "opposites" being "equal to" each other's need, force, action. We must take the *measure* of light, the photon; and we must take the *measure* of dark which is light's opposite. We cannot assign them the same measure number because they are opposites. Therefore, one must measure more, the other less. This brings us to face the asymmetry that is at the very heart of nature. And because we may observe that positive charge is equal to negative charge in the atom, we must make our greater measure number *equal to* our lesser measure number. We are saying that one is equal to, that two is equal to three, and so on. But this is true only as we pose our numbers in *sets*, and say that the two numbers involved are equal to organizing a set, *one set*. A set is equal to itself in being, just as One is.

The first and/or last set that scientists have discovered in the expression of energy, Set Number One, is composed of *the opposite types of neutrinos*. The neutrinos are saved from sameness only because they have opposite direction of spin. In the neutrinos, One shows itself equal to two expressions of energy with opposite spin, each of which must bear the measure number of *one*. Since they are neutral particles, One, wholeness, must be the measure number of *neutrality*. Since neutrinos are the "least" of the particles and are the *only stable neutral particles*, they must be the stuff of which all else is made. So for convenience, Harold referred to them as *degrees of primordial energy*.

Harold acknowledged that "below" the neutrinos there could be smaller particles. A "mirror" reflecting energy "behind the threshold" of the neutrinos might show them to be "gross particles" with a whole series of particles leading up to them. But the "neutrino-principle" as Harold saw it would remain the same. Eventually, two "subneutrinos" would be come upon, diminishing the "quantity" of energy involved in the *alpha set*, but not the fundamental principle it involves.

Harold believed that, since the neutrinos reveal this principle, there was no point in seeking "below" their level. At least, not until we can understand them *at* their level as the fundamental "building blocks" of the elementary particles that scientists deal with today. He dealt with the neutrinos as the primordial degrees of energy of which the units of positive and negative energy are composed, and sought the "measure number" of these units in terms of the number of neutrinos that it takes to compose them.

Since One is the measure number of neutrality, as we measure "dark" or negative, and "light" or positive energy, we must call upon the numbers *two* and *three*. We will start with light so that we can see what we are doing.

A photon is totally involved in action, but light has a bit of "push" so that it must also be *a degree of substance*. Harold refused the idea that motion is possible without some "substance" being involved, if only a very refined substance. A photon does not communicate its mass, but since it exerts pressure, some measure of mass must be present.

The photon is the only particle with Spin number 1. The rest have Spin number 1/2 or 0. If totally involved in action, this body of light must have the capacity to express both types of action or total action. We know there are two types of action because neutrinos have revealed this. There are three aspects involved in a photon: body (potential energy), and two types of action. Therefore, Harold assigned the measure number *three* to positive energy (+). He saw the photon (+) as composed of: one of each type neutrino and one neutrino that is "at rest," constituting a body of energy completely supported by and involved in action. It is this body at rest which gives rise to the *apparent* versus the *unapparent*, to light versus dark. When the photon "disappears," or is "stored," it disintegrates into neutrinos at rest and these cannot be observed or tracked because they are *not involved in action*, nor are they in action themselves.

Neutrinos in rest state is a difficult concept to grasp. But there must be an opposite to action. Harold saw neutrinos at rest forming a substratum of potentially available energy. This substratum constitutes a flux of incipient energy that is called into action when certain conditions arise, and these will be discussed in due course. Neutrinos at rest may be thought of as the corresponding opposite state of matter to that which Einstein described as $E = mc^2$. They are: $-(E = mc^2)$. They are not antimatter. They are matter in a state of antiaction comparable to sleep or hibernation.

We might liken neutrinos in action to "tops" spinning, which, when the spinning ceases, become "tops" at rest, which can be set to respinning. They are energy conveyances and once "filled" with energy they could again express themselves in those terms.

Light, the photon $(+)$, a unit of positive energy, then, is seen to be composed of three degrees of energy, one of which is at rest. Its measure number is *three*.

Dark, or a measure of negative energy $(-)$, must be assigned the measure number *two*. It must be composed of two degrees of primordial energy, one of each of the types of neutrinos, which vests it with the capacity for *dual action*, or expressing either the one way or the other way that its set of values permits. Opposite actions must be thought of in terms of positive versus negative action, which is not synonymous with electrical charge. We may think of positive expression as vertical stance or motion, and negative expression as horizontal stance or motion. The capacity for dual expression does not permit negative energy to *become* positive or apparent energy as light is. But it allows for polarization. Therefore, we associate a single negative value that is involved with an aggregate of neutral energy with *magnetic force*. The capacity of the single negative unit to express in terms of opposite action allows for the polarization of the magnetic field.

If we start with the neutrinos as our primordial degrees of energy and assign three degrees of this energy to a positive unit and two degrees to a negative unit, we see that the measure of one unit of neutral energy is *five*, and one degree of the energy will be at rest. We see, here, that One is equal to five in this "set" of energy values designating wholeness. But this unit of energy $(- + = \text{o})$ cannot communicate in terms of actual mass, because no redundancy is involved in one unit of neutral energy, and a redundancy is required to communicate. When we see an electron as $(- + -)$, a particle with a redundancy of negative units but with less than the two units of neutral energy required for a redundancy, we can see why an electron does not "exactly" have mass and must be thought of more in terms of action.

A unit of neutral energy, $(+ -)$ or (o), cannot be stable. Neutrinos are here taken to be the only stable neutral particles. The unit of neutral energy, $(+ -)$ or (o), by itself cannot communicate anything. In

Harold's view, time's action constantly disorganizes positive and negative energy as units of neutral energy disintegrate into five neutrinos that lapse into degrees of primordial energy in rest state. We say five neutrinos because it requires three of them to form a positive unit $(+)$ and two of them to form a negative unit $(-)$. Loss of neutral energy, for example, neutrons "disintegrating" in this fashion as they lose units of neutral energy, gives rise to the many isotopes found in nature. This sometimes leads to the condition that prompts spontaneous decay, but there are other operations involved in the decay process. Disintegration of neutral energy into degrees of primordial energy in the rest state constantly replenishes nature's store of "potential" energy and allows for the resting of her forces.

As we consider further the neutrino, the first or last or least of mammon that scientists have come upon, we see that "it" turns out to be a *pair*. The Genesis legend tells us that the primordial One (Adam) turns out to be a pair (Adam-Eve), each One, complementary but opposite. We do not know how long before Moses' time man had realized that primordial energy is expressed in terms of One *and* One. And that these primordial ones are of "one flesh" so that their constitution is the same, as is the case with neutrinos. What are they made of? Let us split one or two with a bit of mental energy and find out.

Following the pattern of any one unit of neutral energy, $(+ \ -)$ or (o), as described above, the neutrinos must be composed of one measure of positive and one measure of negative energy. But how can we describe these minute quantities? We can say only that the positive energy is made of three infinitesimal "bits" of the energy that *was sameness*, rearranged to express positive value; and the negative energy is made of two infinitesimal "bits" of this energy, rearranged to express negative value. The neutrinos are neutral particles, but they are also slightly positive in their beings, because in each of them the positive value, measured in terms of its heritage of original energy, is *more*. The positive value is composed of more of this original energy than is the case when original energy is arranged to give rise to negative value. *This one bit more is what differentiates the positive from the negative at this basic level.*

The positive force of a neutrino is not strong, but it is sufficient to have each degree of primordial energy repel each other degree enough to maintain its own "identity" as an entity, until the tensions produced in space cause the individual neutrinos to unite in negative "action," just as Adam and Eve did, forming one unit of negative energy $(-)$.

If it were not for this tiny repelling force in all neutrinos (and in atoms which possess the correspondence to it in their single photon (+) in addition to their neutral energy), matter would disappear into the glue of sameness. The individuality of the "little ones" is doubly insured—there is another force that both unites and holds them separate, which will be discussed later. It is important to point out here that the neutrino and antineutrino are not antiparticles of or to each other. Each has its own antiparticle expression. Because their composition is the same, we must assume that when they lapse into rest state they become actual equals (since only action makes them opposites), so that in rest state they are indistinguishable. And as they go into action, they are capable of going either into left or right spin.

We have now five aspects of the "little ones"—the neutrino and its antiparticle, the antineutrino and its antiparticle, and either neutrino in rest state. There is a correspondence here to the five degrees of energy that it takes to compose one neutral unit of energy.

We are not playing games with numbers. We are seeking a pattern of action and interaction that sets the standard in nature and establishes an image in the Cosmic Imagination with which energy resonates. We seek a formula simple enough and profound enough to tell the story of the neutrinos—and Jesus gave it. He said, "five at issue in one house, three divided against two, and two against three."[117]

We pose the equation: $(3/2 \times 2/3 = 1)$. We liken the $(3/2)$ to the left-handed neutrino and the $(2/3)$ to the right-handed neutrino. Harold saw them as nature's tiniest pair of hands—the veritable stuff of God into which Original Energy *devolved in one act of granulation.* There was no explosion. This granulation was prelude to other divisions that set the stage for creative evolution. In this act of utter self-division, the Absolute destroyed itself as such. But there was a catalyst to prompt it. This catalyst was a portion of *the energy that was,* which was abstracted from *the material that it was to be,* in order that opposite forces $(3/2$ instead of $3/3)$ could arise. This one value that is not expressed in positive or negative terms must be thought of only in terms of mental energy. Therefore, it could not be dealt with in terms of *physical energy, which houses it.* We will discuss mental energy later on. (See p. 214.)

Now, we must consider that the measure numbers of positive and negative energy, three and two, combined, make *five* the measure of One or wholeness. One's measure (five) is, therefore, always greater than either of the components of its union, and the measure of the whole cannot be taken in terms of either component. When units of positive and negative energy are united to produce a body, the absolutely precise measure of the body cannot be taken, because the energy is like "dancing lines" that thread a course through each other; and when these lines unite to produce a body, the length of it will measure longer or shorter depending on how it is traveling through space or how we are viewing it in relation to its motion.

Jesus indicated in his equation that through what might be called "complete cross-action" the asymmetry of (3/2) versus (2/3) converts the "pattern" to symmetry again, as the equation does if written:

$$\frac{3}{2} \times \frac{2}{3} = \frac{6}{6}$$

This pattern of operation is active throughout nature, restoring to wholeness and balance. But the operation does not cease, and the symmetry gives way to the underlying asymmetrical operation, just as (6/6 = 1) and the asymmetrical *alpha set* of One reasserts itself: (−1 vs +1).

Jesus' equation indicates that throughout nature a greater force (3 or 3/2) is working against a lesser force (2 or 2/3), and vice versa, to restore symmetry, effect change, and periodically "balance" the operation. We can see (3/2) as "plus one" and (2/3) as "minus one," again pointing to the principle that One can be dealt with only in terms of *signed number*, so that nature's supreme law must operate upon this principle.

III

Why We Can Say that God Is Love, and that Freedom Entered the Cosmos with the Advent of Negative Energy

We can truly say that *God is love* when we realize that mammon is the stuff of God and neutrinos are the veritable stuff of mammon. They represent the minimum redundancy of neutral energy that holds within itself a bit of Original Energy committed to positive being, and this means everlasting life—they are indestructible.

There is no way to describe a neutrino except in terms of "love," because it represents a union of opposite types of energy (positive and negative) that cannot be put asunder. This is everlasting attraction and satisfaction in being, between opposites that are equal to each other's forces within themselves and within the society of their kind. This is a unity that communicates neutrality—"goodwill toward all."

No wonder "God so loved the world"[118] if it is made of these wondrous particles that act in such harmony. And the world must be made of them, because every number can be reduced to Ones, is composed of Ones, and energy must be as number is, since mathematics describes it so well. But this lovely stuff must have *a place to be*, and this place must be made of the God-stuff that *was* and *is*, and that God granulated into, before the Absolute could lay down its *life* to give birth to life in the universe made of love.

Only if we use our "Cosmic Imagination" can we conceive of an utter division of a degree of energy as small as a neutrino. We cannot actually divide it, but if we stretch it to its utmost limits and pose its forces in diametrically opposite lines, we can create of its five "dots" of energy the perfect symmetry of the cross, which has significance only when the "timbers" are united:

$$\left(\begin{smallmatrix} & \cdot & \\ \cdot & \vdots & \cdot \\ & \cdot & \end{smallmatrix} \right)$$

What we have here is *dimension without body*, or a *condition of energy* that Harold describes as the tissue of *space*, the ultimate expression of energy in and through which all other expressions of energy have their being. This is the third estate of energy. It is *transparent*, as opposed to being *apparent* (positive) or *unapparent* (negative) energy.

Space is a gossamer mesh—at once the greatest and the weakest force in the Cosmos, utterly permissive, utterly rigid. Each "degree" of space is equivalent to one neutrino, its energy utterly *spent and fixed* in this once-only action that cannot undo itself. Space neither acts nor reacts. *It is absolute stillness.* There can be no greater exertion of energy. It is force constant.

But do not forget that it is made of energy that is slightly positive in its nature, although it communicates itself as neutral. Therefore, each "degree" of space is an expression of constant positive force, but this is a secret mammon cannot tell because all mammon can communicate is the redundancy of neutral value, the (2/2) that is involved in the (3/2) of a neutrino's composition.

Space and *matter* actually positive in being? This is a startling doctrine. But it is also very reassuring. The positive repels the positive. Because this is true, space completely and evenly repels (and therefore supports) every body of matter within it. Because space is omnipresent, everywhere and in every direction it reacts against the celestial bodies within it, thereby supporting them without effort, because their positive force is so little by comparison to the total force of space. The "everlasting arms of God" are there. The repelling force of space does not "crush" the bodies it supports; from an inward point of view the force of their slightly positive composition is "repelling" space, or reacting against it; and there are other mitigating circumstances to be explained as we go along.

Perhaps a simple diagram can convey the idea better. (See p. 179.)

In Harold's view, each *measure of space* is equivalent to the utter division of what he calls a Prime Positive bundle of energy, and, therefore, each measure of space possesses an utterly spent positive charge that communicates only as constant positive force. But we cannot be aware of this, *because we never come into direct contact with empty space.*

This constant positive force of space, so overwhelming in its immen-

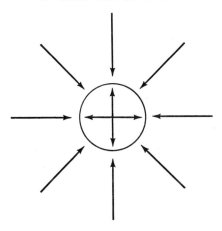

*The positive force of space and the positive force of a celestial
body acting against each other in an omnipresent way.*

sity (so much of the precious stuff of God utterly spent to create it),
would render every body in the universe *motionless* if space were not
involved with other secrets that mammon cannot tell. Infinitely more,
which to Harold meant *more than can be calculated*, of God's energy
was spent to structure space than was left to act within space; and infinitely more of the remaining energy was structured to express in negative
terms than in positive terms. Let us look again at a single unit of negative energy.

A single unit of negative energy ($-$) has no mass at all in *measurable*
or *definable* terms, but it is "something"—it is two degrees of primordial
neutral energy attracted to each other because of opposite spin. We can
visualize it as two minute "cones" of motion, horizontal, spiraling from
a tip, joining and spiraling to a tip.

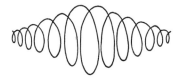

If you take them apart and turn them around to see what this spiral is
made of, it looks like two opposite spirals of energy—which is what
neutrinos are:

179

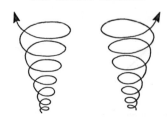

It would be just as easy to pose the spiraling unit of negative energy vertically, which is a clumsy way of saying that inherent in the constitution of one unit of negative energy are two modes of action—opposite. But this small "rod" of energy must act either the one way or the other way. It cannot spiral in both directions at the same time. Either/or is a small degree of freedom, but it is a degree.

Although the negative force is not equal in measure number to the measure number of positive force, it is nevertheless equal to the action of positive force. It may assume the positive role, and some of the negative energy does this as a magnetic field polarizes. Two units of negative energy may neutralize themselves, as one unit acts in a positive way and one unit acts in a negative way: ($|-$). But this arrangement of energy cannot communicate anything. Not even its neutrality, because there is no redundancy; a 2:1 ratio is not involved. Nor can such an arrangement exist in nature except in conjunction with a redundancy of neutral energy, as will be explained later. (See p. 181.)

When an *unapparent* force communicates itself as an electrically neutral "body of strength," Harold says that it possesses a redundancy of neutral energy that it communicates *plus* a single negative unit of energy that it cannot communicate. Such an aggregate of energy values *can express only as a field force.* The organization of such field energy preceded the organization of matter in atomic form.

The building blocks of nature, the neutrinos, were constituted in pairs, opposite ones. The first and most simple organization was their joining to form one unit of negative energy. As the second such conjunction gave rise to two units of negative energy, *a redundancy of negative energy* was created in space. (We will deal only in terms of "one measure" of all that was happening throughout the Cosmos, creating the situation of "darkness was upon the face of the deep.") This was the condition of tension through which light, the photon ($+$), was produced in the "darkness which comprehended it not." This reaction can be discussed only in mathematical terms of the *operation of signed number.* A negative number multiplied by a negative number produces a *positive number*: $(-1 \times -1 = +1)$. Omit the numbers, work only with the signs $(- \times - = +)$, which represent units of energy, and we may arrange the signs to form Harold's symbol for an electron $(- + -)$. This is simply an arrangement of the three signs used in the equation $(-1 \times -1 = +1)$.

Here, we also have Harold's answer as to why the organization of energy in positive or neutral terms, through which matter arises, cannot be observed, and the answer as to why time's entropy arrow points always in the one direction. Energy is organized first in negative, *unapparent* terms. *As* a redundancy of negative energy occurs $(- -)$, a measure of positive energy is automatically and instantaneously organized of three degrees (°) of primordial energy. This happens "at once," before the two units of negative energy can neutralize each other, which is why negative energy arranged as $(\,|-)$ can occur only in conjunction with a redundancy of neutral energy.

We start with the electron $(- + -)$, and as another unit of negative energy forms $(- + - -)$, we see one unit of neutral energy $(- +)$ coupled to a redundancy of negative energy and again the tension calls into play another photon $(+)$. The situation is now $(- + - + -)$. Light is in the darkness, but the light is not apparent because we have a condition in which two units of neutral energy involve one additional unit of negative energy, so that we have only an unapparent field force. The light has not been "divided from the darkness." We will refer to this aggregate composed of five units of energy $(- + - + -)$ simply as negative energy.

In Harold's concept, infinitely more (which means more than can be measured) of the primordial energy organized itself in negative terms than remained to be organized in positive terms. Negative energy is *fluid* in its expression. Genesis speaks of it as the primordial "waters," communicating "darkness, without form."

To see what happens next, we must first go back to Jesus' law of communication. His words indicate that in nature when *more than a two-to-one ratio* (which Harold calls a 50 per cent redundancy) of expression occurs, energy "springs from evil," or the neutral mass (since evil is the symbol of the purely material). Long before Jesus' day, Pythagoras (497 B.C.) had established the harmonious relationship that derives from the ratio of 2:1, operating versus a ratio of 1:2. If Jesus observed the experiment of plucking a single note on a stretched string and then sounding the note one octave higher by shortening the string to exactly half its length, "dancing lines" of energy took shape before his eyes and the concept of how energy's expressions are intensified and *sounded* (communicated) might have come to him.

When we translate the ratios (2:1 vs 1:2) into the symbols for energy represented by the words *yea* and *nay*, we have in the first half of Jesus' equation (Yea, yea) the measure of two positive expressions operating against—what *one* measure? It must be one negative expression that cannot be communicated; but it is there acting to bind the positive energy (+ — +) that gives rise to positive charge. The second half of Jesus' equation (Nay, nay) denotes the ratio of 1:2, which is less than a full measure of communicable mass. Here, two negative values must operate versus the one positive value that binds them (— + —), and this segment expresses negative charge.

Therefore, to *one measure* of wholeness (— +), we must add *half* a measure in order to communicate *positively* (+ — +), and *half* a measure to communicate negatively (— + —). To communicate wholeness itself, we must add one measure of it to another, or *half-again* what appears to be necessary, in order to communicate it in unmistakable terms. Because "half-again" must be added, Harold used the term *50 per cent redundancy* to indicate the measure that is necessary if we would communicate. As the numbers are increased, 4:2, 8:4, etc., the principle does not change. The 2:1 ratio is still expressed.

What happens when we increase the ratio to 3:1? Jesus said that whatsoever is *more* than his formula for communication gives, "springs from evil." And energy springing from evil bespeaks what we today call spontaneous or radioactive decay. But this is a necessary part of the Cosmic plan, as we shall see. Since we are dealing with the smallest quantities of energy, the elementary particles, to attempt through this microscopic analysis to arrive at the macroscopic, a Cosmology, we will trace the next step by observing the reaction of an elementary particle.

We left the situation of negative energy organized into field force, represented as (— + — + —). We have here two units of neutral energy and one unit of negative energy, a 2:1 ratio, or 50 per cent redundancy, which is within the limits of the harmonic law. With the production of one more unit of negative energy, which in turn calls forth the formation of another unit of positive energy, we have a ratio of three neutral units to one negative unit (— + — + — + —). A situation occurs in which there is *more* than a 50 per cent redundancy of neutral energy versus negative energy. In Harold's view, within this aggregate an unstable neutral elementary particle has been formed. Its name is "pi zero." Harold represents it as two units of neutral energy (— + — +).

Pi zero appears and so quickly disappears that in what might be called "no time at all" its place in nature is taken by *two* photons. In this reaction, "God divided the light from the darkness." *Only positive energy takes form.* We can envision this reaction only in terms of mathematics and signed number. A whole or neutral *one* is intrinsically a positive number, so that the reaction that occurs as pi zero arises is equivalent to multiplying a positive number by a positive number, which produces a positive number, or $(+ \times + = +)$. In universal terms, this reaction would not have occurred until most of the primordial energy had been organized in terms of slightly negative, unapparent aggregates of energy. This energy formed "field forces," one measure of which may be represented as $(- + - + -)$, into which additional units of neutral energy were introduced.

We found pi zero $(- + - +)$ occurring in an aggregate of energy represented as $(- + - + - + -)$. (See p. 182.) After pi zero's spontaneous decay into two photons, there is left only an electron. But the electron possesses sufficient negative value to bind the two positive values that arise, so that they do not repel each other. We now have $(+ - + - +)$, or a likeness to what Harold calls a "Prime Positive bundle" of energy, in the midst of likenesses to what he calls "Prime Negative bundles" of energy. We say *likeness* because the Prime bundles as described by Harold are more complex. However, the same principles apply, and our simple bundles are easier to deal with.

We have light in the positive bundle, divided from the darkness of primordial negative energy, but we cannot yet "see" the light because it is cloaked in a redundancy of neutral units of energy, a ratio of two neutral units to one positive unit. Electrical force is also incipient in the positive bundle, but it takes time to express it and time has not yet entered our picture. We are only to the fourth verse in the first chapter of Genesis.

We must account now for the neutrinos used to constitute the negative values in pi zero—what happened to them? As each negative value "let go" the positive value associated with it, the tiny hands that served to form the negative value also let go and lapsed into energy in rest state. Thereby, nature's store of "virtual" energy is replenished. But the four degrees of it contributed by the negative values in pi zero are not sufficient to compensate for two photons sent into action. Six degrees would be required. "Time's action," described by Harold as a negative value acting upon a positive value to reduce both values to five degrees of energy at rest, must enter the picture. As this action occurs, sufficient energy and some to spare has been put to rest, leaving of the aggregate that was a Prime Positive bundle of five units $(+ - + - +)$ only a positive charge $(+ - +)$ in a field of slightly negative energy, *slightly negative* indicating that this field energy does not express a negative *charge*, electrically speaking.

There is now a redundancy of positive energy $(+ - +)$, of light. But this positive charge is not itself the proton that brings on "day." Something else had to happen before the proton could be established, and this may be likened to dividing the "waters from the waters," or the deployment of the slightly negative field energy we left in the state of $(- + - + -)$. The strong force of the positive charge $(+ - +)$ causes a measure of this negative energy to unite with it, so that we now have $(+ - + - + - + -)$, or a "massive" neutral particle, which Harold represents as a *neutron*. He sees the *neutron* as the Adam, or parent particle, a more gross expression of original energy, which is not a stable particle but which disintegrates into stable particles: the proton, electron, and an antineutrino. In this reaction, a negative electric charge has been released. The "waters have been divided from the waters" of slightly negative matrix. Negative energy has been lifted from the "darkness" of primordial energy to become a part of the mass (land) in the midst of it. The parent particle turned out to be: a positive charge, Adam, and a negative charge, Eve, and time's entropy arrow was pointed in the direction of always increasing "random element" as the antineutrino spun away. But what actually happened in the "Adam sleep" that released the negative charge is that the positive charge was "grounded" (as described by Harold on pp. 301-303).

In Harold's view, a proton is a mass that results as the positive charge is made substantive by the reaction of the slightly negative matrix energy. To be made substantive, it must occupy and involve space. Before the atom can appear, a measure of the slightly negative matrix energy must neutralize a measure of positive space, providing what Harold calls a "space chamber" *within* which the primordial pair of charges operate and upon which the pair's *being* or "firmament" depends. "God called the firmament Heaven," and Jesus said that "Heaven" is within.[119] Space is the firmament of the proton, and it takes parent neutral energy to "tie off" this space.

In Harold's view, the proton involves a positive and negative charge as well as a photon. The proton, established in its "firmament," must also have a field in space in order to separate the particle from the flow of the primordial waters of slightly negative energy, providing it with "dry land," or a condition of stability in which the force of space and

184

of matrix energy is attenuated so that the particle itself can act. The field is provided as a measure of the primordial negative energy neutralizes itself, one of its units of negative energy assuming the "positive stance," and thereby provides for the particle a polarized magnetic field. In this operation, again the waters are divided, part of the matrix energy stabilizing itself.

Harold calls the matrix energy "Q" energy. We will be speaking a great deal from now on about Q energy. Harold saw Q energy as the primordial "waters," the primordial "darkness," the matrix or field energy through which creation takes place. As we use the terms, *negative energy, field energy, matrix energy*, we will be referring to Q energy. Please bear in mind that although this energy is slightly negative, it does not express a negative charge, electrically speaking. Harold makes a sharp distinction between negative energy that is "almost neutral" in its make-up, and *electric charge* that the electron expresses, because it is composed of a $2:1$ ratio of negative versus positive units of energy.

When we consider how many divisions of the "waters" the Genesis legend refers to, we can see that Q energy is deployed in many ways and serves many functions. It constitutes field forces. It contains the neutral energy that makes up a neutron, parent energy that "ties off" the space chamber of the proton. The electron that operates with the proton to complete the atom in ground state is embedded in Q energy. In Harold's view this matrix energy flows through space, and constitutes the "Q-force" that will be described. (See p. 187.) And so, having impressed upon our readers that Q energy is involved in all of nature's functions, that it is slightly negative but not sufficiently so to express negative electric charge, we will return to the creation of hydrogen giving rise to "land" or mass within the darkness of primordial waters.

Nature produces hydrogen in the form of the molecule, two atoms bonded so that they operate as one unit. (Again, we come upon a likeness to the Adam-Eve symbol.) In Harold's view, it requires five measures of primordial negative energy, seen as: $[(- + -) (+ - + - + - + -)]$, and called a "Q bundle," reacting with one measure of primordial positive energy, seen as: $[(+ - +) (- + - + - + - +)]$, and called a "P bundle," to form the hydrogen molecule. (See pp. 290-291, 301-304.)

The P bundle is equivalent to a neutron plus a positive charge, and the Q bundle is equivalent to a neutron plus a negative charge. A good deal happens while Adam is in his "deep sleep"—or as the neutron disintegrates—but when the transaction is complete, there remains a negative charge (— + —) left in the field to bond the two atoms, just as the "negative action" of the serpent gave rise to the bonding of Adam and Eve. You may read Harold's own description of the energy transactions. (See pp. 301-304.)

Within the nuclear chamber of each atom, Harold believed that there is a negative charge as well as a positive charge. There is nothing new about this suggestion, but it is not in favor at the moment. In addition, he saw a measure of space providing the atom with a constant positive force that activates the single unit of positive energy it possesses (in addition to its neutralized pair). This gives the nucleus a basis for action within itself. The atom cannot be reduced to the temperature of absolute zero (which would imply the cessation of all action), because this innermost action produces some "heat" (positive action). Varying amounts of primordial energy in rest state may inhabit the nuclear space chamber, but there is a minimum and a maximum density permissible before decay or radiation reactions occur. In the proton there is a ratio of two units of neutral energy to two units of positive energy to one unit of negative energy. The particle has a 50 per cent redundancy of neutral value that gives it mass, and a 50 per cent redundancy of positive value that takes precedence in communication over the neutral energy, so that the particle communicates a positive charge. The single unit of negative energy cannot be communicated.

As the proton is established, it communicates its positive charge. A primordial negative bundle, with its incipient electron, responds and surrounds the proton. The electron in the negative bundle is freed to respond to the strong attraction of positive charge, and the remaining energy in the matrix bundle forms a field-structure upon which the electron can operate. This "call" of the positive nucleus and this "response" from the matrix energy in space, incidentally, is why trapped alpha particles (helium nuclei), which express positive charge, are able to pull electrons apparently out of "thin air."

After the electron is produced *and freed in its field*, other possibilities arise. A single negative unit may form in a location that causes this negative value to be instantly "attached" to the positive unit within the electron. Such a situation would be represented as: $\left(\begin{smallmatrix} & - & \\ - & + & - \end{smallmatrix} \right)$. Another unstable elementary particle enters into nature, because this arrangement transgresses the law. It has a ratio of three negative units to one positive unit. The name of this particle is "mu minus," and it "springs" apart in microseconds, which amounts to almost "no time at all," disintegrating into an electron and a pair of neutrinos.

And once the magnetic field has been established, negative units, such as pi zero releases, may revert to the field, enhancing its strength.

But there is more to the story of freedom of motion entering the Cosmos by means of the action of negative energy—we have not yet finished "dividing the waters from the waters," with which the first ten verses of Genesis are concerned.

Since infinitely more primordial energy was organized in negative terms, consisting of field force, than in positive terms, consisting of aggregates of hydrogen, the call made upon the supply of matrix energy to form these clouds of matter was inconsequential. We must also remember that infinitely more primordial energy was organized as space than was used to organize the matrix energy, which in turn organized the hydrogen. Therefore, matrix energy cannot completely occupy all the space there is.

Therefore, also, we have the first basis for mild action, because as each measure of matrix energy occupies and thereby neutralizes a measure of positive space, its positive attraction for the negative energy is "silenced," and the matrix energy "flows on," creating its own field as it moves. Wherever masses of hydrogen formed, an attraction was posed for the primordial negative energy, because each hydrogen atom is slightly positive. As the negative energy flows around these bodies of energy that involve "inner" space and magnetic fields, which are the "waters which were under the firmament," the flow may be seen as the "waters above the firmament." This flow around the clouds of hydrogen created the constrictive force that began to condense them, and the evolution of the stars began.

Harold calls the matrix energy that flows through space the Q-force. From the beginning until now, it swirls and eddies, seeking space. And it is also always drawn to, through, and around celestial bodies, setting them in motion in the beginning, keeping them in motion, shepherding them toward the central deep of empty space that poses in sum the greatest possible positive attraction for the negative Q-force. The Q-force operates upon the principle of "serendipity." Its goal of filling space cannot be reached, its journey cannot be ended; therefore, it is drawn always first to the nearest mass, because this mass possesses positive attraction, until in embracing it, the Q-force neutralizes the attraction and moves on. At the same time that the central deep of space attracts the Q-force, this deep repels the slightly positive celestial masses, forcing them outward; and they in turn repel each other; so that the complex universal forces of attraction and repulsion give rise to the balanced elliptical motions that are generally found in nature.

Time's action in universal terms began with the flow of the Q-force, which exerts the constant stress of pressure. The flow of this force points time's entropy arrow in one direction because from the beginning and *ad infinitum* the flow goes on and on. Only if this flow of energy stopped could time's arrow be reversed. It cannot be stopped, because the "pattern" of creation constantly repeats itself, in that infinitely more of the energy in rest state that is returned to action is organized in negative and, therefore, unapparent terms. It is the pressure of the Q-force (which gives rise to the concept of "time") that causes the negative value to act upon the positive value, to disorganize both units of energy and return them to rest state. The need to disorganize does not reverse itself any more than man's need for rest reverses itself. These "one-way" aspects of time's action insure that sufficient energy in the system is always "at rest"—enough to be certain that the whole system cannot be "exhausted."

Therefore, freedom to act, freedom to rest, freedom to move within universal motion and fields or to move under the momentum that universal motion sustains, and, to a degree, freedom of choice in determining action, enters the Cosmos with negative energy. A serpent is a pretty good symbol for a unit of negative energy, from tip to tip of its spiraling body, able to spiral vertically and horizontally. The serpent becomes a symbol of the freedom that entered into life and nature through the organizing capacity of all that was potentially "negative" in God. Every bit is precious; nothing of it is to be lost. Not so much as a speck of Cosmic dust can stray beyond the ken of the Q-force. But there is another force also acting to draw all the masses in space together, even as it holds them separate as entities. This force is gravity. What is gravity? And how does it relate to nuclear binding force?

IV

Gravity and Nuclear Binding Force Both Say,
"I Love You, but I Also Love Myself."

Newton gave us the law that describes gravitational force. To Harold, this force could be understood only "if thine eye be single." When we explore creation in terms of examining nature's forces as single units of energy, we can see that gravity is the attraction that units of neutral energy pose for each other. We represent this as:

$$(- + - +)$$
$$(+ - + -)$$

The amount of neutral energy in a body determines the amount of neutral attraction *it can pose or respond to*.

We see from the representation above that each single unit of energy poses attraction for its opposite sign, and together the energy values communicate the attraction of wholeness.

Gravity is the expression of attraction that is posed between bodies of matter in ground state. Each body is composed of ionized and non-ionized atoms, the collection of which is grossly neutral (i.e., positive ions just balance negative electrons). But in Harold's view these masses are not precisely neutral. They communicate neutrality, but they are actually slightly positive, in the sense already indicated (i.e., each atom or positive ion has a unit of positive energy in its midst, and in the case of the positive ion there would be a 2:1 ratio of positive units to negative units).

The play between the attraction of wholeness versus the repulsion between slightly positive bodies is the secret involved in the force of gravity, which mammon cannot tell. The positive energy in the neutral mass cannot be communicated as such. Only the behavior of masses, from atoms to galaxies, reveals it.

189

Neutral energy in the mass communicates the attraction of wholeness, "I love you," and bodies of matter draw together. Until a *critical point* of nearness is reached. Then the force of positive being in the mass asserts itself and begins to dominate, slowing the approaching body down and finally bending its trajectory back. At this critical juncture the interactive force of one positive body sets in motion the process of repulsion, and the trajectory of the approaching particle turns backward.

It is the assertion of the positive "being" of an atom that preserves its integrity versus any other atom and says, "But I also love myself." Therefore, there must be bonding arrangements between atoms—arrangements that can be broken, changed, elaborated. It is the expression of the single positive force versus the complex neutral force that keeps the matter in the universe from drawing together into one big blob.

Gravity is the "socializing" force for the Cosmos, which creates the cities of light—our solar and galactic systems. But measure the distance between "dancing twin stars" and you will find that they are not "cheek to cheek." The dancing is much more modern—there is sufficient distance between them so that each star can "do its own thing."

The distance between stars that appear almost "as one" gives an idea of the strength of the single positive force of each which holds them apart, versus the attraction that draws them together. If we calculate this force in terms of a galaxy, we know why they appear to flee from each other, but maybe they are not fleeing. Attraction brings them too close, then repulsion drives them apart. This goes on constantly, because no celestial mass ever escapes the Q-force, and the pressure exerted by the Q-force tends always to draw the masses together as it moves them toward the centering of universal space, until they come again *within range* of the attraction of each other's neutral energy.

Gravitational force is also posed by the attraction between the neutral energy in the Q-force and the neutral energy in a mass. The neutral energy in the Q-force constitutes the gravitational field of the body as opposed to its polarized magnetic field. The sweep of the Q-force is one of the determining factors in establishing the orbit of a celestial body. Every speck of mass passing through a system influences it. The gravitational field may be altered as the course of the Q-force is altered by any celestial mass that undergoes drastic change within the system or in a neighboring system. For example, a situation might arise that causes the Q-flow to reverse direction and do a full loop, before rejoining the mainstream. And this, in turn, would cause the reversal of the magnetic field, which has happened to earth's magnetic field in the past.

There are many conditions that determine whether one celestial body is apt to collide with another. Near misses occur, but direct hits are the exception and these must be discussed later. (See p. 203.) For example, as a comet passes the sun, it draws near because the nucleus of the comet possesses the greatest "lump sum" of neutral energy. Therefore, it can both pose and respond to gravitational attraction between itself and the sun to a greater degree than the tenuous tail of the comet, which is generally observed to be *away* from the sun. The tail is composed of many particles (such as make up various gases), each posing its own single force of repulsion; and the tail is, therefore, more susceptible to the sun's force of repulsion than it is to the small sum of neutral attraction it can pose or respond to. In each situation, there will always be a greater force operating against a lesser force, and vice versa.

Before we can continue our discussion of gravity, we must turn attention to nuclear binding force, and to another of the white lies mammon has to tell because mammon cannot communicate the whole truth and nothing but the truth. Not when it comes to nuclear binding force, which for some strange reason *becomes a force of repulsion at closest range.*

In Harold's view, nuclear binding force is, like the force of gravity, posed by the attraction of opposite types of energy in the nucleus. The force of repulsion at closest range only appears to be such. There is no actual repelling force. At closest range, opposite and equal attraction stymies further action, so that a force must be applied to overcome the inertia. The condition of equilibrium must be upset. Equilibrium may be represented as: $\left(\begin{array}{c} (- + -) \\ (+ - +) \end{array} \right)$. The energy values are as attracted to the opposite values *within their own groupings* as they are attracted to the opposite values confronting them.

Therefore, we see that at closest range, the attraction of wholeness for wholeness *finishes itself* and becomes the attraction posed by "self-consistency." (This is why electrons do not spiral down and fuse with protons, another of the mysteries of mammon that plague scientists.)

To try to explain the attraction of "self-consistency," we would pose this representation of equal and opposite attraction:

$$(- + -)$$
$$(+ - +)$$

It would be difficult to separate this pair of particles, and it would also be difficult to get them to give up their separate identities and fuse. However, they can be pulled apart. They can also be induced to fuse by posing a sufficiently strong positive attraction in the nucleus. (This happens in a mode of decay known as "K-capture" when an electron is drawn into the nucleus and fuses with the positive charge to produce a neutral particle, thereby causing the substance to transmute into an element with lower atomic number and the same atomic weight as the isotope that reacted.)

We must emphasize that the force of gravity is involved with *critical distance* between two neutral masses. They must be near enough to communicate attraction; but there is a point at which the attraction that neutral energy poses is offset by the force of repulsion arising from the maximum expression of the sum of the single positive forces. Corresponding bodies are then "weightless" in relation to each other. Each is operating under the influence of the Q-force and the gravitational field it poses in relation to the other bodies in the system. The action of coming together or flying apart is stymied. But if a force is applied in sufficient strength to move the bodies closer, then the repelling force is minimized, and the force of attraction takes over, because the bodies are too close for the *sum* of the single positive forces to express itself in maximum terms. The bodies are then drawn together until at contact the repelling force again asserts itself in minimum terms; at this point, the attraction of wholeness also finishes itself into the attraction of self-consistency. Therefore, although the bodies may come into contact—and sometimes break because the mechanical stress is greater than they can withstand, or sometimes melt or burn if the heat stress is sufficient—ordinarily the two bodies do not merge in their entirety into one and the same consistency or substance upon impact. They "bounce apart"—however small the bounce—and come to rest upon a shared field. Inertia then comes into play. But a discussion of gravity's role in inertia and overcoming it must await our discussion of motion.

We may summarize by saying that gravitational and nuclear binding forces are similar but not identical. Neutral energy poses a strong force of attraction, which finishes itself in the stymie of equal and opposite attraction at closest range. But in the case of neutral atoms there is also a single force of repulsion working against the complex force of attraction. And the larger the body, the greater the influence of the Q-force upon it. The complexity of the various forces of attraction and repulsion among the energy systems involved enfolds a multitude of "plus/minus" calculations that serve in the end to maintain and restore to wholeness in accordance with the principle of One. These myriad calculations are synthesized in Newton's universal law of gravity.

Singularity and/or the maintenance of identity is the law under which love operates, in conjunction with the law of complementary action in society because only in society can action take place in meaningful terms. When there is no resistance between units of energy, as would be the case with any two *single* opposite values bound in union (− +), identity cannot be maintained. The units fuse and disintegrate into the singular state of neutrinos at rest, in which the independent being and integrity of matter is vested.

What keeps the units of positive and negative energy that make up a neutral particle from fusing and disintegrating into neutrinos at rest? Again, equal and opposite attraction is involved. We represent this by saying that the units are so arranged that each single unit is equally attracted to the opposite units with which it is engaged, so that this "tension" holds the opposite units apart. Therefore, neutral particles can exist in the nucleus of an atom until stress overcomes the "stymie" and one of the single values acts upon the other to reduce it to neutrinos.

In the nucleus of complex elements, we may envision many arrangements of neutral units of energy, or nucleons, as gravitational attraction draws them together. In neutral particles, there is no singular repelling force that comes into play. In Harold's view, such neutral aggregates are subject to maintaining a 2:1 ratio of active units (exerting force to provide binding energy) versus passive units (constituting the potential energy of the substance). For example, a nucleon with three units of neutral energy operating according to a 2:1 ratio of passivity versus exertion is represented as: (o − + o). The opposite ratio of 1:2 may also be expressed: (− + o − +). All of the energy may be called into action to provide binding force in response to stress (hence the variability of "mass," which is represented by the passive energy), and stress also gives rise to the formation of strange and/or unstable particles (which will be discussed later, see pp. 201-204).

Here, we are dealing with gravity and nuclear binding force. As compression of the energy "squeezes" the potential unit (o) in the representation (− + o − +), overcoming equal and opposite attraction, this unit (o) collapses into its neutrino value, leaving (− + − +). As further compression overcomes equal and opposite attraction, a negative value acts upon a positive value, reducing another neutral unit to its neutrino value, leaving only (− +). There is nothing to prevent these two units of energy (− +) from reacting to reduce themselves to their neutrino value, and this happens immediately. Therefore, a decrease in the dimension of the neutral particle which has been reduced to

($-$ $+$ $-$ $+$) or ($-$ o $+$), automatically brings about an *increase* in the rate of the collapse of the energy. When this "critical dimension" has been reached, collapse of the neutral units of energy takes on the proportions of "two for one." We see this in macroscopic terms as a star begins to collapse slowly at first, and then more and more rapidly.

Within the proton (nucleus of the hydrogen atom), time, as represented by the action of the Q-force, does not come into play. The particle's own magnetic field "encapsulates" it. Because there are no nucleons involved, time's action as it pertains to the reduction of neutral energy within a more complex nucleus does not operate. Therefore, the time-action ceases at small distances; it can have no effect at all upon the one positive value, the photon, enfolded at the heart of the proton. A discussion of proton formation must be reserved until later (see pp. 301-304).

Here we would say that in Harold's theory the mystery of "missing matter" in the universe, which the theory of gravitational collapse does away with, is solved, because he sees the "missing matter" to be neutrinos in rest state, which are simply dormant energy conveyors. As matter "collapses" into neutrinos at rest, replenishing this type of energy in the universe, the process amounts to a "transfusion" of primordial "plasma" into the Q-force (the "time-force"), so that we might say *time's energy is replenished.*

V

The Nature of Space and Motion in Space

Those familiar with the history of physics and astronomy will recognize that Harold's concept of space and field forces is a synthesis of the ideas of Newton, Clerk-Maxwell, and Einstein. It transcends the divided positions and reconciles them without contradicting the insights of men of genius in the past.

As Harold conceived of space, it is as Newton conceived it: a *being* existing in complete emptiness. But Harold's space is also as Clerk-Maxwell conceived it to be: because of the Q energy that operates within it, we can know it only as a "tangible" filled with waves of all kinds, which transmit energy and light, and in Harold's view this tangible property arose through the formation and divisions of primordial negative energy. Einstein believed that we can know space only as a tremendous field of force in which the force of gravity dominates, giving rise to curvature in the path a light ray takes, so that if we followed it to its end, theoretically, it would return us to see ourselves. Harold agrees. Matter does not exist in space apart from the field forces that negative energy provides and through which the positive nature of space is neutralized. Because light is a single positive force, it cannot travel directly through space, also a constant positive force. Light must travel the path of the Q-force, which neutralizes space. Hence the curvature of the Q-force's path is the only property of space that can be apparent through light's action. Light "bends" as the Q-force does. We can "see" the universe and its shape only in terms of light rays, which means we can trace the path of the Q-force through space by following these rays.

This curvature is the "shortest distance between any two points" because this is the only path that can be followed through space by a photon or a slightly positive body such as any neutral mass is. The photons themselves do not ordinarily fly through the air with the greatest of ease. They are conveyed, but we must get into this later (see p. 210).

Einstein believed that space alone remains the vehicle of reality. This view was shared by Harold. To him, *space is the single reality* in the sense that it is *the only absolute state* of material energy's being, *the only force constant* in mammon. Harold did not agree with Einstein that space has "devoured" ether and time, and will swallow up the fields and corpuscles, so that it is a cage in which man is suspended. Harold believed space neither acts nor reacts to time's (the Q-force's) flowing motion; space is *certainty in being*, which enfolds and supports the unified action of its complementary forces.

Space is the "Absolute" that science seeks. Space is as God, the Absolute, in which we live and move and have our being. Space is more and "something other" than the energy that man can measure; he can experience space only in terms of gravitational forces and field forces, wave properties that allow for sound and light. *Only "time," the unapparent flow of the Q-force through space, moves faster than light, because this force creates the path ahead of the light that travels it.* No material object, no form of positive energy, can outdistance time as it "leads" light through space.

We have spoken a good deal of motion and action. But we have not yet said what it is—what makes it possible. The mechanical forces and motions that we observe in daily living, and deal with in classical physics, are somehow taking place within the body of motion the universe is thought to be, from spiraling neutrinos to galaxies spiraling through the night. In Harold's view, motion is a matter of cross-action between opposite types of energy. Before explaining this, let us take a look at the Cosmos in action as modern physics conceives it to be.

Everything in the Cosmos, including itself, is thought to be interpenetrating fields of energy, and the fields are forces and/or wave actions, which somehow both are and are not particles. But then, particles themselves are thought to be simply motions. It is all a matter of action. But there comes a point when the mathematicians cannot get hold of the action—it is simply accomplished, in that it must be determined to be a series of positions accomplished or a series of "rests." But what is accomplishing what?

It all sounds suspiciously like pure magic or pure nonsense. It is amusing to realize that in the end science bases the Cosmos and all that is happening within it upon the hocus pocus of nothing substantial moving upon nothing substantial by means of a series of rests wherein a "body" gets there and does God knows what—maybe. But a body, real substance, was not there in the first place—how can it be there in the second place?

This generation says, "Tell it as it is." Harold replies that there is no such "thing" as nothing in action, acting upon nothing, traveling through space which is nothing, the action itself having no basis of cause. A wave train of energy is something substantial acting upon something substantial—in short, the whole universe is a matter of varying degrees of substance in action upon and through inactive substance. The real "fixed stuff" is space, and every atom involves it. No one can say exactly what attraction and repulsion are, but attraction causes particles and units of the primordial substance to move, and repulsion poses enough resistance to provide the friction necessary to hold the course and make progress real.

In Harold's view, motion is a "mix" of being (position) and action (change of position). The substance that moves is a mix of positive and negative units of energy. This mix is moving through a field that is also a mix of positive and negative energy. The negative units of energy in the moving body "reach ahead" to secure a hold upon positive units in the field; they secure their positions before the positive units are "pulled up," and come to rest upon a negative value in the field. At no time are all the forces in a moving body in action; at no time are all the forces at rest; at no time is the particle unsecured in its field. At the limit, you must measure this motion either in terms of the action of the negative units changing position (velocity) or in terms of the holding positive units (position). The particle *taken as a whole* is neither moving nor still. The negative units in action are not material energy in the sense of being apparent energy with measurable mass. This action cannot be observed. The motion of the body appears, therefore, to be a series of positions accomplished, or a series of rests. The principle of indeterminacy is involved. This principle again reflects the principle of One's indeterminacy, except as its measure is treated with in positive and negative terms, so that balance is sustained through what appears to be imbalance in the operation.

As particles or bodies of matter move through space fields, act, and interact, the substance that is set in motion, so that wave trains of energy are propagated, is the emulsion of energy in rest state. This is the medium in which the "net" of field units moves. We may think of the waving "net" of field forces as the ether, and the emulsion of energy at rest as the subether. As a light wave group travels through the field, the units of energy encounter some resistance as like units confront each other.

The greatest conductivity bespeaks an alignment of units of energy that offers the least resistance, as though a negative charge is always confronting the *equivalence* of a positive charge secured in the field toward which it moves with greatest ease. But a force of repulsion would still exist between the positive values in the field-equivalence of positive charge, on the one hand, and the positive value in the negative charge, on the other hand.

As a light wave group travels, it, too, is traveling upon a field composed of opposite forces. But a discussion of this, and of Harold's ideas regarding the absorption and radiation of light, can be dealt with better after we have discussed the structure of inner space in the atom, and its content, as well as material energy's reaction to stress.

VI

A Day in the Life of an Atom

As we explore atomic matter, we can understand it better if we are anthropomorphic enough to hold in mind the construction of a living cell. We know that there are four components out of which the DNA of every cell is arranged, and the DNA is in the nucleus of the cell. This "coil" carries the code script, and governs the life of the cell. Endless arrangements of these four building blocks are possible.

To Harold, the fact that there are *four* natural modes of decay, insofar as the elements are concerned, means that there are four types of inorganic nuclear building blocks, each one exhibiting its unique mode of decay. Therefore, an inorganic correspondence to organic DNA arises as the more complex elements form.

But first, the nuclear blocks themselves must be constituted. Atomic number is indicated by the letter Z. The first nuclear block is hydrogen, Z 1, the proton, $_1H^1$. It may absorb a neutron, or two protons may interact to become a deuteron or heavy hydrogen, $_1H^2$. This is the second nuclear block, which Harold calls Z 1 + 0. We have here two Z 1 "cores," as Harold calls them. He describes the several ways in which the Z 1 cores may interact to produce helium, $_2He^4$, in Harold's terms, Z 2 + 00, and "light" helium, $_2He^3$, Z 2 + 0. These primordial nuclei represent the four component blocks of inorganic DNA, out of which all other elements are constituted. Lithium, for example, would be an arrangement of two or three of the cores. Its properties would depend upon its "Z" structure (not atomic weight), which could be Z 1 + Z 1 + Z 1, or Z 1 + Z 2, or Z 2 + Z 1. Harold did not describe the composition of elements other than hydrogen and helium, but he indicated that all other nuclei are composed of arrangements of two or more of the four nuclei described above.

In Harold's concept, as a neutron is absorbed into the nucleus, a gamma ray may be emitted, or some of the energy may be disorganized as it "melts" into neutrinos in rest state. This also happens as nuclei fuse, and this is one of the reasons why atomic weight does not increase precisely by the weight of a neutron as measured by a neutron's weight outside the nucleus. Therefore, Harold differentiates between a neutron and the nucleon it becomes after absorption.

As Harold describes the formation of the hydrogen molecule (H_2), he poses its actual bond as a negative charge of energy in the joint field the atoms occupy. The negative energy attracts the slightly positive atoms, which communicate only their redundancies of neutral energy. This negative charge, left over when the H_2 molecule was formed, was not left in the field for the sake of convenience. The concept of the field-bond fits the arithmetic *and* the facts of the case when the bonding energy of *one* hydrogen atom is considered. In Harold's view, because the bond of molecular hydrogen involves a field-bond that is not within either atom, it adds to the bonding energy of the molecule; and this explains why a single atom of hydrogen does not contribute exactly half of hydrogen's calculated bond energy as determined by pulling apart the hydrogen molecule. The field-bond cannot communicate its presence, and when the molecular field is disorganized or disengaged, the bond is gone.

The natural and induced modes of decay are described by Harold in the unfinished manuscript he left. The processes that are observed by physicists are described, and Harold's translation of the phenomena into his numerical concepts of positive, negative, and neutral units of energy fit the empirical data as neatly as the glass slipper fit Cinderella's foot. There is an explanation of what happens and why, but this material should be read in its original form. It is too complex to condense (see pp. 321-325).

Only a person who is familiar with the intricate, complex, baffling reactions that occur in the decay processes could appreciate how intriguing it is to find a hypothesis that explains these mysteries and is not itself self-contradictory.

Our purpose here is to bring forward the principles upon which Harold's hypothesis rests. One such principle is that *stress causes energy to turn from positive to negative to neutral expression*. We see this "turning" in Jesus' law of communication: Yea, yea; nay, nay. The formula reads: from positive, to negative, to a neutral statement that in the end "says nothing," as energy in rest state does because it cannot communicate.

Time's action, or the pressure of the Q-force, produces stress in nature.

As we examine the reactions of inorganic matter to stress, we must be anthropomorphic enough to hold in mind the body's reaction to stress. We can imagine, then, the elementary particles that make up an atom following the pattern of "alarm, resistance, adaptation" studied by Hans Selye in his book, *The Story of the Adaptation Syndrome.* Or, if there is overresistance, they reach a state of exhaustion. Or, if the stress is prolonged or increased, exhaustion ensues.

Here, we come to another important principle in Harold's concept. *Antiparticles are particles in alarm/resistance state; therefore, antimatter is a stress reaction.* Antimatter does not exist in the universe as an "opposite" type of matter or another "estate" of matter. It occurs when particles or massive bodies are subjected to duress. If a particle and its antiparticle come together, they destroy each other's organization.

The nature and degree of the stress determines the production of the antiparticles, and also the products of induced decay and particle collisions.

Antiparticles are possible because the aggregates of energy possess opposite units of energy, and under stress conditions the energy groups can give expression to these hidden values. The aggregates also contain negative units that can *act* in positive or negative terms, enhancing the positive or neutralizing the negative expression of the group.

This is why, for example, an electron $(- + -)$ can express a positive charge, becoming a positron. It cannot express as a *proton*, but as a positive charge of electrical energy. When both of its negative units assume the positive "stance," the particle does not disintegrate, as a particle composed of three positive units would, since like units repel each other; this is because the negative units are still negative units, and the positive unit binds them. If the real nature and constitution of an electron is a mystery to scientists, the occurrence of its antiparticle, the positron, is a greater mystery. See "Electra," the electron: $(- + -)$. Sometimes, when she is taking her rest, she looks like this: $(- o)$, a tiny magnet. But when she is extremely alarmed or hurt or angry, she looks like this: $(| + |)$, a positron.

If she attracts a placid sister when she is in alarm state, the positron/electron reaction usually or sometimes results in both particles emitting their bundles of light, and their negative energy dissolves into rest state. But in the normal course of events, or when the stress is such that Electra can cope with it gracefully, she reacts to the situation by emitting her quantum of light $(+)$. As this happens, she is in the fine state of tension $(- -)$ that calls forth from nature a "replacement seed," another photon to take its place, so that her countenance is restored in the act of losing it, before she can go "all to pieces or fly apart." Electron: $(- + -)$.

The faces of the proton and antiproton are too complex to sketch easily. Harold describes them in detail in his hypothesis. The photon, and pi zero, which releases the photons from the "darkness" of primordial waters, are each their own antiparticles. When the photon is disorganized, it lapses into the "little ones" in rest state. And this is the end that all stressed energy reaches under duress or in time.

Unstable particles are a "temporary holding" of energy. The more massive ones disintegrate into unstable particles, which in turn disintegrate into a mixture of stable and unstable particles—always in the direction of producing less massive products. In Harold's view, this is because in each transaction some of the energy lapses into rest state. This happens in such inconceivably short "split seconds" that a day in the life of atomic matter or elementary particles can be a long time indeed, if measured by the events that can take place in a large mass—or it can be indeed short if measured by the time it takes a particle or an atom to react.

In Harold's view, the "alarm" reaction is *positive* (i.e., positive values go into action, thereby producing heat, or increased temperature, or radiation of energy). The "resistance" reaction is *negative* (i.e., negative values take over the expression of the particle's energy, thereby inducing cooling, or decreased temperature, or liquefaction, depending upon the type of stress and the material involved). The "adaptation" reaction begins, in the most exact sense, with the response of the positive and/or negative values, but as stress continues "adaptation" gives rise to *neutral* expression (i.e., random motion as in the gaseous state, or "fixed forces" as in the crystalline state—again, depending upon the type of stress and the material involved). As stress continues or is increased, "over-resistance" is expressed in terms of intensification of the "alarm" or "resistance" syndrome, which tends in the end to produce neutral and/or random expression, as in a plasma or supercooled substance. The principle involved, as Harold saw it, is that under stress energy "translates" its expression from positive to negative to neutral, or from negative to positive to neutral, depending upon the material involved and the type of stress. "Exhaustion" accompanies the course of stress, which means that some of the energy used in the whole process (either that used to stress or that being stressed) is reduced to neutrinos that lapse into rest state, which is a neutral state insofar as expression or being is concerned.

Heating indicates positive expression. Cooling indicates negative expression. In supercooled substances, the electron shifts into positron expression so that it can travel through the "negative atmosphere" with minimum resistance; but the slightest alteration in the nature of the stress, such as the positron's arriving at its destination, or being stopped, or confronting a positive pole, causes the electron instantly to reverse itself or revert to negative expression so that it appears in its natural state.

According to Harold, "adaptation" may take a variety of states—every degree of "tensile being" ranging between water and diamond hard, ranging from "crazy putty" and rubber to brittle glass or plastics with all sorts of different qualities.

Water was energy's most triumphant adaptation—the adaptation that inorganic material had to make in response to general Cosmic stress before, in the chaotic conditions of the early universe, living material could evolve. And water is actually the *minimum* expression of the principle that in its maximum expression gives rise to *antimatter*. Water is "antimatter" in the sense that although it is composed of "solid stuff," it is "antisolid" in behavior, ordinarily giving expression to the negative energy in its make-up so that it remains pliable and free.

The idea of bodies of antimatter colliding with matter in the universe, leading to the utter disorganization of both types of material, is terrifying. But water is "anti" expression at the minimum, and this is life-giving. Each drop of rain that falls represents a collision of celestial masses. Water, by giving expression to its negative energy, obscures the slightly positive nature of its material substance, thereby minimizing the repelling force between masses of matter.

Water adapts readily to stress without losing or exhausting itself in the process. Living material depends on this "learning" in the inorganic realm. Therefore, learning how to adapt to stress is the primordial lesson all living material must learn.

Insofar as antimatter's being formed in celestial systems is concerned, Harold believed that within the smaller systems which operate within the larger systems, it is possible for very small masses of antimatter (in astronomical terms) to form in response to stress and to be swept into collision with a larger mass of matter. He believed that celestial collisions also occur when a smaller body (that collides with the larger body) is composed predominantly of negative particles (a mass that has electrons added to its normal complement, which is equal in number to the protons involved). For example, hydrogen can support two electrons. We represent this in terms of the electrons' being attached to a positive charge:

$$(+ \; - \; +)$$
$$(- + -) \quad (- + -)$$

We can see that there is sufficient positive energy to bind them. The "surface" of such a negative particle communicates the negative. But when we remember that at the heart of the proton itself, hidden behind its neutral energy, there is a single photon $(+)$, we see that, in effect, the added electron *neutralizes the mass* because a negative unit that balances the photon has been added. The positive repelling force between the negative particle and the neutral mass it approaches (which is slightly positive in its being) is not effective. Only the attraction between bodies of neutral energy is communicated. Therefore, there is an *abnormal impact.*

Or collisions between celestial masses may occur under such stress as causes *the smaller body* to express completely in antiparticle terms so that it becomes antimatter, and there is nothing to prohibit the "opposite" masses from coming together. Contact would be abnormal. Such a body of antimatter would take its like toll of the receiving body. Itself and its equivalence would convert to energy, leaving only a scar upon the terrain as the energy disintegrated into rest state. In the chaotic time of early universal evolution, countless such impacts must have occurred, so that as much matter as is in evidence was converted to neutrinos in rest state, transfusing the universal body of Q energy with the plasma it must have, and *reducing the amount of matter in expression to a manageable amount.*

Every day in the life of an atom it, too, must reduce the amount of matter in action within it to a manageable amount. How it reacts depends on how many nucleons it may have lost via time's action and how many neutrons it may have absorbed, as well as how efficient its arrangement is for the absorption and emission of light. And, of course, the body of any living thing operates under the same principle.

As for a day in the life of the Cosmos, although it is not in itself a "macro-creature," or a supergiant organism, the Cosmic System operates on what may be called the "living" principle. The Q energy that courses through it may be likened to the blood that courses through the vascular system of a body, bringing sustenance to the organs within it, and carrying away the "waste." Therefore, *in principle,* the Cosmos operates like a living system and is itself as "alive" as the energy within it, from proton to man. In Harold's view, it is a living universe, because it is a system capable of supporting the living systems within it everlastingly. Let us discuss next the "ways and means."

VII

Harold's Theory of the Living Universe, Wherein a Sun May Have Its Cake and Eat It, Too

Today, it is thought that our sun is constantly "burning" its hydrogen, and is headed for eventual "death" as its internal supply is consumed. A process known as the proton-proton chain (wherein a series of nuclear reactions produce helium and release energy) is thought to be responsible, for the most part, for the sun's heat-giving activity. Other reactions are probably involved, such as the carbon cycle in which the carbon isotope that reacted initially is regenerated at the end of the process. In each case hydrogen is not generated. It is "consumed."

Harold took another view. He believed that some types of stars evolve to the point that they become *energy reactors*, in the sense that they *produce* each day the hydrogen they consume and more—spewing out the excess material that builds up within them. In the process, the Q energy in the universe is also replenished.

In Harold's view, hydrogen is produced in a star such as our sun through the decay of neutrons, and also in nuclear reactions wherein isotopes absorb neutrons and release protons, the absorbing isotope transmuting to lower atomic number and in time undergoing beta decay in which the initially reacting isotope is regenerated. The *fuel* required for both processes is *neutrons*, and every measure of Q energy contains the equivalent of a neutron plus a negative charge. The Q-force, therefore, brings to the celestial body the materials it needs, much as the blood does in our bodies. And the Q-force carries away the waste, which time disposes of by reducing the matter to rest state in the form of pure neutrino energy. You may read Harold's own description of this process (see pp. 332-335).

Harold believed that our sun has reached this "steady state," wherein it produces fuel to replace the fuel it consumes. Not all celestial bodies will become such energy reactors, and the universe has not yet produced all that will be. Some stars will run their course without developing life-bearing planetary systems. These act much as "buoys" in the celestial seas, setting the course of the Q-flow. Only certain types of second-generation stars, which begin a rebirth with a sufficient quantity of elements other than hydrogen, are susceptible to becoming reactors. The transition from star to energy reactor must occur before more than 50 per cent of the star's hydrogen is radiated—at the period of what might be called the "half-life" of the star, which our sun has reached. A star can become an energy reactor only after sufficient helium has been produced to stabilize the situation.

If Harold's idea of a star reaching a "steady state" and becoming an energy reactor seems "farfetched," let us remember that scientists are now working to perfect "breeder reactors," which operate in one of two ways. One way depends on the neutrons that are emitted in decay processes of fissionable material, some of which, slowed down by inert material in the "mix," are used again to repeat the process. Or neutrons may be injected into a mix of fissionable and inert material. There are, of course, other requirements concerning size, temperature, etc. We are concerned with the principle involved. In either case, neutrons are the fuel that is needed to keep the reactors going.

Harold does not mention "breeder reactors." The point he would make is that nature has devised energy reactors that produce hydrogen from the matrix energy that gave rise to it in the first place. This, he saw to be an unending "stream" of energy, which the Q-force brings to the sun. Each measure of it contains a neutron equivalence that is released. If the neutrons do not react with other substances in the sun, then they decay into the components of hydrogen: a proton and an electron. Therefore, in neutron decay, hydrogen is produced.

When a solar system's sun reaches the steady state that an energy reactor represents, the evolution of its planets proceeds in steady course until organic life becomes possible on some of them, while others act as "decoys" to mitigate the force of Q energy as its flow interpenetrates the system.

In Harold's cosmogony, again we see that all other cosmogonies are gathered in a grand synthesis. But, like the religions, these theories must transcend their ideas of the alpha and/or omega state of this marvelous creation in order to fit into his view of the living universe. Let us look now at the major theories that vie with each other today.

The explosion theory, which holds that the universe began in one great explosion of a centralized mass of energy, has its counterpart in the religious idea of God's casting Satan out of heaven. In Harold's theory of the living universe, we must see this beginning in terms of an explosion so quiet, so gentle, that the whole body of the Original Energy melted like a snowflake in the hand as it granulated into "God as an irreducible number of indestructible elementary particles." In the course of the reorganization of this energy, the galaxies of matter arose; they appear to flee away from each other, but they return to our view as surely as light does in Einstein's curved path of light, which must track back in time to ourselves.

The expansion-contraction theory comes into the picture because, in Harold's view, the Q-force working against the constant force of space gives rise to a recurring expansion and contraction of the distance between galaxies, as the force of space sends them outward and the centering action of the Q-flow turns them inward. But this expansion and contraction is as nontraumatic to the whole Cosmos as breathing is to man. It indicates simply that this is a living, breathing Cosmic being.

The steady-state theory contributes the concept of the eternal creation of matter, which in Harold's theory begins with the regathering of primordial units of neutrino energy into quanta of light. To the concept of the universe having no beginning and no end, Harold would say, yes and no. We cannot know what that prior body of the Original Energy was like. Nor can we envision a beginning for it. But we can envision a beginning to the universe as we can know it—a beginning of time's action through which this creation is being reorganized and perpetual creation is being sustained. We can envision an *end* to the *energy that was* because it can now never return to its former state. We can envision an end—not to change or the pulsing life of the universe—but to the processes of universal evolution, when the arrangement of the bodies within it and their course through space has reached the optimum state. *A steady state will be reached as the course of the Q-force flowing through space holds steady, because the systems within it have reached steady state.* The Q-force's path will then form a Cosmic "El Camino Real" leading to other solar and galactic systems—the Q-force itself to be used as the wind was used to convey men across the oceans. Time's action will not cease, so that time is everlasting. It measures change, insists upon it eternally.

The static universe theory contributes to the concept that matter is continually being used and reused. In Harold's view, the matter involved is the primordial stuff, the neutrinos. Harold's concept of a star reaching a steady state as a life-giving energy reactor gives purpose and meaning to universal evolution. The static universe theory is in agreement with Harold's in that it proposes that the universe is not expanding, there was no violent explosion, the galaxies will not end in isolation. But this theory does not allow for the "becoming" that is an essential part of Harold's theory.

The electric universe theory, proposed by Lyttleton and Bondi, was based on the assumption that the positive charge is not exactly equal to the negative charge of the electron.[120] Here, Harold's measure of the positive unit of energy as *three* versus the measure of the negative unit as *two* supports the contention. The positive is the *more*, but the negative force is *equal to* its action.

In Harold's theory of the living universe, once a solar system is established, in the sense that its sun has reached a steady state, maximum stress such as is required to produce celestial collisions cannot occur within it except in minimal terms, or in the expression of very small bodies of antimatter. This is because the system as a whole is harmonious; the bodies within it are symbiotic. And every move made within the system and within the universe *diminishes the destructive potential* in the power it enfolds and expresses, until the destructive potential is reduced to the desirable minimum.

What Harold understood, and what he believed Jesus perceived, was that "heaven," as each of us looks up to behold it, is passing away. And so is the earth of our time. But this does not happen as men expected it to happen in Jesus' day, nor as the astronomers expect it to happen today. In the midst of the passing, there is always rebirth, renewal, re-creation, which leads to the everlasting life of the celestial bodies that are established *in* time, as our sun and planet are. In the passing away of the cells, the body is renewed—and so it is with this Planet Earth. The passing away of the early continent that became the Americas, Europe, and Africa may have been much like the division of a cell into segments. The continent may have split early in the life of the planet as the waters "under this firmament" (earth's fluid center) shifted in an unimaginably large and Stygian tidal wave in response to some development in the sun; and thereafter the segments pushed apart as the slightly positive masses repelled each other, until the "push-pull" of gravity stabilized their positions.

Synthesizing the five cosmogonies into a cosmology that is greater than the sum of its parts was to Harold a greater necessity than dealing with the disputes in religion. *Because if the religion of tomorrow is to be in truth a universal religion, it must be Cosmic in every sense and it must project a living universe in the process of becoming, able to sustain life everlasting.* Otherwise the religion can have no meaning, and science has no meaning; and neither the religion nor science would accord with the intuition, the certainty of unending life, in man, the book in which the story of creation is written.

But Harold did not develop his hypothesis from the strands of wishful thinking. Step by step he put together the pieces of the puzzle of physics and astronomy, the pieces made of observations and empirical data. Looking at them in terms of positive, negative, and neutral energy— what we know about it and how it behaves—the outlines of a new faith in God, man, and nature appeared. (See Book III, pp. 336-339.)

It is easy to see that Oliver Reiser's concept of Cosmic Humanism could, by the nature of the name, provide a framework large enough to house Harold's cosmology. But we must light this structure before we can see what a mansion it truly is.

VIII

Light Enfolds Its Own Drama:
A Magnificent Contradiction

Today, there is a "magnificent contradiction" in physicists' theories of what light is. On the one hand, it is described as a wave group action. On the other hand, it is described as a "corpuscle," a photon. Both theories are workable. In some situations the wave theory applies; in other situations, the particle theory applies. But this is not a comfortable situation for scientists—their whole edifice resting on two theories that contradict each other. And yet, does not nature operate by utilizing contradictions?—positive/negative energy, light/dark, heat/cold, male/female, etc.

Harold's theory of light provides a simple and profound synthesis of the opposing theories of light. He represents the light wave group as a 50 per cent redundancy of neutral energy enfolding a single unit of positive energy $(+ - + - +)$. There is a ratio of three positive units to two negative units in operation. Therefore, there is a difference in the frequencies of the wave trains. One wave train has a greater frequency than the other. This follows because in primordial energy the negative unit is less than the positive unit.

As the three positive units of energy "work against" the two negative units of energy, the negative units open to secure one positive unit at the *center* of the group. In this act of reinforcing each other at the center, a boundary for the group is drawn and the wave group itself becomes "like a particle." If we enlarge our picture, using black dots for units of negative energy and white dots for units of positive energy, we can represent the action as follows:

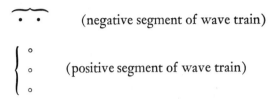

                             (negative segment of wave train)

                             (positive segment of wave train)

As the positive segment moves through the negative segment, we *define* a corpuscle of light:

If we picture this reaction in positive and negative symbols, we see it as an electron conveying a photon:

$$\begin{array}{c} + \\ (- + -) \\ + \end{array}$$

But we would have to surround this configuration with other units of positive and negative energy that make up the field through which the wave group operates. Otherwise, our positive values would repel. We must also understand that the "threading process" is continuous, as though the strand of light were being drawn through the "eye of the needle," zero field intensity, periodically. But if we stopped this action at any one point, an electron would be "stopped in its tracks." As this happens, we still have a light wave group $(- + -)$, in which there is still a difference in the measure of the frequencies involved.

The light becomes "corpuscular" as the photon is "bumped out" of the *electron*, or as it is drawn into an *atom*. As this happens, the negative tension causes the formation of another photon to take its place, this photon being drawn up and into action from the "uniform chance of energy" which is the flux of neutrino energy in rest state, spread throughout all we can experience of space. But if the central photon $(+)$ is lost from the light *wave group*, then the remaining units of energy in the wave group, which collectively constitute simply neutral energy, revert to the general field.

The photon is freed from its "negative cradle" as it enters the atom, and there the interaction in the space chamber between the atom's own single measure of positive energy and the light that enters begins the inward drama which proceeds according to quantum rules. The "even chance" of energy is spread inside the atom in the field upon which its electrons play and also upon the larger field of space. But it is the "virtual" energy in the atom's space chamber, neutrinos in rest state, that causes certain of the decay processes which serve to relieve the atom of some of its excess "riches" because there is a maximum that it can handle. In Harold's view, five degrees of this energy is all that one space chamber can hold. Inward stress arises from too much, or too little, reserve energy.

Harold did not name his theory of light. Probably, it should be called the wave-particle theory of light since it reconciles the two theories that appear to stand opposed and actually do not—as is the case with Jesus, symbol of light defined, and Judas Iscariot, friend who opened himself to the role of negative action so necessary to the drama. As the negative energy drops its "hold" on the particle of light and betrays the presence of the photon in its midst, there is set up within the negative force the tension that leads to its purchase of a bit of "earth," primordial neutral energy. But in this act, the negative force disappears from the scene—just as Judas did—and just as the electron disappears into the general field, the "potter's field" of space, until it is called into action again.

In a light wave train, the two types of energy (the unequal frequencies represented by the black and white dots in our diagram) interfere, for the most part, but complete their action *in phase*—just as Judas and Jesus complete their actions finally "in phase."

Harold's wave-particle theory of light depends, of course, on the concept of the *resurrection of light*. He believed that Jesus realized that the secret of creation rests in the *resurrection of light*, and this is why the Resurrection drama was essential to Jesus' dramatization and symbolization of light and its action.

Harold believed that just as in the legend the phoenix arises from its own ashes, so the neutrinos, "ashes of the universe," rise again to light the world when negative tension prompts them to this action—and the radiant spirit of Jesus rises again and again through the centuries to light the minds of men.

This brings us to the subject of mental energy.

To Harold, mental energy was "something"—it was not "nothing acting upon and through nothing," any more than a photon of physical light is "nonmaterial," although its degree of mass cannot be communicated. Mental energy is a still further refinement and a different structuring of the ONE Original Energy that was Parent. And there is structured into the material or physical universe energy that is refined enough to operate with it.

IX

The Nature of Mental Energy

Harold used the term *mental energy* to include every aspect of intelligence, imagination, psychic energy, sensory and extrasensory perception. To him, mental energy is material, real, in that it is drawn from the same Original Parent Substance of which all else is constituted. As mental energy is radiated and absorbed, it is sensed. Measurable effects are produced, but mental energy is so refined that our laboratory instruments are not geared to deal with it, although the brain wave patterns of man can now be recorded.

Someday a detector fine enough to pick up mental waves will be devised—although we must also say that there is no expression of energy in which mind and matter are not met, so that in this sense every detection of any kind of wave is a detection of mental energy expressing itself throughout creation.

Indeed, we may go so far as to say that nature may have provided us with a detector fine enough to pick up mental waves—plant life. In the May–June 1969 issue of *Main Currents in Modern Thought*, F. L. Kunz discusses the research done by Clive Backster that shows that plants register apprehension, fear, pleasure, and relief. Mr. Kunz says:

> [The research] establishes the fact that plants are sentient, that they have what we can only (while avoiding undue anthropomorphism) refer to as "feelings." . . .
>
> Mr. Backster's experiments have shown that house plants . . . register apprehension when a dog passes by, react violently when live shrimp are dumped into boiling water, and receive signals from the dying cells in the drying blood of an accidentally cut finger. They appear to respond to distress signals issued in response to threats against any member of the living community. What is more, they in some way are able to receive signals over a considerable distance, for they have registered Mr.

Backster's intent to return to his office when he was fifteen miles away. . . .

Once we have brought ourselves to accept the authenticity of such evidence—based upon Mr. Backster's unimpeachable reputation as an interrogation expert, initiator of the Backster Zone Comparison polygraph procedure which is the technique standard at the U. S. Army Polygraph school—its significance appears to be compound. . . .

Backster reports that he has "tried unsuccessfully to block whatever signal is being received by using a Faraday screen, screen cage, and even lead-lined containers. Still the communication continues. It seems that the signal may not even fall within our electrodynamic spectrum." . . . Now that we know that plants are sentient, and that they respond (in some appropriate but as yet unknown way) to emotions, both beneficial and menacing, delivered from without, the way is open to establish the existence of a life force-field. The question will be: What is that particular force? As force is variously defined even in physics, the inquiry is wide open.[121]

Based on Harold's view, we would say that mental energy is being *registered* by the plants. But before going further, we must discuss the nature of mental energy.

To determine the nature of mental energy, we must look backward in time to before the beginning of it, and try to determine the measure number of the Absolute One that *was* and acted upon itself; so that "after this," the measure number of One became *five*, divided to reflect the measure numbers of positive One (3) and of negative One (2), which operate versus each other to produce wholeness, unity, One. Absoluteness (or symmetry) reigned, prior to this division, and absoluteness implies sameness, which must be represented in an equation as: $(3/3 \times 3/3 = 1)$, giving the Original One the measure number of *six*, divided to reflect *sameness or symmetry*.

Something was abstracted from the side of the "ledger" that we call "negative" in its reduced state. And this energy was reorganized to provide something of value *that cannot be compared to anything apparent and material* because the quality of negative energy is that it is *unapparent* until it reveals itself in action.

(Here we would say: scientists understand concepts of positive energy, and the action of most physical processes is expressed in terms of potential and kinetic energy, the sum of which they look upon as a positive and, if conserving forces are acting, as a constant. If energy is dissipated, this sum can be reduced to zero, but it cannot go further into the negative realm. However, Harold considered negative energy, or the "function of the negative," to be associated with magnetic fields, etc.)

We return now to the original state of absoluteness, and the "something" that must have been abstracted from the side of the "ledger" that we call "negative" in its reduced state. This missing bit of absolute energy, which was extracted from "sameness"—or a condition in which there were no actual opposites—must be energy that is *actually neutral*. It is neutral in a way that no other energy we experience can be, because opposite types of energy arose as a *result* of its abstraction and thereafter joined in union to give rise to a new type of neutrality in which sameness joined to sameness is not tolerable, just as a union of two like signs (++) is not tolerable. We know that like signs (sameness) repel.

Mental energy must be represented in this one degree that was abstracted from the original *One* measure, and it expresses sameness that was in the beginning, before otherness arose; it expresses also likeness attracted to likeness, which is operative in life.

Harold did not name this mental particle, but let us call it a "psychon." We can see now that although it is material, in the sense that it is a part of the original substance, it is altogether different from mammon or what we experience as material energy, so that in this sense, it is altogether nonmaterial. But mammon *serves it* as we shall see later on, so that mental energy is both sensory and nonsensory in the ordinary use of these terms.

Mental energy is one degree of energy so "programed" or instructed originally that it cannot *itself* express in positive or in negative terms. But the psychon is the mental light that is involved in a thought wave, and a *thought wave* may be programed by the psychon it carries to express in positive or negative terms, because mammon's energy is involved in the mental wave group. Before discussing this group action, we must examine the psychon in more detail.

Harold saw "mental light" as energy in the fourth estate. It is *parent energy*, expressed throughout as the "mind of nature," as opposed to the *transparent* energy of space, and *unapparent* negative energy (field forces), and *apparent* energy (light and mass). The psychon is an indivisible unit of energy that bifurcates but does not actually separate. Within itself, it is a cleavage that is not complete. The particle is "as one," but its ability to bifurcate without separating provides it with a *three-point property* that allows it to express in the perfect harmony associated with the Pythagorean ratio of (2:1 vs 1:2).

Because there is nothing to resist mental energy, as it acts it bifurcates and *resists itself*. Here, we have *responsibility* entering into the state of freedom and the action of mental energy. We see this represented as intellect and intuition separate and confront each other: the one aspect of mind must recognize the other aspect of mind as a likeness, in the image each presents, before the strands cross-act to reflect upon a point of truth or reality, in principle.

Within itself, the psychon is constituted of *actually equal measures* of mental energy coupled by the one-point each partakes of. This is a union of One and One that may be described as "I and the Father are one." In nature, we see the likeness to mental energy in the two like hydrogen atoms bonded in the hydrogen *molecule* (which is the way hydrogen arises in nature—i.e., H_2). But this molecule may be put asunder. The psychon itself cannot be divided—and in nature we see this quality of indivisibility repeated in the neutrino—but the psychon may couple with other psychons to produce mental molecules or complex chains of thought.

Because the psychon involves the pattern both of what *was* and what *is*, it involves the "minus/plus" or "absent/present" principle involved in the principle of One, wherein complementary forces are involved in dynamic action. It may, therefore, be seen to be a "binary system" within itself that may be programed to disseminate simple or complex messages directed in a negative or positive way—"nay" or "yea." But it cannot actually *become* negative or positive in being—or neutral in the sense that a neutrino is, communicating neutrality although its constitution is slightly positive. A psychon remains what it is. And just as a photon may spin off from its "negative cradle," so a psychon may travel on its own.

Because a psychon is actually neutral, mental energy can travel directly through space in a straight or tangential line, penetrating anything, everything. *It is, therefore, independent of the Q-force.* This means that mental energy can move faster than time (faster than light, which must follow the path of the Q-force) and be there when the light arrives to interact with it, expressing the phenomena we associate with ESP. But mental energy may also travel with ease through the fields that light travels.

As we think of a psychon moving directly through the tissue of space, there is only its own self-resisting action that steadies its course. We may envision the mental particle fixing itself upon a point in the mesh of space and opening itself to reach ahead to secure another point along the way. Like all else in motion, it is never altogether moving nor altogether still. Its three-point property allows for one-point to be at rest as two-points are in action. Therefore, mental energy provides for the capacity to, "Be still and know that I am God," and for the constant involvement in action of mental energy, "the Lord" that neither "slumbers nor sleeps."

As we consider the Absolute One, with measure number *six*, we see that for every possible measure of positive (+) and negative (−) energy in creation, there is a psychon. Since infinitely more of the primordial energy was used to create space than was left to act within it, there are more psychons in the universe than there are physical neutrinos. Therefore, mental energy, like neutrino energy in rest state, constitutes a flux or field that pervades all we can know physically of space, and more: space itself. It can penetrate without resistance any aggregate of energy values; it can move with no resistance through any field; and it offers no resistance to the material energy that moves through its flux.

To Harold, although mental energy may move directly through space in actual straight-line motion, this is not the norm. Ordinarily, mental energy and physical energy "cross-act" to give rise to normal perception. To put this another way, just as light acts both in corpuscular and in wave group terms, so mental light may take an independent path through empty space; but ordinarily mental light travels as part of a wave group through the natural medium, neutrino energy in rest state.

The components of a mental light wave group are seen by Harold to be two neutrinos totally involving a psychon in action and conveying it. Neutrinos travel at the speed of light and flow through the earth with ease. They do not react readily with matter in observable ways. (Scientists try to "trap" neutrino reactions deep inside mines.) In Harold's view, as neutrinos convey mental energy, they travel through a field of themselves in rest state. This field, like the neutrino itself, is constituted of opposite values posed in small enough size that the necessary adhesion to hold a steady course is there.

Like the photon, which also involves two neutrinos enfolding a third in action, mental light (the psychon) is "embodied" in action. The psychon, however, cannot be "seen" because it is without dimension and definition in its structure; whereas the neutrino at rest that the photon enfolds has the five-point composition of One and therefore has definition and dimension, although it does not have communicable mass.

Because two neutrinos are engaged with a psychon to form a mental light wave group, the group forms a *singular unit of negative energy* that may act in a negative or positive way. Because there is more mental than material energy (apart from space) in expression, we must conclude that every single unit of negative energy incorporates a psychon. Herein, mental and material energy meet, and herein we have the "mind of nature" operating throughout the Cosmos. For this reason, negative energy has a degree of choice and the "mental capacity" to be the organizer of positive energy (light and mass); it also has the "mental capacity" to perform the "time actions" that Harold sees negative energy and the Q-force to perform.

This does not mean that negative energy is "mental" and positive energy is "physical." It means that mental energy, the psychon, is bound up in the constitution of a unit of negative energy (—), which has the measure number *two*; and negative energy is bound up in the constitution of positive energy (+), which has the measure number *three*, just as the number *two* is inherent in the number *three*. Therefore, mind and matter are as one, mental energy preceding negative energy, and negative energy preceding positive energy—and neutral energy, which involves the opposite forces, preceding the expression of either force. Neutral energy expressed as neutrinos was preceded by actually neutral energy expressed now as psychons, which may be seen as the Holy Spirit of God, Cosmic Mind, which permeates the Cosmos.

A mental light wave group is patterned after an electron, in that three distinct particles of energy are acting in concert: two neutrinos and a psychon, but all three of the particles involved are neutral. The thought wave group establishes the pattern of the electron, which in itself is a light wave group. Just as the electron may emit or release the photon it enfolds, so the neutrinos involved in a thought wave group may release the psychon they convey.

Because a unit of negative energy can express only in terms of wavemotion, the singular negative unit that comprises a thought wave group expresses mental energy only in propagation of wave trains in the emulsion of neutrinos in rest state. Only in inner and outer space that is empty of the Q-force's energy can the psychon act in terms of a "mental quantum," which regulates the actions of inner and outer thought wave groups much as the light at the heart of the atom regulates the actions of the electrons girdling the nucleus according to quantum rules.

The "mind of nature" obeys natural law. The code script has been written into the constitution of mental energy (psychons) and mammon (neutrinos). Harold indicated only that mental energy is multiplied and programed in ever more complex ways as the elements and organic materials build up—and that to the degree that man is a material creature and a conditioned animal, his mental energy is programed for him automatically.

Man is an animal. But he is also much *more* than an animal—as his mental processes attest. For example, according to Sally Carrighar, author of *Wild Heritage,* insanity appears to be a state peculiar to Homo sapiens. She says, "Insanity is a human development," and Harold asks:

> From whence in nature's sane world does man's distinguishing characteristic of susceptibility to madness come? Does this susceptibility cast the clue that man's mind is offspring of a mind that does not express itself to the full in any other form in nature? Is madness the culmination of evil that man must know if he would become as God with dominion over evil, over himself, his flesh, his life? Must he know madness in order to be "salted," *immunized* against this, the final expression of evil, so that there remains to him only the possibility of expressing it at the minimum whereupon it turns to good, becoming the ingenious in the mind that man is? Must death remain a part of life until man is no longer susceptible to madness, evil's culmination?[122]

We know how closely genius borders on madness, and vice versa. What gives rise to the sometimes blinding brilliance of this light that flickers in the mind of man?

Harold believed that a very special mental unit programs the psychons that are involved in the expression of human mental energy. Before discussing this special unit, let us again narrow our vision to consider the nature of One.

So far, in following our arithmetical path, we have called upon the odd division of One $(3/2 \times 2/3 = 1)$, and the even division of One $(3/3 \times 3/3 = 1)$, and the simple division of One $(1/1 = 1)$, so that now we must call upon the mathematical concept of the multiplication of One $(1 \times 1 = 1)$. One may multiply itself by itself *ad infinitum* and the product will never be more than One.

Therefore, the one mental particle may be "multiplied" in nature in its more complex forms, and mental energy may also be multiplied again to produce a human mental unit that both enfolds the natural mind and moves beyond it.

In Harold's view, into a precious few degrees of the mental energy of Absolute God was given an added measure of mental energy through the *multiplying* of mental power. (In dealing with One, we do not call upon simple addition and subtraction because this would step beyond the *alpha,* involving us with the *beta,* and we must hold to the course that single vision commands.)

We say that Parent Energy was multiplied in these few mental units, providing each with a sufficient amount *to constitute a redundancy that can communicate as nothing else in nature can.* Therefore, these units can program the psychons in a way that nature's mind cannot. Harold believed that the last iota of Parent Energy's power—God's power—that could be shared was given into these few "cerebral cells," which possess sufficient mental energy to communicate in *words*. This power gives to man the capacity to create in his own right—to be the programer rather than merely a programed animal in nature's fold, although man is subject to natural law, and his development is insured through the operation of the principle of evolution.

Into the "cerebral cells" that we call mankind, the Cosmic Mind gave all that it is possible to give. Love can do no more. God speaks now, acts now, through man and nature, both operating under the perfect principle of One.

Harold did not name the "cerebral cell" that carries the seminal mental energy of God. He saw it as the fifth estate of energy—as derivative of Parent Energy it is *Son* energy; as derivative of Mental Energy it is the Word, *Logos* energy. Let us call this cell a *Logon*.

Each Logon carries within itself the whole plan of creation, just as each cell of the body carries the whole code script. The Logons have been in existence since the beginning, and each is establishing its own world of being following the blueprint of Cosmic devolution and reorganization through evolution. Logons can be neither created nor destroyed. If Homo sapiens on this Planet Earth destroyed his generation, mankind would arise again from Cosmic dust—life would restate itself, and Homo sapiens' generation would again appear because this generation represents a necessary step in Life's development.

The energy in the Logon is divided into complementary factors in dynamic union, giving each cell the sense of itself "as God" in independent being—or a full measure of Father-being and knowledge—and giving it also a sense of itself "as man" or Son in Society where love can recognize itself, express itself, and re-create itself endlessly.

The Father-Son energy operates in the Logons as DNA does in the human cell, programing the psychons that are sent into the world of consciousness to build and sustain its "body," just as Messenger-RNA is sent from the nucleus into the world of cytoplasm surrounding it. The God-consciousness of the Logon is "seated" in man's inner kingdom, the *unconscious* realm. The Father-energy carries the code script; the Son-energy "reads it" and programs the psychons. Just as there are many types of RNA distributed throughout the cell, so the units of mental light are distributed throughout the whole body of consciousness. Man's psychons, programed by his Logon, may be thought of as mental-RNA.

The DNA of the human cell does not leave the nucleus. Messenger-

RNA is sent from the nucleus into the surrounding cytoplasm to imprint upon ribosomal-RNA the chemical words that govern and sustain the life of the cell.

Jesus was symbol of light (physical) and of the "light of men"— therefore, symbol of the photon and of the psychon, programed by Son-consciousness to carry the Father-consciousness into the world of conscious personality, the "mental cytoplasm." Harold shows that Jesus' words and drama pose a perfect parallel to the intricate operation of DNA and the various types of RNA that operate in the life of the cell.[123] This can be no accident. There is a similarity in the underlying patterns in nature. There are parallels between the operation of inorganic, organic, and mental energy.

A Logon cannot *fuse* with any other type of energy, not even its own kind. Singularity is its law; it must be self-possessed. But it acts easily in concert with other Logons and with the universal whole. Only human-kind possess Logos energy. Man, the programer, does not behave in terms of the conditioned behavior that all else in nature's realm expresses. Man shares in programed behavior only to the degree that it relieves his crea-tive potential of the necessity to give thought to that which is better expressed automatically—such as breathing, and countless other reactions that allow him to function smoothly.

Each of us is a Logon. We radiate ideas or thoughts—the psychons of mental energy that we have programed, or instructed. These may influ-ence other Logons. But just as something within the atom must make itself equal to the photon before light can enter, so something in man's "cerebral cell" must make itself equal to the idea that is projected, before mental light can enter consciousness. Only as this ratio of "two to one"—or two ideas becoming as one—is established, can mental energy communicate. Therefore, mental energy with which we cannot or will not establish a "redundancy" cannot penetrate our minds. We cannot observe our mental processes because we are too completely involved in them. But we can observe the action of physical light in which a like pattern operates. Mammon is the mirror through which we may observe ourselves.

As we absorb mental light, we use the energy to grow a "body of con-sciousness" by means of a process that must be similar to photosynthesis. Just as the plan of each mutation is enfolded in its seed, so as the body of our consciousness mutates, its new form is enfolded in the Logon's script.

For centuries man has "programed" organic energy to a great degree in the development of agriculture. Only recently has he begun to learn to program inorganic energy to any great degree. But his greatest triumph will come when he learns more about programing the mental energy at his command so that he will function in optimum terms both as an individual and in society.

We come now to the last aspect of One, *God*. In Harold's view, all of nature including space, all psychons, and all Logons do not add up to God. God is *more* than this. *And there is a mathematical necessity as well as many scientific observations that require us to say this. Harold did not introduce God into his scheme of things because of wishful thinking, or loyalty to religion. To be mathematically and scientifically correct, he had to include the concept of God, One, Whole.*

We know now that the whole is greater than the sum of its parts. There is some intrinsic value in wholeness—*a value that cannot be shared* because it is lost in the process of division. Mammon has taught us that the original whole is like Humpty Dumpty. When atoms are split or fused, energy escapes. There is a mystery to wholeness that we cannot quite lay hold of. The best word to describe it is *Synergy*. Whole systems express unique behavior that is unpredicted by the behavior of any of their component functions when taken separately. Or we may say that the combined action of several elements taken together is greater than the sum of them taken separately.

God is Cosmic Synergism—Synergy of all that was, is, and is to be—operating in the *undivided whole*. We say the undivided whole because the divisions we have discussed are *inner divisions*. The Cosmos is One. There is *nothing to divide it*, from an objective point of view. Its wholeness (God) remains, whatever the form its subjective and inner divisions take. We cannot escape the simple fact of the wholeness, the oneness, of the Cosmos—enfolding a body of consciousness that is complete. From a Cosmic standpoint, nothing can be added, nothing can be taken away, and every iota of its substance is conscious to *a degree*. Therefore, God —unlike man—is not presently building a body of consciousness of his own.

Harold would give no other name except *God* to the whole that is greater than the sum of its parts. To him, this One, only, unit of total mental energy centers in the deep of space and is the energy that lies beyond the outermost limits of space. It is the perfect sphere of being that *was*, which man dreams of, enfolding the sphere of beings that *are* and *will be*. If this generation insists upon a new name for God, we can call this total consciousness, of which there is but one unit, the *Cosmon*.

In its centering and reach we have the mental pattern for the nucleus of atom and cell, and the intrinsic, indefinable preciousness of wholeness, which escapes us when we lose it.

The wholeness of God, the Cosmon, is the one aspect of God that could not be shared with man. Man cannot know, cannot imagine, in this generation at least, what the whole of Cosmic Being *was* before the universal action that he may observe and comprehend began. What catalyst could have effected its inner disorganization that allowed for the reorganization that we call evolution? The Cosmon was vested with word power, which has at the minimum the two aspects of sound and mental light. Today, we know that high frequency sound is used to separate or break down many physical and biological objects. Also, through use of sound waves, fuel and its rate of consumption can be controlled. If sound alone can do these things, sound and mental light can do more. We can surmise only that Cosmic mental light must have somehow broken the Cosmic mental sound barrier, creating a "mental sonic boom" that utterly granulated all that was into neutrinos, psychons, and Logons, setting in process all that was to be. The mental catalyst that began it must have been a Cosmic belly laugh that ended in a shout of joy: "Freedom!"—because that is what mental energy expresses.

Only mental energy is free actually and in reality to conceive the straight lines and perfect spheres that Euclid drew so marvelously. These conceptions must have *a basis in reality or else they could not arise in the mind and be so workable.* Think of all that man still accomplishes through use of Euclidean geometry. Euclid was not exactly "with it," since we know today that it takes non-Euclidean geometry and much else to deal with the physical universe and energy as it really operates. But Euclidean geometry must describe with mathematical precision some function that actually takes place in terms of energy, *or else mathematics and energy could not speak each other's language so well.*

Euclidean geometry describes the actions and conceptions possible to mental energy, which is just as real as any other kind. Mental energy says to physical energy, "Be ye perfect" even as God (parent energy) was perfect and is now perfect in the operation of the principle of One. But Euclidean geometry in its attempt to reach perfection made no allowance for God. And there it lost touch with *the single reality of the whole* —that it cannot be divided and put together again without the principle of "minus something/plus something" entering the picture, so that the whole is greater than the sum of its parts. God is *the single reality*— greater than, different from, the material (neutrinonic) and/or mental (psychonic and Logonic) energy It enfolds.

The question of the whole versus the sum of the parts troubled many brilliant men long before non-Euclidean geometry was developed. The whole must first be divided before its parts can be summed, and this is equivalent to the division of zero, which represents the whole and designates wholeness when used with numbers. To say that zero divided by zero equals zero $(0/0 = 0)$ is equivalent to insisting that Euclid's axiom —the whole is equal to the sum of its parts—describes *reality* in all its depths. We know today that this is not unequivocally the case.

Harold saw that to divide zero is equivalent to multiplying negative Ones: $(-1 \times -1 = +1)$, because as we divide any whole (or point of departure in reckoning) two Ones appear, each minus the quality of the erstwhile estate, each plus the intrinsic value of the new entity that has been established. He believed that Jesus realized this and saw that division and/or multiplication of the negative produces the *positive* $(+)$, and that division of zero or the whole requires the operation of *signed number,* beginning with One. He saw that we can understand zero or the whole only as we see it to be a *correspondence* to One, so that One must be described as: $(-1 \; 0 \; +1)$. In Jesus' day, mathematicians were not dealing with signed number; but certain statements made by Jesus indicated to Harold that Jesus understood the meaning of zero and of signed number, which he may have discerned or learned from Hindu mathematicians who introduced the concepts to the Western world in a later period.[124]

Zero implies *naught,* as well as point of departure in reckoning, because the "secret" of wholeness cannot actually be revealed. Its mystery eludes us because it is inexhaustible. Each one is vested with the mystery of wholeness—of God. Jesus took into account in his reckoning the inexpressible mystery of wholeness which when divided insists upon the operation of One in terms of signed number: absent/present, or minus/plus. We know today that $(-1 \times -1 = +1)$ and that $(+1 \times +1 = +1)$. We can get only a positive answer, a signal that says "more" or "plus" or "yes." To symbolize this answer, one must employ the cross $(+)$, which is also the symbol of positive energy: light.

Mental light, like physical light, must be propagated according to similar patterns of operation. It, too, must be dealt with in terms of a wave and a particle action. Just as inside the atom the "quantum" rules take over, so within one's mind the psychon operates as a unit of energy. As thought is projected, mental wave group action takes over—and wave group action conveys the patterns of thought that are brought to the shores of our consciousness.

Oliver Reiser seeks the Psi-belt that surrounds the planet and provides a psychosphere for the Celestial Child (see p. 12). We suggest that the logos of the planet is where we find the logos of the cell—in the nucleus. In the case of earth, this would be in its liquid core. Here, there may well be a fluid with the properties of a superdispersive medium wherein new types of field influences occur. As the neutrinos move readily through the earth, so thought waves may also. Their approach to our planetary center may create the wave patterns that spread outward, involving all the layers of the earth's cover, finishing in the outermost reach of earth's magnetic field into a Psi-belt of thought.

In the interior of the planet, the effect of the Q-force is reduced to virtually nothing; here, magnetic energy and its force or guidelines predominate. The mental wave trains that are propagated in this subfield may set in motion the plasma of neutrino energy at rest, which permeates our environment, providing the oscillating source that causes mental light to arise in the outermost magnetic field—or even the gravitational field that the Q-force determines. The psychosphere of the planet would then be a pattern that follows the structure of the Cosmon. Recent Mariner missions to Mars appear to indicate that the earth may be unique among our planets, both in its magnetic field and in the presence of life. In consequence, it may well be that the two are related in some fashion.

But whatever the answer to the psychosphere of the planet, mental light can move only to the "edge of space"—it cannot penetrate the Cosmic Mind that enfolds space. Therefore, not a single psychon can escape the Cosmic Being.

Harold saw this "Cosmic Being" as a *living system*. A living system, as opposed to a "macro-organism," may be likened to the ocean. The *ocean itself* is not alive in the sense that its contents are alive—and yet when the "container and its contents" are taken together, as the ocean must be taken as a whole, we are dealing with a living system or entity. The droplets of water in the ocean are alive with plankton; even the inorganic elements of which the ocean is also composed are expressing the consciousness we associate with elementary particles that can somehow recognize their like and opposite signs, behaving accordingly. Every organism within the ocean expresses to greater or lesser degree "fear and faith," or "desire and satisfaction," but the ocean itself does not feel such as this. The ocean itself is a pattern of operation governed by the laws of nature; these laws are structured to keep it always a viable system for the organisms that operate within it.

The Cosmic Mind, the one Cosmon, is now a pattern of operation that has been laid down in neutrinonic, psychonic, and Logonic energy.

Within this Cosmic environmental pattern all things are possible; the system is inexhaustible. The effect of the slightest change is felt throughout the whole, because each expression of the primordial Cosmic energy and the whole structure of the environment carry the necessary code script that allows each change to be resonated throughout the whole. The laws that govern this living system then evoke the accommodating, alleviating, or compensating actions within the system to deal with the situation (just as Logonic energy is now beginning to deal with environmental pollution).

As this book is being written, the claim is being made of the detection of waves, by Dr. Joseph Weber of the University of Maryland, which appear most certainly to be gravitational waves. The momentous discovery may support Einstein's theory of general relativity; and if the claim is upheld, scientists have at hand the means to learn tremendously more about the Cosmos. Dr. Weber believes the waves are coming from developing or collapsing stars somewhere in the Milky Way, of which earth is a part.[125]

How would Dr. Weber's magnificent accomplishment—if confirmed—fit into Harold's theory of the living universe? Harmoniously. In Harold's view, the field of neutrino energy in rest state, in which all star systems are submerged (since this energy permeates the Q-force's path and flow), is the medium in which wave trains of energy even finer than those we call gravitational waves are propagated by the action of energy: wave trains of mental energy.

As said before, in discussing Clive Backster's experiment, plant life may now provide detectors sensitive enough to register mental energy. (See p. 214.) Harold's answer to the Backster experiment would be that the plants are registering the mental reactions of the organisms with which they are tested—primitive or sophisticated thought waves that are conveyed by the neutrino-psychon group through the field of neutrinos in rest state. The neutrino-psychon group could pass readily through the barriers that Backster erected; the thought wave would constitute a signal too "fine" to fall within the electrodynamic spectrum.

Backster's discovery tends to confirm Harold's postulates, which are, perhaps, the only ones at hand that offer a solution to the mystery. The discovery also brings us to consider again Jesus' words that the "flesh availeth nothing"—it is the spirit (mental/psychic energy) that gives life.[126] Underlying every manifestation in the universe is the mind of God, which has multiplied itself most abundantly in the mind of man, the Son cell, but also "quickens" even a leaf. If we consider all the im-

227

plications in Harold's concept of mental energy, we must acknowledge that the plant-receptor is endowed with a certain degree of the mind of nature, which is inherent in matter.

In "Mind, Matter, and Quanta,"[127] Andrew A. Cochran writes, "The stream of conscious thought in the mind of a man is one of the incontrovertible facts of his existence, yet it is not included in the present conceptual framework of science. We still do not understand the difference between living and lifeless matter. . . . Man is both matter and mind, while atoms and the fundamental particles of matter are both particle and waves. If one suspected that a rudimentary degree of life were possessed by all matter, he would naturally suspect that the dual aspects of man are a direct result of the dual aspects of the matter from which he is made, and that the mind of man and the wave properties of an electron are two extremes of the same thing: the mind properties of matter. . . ."

Since, in Harold's view of energy, the negative unit enfolds the unit of mental energy—and the negative unit's action must be associated with wave properties, and with action that gives rise to cold versus hot—Cochran's postulations are congenial. Cochran says:

> What nature has been trying to say, through the revolution in physics and the emergence of quantum mechanics, may be that all matter has a rudimentary degree of mind, that man is a direct result of this fundamental property of matter, and that quantum mechanics is a mathematical description of the dual mind-particle properties of matter.

To Harold, such a statement would not support a blind, nihilistic materialism—and it is not here intended to say that Cochran holds such a view. Cochran's statement would support what Harold called the "divine materialism" offered by Jesus, who said that matter, even a *stone*, is alive with the same potential man possesses: *mind*. Because if from a stone God can "raise up life," this is the implication. Also implied in Jesus' words is that every expression of energy in the Cosmos is an expression of the universal mental energy we call God, as well as God's substance, and is therefore responsive to the Cosmon—the indivisible mental pattern enfolding a living universe.

Cochran says, "Science will never create life in a test tube. Life is already created and is all around us; all a scientist can do is rearrange it." Harold's philosophy is in agreement—but he would add that rearrangements must be within the limits of natural law *and* they must serve life's large *purpose* to evolve into an optimum state of being and change. Where does purpose enter the picture? Cochran writes:

When matter is cooled almost to absolute zero, its thermal disorder is removed and its wave properties become strongly predominant. . . . When liquid helium . . . is cooled below 2.18°K., it is still a liquid but strange new properties appear which are not found in any other liquid. . . . The reason the behavior of helium II [helium cooled to a superfluid state] seems peculiar is simply that its phenomenal mobility and odd behavior are suggestive of life. In climbing up and down the test tube, it acts as though it has purpose.

Harold's description of the constitution of atomic matter stops with helium. Perhaps he, too, recognized purpose in the behavior of helium II, and saw that no more is needed than living material with inherent mental capacity so that purposeful (versus random) action is possible to it. But this is speculation. Harold did not mention helium II. He speaks of a star's having to produce sufficient helium before it can become an energy reactor that creates the hydrogen it radiates. It is intriguing to think that the star's mental energy and purposeful nature must be sufficiently multiplied by way of increasing its helium content before it can itself become a system capable of maintaining its own life-giving qualities *ad infinitum*.

Harold's concept of mental energy seems to fit smoothly with Cochran's statements regarding wave properties. Cochran says, "Life seems to be an intrinsic property of matter that is most evident in the lowest quantum state, when its 'wave' properties are most predominant and it is unaffected by thermal disorder. . . ." And he points out that the "wave function contains interference terms that have real physical significance; unlike any other probability function that we know, the wave function interferes with itself. How can we understand a probability function that interferes with itself? . . . Thought processes involve probabilities that interfere with and modify each other." In Harold's concept, the mental particles, having nothing to resist them, resist themselves. Therefore, a thought wave, singular expression of negative energy that it may be, contains its own "interference terms"—and, as with every expression of energy, in Harold's view the thought wave group has "real physical significance," although it does not have measurable mass or a *defined point* of being.

Cochran says, "Our line of thought leads to a dual mind-particle concept of the electron, rather than the dual wave-particle concept." Harold saw the electron as a dual mind-particle because the unit of positive energy (+) associated with the two units of negative energy is a *particle involved* between opposing lines of force, and the two negative units are expressions of energy that can be associated only with wave properties and mental energy. Because there are two negative units in an electron, both dual wave functions and "dual mind" (interference) properties would be possible. Harold's representation of an electron (— + —) seems more nearly to picture its properties than any other symbol yet devised.

In Cochran's challenging article, he says that "Causality in classical physics was conceived as absolute, and as arising external to the particle or body under consideration. . . . This concept of absolute, external causality was found to be erroneous, and has been discarded in modern quantum physics. Causal forces are now considered to arise within each particle and to be limited, not absolute, in scope." Here, we see the correspondence to Harold's theme that in life the absolute can no longer be expressed—*absolute action* cannot take place. Nevertheless, absolute states remain. There is space, which neither acts nor reacts (once its self-resisting expansion is complete), but is a force constant. And there is the Cosmon, the whole that cannot be divided from an external point of view, the mental pattern in which is laid down what *was, is,* and *is to be.*

In the above quotation from Cochran, we see also that *classical physics* is in one-to-one correspondence with "classical religion," in which God was seen as the *Absolute in action,* external to nature and humankind, which "He" manipulated as "He" would. Cochran sees that the proponents of exogenetic (external) causes may be influenced by their belief in a "Deity that is external to man and to man's world" and that such theories have proved to be more primitive, scientifically speaking, than endogenetic theories which hold that *causal factors arise from within.*

Harold saw that 2,000 years ago Jesus proclaimed that true religion (God-consciousness) arises from an *endogenetic factor*: God is not external to man, not external to mammon; God is the substance and living quality that each particle of energy is, multiplied in the constitution of humankind to be the divinely conceived expression of Life.

In science today, concepts arising from classical physics are very much with us, and so are the concepts arising from classical religions. But classical physics gives way to quantum physics. Scientists and theologians must allow classical religion to give way to *quantum religion,* which will evolve into the divine materialism, the Cosmic Humanism, that will be upon us when we are forced by the findings of science itself to attribute a degree of life to the least particle of energy in the universe. It looks as though quantum mechanics insists upon this view. If this be so, is this not a living universe?

When classical religion is ready to give over to quantum religion, it will find the *psychic* quantum mechanics revealed by Jesus, symbolizing the action of one's inner light in terms of Son of man, outlined in *The Shining Stranger*.

Harold saw that *Jesus gave us quantum religion,* which must be given in terms of "one, only," because the quantum measure, the one "atom of action," is "one, only." This religion could not be understood and Jesus could not be correctly interpreted until countless scientists had built a temple of classical physics to match the temple of classical religion that held sway for so many centuries *and both of these temples had given way* to mankind's ever enlarging understanding of reality in all its depths.

Religion will not disappear in tomorrow's world, which will be structured by science and technology. Far from it. Already the day is rapidly approaching when a scientist who does not accept *quantum religion*— the endogenetic God-consciousness in each human being—will be recognized to have failed to understand even the material of which man is made, its mental and purposeful nature that belies nihilism in countless ways. Such a scientist will be recognized to be a classical religionist, whether he accepts the doctrine or not, because he will still belong to the past in which God was thought of as the bearded one in the sky going about his exogenetic business.

God-consciousness in man is the *growth factor,* the endogenetic psychic factor that is called by many names and is symbolized in each great religious figure. Science cannot deny that there is a *growth factor* in mankind, which has led this species immeasurably further than any other species man is aware of. Nor can science deny that man is just now beginning to be aware of his own potential for further growth.

Harold chose the term *Authority-Ego* to designate God-consciousness, the growth factor, in man. At first glance, Authority-Ego may call up exogenetic implications. But not so if the word *authority* is understood. It comes from the Latin *auctor* (author), which is based upon the verb *augere* (to grow). Each possesses within himself the Authority-Ego, author empowered with the word, committed to the growth of consciousness—unto each his own endogenetic measure of the power, grace, and glory that was and is God and nature.

We cannot altogether penetrate the mystery, the secret, of the wholeness, indivisible, that is the Cosmos. But is not this much mystery a necessary ingredient to make life tolerable in Homo sapiens' generation?

God lives *in the human sense* only in each degree of Logonic energy expressed throughout the universe. Insofar as we know for sure, only in the mind of mankind upon Planet Earth. Each Logon is uniquely structured to resonate with the Cosmon, each one is in one-to-one correspondence with each other one and with the one whole pattern of creation.

Conservation principles tell us that not so much as a neutrino can be lost—that energy cannot be created or destroyed. In speaking of the "little ones" in life, the children, Jesus said that it is not the will of the Father, God, that a single one of them be lost.[128] If not so much as a neutrino can be lost, how much more precious than this physical energy must be every Logon that possesses the mental energy of One multiplied into the creative potential that was with God in the beginning: Word power.

We will use a little word power now to pose and answer ten questions plaguing physicists. Questions by Reiser—answers by Harold, via Babcock's interpretation.

Ten Questions, Ten Answers

In *Cosmic Humanism*, Reiser poses ten of the major problems that confront astronomers and physicists. He wonders if it is possible to solve any of them without solving all of them.[129] Harold's theory of the living universe, and his wave-particle theory of light would answer them as follows:

Question 1. How can matter be made up of indivisible particles? If these particles have a finite radius, why can't they be subdivided?

Answer: Division of energy is finished in the neutrinos (or possibly "smaller" neutrino-like particles), separated into neutral units in opposite action. Neutrinos cannot be subdivided, because there is no particle in the physical realm small enough to penetrate them. Only mental energy is fine enough to interact with them, fine enough to pass through them without disturbing their structure. Endless division is senseless, meaningless, and nature is not.

Question 2. Why is the number of elementary particles restricted to a specified few? Why are there a limited number of classes of particles . . . ? Is it possible that new types of particles may be produced in the future?

Answer: There are only five stable particles in nature. They represent the five measures of One: the two neutrinos, the electron, proton, and photon. In them each class of particles (leptons, bosons, baryons) is represented. All other elementary particles are simply some combination of the five stable particles (and/or the parent particle, the neutron), and they arise in response to stress. It is possible that other stress reactions (unstable particles) may be observed; it is unlikely that other stable particles will be discovered. There are only three classes of elementary particles, because three is one of the measures of One. There are two classes of mental particles: psychons and Logons. Five classes altogether.

Question 3. Why do all charged particles—electrons, protons, and the rest—carry the same charge for the same type particle?

Answer: Charge as such represents a redundancy of positive or negative value. It is the 50 per cent redundancy of negative value in the electron (− + −) that produces the negative charge. It is the 50 per cent redundancy of positive value in a proton's positive charge (+ − +) that produces positive charge. In more massive nuclei, the 2:1 versus 1:2 ratio remains the same, whether we are dealing with 4(+)/2(−), 8(+)/4(−), etc., and therefore the 50 per cent redundancy that gives rise to charge remains the same. Each single unit of energy is exactly like its counterparts in its make-up and its measure of primordial energy.

Question 4. Why do all bodies made up of such particles produce gravitational fields?

Answer: Because such particles possess neutral energy, and gravity is the attraction of opposite types of energy that compose neutral units. But gravity is a complex force.

From the macroscopic view, gravity is the *sum* of the attraction of neutral energy between two bodies; *minus* the repelling force between two bodies communicating neutrality, because each body is actually slightly positive in its constitution; *plus* the pressure of the Q-force flowing through space.

Q energy is attracted to the "density" of positive attraction represented by the mass *and* the space it enfolds in every positive ion that composes it. *The enveloping flow of Q energy creates the gravitational field.* Because space is slightly positive and neutral masses are slightly positive, not even a neutrino can operate in space apart from the gravitational and magnetic field, and the *general field upon which the Q-force itself moves.*

Question 5. How is it possible for matter to move through space?

Answer: All particles and all bodies of matter are composed of measures of positive and negative energy, beginning with the neutrinos. In "submicroscopic" terms, at no one time are all the measures of energy moving. Part of the energy is "holding" to a unit of an opposite type in the field, and part is drawn forward toward an opposite unit and is in action. Not until the position of the "reaching" energy is secured does the "holding" energy move forward. "Holding" energy acts as the fulcrum from which "acting" energy can "take off." The condition of stillness versus action makes motion possible.

In "macroscopic" terms, all bodies in space move under the impetus of their own momentum, according to Galileo's law of inertia, because the Q-force is constantly moving upon the bodies to maintain them in motion. If they come to rest upon some other mass, inertia is expressed. Inertia is another aspect of gravity, or the binding attraction between the positive and negative energy in the mass and the positive and negative energy in the field upon which the body rests. As a force is applied to separate the resting body, the force of repulsion between the two positive masses makes its minimum expression, enabling the resting body to move. At this range, the force of attraction between the neutral energy is the greater force. Gravity is not overcome until the distance between the two bodies is such that the complex force of attraction diminishes; at this point the singular force, the positive force, that each body possesses, begins to express itself, and the body becomes a "vehicle" in its own right, subject to the flow of the Q-force.

Question 6. How is it possible for particles to behave like waves?
Answer: The negative units of energy in a particle operate in wave motion, as they express first one way and then the other way, horizontally, vertically. The shift creates the wave pattern in the flux of virtual energy. We picture this:

Question 7. How is it possible for energy to behave like a particle?
Answer: A unit of positive energy *is a particle.* The photon is composed of three degrees of neutrino energy (i.e., three neutrinos), one of which is a rest mass enfolded in the opposite spirals of energy. A magnificent picture of spiraling motion enfolding energy into a body of light may be observed in "supermacroscopic" terms in the evolution of spiral nebulae, as given by Rudolf Thiel in his book, *And There Was Light.*[130]

Question 8. How is it possible to unite gravitational phenomena (of particle physics) and electromagnetic theory (wave physics) in one comprehensive theory of physical reality?
Answer: By describing nature in the only basic and certain terms we have: positive, negative, neutral energy. Gravitational phenomena describe energy in terms of its positive and neutral characteristics; electromagnetic theory describes energy in terms of its negative and

neutral characteristics. Since units of positive and negative energy are different and opposite, they cannot be dealt with in terms of sameness. We have oversimplified in thinking of the expression of the opposite types of energy only in terms of electrical charge. Each type unit is in itself a complex force, and there are greater and lesser degrees of the force involved in all phenomena. The minimum expression of a force cannot exhibit the same qualities as the maximum expression of a force.

We have failed to comprehend the portent of our recognition that all of nature is simply a communications system. It becomes of prime importance to understand how greater and lesser forces communicate—or *do not communicate*. Redundancy is essential to communication. This must be true also in the Cosmic communication system, insofar as energy's communication is concerned.

Particle and wave physics are combined into one comprehensive theory in the description of an electron as a particle composed of two units of negative energy and one unit of positive energy, so that light is a particle involved in the wave motion produced by negative energy, the positive particle obscured by the redundancy of negative energy operating with it, until the positive unit is released as it enters the atom, to operate therein according to "quantum rules."

A comprehensive theory must be based on the basic principle we know to be operating in nature. In the interaction of positive and negative energy, neutral or "balanced" energy is produced. Any theory that fails to take account of maintenance of "balance" in every aspect of the Cosmic system is out of line with the underlying principle of mathematics, which depends upon *balance*. An infinite number of *imbalances* can be expressed, and these are an integral part of the mathematical process. But balance is regained because nature operates only in "sets" of energy (positive and negative); and balance versus imbalance must be dealt with in mathematics in terms of "sets," such as, for every odd number there is an even number *ad infinitum*. The "primordial" set is *One* operating as signed number: $(-1$ vs $+1)$ giving rise always to One, in balance, wholeness restored.

It does not take faith, it takes common sense, to read from our most certain observations that opposite actions constantly occur. If this is so, the measure of the disorganization of energy is offset by the measure of the organization of energy into usable fuel.

A theory comprehensive enough to deal with underlying reality must be based on restoration to balance and wholeness through cross-action between the asymmetries that produce symmetry, as would be the case when fractional expressions are posed against each other: $(3/2 \times 2/3 = 1)$.

Question 9. What is the binding energy which holds particles together in atomic nuclei to form atoms, molecules, and so on? What is the "dimensional binder" which synthesizes aggregates of particles into superaggregates to produce the higher levels of the ladder of emergent evolution?

Answer: Attraction of opposite units of energy accounts for all binding energy, although this attraction may be described in different ways, such as electron sharing, etc. Opposite units of energy are involved in the nuclei, and in the field, and in field forces. The attraction between neutral masses, as well as negative field-bonds that pose attraction for the slightly positive atoms, give rise to aggregates and superaggregates.

The repelling force of the single positive unit in each atom insures its independent being, even though it may be bonded to form a molecular group.

In alpha decay, as well as in other modes of decay, two distinct elements are produced. The development of two single positive units of energy from the "virtual energy" in the transmuting mass provides the repelling force that separates the mass into two atoms.

In macroscopic terms, the physical division of masses breaks the field bonding and produces two bodies that are then operating under the law of gravity wherein the sum of the attractive forces between them is diminished by the sum of the positive forces of each body repelling the other. And once a macroscopic break of any sort is effected, the matrix energy brings to bear upon the parts, acting as the dimensional binder by exerting a compressing force that establishes the individuality of the "pieces."

Question 10. How can the universe be finite in space and time, if reason demonstrates that it must be infinite; or infinite, if experiment shows that it must be finite?

Answer: Infinite must be defined simply as more than can be measured or used through the course of any event or through the course of all events, either physically or mathematically, which is to say, more than can be measured or used by Homo sapiens' consciousness.

Infinite, therefore, is without calculable self-limitation; but the limitation of human consciousness puts a finite limit on man's capacity for experiment, mentally or literally, with Cosmic energy as a whole. Mental energy expresses the limit in calculation of the finite through the mathematical precept that any one number can be divided into fractional expression endlessly, but cannot be reduced to zero. Mental energy therefore circumscribes the Cosmos but cannot reach the "infinite" or "zero condition." The division of zero is equivalent to the division of the whole, which produces two negative quantities, or $(-/- = +)$ or "more." Further division of this result is equivalent to $(+/+ = +)$ or "more." The universe is not finite in space and time. It is always *more* than can be measured or calculated.

Experiment has not yet shown that the universe must be finite. Energy operates under finite law that provides for its infinite operation in time and space, and in terms of rest and action, through a process of disorganization and reorganization. Calculations have demonstrated that the division of energy into elementary particles comes to rest in the neutrinos; and experiment shows that light is somehow regathered into a quantum of energy despite the fact that the energy appears to dissipate beyond recovery.

Pressure causes the organization of negative energy, which produces the negative tension that organizes a positive unit of energy from neutrinos in rest state, which permeate the space we can experience. Q energy in space "grounds" the positive charges that arise, organizing them into protons. Fuel is organized in nuclear reactions when Q energy in space feeds through the energy reactors (that all atoms are, and some stars become) and releases neutrons to react with elements that produce protons in decay reactions, or when the neutrons decay, producing hydrogen, $_1H^1$.

Time may be understood in the same way Einstein understood that the curvature of space could be followed only with the aid of light rays, which in the end would circle round to show us ourselves. "Time's entropy arrow" never ceases to travel, so that in this sense it moves always in the direction of "next," or *future*. In its course, it brings the system back to the state of wholeness in each cycle it completes, showing us ourselves here-now in a universe able to sustain life.

The universe both is and is coming to be. In some of its aspects it is finite, and in others it is infinite. For example, there is a finite quantity of Cosmic energy, which is subject to changing arrangement infinitely. The original organization of absolute power had to be disorganized through the expression of the destructive potential before it could be reorganized *to express its constructive potential endlessly*. Disorganization of the original state has been accomplished in nature. Its reorganization continues. With every move made, the destructive potential is lessened, and the Cosmos moves nearer to its state of optimum being.

We have come now to the end of Reiser's ten questions. But Harold's hypothesis sheds light on other baffling questions that confront physicists. We will discuss only one more: the meaning of the shift of spectral lines. This puzzle gives substance to Harold's postulation of a Q-force flowing through space and to the postulation that neutral masses are slightly positive in their constitution.

Spectrum analysis of a celestial body reveals the elements that compose it, and until comparatively recently it was thought that such analysis could reveal whether a star was moving toward earth, or away from it, and at what speed. A shift in spectral lines toward the violet end of the spectrum indicated motion toward us; a shift toward the red end meant motion away from us. According to this interpretation, the galaxies are rushing away from each other, so that a Stygian night will enfold us. Then spectrum analysis of binary stars that must move together upset the applecart.

For example, in the case of Sirius, the Fraunhofer lines show a shift toward the violet end of the spectrum, indicating that Sirius is approaching us at a speed of five miles per second. But Sirius has a very small companion, and its lines are shifted toward the red end of the spectrum, indicating that it is moving away from us. How could this be, since they must travel together? Then it was discovered that the red shift has some connection with temperature.

According to Harold's theory, the force of gravity that attracts one body to the other also involves the repelling force of the hidden positive nature of all masses. This force of positive versus positive generates positive action, which means *heat*. Therefore, the measure of the positive energy in the star would be a factor in determining the temperature it could reach. The density of the body would also be a factor, since a tenuous body, although large, would not necessarily possess the same number of protons as a small dense body. And the Q-flow of matrix energy through and around the body would be a factor, since the effect of negative energy is cooling—the negative energy neutralizes or reduces the action of positive force as it flows through a mass freely. Whereas, as it comes upon a dense mass, of Q-effect is compression, which keeps the positive action going at full speed. The effect of the Q-force upon Sirius, plus the effect of the positive force of its tiny companion evoking positive response, serves to keep the fires of Sirius kindled to produce white heat or light. Therefore, the shift of spectral lines would indicate the speed at which the units of positive energy in each body are operating, each "kindled" by the action of the other and by the compressing force of Q energy.

It may be that motion toward or away from us is not involved other than to indicate the direction the Q-force takes as it swirls through and around the masses. It may approach Sirius headed in our direction and sweep around the small companion star heading away from us, making it appear that one star is moving toward us, the other away from us. The idea of a flow of energy moving both toward and away from us as it encircles binary stars is plausible; the idea of binary stars moving in opposite directions is not.

In Harold's view, the force of repulsion between galaxies of matter separated them in the beginning and holds them apart. In the galaxies, and in each solar system, the positive force of each body kindles the other. The planets, for example, act upon the sun to keep its "fires" going at a desirable temperature to produce the necessary hydrogen. The attraction of neutral energy draws the bodies together until they reach "critical range." Then they kindle, and heat and light arise from the "darkness" of primordial negative "waters."

Establishment of optimum distance between celestial masses may still be taking place; so that in this action, the "becoming" of order within the Cosmos may be progressing.

XI

Jesus Brought the Light of Asia to the Greco-Roman World in Which Science Was Making Its Stand

Harold's symbol incorporates the Yin-Yang symbol at the center of a Cross of light rays. This composition acknowledges the light of Asia, which Harold believed Jesus incorporated in his teaching and acknowledged in his birth legend in poetic terms that would ring through the centuries. Three wise men came from the East, bearing precious gifts—*amber* was among them. Electricity was first known as the "amber effect." The legend says that the wise men acted as lifesavers for the "infant" truth that was to be expressed through the man Jesus, whose own enlightenment (star) arose in the East.

If Jesus journeyed through Asia in early manhood, as Harold postulates, then he would have been introduced to the wisdom of China enfolded in the Yin-Yang symbol, and in the *I Ching*, the *Book of Changes*. Let us look first at the symbol. It indicates that many men other than Moses and Jesus have understood the underlying principles that operate throughout nature in terms of opposite types of energy interacting.

In the above symbol, the Yin (feminine or negative principle) and the Yang (masculine or positive principle) are described as complementary and interpenetrating, as indicated by the white dot in the black segment and vice versa. The sphere, which incorporates the opposite principles that do not operate apart from each other in *any* expression of energy, represents wholeness. Many principles are enfolded in the symbol:

(1) There is no purely positive, no purely negative energy (the opposite colored dots in each segment), and, therefore, there is no "absolute" expression of either type of energy.

(2) Every manifestation of energy must be some arrangement of primordial neutral force, such as the symbol is when taken as a whole.

(3) We see that the forces are "equal to" each other in the operation of the whole, but they are not the same. (Has the role of woman been degraded all over the globe because something in consciousness insists that the measure of the negative is less than the measure of the positive?) Look again, and you will see that Harold's Yin-Yang symbol involves a larger black area, giving to this positive expression a ratio of 3:2 versus the white or negative expression. He could do this without degrading the feminine role because he saw the Yin-Yang symbol as a representation of the neutrinos, opposites and equals, as the ancient symbol implies.

(4) The positive energy is expressed as "light" in the darkness, and as the "darkness" of mass in the light. The white dot in the black becomes a representation of our sun; the black dot in the white becomes a representation of earth. The flow of energy in the system around these bodies, as well as the curvature of space as determined by the way light travels through it, is indicated in the sweep of the curves, which returns the eye to the starting point. We have here light involved with the sweep of a wave formation; light involved as a corpuscle; light involved in the blackest of matter (pitchblende). Light and mental light.

(5) We have also a symbol that incorporates the concept of gravity in the relationship between the two dots of "sun" and "earth" or all other types of bodies.

(6) We have also what may be seen as the "cross-section" of a double helix.

In short, this is a marvelous symbol, which incorporates basic principles and the underlying, interpenetrating actions in nature. Let us consider now the *I Ching*.

The *Book of Changes* is based upon the principle of evolution—all things must change. And there is an immutable law that says this process must begin anew with every "end": or, as change establishes an arrangement, change also operates upon the new arrangement, so that the process of "being" is also a process of change. This mathematically based sacred writ that is truth-bearer to millions is viewed as a "psychic computer" by José Arguëlles.[131] When consulted, this book works much as a computer works. The *I Ching* states with authority, just as Jesus did, that all things are made anew. But more is implied. Man, who writes and computes with the *Book of Changes*, is himself the "book" in which all is written. If he would understand the innermost and hidden secrets of nature, he must discover them by looking into human nature and not outside himself.

Jesus could have drawn upon the great symbol and book, measuring these against the symbology of Genesis, to come to a deeper understanding of the reality that underlies appearances. He could have realized that if the anthropomorphic approach was to be followed, it must be *completely followed*. He must become the representation of what he was to convey.

Jesus did not have to look beyond the human race to see that opposite types of energy are enveloped in the *neutral energy that dominates the "gender"* first and last, as embryo and in senility. The family situation grows into all the complexities involved in the force we call gravitation. But the basic law of singularity must assert itself as the proximity or binding force becomes oppressive. Only *adult* male and female can play a "charged" role; antiexpression in either sex is evidenced in life as a result of stress. Home ground always expresses the magnetic attraction with which life initially endowed it; but the actual home ground to which all energy returns is the potter's field of space. Of all the forces in expression, "nuclear binding energy," which allows for self-possession, self-union, is the greatest, and the "least."

Man cannot operate apart from nature. Therefore, there must be an underlying similarity between nature's expression and human expression.

The partially anthropomorphic approach fails. It had failed in Jesus' day when mankind had tried to understand Cosmic being and Cosmic energy (God) by casting God outside human life (not placing Cosmic being and energy within it), and then endowing the "Cosmic extraction" with the worst that man knows to be true of the adult male and/or female. In the theologies man developed from the play of opposites depicted and symbolized in his sacred writings, he endowed Parent Being with qualities that strike even a child as unjust, impractical, inefficient, and intolerable.

Jesus' doctrine and his scientific view is simply that God's Parent Energy is not outside man, and man is not outside nature. Nature is an expression of the unending life and love of Parent Being, uniquely expressed in mankind, who is similarly endowed. Not one life, not one iota of this whole divine creation, is ever to be lost.

243

Jesus saw that the life of the universe depends upon light. And that light may be extinguished as the energy composing it is laid to rest; but that light is resurrected whenever two or three of the primordial units of neutral energy, "little ones," are "gathered together" in the name of One, the quantum of light.

Harold's cosmology, which follows the path that the doctrine and drama of Jesus cut through the mystery of the Cosmos, will be difficult to "prove" because no one will be able to lay hands on a sleeping neutrino. Nature does not lift the veil and show her babes at rest. As time raises the curtain, light brings the siblings into action.

And so, in the end, the theory of the living universe must elicit faith —not proof—(but proof is implicit in any theory that matches empirical data and observations of nature, explaining these in terms that are not self-contradictory). The faith that is required is *faith in mathematics*, based on the observation that mathematics most accurately describes energy and its reactions, and that the two operations share common properties and synonymous meaning. Mathematics is basically constructive, infinitely workable, and must deal justly with itself and mammon if it is to work at all. If a mathematician ever succeeds in putting the number One out of commission, then and then only would there be reason to believe the universe is dying. But divide as you will, $1/2$, $1/3$, etc., One remains stated. The absent measure is the inverted fractional expression underlying the fractional expression that has been produced; and One constantly organizes its own forces that maintain it in unity, balance, and wholeness. God is not dead. God = One. The Cosmos is not dying. Cosmos = One. *The Whole, One, God, remains greater than the sum of its parts.*

XII

To What Shall We Compare the Reign of God?

Before bringing to a close our presentation of Harold's theory, we would like to pose certain of his concepts against Einstein's geometry of space-time. We will draw upon Dr. John A. Wheeler's and Seymour Tilson's presentation of Einstein's ideas (and development of them) in an article, "The Dynamics of Space-Time."[132] The article begins:

> Is the physical universe made of matter, or is it made of mathematics? To put the question another way—is space-time only an empty arena within which real fields and particles play out their drama; or is the four-dimensional continuum of space-time all there is? No questions are more central than these to the master plan of physics, the plan which seeks to unify into one harmonious whole phenomena so apparently diverse in scale and kind as elementary particles, neutrinos, electromagnetic fields, gravitation, and galaxies.

To the first question, Harold would answer that the physical universe is made of actual substance. This substance and its operation correspond exactly to the operation of mathematics. Indeed, simple arithmetic must be used to describe this substance in its most fundamental state, because the energy operates as signed number does and in terms of sets of energy. Mathematics may also be seen to be *substance in action*, the mathematical substance being the most highly refined type of energy derived from the original source—i.e., mental energy is "something," rather than "nothing." In the article, it is stated:

> In a matter-free universe the stuff of space-time, literally nothing but geometry, turns out to be a remarkably malleable primordial dough.

Harold saw that we cannot enlarge our understanding if we attempt to speak of a *matter-free* universe and then pose the concept of space-time's being *stuff*. If stuff of any sort is involved, then substance is involved.

We must understand the substance of space-time as degrees of energy that do not have *measurable mass* until the amount of energy involved is multiplied or concentrated in sufficient quantity to come within range of our sensors, senses, and ability to comprehend. In Harold's view, the "malleable primordial dough" is the emulsion of neutrinos at rest, which pervades all we can know of space. The article says of this dough:

> [It is] catalyzed only by energy and by the fertile yeast of mathematical imagination. It rises—here into a slowly curving section that has all the attributes of a gravitational field, there into a rippled configuration indistinguishable from an electromagnetic field, and elsewhere into knotted regions of intense curvature that manifest concentrations of charge and of mass-energy and behave like particles.

To Harold, the dough itself must be made of specks of "something"—just as commonplace dough is made of specks of wheat or meal. These specks rise to form the units of negative and positive energy that in turn catalyze the stuff of space-time (neutrinos at rest) only in terms of energy or wave motion. It is this net of energy values, the aggregate slightly negative, expressing only in terms of motion (as opposed to mass or light), which forms the electromagnetic and gravitational fields.

The lines of force formed by this matrix energy, which Harold called the Q-force, have neither beginning nor end in the space-time continuum we experience, because the free-flowing energy moves upon its self-constituted field, which remains as it flows on. Space is multiply connected by this flow and by the fields this energy creates. The flow of Q energy is identified with *time's* action. We cannot experience space separated from time because we cannot operate in space except as we operate on the flow of Q energy. The matrix energy arising from the malleable primordial dough in turn organizes matter, the "knotted" regions of intense curvature, which then behave like particles. In the article, we read:

> Electric lines of force (which in empty space have neither beginning nor end) similarly are trapped in any "wormhole" or "handle" of the geometry. . . . Into the wormhole from all directions converge electric lines of force, their number in any particular wormhole unchanging with time. This number represents the charge associated with the wormhole: To an observer on one side of the wormhole—the inlet side—this number represents negative charge; to an observer counting lines of force that emerge from the other side of the wormhole, the same number represents positive charge. Thus, in this geometrodynamic conception the zero total charge of the universe is automatically guaranteed. . . .

But this simple picture of electric charge is out of the question in a world free of wormholes. So it's natural to ask—is the physical world singly connected or is it multiply connected?

We are dealing here with a wormhole that is somewhat like a doughnut —"no one has yet seen the mouth of a wormhole."

First, we will say that in Harold's view, such a doughnut or wormhole would be doubly connected on its surface by the lines of force of the surrounding Q energy. The horizontal line would represent the negative; the vertical line would represent the positive. The "net" of Q energy's values, seen as $(-+-+-+-+-+-)$, could be so deployed as to provide a correspondence to both positive and negative charge: i.e., $(+--+)$ and $(-+-)$, with energy that communicates neutrality remaining: $(-+-+-)$.

But more important to this wormhole concept is Harold's concept of proton formation. In order to produce atomic matter, Q energy in space must delineate a measure of space, thereby creating a wormhole in the stuff of space-time that allows the positive nature of space to express itself. Harold called the wormhole the space chamber of the nucleus; it is the space chamber that constitutes an atomic particle. When stress causes matrix energy to release its hold on this chamber, atomic matter ceases to be, and the energy subsides into the net of Q energy in space, so that nothing is left behind but wave motion, or curved space. This is not empty space because the *curvature* bespeaks the presence of Q energy. The proton is not an independent entity in space in the sense that it is independent of space-time, because space energy gives it its being and time energy (Q energy) enfolds this space. The proton is an independent entity only in relation to another proton. If we could stop the motion picture and see what the wormholes or protons look like, they might appear much as the fine holes that make up a slice of bread. The holes are "pure geometry," independent of each other, yet because of them, the slice is multiply connected.

As the elements are built up, we will have to envision these and molecular matter in terms of every shape of coffee cake we can envision, stretching and shaping our wormholes from doughnuts into twists, etc., all multiply connected by Q energy, which also connects and enfolds galaxies of matter.

The doughnut or wormhole that begins and ends all such is the neutrino in rest state, in which the pattern is laid, and of which all else is made. Because it is a neutral particle with zero charge, the total charge of the universe is zero, insofar as material energy or the stuff of space-time is concerned. As this stuff is shaped and multiplied to form particles, there is more than enough negative matrix energy to supply each positive charge with its negative partner. Therefore, in more gross form, total electric charge is zero. We can experience space only in conjunction with time; therefore, space (positive energy) is neutralized by time energy (negative), so that the universe as we can experience it has zero "charge" of any sort.

But empty space which we cannot experience is positively charged; and because there is more of it than there is negative matrix energy to fill it, the Cosmos is positive in its being. Now listen to this explanation taken from Wheeler's and Tilson's article:

> [Einstein's] structural law of space-time has a most important consequence for all of physics. It means that *geometry is a dynamic entity in itself*, with the same kind of ability to store energy and to carry energy as that which belongs to elastic materials and electromagnetic waves!

Harold's parallel idea (at least to a degree) is the concept of the reality of space as a form of energy that is expressed in terms of: *dimension without body*. He saw a measure of space as "pure geometry," as an entity capable of storing energy and of becoming a dynamic entity when a wormhole of it is delineated to constitute a proton. Here, we must come to terms again with pure geometry (or space) as the ultimately refined physical expression of primordial energy, although too rarefied to be dealt with in terms of what we think of as physical energy. Nevertheless, space is a condition of primordial energy upon which all else depends for its being and expression.

Q energy is also dimension without body in terms of measurable mass. It is, nevertheless, substance that has strength. We might say that the elementary wormhole, the neutrino, is also dimension without mass in calculable terms, so that in this sense, it is pure geometry—or indestructible and yet malleable three-dimensional being, upon and through which the fourth dimension, time or Q energy, operates.

We may think of the universe as the ultimate doughnut or wormhole within which is enfolded every expression of matter and the dough from which it is made. This macro-doughnut is delineated by the circumscribing flow of matrix energy. As it moves from galaxy to galaxy, it carves curving paths through space, which form universal wave motions because the energy is attracted both to central space and to celestial bodies; therefore, it operates through space that is empty of matter save for the Cosmic Dust or stuff of space-time. Light follows the path of the Q-force, which bends it toward a celestial body such as our sun (to which the Q-force is attracted), even as the positive nature of the sun repels and thereby deflects the positive energy that light is. It is the push-pull of attraction and repulsion in macroscopic and submicroscopic terms that causes the path of light to curve.

In this picture of the universe, we have delineated within the Cosmic Whole what we may know of it physically. Space, empty of Q energy and matter, remains: pure geometry able to store energy and exert it as a constant force to support the universe we can know. Within this pure geometry of space, systems within systems *ad infinitum* operate. As Wheeler and Tilson explain it:

> The dynamics of the universe deals with distances of the order of 10^{28} cm. Elementary particles within atomic nuclei, in contrast, average 10^{-13} cm. in size. And yet both of these distances are enormous in contrast to the lowest limiting distance for quantum fluctuations in geometry . . . sometimes called Planck's length.

In order to see the inescapable connections between the disparate worlds of very small distances and very great distances, Wheeler and Tilson compare the geometry of the universe with the shape of a great ocean wave:

> As the wave moves into shallow water it curves up more and more strongly. Finally it develops a crest—a zone of infinite curvature—at which point it breaks up into foam. . . . In the case of the ocean wave the usual simple hydrodynamical equations lose their power to predict beyond the moment of infinite curvature of the crest. Only when the equations include a new effect—capillarity—having to do with physics at small distances, do they reveal that the curvature does not become infinite along the crest. And only then can one analyze the development of droplets at the crest and further dynamical evolution of the wave. When a closed model universe similarly endowed with only large-scale curvature evolves in time in accordance with Einstein's equations, like the wave it too develops a highly localized region of infinitely sharp curvature. And a new effect comes into being at this "wave crest" of the evolving universe, an effect which involves Planck's quantum of action and Planck's miniscule limiting length. Is this effect the creation of matter? No one knows. But no alternative is evident.

Let us go back for a moment to consider that in Harold's theory as the matrix energy of space develops a crest and breaks up into foam, the droplets we are dealing with are neutrinos in rest state. At this point, "negative tension" arises because of a *reversal* in the progress of curvature that is "positively" proceeding toward infinite curvature. We must deal with this *shift* in terms of action's shifting to express in *opposite* terms: i.e., from maximum to minimum expression, because action cannot be expressed in "absolute" terms, such as "forever positive" or "forever negative" or "infinite curvature" would imply. In Harold's terms, "cresting" signifies intense pressure and this produces negative units of energy (Planck's miniscule limiting length), which in turn produce the negative tension that evokes positive units of energy (Planck's quantum of action) from the substance of space-time (neutrinos at rest).

This effect, which must be seen as the mathematical equivalent to multiplying and/or dividing $(+1)$ or (-1), is responsible for the creation of the fundamental units of energy that compose matter.

The neutrinos in rest state that permeate all we can experience of space constitute both the units of energy from which matter arises and also what appears to us to be space, or space-time. The supply of this energy is inexhaustible, because even as tension and pressure cause the formation of units of physical energy, so tension and pressure cause these units of energy to disappear as they lapse into the stuff of space-time. Harold's concept of this operation conforms to the principle of reversibility that rules in most domains of physics.

If a process can go in one direction, it can also proceed in the other. In Harold's view, the principle of reversibility must come into action in the expansion and contraction of the universe. The question becomes, to what degree does it expand, to what degree does it contract, and how *traumatic* is this effect? In Einstein's view, it is indeed traumatic. As Wheeler and Tilson put it:

> At the end lies the mysterious fate [of a collapsing star] which also awaits Einstein's collapsing universe. There is no difference in relativity theory between the star's collapse and the collapse of the universe. In both cases the curvature of the geometry increases without limit; in both cases quantum effects must come in before curvature reaches infinity. In both cases the conclusion seems unavoidable that matter must be crushed out of existence, whatever our ignorance about the quantum details of the mechanism.

It was *our ignorance about the quantum details* that Harold tackled, holding in mind the principle of reversibility. Whatever caused the photon to arise in nature must be a reversible process that repeats the cycle *ad infinitum*, so that matter is constantly disorganized and constantly organized. The universe cannot collapse because space cannot collapse; and the Q-force that gives rise to curvature cannot cease its action. The Q-force (slightly negative matrix energy) is both the organizer and the disorganizer of matter.

Only mental energy can reach into the infinity of space, because only mental energy is actually neutral. Expansion as the term applies to space itself is not reversible.

Wheeler and Tilson present an intriguing picture of reversibility as it pertains to what goes on in space:

> Imagine having on hand, some years from now, a motion picture of a collapsing star. And imagine we can see the neutrinos and gravitational radiation streaming out as matter dissolves away. It presents a fantastic scene when run backwards. Sufficiently many neutrinos of the right helicity, and enough gravitational radiation, coming together from all directions—into one region of space over a short time interval—magically materialize into nuclear matter!

This, simply, is Harold's picture of the beginning of creation as we experience it. But it is not the beginning of the Original Cosmic Energy and Being that devolved into neutrinonic degrees of energy and into the pure geometry of space (both states of energy slightly positive in nature), so that the repelling force between these states of matter (space's overwhelmingly the greater) compressed the substance. This compression created the condition in which negative and positive units of energy arose in the clouds of neutrino energy that were left suspended as the pure geometry of space also arose.

If we can run our motion picture of the star back to its beginning by reversing the direction and see the neutrinos that were streaming away from it begin to reconverge into matter, is it not feasible to say, as Harold did, that neutrinos of energy are the building blocks from which all matter is constituted and to which all matter returns? And if the principle of reversibility rules in most domains of physics, is it not feasible to say, as Harold did, that the energy that is put to rest is also drawn back into action so that matter is constantly re-created, even as it is constantly disorganized? When we know that expansion and contraction is the principle upon which all living things operate, is it not feasible to believe that there is a universal *breathing* motion in a living universe?—nothing traumatic about it.

In Harold's theory, as in Einstein's, it is unavoidable that matter must be crushed out of existence; but in Harold's view it is also unavoidable that it must also be drawn again into existence. The rate of change and the balance between resting and active energy become the important considerations. Both men saw that this universe is evolving and that evolution implies that some end or goal be reached. Harold believed that mathematics itself gives the answer as to what that goal is: an endlessly operative, balancing and balanced system which is progressing toward the optimum state and rate of *constructive change*.

Until we can say with absolute certainty that the universe originated from one mass exploding, we cannot say that the principle of reversibility will return the universe to one mass of crushed matter or to any type of absolute state. Not even an Einsteinian insight into nature could say with certainty that the universe arose from one mass and will collapse again into such a state. Or that what evolves and devolves in the operation of space-time is not a cyclic and nontraumatic operation.

Einstein gave us a marvelous *synthesis of geometries*. As Wheeler and Tilson put it:

> . . . geometry of an unexpectedly rich and dynamic kind . . . it was Einstein's general relativity that gave geometry a life of its own.

In so doing, did he not give the *Cosmos* a life of its own?

In a later article by Wheeler (1968), dealing with "Our Universe: The Known and The Unknown,"[133] we can see how much progress has been made in a few years toward assimilating Einstein's ideas and equations—and how many more questions have, as a consequence, opened up. In this article, Wheeler deals with the two kinds of gravitational collapse of stars and relates this to the expansion and recontraction of the universe. He says of a supernova, "What gives one any right to think that he can work out the story of the collapse with any reliability? It is one thing to analyze a star as nearly static as the sun. Is it not quite another matter to forecast the fantastic dynamics of a supernova?"

One must wonder what turn Einstein's thought would have taken if he had conceived of such a *nearly static star* as our sun having achieved a steady state, in which the complex forces of gravity had reached near optimum expression, allowing the star to "react" to the energy that courses through and around it? But this idea could not have occurred unless the singular force of repulsion that is involved with the complex force of attraction in the phenomenon we call gravity had established itself in his mind.

What evidence is there for this singular force? The facts that "quantum rules" apply as light is absorbed and emitted—and that there are quantum fluctuations in the geometry of space—seem to support Harold's postulation that the single positive value (the photon) is at the heart of every atom, giving rise to a singular positive force that also expresses itself in celestial terms.

Wheeler says:

> If the quantum principle and relativity are the two over-arching principles of twentieth-century physics, then the union of these two principles that we have today in "quantized general relativity" or "quantum geometrodynamics" is a body of knowledge of exceptional interest and nowhere more so than in the consideration of gravitational collapse. Appreciable as have been the difficulties in getting hold of the mathematics of quantum geometrodynamics, a simple conceptual difficulty cost us greater trouble in these years since Einstein's death. Relativity, by treating time as a fourth coordinate comparable in quality to the other three, had brought a great new unity into the description of nature. Einstein gave us space-time in place of space. Nothing has been harder to learn than the necessity to go back from space-time to space.

This, of course, is what Harold did. He went back to *space alone*, considering it in terms of a singular expression of energy. We do not know exactly how long ago, but presumably not later than the mid-1950's.

Whereas Harold saw that we can *experience* space only in terms of the curvature deriving from the action of the energy he called the Q-force, which involves space with time's action and gives us space-time as an inseparable condition when we are dealing with appearances of reality, he also saw that space itself—three-dimensional space—is the constant and the basis of the reality that underlies appearances. Although Harold separated space and time, he saw them as complementary forces. Because space is positive force constant, it is responsible for universal dynamics, but it is not itself in action. Harold's concept of space is to a degree similar to what Wheeler refers to as superspace, in that Harold, too, would say, as Wheeler does, that "each 'point' in superspace symbolizes and stands for an entire three-dimensional geometry."

Harold saw that there are microscopic and macroscopic states in which time's action is not involved: microscopically, within the nucleus of the hydrogen atom, and macroscopically, in the space that the Q-force does not occupy. Therefore, there are areas of actually empty space in the Cosmos in which there is no such thing as the manifold of space-time. Because each point in this space not only symbolizes an entire three-dimensional geometry, but also stands for a measure of constant positive force, space is "self-repelling." And herein may rest the secret of the *expansion of the universe.* Harold said that space itself may still be self-reacting, because each measure of its constant positive being must repel each other measure until the force of repulsion is spent in every direction —or this self-reaction may now be complete. *When this force is spent in every direction, there will be no force of attraction to draw space together again. Hence, space itself cannot collapse.*

Since there is so much more space than matter operative within space, the outermost "band of space" acts as a repelling force to turn inward the galaxies of matter that move outward concomitant with the expansion of space. This force, acting in conjunction with the Q-force, which is drawn toward the central deep of space with its greater positive attraction, serves to keep the celestial masses from such separation as would enfold each of them in a Stygian night.

We must think of the expansion of the universe both in terms of the expansion of space and of the galaxies fleeing from each other until the force of repulsion between their slightly positive masses is spent and the Q-force draws them into society again. After which, the gentle expansion-contraction allows the universe to "breathe."

Wheeler says, "If there is no such thing as 'the' geometry of space at small distances, then it is also true that there is no such thing as 'the' universe at large distances." In Harold's view, there is no such thing as "the" *geometry of space* in, for example, one unit of negative energy (—), which may be likened to Planck's length (minimum). There is insufficient "dimension." The universe—in terms of space at large distances—is not "the" geometry of the Cosmos. "The Geometry" is laid down in the Cosmon, the Cosmic Mental Pattern that provides for the expression of all possible geometries *and enfolds space that cannot completely occupy it,* just as the Q-force of "Time" cannot completely occupy space.

As we return now to the concept of space without time, Wheeler says, "Space is to be compared to nothing so much as a carpet of foam spread out upon the floor. The carpet of foam looks smooth to a casual glance. But closer inspection shows that it is made of millions of tiny bubbles, and a still closer view shows that the bubbles are continually bursting and new ones being formed." In Harold's view, the carpet of foam in which the bubbles are bursting and being formed is equivalent to neutrinonic energy pervading the entire area of space with which we can deal, and the carpet of foam would reach from floor to ceiling. In submicroscopic terms, the bubbles bursting and being formed, creating holes and gossamer spheres of light, would correspond to the neutrinos going into and out of rest state.

In microscopic terms, the implosion and explosion of the bubbles in the foam is the disorganization and reorganization of the photons. The bubbles are light (a single positive unit), the holes are dark (a single negative unit), and neutrino energy in rest state is the "glue" that combines the bubbles and the holes into the yeasty action that characterizes the foam of space as we can know or experience space.

The foam permeates our space, but the floor and the ceiling are also to be reckoned with. They are equivalent to space—empty of foam—fixed, perfectly still, not acting or reacting. No doubt, it will be as hard to divide the foam from space (its floor and ceiling) as it was to divide space and time.

Let us look now at a collapsing star, of the sort that ends as a "black hole" in space. In Harold's view, *a black hole is a "whirlpool" of matrix energy* (Q energy that communicates neutrality but is slightly negative in its constitution) into which atomic matter *devolves,* beginning with the collapse of a proton as stress gives rise to negative expression within its space chamber. Black holes indicate that systems within systems within the Cosmic system may revert to the "initial condition"—"without form and void; darkness upon the face of the deep." *Void* means "empty space," so that we may translate this: nonatomic or matrix energy, slightly negative, which does not *involve* in each unit of it the geometry of a three-dimensional space chamber, as a proton does. Because so much neutral energy makes up matrix energy, the black hole will express gravitational attraction.

The incomplete collapse of a less massive star may result in the formation of a neutron star. In Harold's view, neutrons may arise as a proton is destroyed, because its energy loses its hold on its space chamber. "Firmament" is no longer an intrinsic part of its composition. Such a mass of neutrons would finally reach the point where equal and opposite attraction would mitigate, or slow down, the further collapse of the material into its neutrino equivalence. Disintegration of neutrons into protons, electrons, and antineutrinos must also take place.

In either case—the star that collapses into a "black hole," or the neutron star—the mass of energy would continue to be subject to the universal Q-force flowing through space. In time, the Q-force could unravel the "knots" in the net of field energy caught in the whirlpool of darkness. Or continued Q pressure could dissolve the neutron star. The "whirlpools" may actually be "wound skeins of energy" upon which the

Q-force draws. And it is possible that islands of empty space surround these seething pools of energy or stand between them and their nearest companions—the space providing the singular force of repulsion that the star lost as its atomic material collapsed, so that a companion star is not drawn into the pool of gravitational attraction. But we dare not take Harold's unfinished hypothesis too far—and such as this was not mentioned by him.

Here, we say only that in observing celestial phenomena, scientists will be acting like Chicken Little—declaring that the skies were falling because an acorn dropped on his head—if they ignore evidence at hand and declare that the universe itself is collapsing. Evidence at hand is our "nearly static sun"—countless billions like it within our ken—which is life-giving. Harold's concern was with such second-generation stars, and the belief that they had reached or could reach a steady state. Insofar as a collapsing universe is concerned, he saw this as an impossibility because of the nature of space (apart from time), and of matter, and of time's action through which all things are made anew, eternally, infinitely.

According to Wheeler, to the physicists, "A prediction that is infinity is not a prediction. Something has gone wrong." When Harold's answer was "infinity," it indicated to him that he had come again upon the operation of the principle of One, as number, infinitely workable, inexhaustible, its potential always *more* than can be measured.

Wheeler says that the problems scientists are dealing with are theological in character because the "initial condition" of the physical universe must be taken into consideration. And he adds this interesting comment:

> My colleague, Frederick Mote, a distinguished student of Chinese history and philosophy, in a recent address attributed the difference between Chinese outlooks and sense of values and those of the West to nothing more central than their different view of cosmology.

To Harold, the initial and infinite condition of physical energy, insofar as we can deal with the problem, is space and the "dissolving" of matter into neutrinos. These he saw as the alpha and omega particles that give rise to darkness and to light when the photon is called into action.

According to Wheeler, "Einstein, who did so much to bring the quantum principle to fruition in his earlier years, disowned it in his later years." (One is reminded of Marx's, "I am not a Marxist.") Perhaps Einstein realized that the quantum principle, valuable as it is, was somehow on the surface of the reality he sought in depth. As energy tells the story, we come to the end of division not in the one quantum of action, but in the pair of neutrinos—opposites, so that one may be called negative in the sense that the left hand is, and one may be called positive in the sense that the right hand is. And between them they can enfold all that is left of the actual initial condition of the universe, a psychon, or *mental light*, that carries within it the mystery of undivided wholeness, or God.

Jesus, *symbol of light*, said, "where two or three are gathered together in my name, there am I in the midst of them."[134] One must wonder what Einstein's thought patterns would have woven if he had had the concept of the resurrection of "light," and that where "two or three" are "gathered" in the name of "light," the One arises in their midst. Is not the One the photon? Are not all of us children, "little ones" in the Cosmic system? And if there is a psychic parallel to the operation in the physical realm, do not the "little ones" in the table of elementary particles gather by twos to produce the negative tension that calls the photon into action and by threes gather into one measure of light?

We catch only glimpses of Einstein's religious convictions. Few men who peer into the deepest secrets of the universe can muster twenty-twenty vision with no astigmatism. They must contend with the prejudices of the conscious mind that acts in unison with the realizations arising from the *unconscious*, which alone brings "singular vision" such as Jesus exercised after committing himself in consciousness to the glory, grace, and reality of the natural in life. We do not know how Einstein, who gave the world so incredibly much in the way of enlightenment, contended within himself—what made him disown the quantum principle, without which it is difficult today even to think of the word *physics*. We can only be grateful to him, as certainly Harold was, and to men like Wheeler, who bring the ongoing synthesis of astronomy and physics to the layman insofar as they can.

Judaic beliefs must have had some influence upon Einstein's thinking. As Wheeler points out, "One cannot escape the fact that theological considerations have their influence on human actions." This must include scientists, who cannot altogether erase what has been "programed" into their minds in childhood. Resurrected and everlasting life for the individual is not dominant and basic in Judaic doctrine. But this concept is dominant and basic in the religious expression of the overwhelming majority of Homo sapiens, although expressed in varying ways. Jesus, too, was influenced by Judaic theological considerations in which his mind had been steeped. But he took a wider view, because he embraced in his doctrine the whole of the expression of God-consciousness in man, as it was expressed "in spirit and in truth"—intuitively and intellectually.

Today, the question of the creator and creation—of logical and/or chronological relationships—remains. Wheeler says:

> One cannot touch thus peripherally on "theology" without recalling the great debates of long ago. One cannot forget that they eventually opened the door to modern science, which demands that we communicate with one another in understandable words, free of all mysticism.

Harold attempts to communicate in simple words, as free of mysticism as the mystery of arithmetic and geometry, and the data of astronomy and physics, will permit.

The words of Frederick Mote, quoted by Wheeler (see p. 256), support Harold's view that a unified planetary consciousness, *a real community of belief*, depends as much, if not more, *on transcending the opposing and nihilistic cosmologies as it depends on transcending opposing religious views*. Unless the universe is a living system able to support and engender life everlastingly, religion has no meaning, no basis. When we have accomplished these two transcending syntheses, we will be ready for the synthesis of science and religion, which we must have before human consciousness can gather into the planetary consciousness of humankind.

We have journeyed out into space and time, discussing concepts that have meaning perhaps only to a physicist, although they may be described in terms as mundane as a doughnut. But we have not dealt with lifeless mathematics. In *One, Two, Three . . . Infinity*, George Gamow discusses the properties of space, showing us how to "turn a double apple eaten by a worm into a good doughnut," and reminds us that:

> Your body also has the shape of a doughnut, though you probably never thought about it. In fact, in the very early stage of its development (embryonic stage) every living organism passes the stage known as "gastrula," in which it possesses a spherical shape with a broad channel going across it. . . . In fully developed organisms the internal channel becomes much thinner and more complicated, but the principle remains the same: and all geometrical properties of a doughnut remain unchanged. Well, since you are a doughnut. . . .[135]

Try to understand how completely kneaded into the primordial dough of space-time the creative life principle is. And ask yourself if man is not the book in which is written the whole story of creation. How can we take other than an anthropomorphic view when our embryonic minds shape us in the beginning as the stuff of space-time shapes itself? This knowledge is still with us—if we but knew how to tap this fount.

From whence did Einstein's rare vision come? His view of the Cosmos and its operation can be indeed well described as:

> A matter-free universe that nevertheless must be thought of in terms of the "stuff" of space-time—a remarkably malleable *primordial dough*, catalyzed only by energy and by the *fertile yeast* of mathematical imagination.

This brings to mind the description Jesus gave long ago when he was trying to explain what the life and action of the whole Cosmos is like:

> To what shall I compare the Reign of God? It is like dough, which a woman took and buried in three pecks of flour, till all of it was leavened.
>
> (Matt. 13:33)

Scientists today, in their efforts to explain the action of Cosmic Energy, draw upon the same words and ideas Jesus used. Does this not indicate that they have not yet moved *beyond* Jesus' realization of the nature of Cosmic Operation? The more important question is—do they as yet understand *all* that he expressed? The only way it could have been conveyed was in poetic word, symbol, and drama.

XIII

Synthesis—Organic Life Enters the Picture

In Harold's view, the evolution of consciousness and human society follows the pattern of the evolution of the Cosmos. Each move diminishes the destructive potential and increases the constructive potential that will in time give rise to true humanity among mankind, and to everlasting life in an indestructible body brought forth and maintained because an incorruptible body of consciousness will express it.

This is "divine materialism" that places mankind in one-to-one correspondence with the least, not the greatest, expression in nature: equal and opposite neutrinos. But are they not "the most"! Each is an indestructible self-union, which has everlasting life and a large measure of liberty. Each is an expression of love in being which periodically joins with other particles of like kind to produce light and dark, both necessary to life. Such a divine materialism transcends pantheism and becomes a modern Trinity: God-in-nature (Father), God-in-man (Son), and the remaining One, the Cosmon (Holy Spirit, wholistic mind of God).

Although human mental energy is seen to be drawn from the same one source that all other types of energy are drawn from, mankind's mind is not of the same "estate" as nature's—nor of the *One Cosmon* programing the universe and resonating with the human mind. God *builds* no body of consciousness that is "his own." The code script for this operation is given to man. The code script also remains in God, and God remains one measure of full consciousness to which nothing may be added, nothing subtracted. The wholeness of this One resonates with the minds into which word power has been given, promising to each the glory of everlasting life, as and when its own body of consciousness, which each is building, is complete.

Because this planet is the ground upon which human life took form, the planet itself has life with human characteristics in the Cosmos. It is dispersing into space mental energy patterns taken shape in words, spoken and written; and these patterns are unlike any other in the universe *if* this be the only planet on which human life exists. If not, these patterns are communicating that the planet is alive. Coherent communication will be established when the East-West "lobes of thought," symbolized in the Yin-Yang, establish within each other a "pole" of the other's ideas— just as the Yin-Yang symbol shows the complementary action and the opposite poles of thought established in the midst of each type of thought. The tilt of this mental axis must, like the earth's, be tangential to North-South, involving in the polarity every point on the compass.

Today's technology permits man to put in orbit around the earth an actual "body of enlightenment"—a global satellite communications system such as Oliver Reiser envisions in his Project Prometheus-Krishna. Such a celestial sphere will be the *Temple of Cosmic Humanism*. It must speak in a language that all can understand—the language of man. And retrospection of the light of men in centuries past must bathe the mind of the world today, even as men of the present project their light. Wherever the planet's logos field may be, the important thing is to harmonize East-West, North-South ideas and thought patterns, so that a free flow of thought and belief will in time establish a community of harmonious information that our World Brain thinks and speaks into space. And if our Celestial Child knew how to send its messages using the most efficient redundancy in expression, there would be a better chance of its being heard. But we must be able to lift our minds and voices in synthesis of belief, regardless of the particularized and individual expressions of it, before we will be able to speak *a word* in Cosmic terms. A word is a synthesis. Today, the Celestial Child babbles and wails, tomorrow it will talk.

Cosmic Humanism is a good name for Harold's concept of man, God, nature. But Oliver Reiser must be the one to say whether Harold's concept can fit into the structure of Cosmic Humanism as outlined by Reiser. This would involve taking a new view of the universe, of physics and astronomy, as well as a new view of religion as a primitive but sophisticated expression of scientific and psychological truth, and a new view of psychology or the psychic structure of each person that places him in the role of God-Son as surely as Jesus played it.

Reiser's Cosmic Humanism and Harold's divine materialism are to a great degree complementary. Because each is synthesis, the philosophy enters everywhere but is at home nowhere in the differentiated organizations of today's society. Neither doctrine can be completed, wrapped up neatly. The ideas may be precised and supported. But both doctrines demand their own evolution to keep pace with knowledge.

A valid doctrine must always be a little beyond the shoreline of common consciousness, inviting man to explore the deeps of himself and the Cosmos. It can have no mode of worship—except however love and laughter come, bringing with them beauty and certainty in being which evoke appreciation of the universe and all within it.

We have not been able to say what positive attraction is—but we can see the unit of positive energy as a body of pure substance involved in action. This has appeal. We can see negative attraction as the appeal that freedom of action poses. We can see neutral attraction as the appeal of self-possession while in the company of others with whom we can act in concert and in harmony.

Although we have given mental energy a "form" and a basis for operation, we have not been able to say what it is, or what word power is. Mankind is too involved in the play of this energy to be able to observe it, as he can observe physical energy in play. We are like a person coming out of deep anesthesia or coming to after a knockout blow, so that full consciousness is not upon us as yet. It is as though we are experiencing in slow motion that which happened to God as God became "us" and we became "it" in such a flash that unless we experience this action in slow motion we cannot come into full consciousness of ourselves and what happened.

We do not know what mental energy in "slow motion" is programing into life as it programs out the destructive potential and recasts evil into something of value. Maybe other senses are to be developed. Or those we have are to be enriched. Homo sapiens may be the generation of man that is to learn the meaning of colors—how they work and what they mean in terms of the influence they have upon being. Or our generation may be the one that must experience to the utmost the function of *tone* —the variety of sound and its effects. Or, movement itself produces a synthesized sensation that cannot be precisely identified with any of the senses. Perhaps we must experience to the fullest independent motion, but learn to act in concert and, as an infinite variety of instruments, each participate to raise a symphony of consciousness worthy of Cosmic communication. There is so much we must experience and know before we can experience more, know more!

If every answer did not present its more intriguing problem, we would soon be bored. And if by the time we can state the problem we did not have the answer within our reach, we would soon despair. And so we turn to another problem, another answer that is scarcely more than hinted at in Harold's unfinished hypothesis.

We have brought the living cell into the picture, but we have not dealt with the question of what arrangement of energy could introduce into the scheme of positive and negative operation a force that would give a substance the living quality that organic matter has. Living material is antientropic. It organizes substance into ever more complex forms.

Harold spoke briefly of a particle he called "p-1," and saw to be a "coefficient" of energy that allows for the conversion to the organic state and makes possible a whole new series of "living elementary particles," proteins, amino acids, etc. The p-1 particle is constituted by a synthesis of all the physical forces that are in play in the reorganization of the energy of Original God. This means that the particle has a measure of positive energy, a measure of negative energy, and a measure of *stable* neutral energy, a neutrino—which Harold represented as (*) when in action, and as (°) when at rest. Therefore, a p-1 particle would be represented as (— ∘ +) or as (— * +). Its ratio is (1:1:1). Or, if we use the measure numbers for the units of negative and positive energy, the ratio is (2:1:3).

The neutrino value in the p-1 particle provides the binding energy and prevents time's action wherein the negative and positive units of energy react to disorganize each other into virtual energy. The rate of disorganization of energy is slowed—time's action is tempered. Growth into more complex forms with a reasonable degree of stability becomes possible.

The point Harold wanted to make was that *one iota of energy* can make all the difference there is between the organic and inorganic, as we shall see when we observe the p-1 particle. It gives to an aggregate of energy a *neutral particle* that can attract the "food" it needs and create such "links" of inorganic and organic substance as blood is —a simple protein and an iron-containing material. The p-1 particle, seen as (— ∘ +), has sufficient negative (horizontal) value to attract a photon. As the photon enters and activates the neutrino, the neutrino reduces the photon to its neutrino equivalence of energy in rest state. Because the p-1 particle can be slightly more negative than neutral, it can absorb the light it attracts, and convert the "stuff" of it to neutrinos which transfuse the aggregate with the *plasma* of nature's blood, so that neutrinonic energy courses through the system providing it with the *energy potential* it needs for organization and growth.

Neutrinos react with matter only rarely. However, in Harold's view, once the p-1 particle has been formed, reproduction of the p-1 units within an aggregate of energy increases rapidly. And although the organic substances that are produced by the coefficients break down, the p-1 particles themselves are long-lived. Therefore, once the possibility of organic life has been established, the probability is that it will continue to flourish or at least persist even under extremely stressful conditions.

Harold concluded that neutrinos react with other material only rarely because the particles are programed to produce positive and negative units of energy. Also, because the forces of attraction and repulsion in the neutrinos are so diminished, and in the sum the particle presents such a small degree of neutral energy that it has little capacity to respond to the gross expression of these forces in nature. Otherwise, since all in existence is so submerged in neutrino energy, chaos would ensue and soon there would be only one absolute mass.

Neutrino energy is the "food" that the material realm needs for sustenance, and this realm is fed this food *only as light is ingested and absorbed*, as it is reduced to its neutrino equivalence.

All living things, therefore, *feed upon the body of light and drink its blood*. Light is the actual substance life lives upon—and this, Jesus, as symbol of light, conveyed in the drama of the Last Supper. Today, we call this drama photosynthesis.

The drama of the Last Supper also conveys that we must partake of the flesh and blood of a *brother-being* to come into life, and that every human being is a brother-being to every other. The real parent-child relationship exists only between God and mankind. As the ovum partakes of the sperm and then draws its sustenance from the blood of its host, the holy communion of life is kept.

As we face the mystery of sexuality, particularly in human beings, which unlike other mammals constantly express and respond to the attraction posed by the opposite sex, embryological research indicates that the creation story, in which Eve is drawn from the body of Adam, must be reversed. Dr. Mary Jane Sherfey says that the findings call for an "Adam out of Eve" myth,[136] because *all* mammalian embryos are anatomically female during the early stages of fetal life. In embryos that develop into males, the increasing production of androgen gradually overcomes the innate female anatomy and the maternal estrogens, changing the direction of the growth of female structures into the direction of the growth of male structures, which are completely developed by the end of the third month of pregnancy.

This embryological process is congruent with Harold's concept that negative (and/or female) energy is first organized, and through its involvement of mental energy and its organizational power, positive (and/or male) energy is organized. If superiority is to be based on primacy, then the embryological facts are no doubt a blow to male vanity. But Harold's view does not offer either sex superiority based on primacy. He saw that preceding the organization of negative energy is the primordial organization of energy into a neutral union that must involve both types of energy—the neutrinos, to which he likens man and woman. Therefore, all in existence is "bisexual" in the sense that "bits" of positive and negative energy in neutrinos are involved in every expression of energy. In these *alpha* and *omega* particles there is no "primacy" for the one type or the other, and each is a union of positive and negative energy.

The creation story must indeed be changed if Adam is seen simply as a male, because then the legend would be out of line with the facts that science has laid before us. But Adam cannot be seen as a male—at least, not in Eden. Adam is a duo from the beginning: Man and Woman, and God is parent of this life. This duo may be seen as a correspondence to the neutrinos; or Adam may be seen as the neutron's correspondent, since this particle disintegrates into a pair of charges; or Adam/Eve may be seen in correspondence to the hydrogen molecule in which a neutral pair share a field. But most important, in Eden, Adam in the beginning must be seen as a "body of consciousness," which expresses its *own physical body* to which it is mated until death—and the creation story tells us that inherent in this body of consciousness is both maleness and femaleness. And so it is with the body it expresses. We know that embryologically speaking it is correct to say that the penis is an exaggerated clitoris, etc., so that maleness is enfolded in femaleness, and femaleness underlies maleness in expression.

What we confront in humankind, in each sex, are two types of expression enfolded in the wholeness of each gender, each as One. The creation story tries to tell us that each of us, regardless of our sex, is a part of the new generation that arose with the advent of positive energy as the several divisions of the primordial waters of matrix energy gave rise to it and to light. And since maleness is the mark of the new generation, we are *brother-beings*.

If we try to determine what causes the increase of androgens which turn femaleness into maleness, we are told that this happens if the genetic code so dictates. But how was this genetic code written? When and how in life's processes did cells arise carrying the genetic code that would dictate *maleness able to reproduce itself?*

At some point in the development of living creatures, through the division and rejoining of primordial daughter cells that divided to become two cells, the cells began to fertilize each other. But sexuality as we know it did not come into the picture until through some type of cross-action, multiplying and dividing of the negative or female cells, the positive or male cell was produced—just as mathematically ($-1/-1 = +1$) or ($-1 \times -1 = +1$). There must have been a *primordial* "virgin birth"—an unconscious act that parallels parthenogenesis—which produced a male cell able to reproduce its kind.

Not until Adam was driven from the "womb of life"—or its nonsexual, "garden" culture—and into the world, did he *become* such a cell of maleness, evoked through the "cross-action" of Eve and the serpent, both symbols of negative energy. Adam, symbol of a new generation of life, bore the seed of maleness and femaleness within him—just as Adam as symbol of a body of consciousness was originally composed of the masculine and feminine aspects of being: Adam-Eve.

Precious, indeed, must have been the first male cells in nature's realm. And wherever the male was produced, his environment was stocked with daughter cells ready to receive him. Hence, Cain and Seth had no trouble finding "wives."

And so the story of creation begins again. It will not end.

Harold infused his scientific writings with the spirit of an artist—an artist of life, which he saw Jesus to be. In art, we have the greatest synthesis—which often can speak more surely than words—so we shall call upon it. Although Harold's concept of the living universe has not, to the knowledge of those working on his manuscripts, been stated before, it has, perhaps, been painted more effectively than it has been presented here—in Vincent Van Gogh's *Starry Night*:

> ". . . expressing light by opposing it to dark" and ". . . sky and earth form one whole, they belong to each other. . . ."

H. R. Graetz, author of *The Symbolic Language of Vincent Van Gogh,*‡ from whose book the quotation above was taken, says that this picture is Van Gogh's spiritual testament:

> . . . his message of a conception that *does not pass in the passing,* communicated in a change of form, a metamorphosis . . . "as necessary as the renewal of the green in spring. . . ."

‡ (New York: McGraw-Hill, 1963), pp. 200, 213, quoting Vincent Van Gogh.

Certainly the poet—artist whose medium is words—with a few strokes of his pen can paint in unforgettable lines a portrait of the neutrinos upon which Harold based his theory of the living universe:

> Out of the dimness opposite equals advance—
> Always substance and increase, always a knit of identity—
> Always distinction—
> Always a breed of life.

Walt Whitman
Leaves of Grass

ADDENDUM

We have said that to our knowledge Harold's concept of the living universe has not been stated before. But as this book goes to press, we cannot say this without qualification. Another book has just been published which will be of profound interest to scientists the world over— *Psychic Discoveries Behind the Iron Curtain* by Sheila Ostrander and Lynn Schroeder (Prentice-Hall, Inc.)—and in it is reported the work of one of Russia's most renowned astrophysicists, Dr. Nikolai Kozyrev. He proposes, as Harold did, that *time* is a form of energy. Kozyrev has measured this energy and described some of its properties. In view of the brilliant predictions he made about the moon, Venus, and Mars, proved by later space probes, physicists must give serious consideration to his work.

We find it both startling and gratifying that Kozyrev's description of time energy so closely parallels Harold's description of Q energy (which he called time energy) that the two men present in broad terms many of the same concepts. Space does not permit us to present these parallels in detail; we hope the reader will refer to Chapter 13, "Time—A New Frontier," in the above mentioned book. But some of the most salient and "far out" points of contact may be presented briefly.

Just as Harold said Q energy is immediately everywhere and links all things in the universe, so Kozyrev describes time energy.

Harold said that the "density" of Q energy involving a mass depends upon the gravity and/or density of the matter. So says Kozyrev of time energy.

A characteristic of Q energy is that it has a flow pattern which Harold refers to as the Q-force flowing throughout the universe. Kozyrev discovered that a characteristic of the energy he calls time has a flow pattern.

Just as Harold projects an asymmetrical operation throughout nature, so Kozyrev finds an asymmetrical property associated with time energy. Time energy is denser near the receiver of an action and thinner near the sender.

And just as Harold insisted that all phenomena must first be understood in terms of positive (more) and negative (less) "value," so Kozyrev associates the flow of time energy with positive and negative patterns. In a left-hand rotating system (for Harold, a system with measure number 3/2 or 3) the time flow is positive—it adds energy or gives rise to "more." In a right-hand rotating system (for Harold, a system with measure number 2/3 or 2) the time flow is negative, giving rise to "less."

Kozyrev says that time energy not only has a pattern of flow, but also a *rate* of flow. Harold suggested that the red shift might well indicate the *rate* of the Q-flow around celestial bodies.

Kozyrev says that as the rate of the time flow through a substance changes, weight is lost. In Harold's concept, the "time action" that is constantly taking place because of the influence of the Q-force upon a body causes a negative value to act upon a positive value, reducing this unit of neutral energy (which gives rise to weight) to "weightlessness" —i.e., the unit of neutral energy disintegrates into neutrinos in rest state —and this causes the body or isotope to lose atomic weight.

The most "far out" and therefore most astounding point of contact between the thought of Harold and Kozyrev is that nuclear reactions in stars do not play "first fiddle" in providing the energy that maintains the system. Both men postulate that all material systems are the sources of energy which feed the general current of time energy, and it in turn influences the material systems. Stars get some of their energy from time's current in which they are enveloped. This, of course, was Harold's view of how the life of our sun in particular and the universe in general is maintained.

Although today science makes no distinction between past and future, both Harold and Kozyrev believe that the thread of time progressing from past to future is not a "strip of film" that can be run backward. For Harold, time's action involves disorganization, organization, and *reorganization* of universal energy. The reorganization cannot be *undone*, and will progress until the whole system reaches its optimum state.

The report of Kozyrev's work in *Psychic Discoveries Behind the Iron Curtain* is focused upon its implications for an explanation of the transmission of mental energy as a form of measurable physical energy, a tangible property. We must leave it to our readers to think again of Harold's concept of psychic energy and its relationship to Q energy, which brings his thought in line with Kozyrev's: time is a form of energy that participates in all things that happen in the universe as we can experience it, and allows for psychic happenings; but it does not "carry" mental energy (telepathy) in the usual sense of the word because time energy does not propagate, being immediately present everywhere.

Dr. Albert Wilson of the Douglas Research Laboratories in California is quoted as saying of Kozyrev's work, "I feel that something very much like what Kozyrev has hypothesized will be established in physical theory within the next decade or two. Its implications will be revolutionary. It could take a generation of work before the leap he has taken can be incorporated into the body of scientific knowledge. Whether right or wrong, it is the type of imaginative speculation that points to a new way of viewing the world and this is always highly valuable."

Also quoted is another prominent Western scientist who has proposed the idea that time has quantitatively measurable characteristics—Dr. Charles A. Muses. He says, "We shall eventually see that time may be defined as the ultimate causal pattern of all energy release." This is the basis of Harold's hypothesis, first published in 1966, although it had been in our hands a number of years prior to that time.

It does not matter who first states an idea. What really matters is that parallel lines of thought meet in the infinity of the pioneering minds of those men who dare to think in Cosmic and affirmative terms. The work of one lends substance to the work of the other until, in time, they become like double stars, developing the same brightness, the same spectral lines, the same radius—or, should we not say, the same faith in the Cosmos, which is God.

Quotations by Dr. Wilson and Dr. Muses may be found on p. 165 of *Psychic Discoveries Behind the Iron Curtain* (Englewood Cliffs, N.J.: Prentice-Hall, Inc., 1970).

XIV

A Word about Harold

Here, this section of our book draws to a close. In the concluding portion, the unknown author, Preston Harold, speaks again for himself, in his own words, through the manuscript he left, *On the Nature of Universal Cross-Action*.

Although the hypothesis is written in nontechnical and nonmathematical language insofar as possible, it will be of interest primarily to those with some knowledge of nuclear physics. The major points have been presented. However, there is much material that has not been introduced. Also, Harold approaches from the standpoint of the creation of Prime Bundles of energy, rather than from the translation of the first ten verses of Genesis into universal energy in action in terms of elementary particles.

Our description has been drawn largely from material that was not printed in the hypothesis, but was a part of the original notes. These were not organized in such a way that it was possible to determine just how the author would have introduced and developed his ideas. In the chapter, *On the Nature of Universal Cross-Action*, Harold does not introduce the subject of religion or Jesus until very near the end. In the notes he left regarding the beginning of the universe, the Genesis equation is introduced at the beginning. Whether justice has been done to Harold's concepts in this presentation of them, with only memory to call upon, will remain a question. But, if nothing else, this effort may make Harold's own words easier to understand.

In *The Stranger*, Harold says that he set out to see if a sustainable belief, congruent with the demands of both reason and intuition, would emerge from a re-evaluation of Jesus, after his words, works, and drama had been measured against all kinds of experience, observable phenomena, and the most advanced scientific knowledge. We can see that Harold's faith in Jesus as a man of complete integrity, in touch always with reality in all its depths and heights, grew with each measure made of Jesus' revelation. For this reason, Harold came in the end to have complete faith in Jesus' doctrine as it pertains to God, man, and natural phenomena.

Many men of intellect, many guided by intuition, follow Jesus in blind faith, exhibiting great devotion. Harold's was not a blind faith. His was a *seeing belief*. He followed Jesus with singular devotion and integrity wherever the comprehensible path of One led, until he had fashioned a panoply of fact to shield the Gospels and their message.

In today's world, it is no longer enough to follow anyone or any ideology in blind faith, no longer enough to apologize and rationalize with devotion. Christians, secular or otherwise, are doing no more.

Harold's plea was for Christianity to open its eyes and mind to behold the magnificence of the man it rests upon. And to exercise the intellect at its command to precise Jesus' doctrine so that it will be intelligible *in relation to modern knowledge*—not to endlessly translate the Bible into ever less beautiful and less poetic language.

And to Israel, Jesus' own people, enough of whom *received him* to insure that his message would be given to the world, Harold says, "Come, let us reason together." Messiah comes when and as truth comes into conscious expression in the mind of mankind. Messiah's must be a "planetary" coming in the birth of the unified consciousness of this Celestial Child.

In Jesus' day, *his own*—the learned, the mathematicians, the astronomers—*received him not,* because his insights were too advanced to elicit their understanding. Harold again presents Jesus' work in the temple of understanding that scientists have structured. We shall have to wait and see if they are as yet ready to receive him.

BOOK THREE

ON THE NATURE OF
UNIVERSAL CROSS-ACTION

by Preston Harold

I

Using ordinary language, we present our hypothesis in nonmathematical terms, so that the discussion may be followed with ease by a person having very little knowledge of nuclear physics.

Our view rests on the premise that there is but *one* energy *asymmetrically* divided to express through opposite forces: negative and positive. In our view, there is no purely positive, no purely negative energy, and there is no purely neutral energy in the sense of a union of exactly equal amounts of opposite force. We believe that the negative and positive forces that *communicate as such* are asymmetrical arrangements involving both forces, giving rise to *redundant* expressions of the one or the other force.

We deal primarily with the *internal structure* of those "bundles of energy," the elementary particles, each of which we see as "manyness" in itself: i.e., as a special multiplicity of positive *and* negative energy. Using simple symbols, we describe them, and the internal structure of an atom, in terms of negative and positive *value* only. A particle's exhibition of, or communication of, positive, negative, and neutral properties depends upon its *redundancy*. Whatever is redundant in the aggregate is communicated. Thus, we believe, the *being*, or value count, of a particle or force may differ from its *communication*: i.e., a particle composed of a number of positive and negative values may have one more positive value than it has negative values, or vice versa; but the *neutral value to be realized from a combination of positive and negative values* will give it a *neutral redundancy* and this redundancy, rather than its "net" positive or "net" negative value in count, will be communicated.

In order for an aggregate of values to express charge or mass, a *redundancy* of some value (positive, negative, or neutral) must be present. If the aggregate does not possess a redundancy of some sort in its value count, nothing in the way of charge or mass will be communicated.

The "value force" we deal with is independent of electrical charge: i.e., it is seen as a *singular force* versus a *redundant or complex force* which we believe electrical charge to be, as will be explained in our discussion of the special multiplicity of the various particles. The singular force of the positive ($+$) and negative ($-$) values operates, however, on the same principle as that of electrical force: i.e., of attraction between opposite *values* and repulsion between like *values*. We do not discuss forces in technical terms of strong forces versus weak forces; our concern is with the *constitution* of the various forces operative in nature.

We speak of binding energy, but not in the technical sense of its being the amount of energy that must be supplied to pull apart all the nucleons in a nucleus. We speak instead of the attraction of opposite values, $(+)$ and $(-)$, for each other that "binds" different arrays of values into particles and also "binds" particles in the nucleus. This "binding" force becomes negligible as distance between particles increases, and it becomes a *force of repulsion* in relation to any other particle at the minimum distance between them before they must react, or in "immediate" terms, as will be explained in Section III when the internal operation of an atom is discussed.

No one can say *why* like charges repel and opposite charges attract; the principle was drawn from the results observed when like and opposite charges come together. We cannot say *why* energy tends to react in the way we describe in the several transactions we use to illustrate our view. We say only that we read in the results observed in the laboratory the principles we will try to elucidate.

We "spell out" our concept of the multiplicity of various particles using the symbols: $(-)$ negative, $(+)$ positive, and several simple symbols to represent the neutral energy possible in their combination which will be explained as we go along. Here, we would say that the neutral value to be realized from the combination of a single negative and a single positive value is symbolized as (o), or *one* measure of neutral energy. We speak of such neutral energy, as well as other *degrees* of neutral energy as "potential energy," but not in the technical sense. We use the word *potential* in the sense of latent and/or possible as opposed to realized, seeing potential energy as energy composed of an equal number of single positive $(+)$ and negative $(-)$ values that may express in terms of force, i.e., $(+ -)$, or in terms of "rest mass," i.e., (o), but the values cannot simultaneously express as both.

We attempt to present a new view of matter, but our symbolic arrangements do not represent actual arrangements any more than spelling "baseball" presents a mechanical model of such a ball or lists its properties or describes it in terms of any number of dimensions in a space of any number of dimensions. Or, we might say, the parts of a dissected frog laid out upon a board and themselves dissected no more present a true picture of the living animal than do our dissected elementary particles and atoms present a "living" picture of these entities.

When used with numbers, our symbols do not designate signed numbers. Therefore, the order is reversed and the symbols are contained in parentheses. The numbers represent proportional amounts of the qualities involved: for example, $2(-)/1(+)$ represents twice as much negative value as positive value in the arrangement. Wherever practical we use the symbols so that the *ratios* may be seen at a glance: for example, $(- + -)$ represents a *ratio* of $2(-)/1(+)$. Such a bundle of energy is also equivalent to one negative measure versus one neutral measure (o), or a ratio of $1(-)/1(o)$, or $(- o)$. Since no neutral redundancy is present, this aggregate would communicate itself in terms of the *redundancy that is present in its value count*: i.e., in terms of negative energy.

We see this ratio, $(- + -)$, to constitute the basic *negative charge*: an electron. Its 50 per cent redundancy of negative value gives it one measure of negative electrical charge. The positive value in it allows for its expression in positive terms, as will be explained later on when antiparticles are discussed. Thus, we see negative electrical charge as a complex force and not as a singular force or one measure of negative $(-)$ energy.

We see a ratio of $2(+)/1(-)$, or $(+ - +)$, as the basic *positive charge* associated with a proton. Its 50 per cent redundancy of positive value gives it one measure of positive electrical charge. It may be seen also as a ratio of $1(+)/1(o)$, or $(+ o)$, and it communicates the redundancy that is present in its value count: i.e., in terms of positive energy. The negative value in it allows for its expression in negative or "anti" terms. We do *not* see this bundle $(+ - +)$ as the nucleus of hydrogen $_1H^1$, but as *the unit of positive charge associated with it*.

Thus, the electron's structure $(- + -)$ is completely opposite from that of a basic unit of positive charge $(+ - +)$. And a positron, antiparticle of the electron, is equally different in its structure from a basic unit of positive charge, for, in our view, a positron is an electron giving expression to its inherent positive value in response to stress. Before attempting to discuss further the make-up of the particles that allows for certain aspects of their behavior, we must discuss other concepts basic to our hypothesis.

A modern theory postulates that there are three quarks, each with corresponding antiquark, and these as yet undiscovered particles are the fundamental units of which the elementary particles are made.[137] We do not dispute this theory. Indeed, we incline toward it. But we believe the quarks themselves must be organized of aggregates of positive and negative value, and these in turn must be made of *one* fundamental building block, which is at the root of matter. Here, the question of what the one fundamental building block is made of must arise. Because organization itself involves the concept of "and," we believe the primordial organization of matter and/or energy involves the organization of "one and one," or a division of the *one* energy into *opposites*, which are, paradoxically, the *same* in being.

We see the one fundamental building block as the smallest particle, the neutrinos which must be seen as "one and one." The neutrino and the antineutrino are each "real." Their "existence" can be calculated mathematically, but the particles themselves have no measurable mass or charge: they cannot be observed directly; only the products of their interactions can be observed; one has a right-handed spin, while the other's is left-handed. The neutrino-antineutrino particles constitute, in our view, the primordial organization of matter and/or energy into "one and one." We symbolize the neutrino and/or antineutrino as: (*), seeing these particles as a union of positive and negative energy which cannot be put asunder.

The union of the positive and negative energy in the neutrino and/or the antineutrino may be likened to the Yin-Yang symbol:

But in our view the symbol must be altered to show the "black" or positive element to be a *trace more* than the "white" or negative element, because in its "manyness," we believe that *positive energy* is constituted of *more* of the *one* energy than negative energy possesses. Or, we might say, *exactly equal* amounts of the *one* energy would not constitute *opposites*.

Our concept rests on simple mathematical principles: a negative number divided by a negative number and/or a positive number divided by a positive number produces a positive number; *odd* numbers versus *even* numbers give rise to *opposite kinds* of numbers, but all numbers are alike in that they are divisible into *ones*; opposite kinds of numbers cannot be composed of an *equal* number of *ones*. As our concept is explained, application of these principles to the expression of energy will become evident. Here, we say that we believe neutral energy is composed of opposite types of energy, i.e., positive and negative, and that opposite types of energy cannot be composed of an equal amount of the *one* energy.

We believe positive energy involves *three* aspects of the *one* energy, and negative energy involves *two* aspects of the *one* energy. We assign to both the neutrino and the antineutrino three "bits" of positive energy and two "bits" of negative energy, so that in our view there is no absolutely neutral energy in the sense of a union of *exactly equal amounts of opposite value*. Neutral energy is thus asymmetrical, and the neutrinos are as "neutral" as it is possible for the *one* energy to be. They are also the least expression of the *one* energy in comprehensible terms, an indissoluble union of its opposite aspects.

We say the neutrinos have "bits" of positive and negative energy because we believe that they have less than a full measure of either type energy, a *trace only* of each type, and this trace is too diminished to be active and/or expressible and/or comprehensible in terms of positive and negative energy as such, so that only in the *union* of these "bits" is the energy comprehensible in terms of a particle. In our view, the neutrinos cannot be destroyed, and they do not disintegrate. But they can "contract" or "lapse" to form a degree of potential energy. This potential is too small to measure as mass in the ordinary sense of the word, so that the lapsed neutrinos must be thought of as a degree of incipient mass, a hypothetical particle, or as "virtual energy."

We see such "virtual energy" as indistinguishable from space, a space property; it is the creative potential *in* what might be called the sub-subaether; but *it is not itself space*. We call the lapsed neutrinos not a *measure of* but nevertheless a *degree of* potential energy, which we symbolize as: (°), in order to distinguish between this state and the neutrinos in action, which we symbolize as: (*). Because the neutrinos have a trace more of positive energy and like values repel, each degree of potential energy (°) repels each other degree (°) sufficiently to maintain itself as a discrete entity in the absence of stress. We believe space is permeated, but not necessarily at any or all points saturated, with these hypothetical particles.

In our view, as either a neutrino or an antineutrino lapses, it lapses into one degree (°) or the *same degree* of potential energy. Hereby, symmetry and the *unity of one* are regained: i.e., each of the fundamental units lapses into the same degree (°) of potential energy, which in turn can lend itself to the expression of either neutrino or antineutrino, so that this degree (°) is "ambidextrous."

We liken the neutrino and antineutrino to nature's smallest pair of *hands.* The corresponding antiparticles of the smallest particles may be likened to reversing the direction of one's thumb as he turns his left hand so that the palm faces upward; but this does not make of his left hand a right hand; and so it would be with the corresponding antiparticle of the right-handed particle. Therefore, there are two kinds of neutro-antineutrino pairs.[188] In our view, each of the neutrinos may *act* as its own antiparticle: i.e., reverse its *expression* and/or its "countenance," but this does not alter its *constitution*; and this principle applies to all antiparticles, as will be discussed in more detail later on.

Thus, our concept of the two kinds of neutro-antineutrino pairs comes to rest in a trinity principle that allows us to present the neutrino, the antineutrino, and the degree (°) of potential energy that each lapses into as three aspects of the *one* fundamental building block in nature. Just as the left hand does not readily perform the functions the right hand performs, and vice versa, so the two kinds of neutrinos give rise to different reactions. In our view, the neutrinos are primordial. They *were* formed in a past reorganization of the *one* energy, and they cannot now be formed. They may be emitted in decay processes or in stress reactions, but they are not thereby "produced": i.e., they form the particles and/or values that react.

To "create" opposite forces and/or values, i.e., "real" positive and negative energy *expressed as such*, we assign three degrees (°) of potential energy to a positive value (+), and two degrees (°) of potential energy to a negative value (−). We believe that reactions of the neutrinos form these values, but the reactions take place only as degrees (°) of "virtual energy" react in response to stress to form them.

Because the neutrino and antineutrino are opposites in expression and equals in being, two of the values (°) can go into action (*) and combine to form a "line of force," or a negative value (−); whereas at rest (°) the aspect of like *being* comes into play and the degrees (°) of potential energy repel sufficiently to maintain their discreteness. Just as, mathematically, a negative number divided by a negative number produces a positive number ($-/- = +$), so in our view as four neutrino-values react to form a double negative (− −), this energy "commands" the

reaction of *three* degrees (°) of potential energy to form a positive value
(+). We believe that in this transaction two neutrinos exchange values,
their "bits" of energy forming a positive or "vertical" force and also a
negative or "horizontal" force, the two opposing forces serving to enfold
the third neutrino value, which is a degree (°) of potential energy. Thus,
the positive value (+) is seen as "being-in-action." But its *being*, or the
degree (°) of potential energy, cannot be calculated as mass or as potential energy in the technical sense of the word.

In our concept, a *single and lone* positive value (+) represents the
photon, which is its own antiparticle. The photon, a measure of light
which is at the root of creation, will not express *itself* in "anti" terms.
Only as it disappears does it express in terms of "anti-positive-being."
Thus, we see light as a single measure of positive *value* versus positive
charge, and as the root of visible versus invisible energy. The photon
(+) does not *communicate* itself as a positive particle because, unlike
positive charge (+ — +), it is *not a redundant expression of positive
value*. Although *complex in being*, the photon (+) constitutes *a singular force*.

The "event" of the photon, as three degrees (°) of "virtual energy"
react to form it, cannot be calculated: i.e., a calculable event or mass
must involve a minimum of five degrees (°) of energy; and for five
degrees (°) of energy to be represented, a single positive and a single
negative value must join: (+ — = o). Thus, we say that the neutrino
transactions "happen" at the speed of light, in the *now* which is "past"
before it can be grasped, so that light (+) occurs and moves from the
"now-past" to the always "now-here" future, pointing time's arrow from
past to future. In our view, the "event" of light "happens" at a threshold
in space below that which we can experience before we can observe it.
And so it is as the photon disappears, in our view cascading into three
degrees (°) of energy indistinguishable from space, so that it is "now-
gone."

As space becomes saturated with potential energy (°), "crowding"
overcomes the *minimum repelling force* which exists only between hypothetical particles (°), so that they fuse, two by two, to create the double
negative situation (— —) through which, in turn, an electron is created:
i.e., (— —) becomes (— + —). Stress may cause an electron to emit
its photon (+), but as it does so the double negative situation (— —)
is posed, and this commands the reaction wherein three degrees (°) of
potential energy combine to provide a positive value (+). Thus, the
basic negative charge is never without a positive value: if it emits its
photon, another photon "takes place."

The two degrees (°) of energy that in our view fuse to give rise to a single negative value (—) create a measure of magnetic force, not a "visible" particle or a particle as such: i.e., we see a "net" negative value (—) in an aggregate of values, or negative values in a one-to-one ratio with positive values, or negative values in a grouping that does *not* possess a 50 per cent redundancy of negative value, to constitute magnetic force. The 50 per cent redundancy of negative value in the electron's arrangement provides for its measure as one unit of negative *charge*. A single measure of negative energy does not communicate itself as negative in the ordinary sense, because it is *not* a negative redundancy. Although less complex in being than a positive value, we see a single negative value as a force that can express in dual terms.

This is to say, we believe a single negative value (—) can be its own "opposite," whereas a positive value (+) must always be "itself-in-action" until it disappears. We believe the single negative value (—) may express in negative terms, which we symbolize as horizontally, or it may express in positive terms, which we symbolize as vertically, since we must "pin our values to the board" in order to examine them. *At the minimum*, we see "sameness" to be represented by the horizontal line or force, and "otherness" to be represented by the vertical line or force. Thus, the "horizontal" or "sameness" repels the "horizontal," and the "vertical" or "otherness" repels the "vertical," but "sameness" and "otherness" are attracted to each other and both are expressed in the positive value (+) which also states itself as whole: i.e., incorporates a degree (°) of potential mass.

The ability of negative values to be their own opposites gives to the magnetic force or field opposite ends, or poles. The ability of these values to be their own opposites allows two of them to behave also in neutral terms as one assumes the positive stance and the other the negative stance. Their ability to express as negative, positive, or neutral force allows them to alter the "complexion" of an aggregate of energy that is neutral in value count: i.e., composed of an equal number of positive and negative values. Thus, how such a mass expresses itself depends on the arrangement and expression of these values. The single negative value (—), then, must be seen as a dual force capable of giving rise to a trinity of expressions.

Because conditions and requirements to produce positive and negative values vary, and because there are two types of neutrino reactions as well as two kinds of neutrinos, paradoxical reactions arise. Neutrinos released when a charged pion decays can produce muons but no electrons, but neutrinos released when a neutron decays can produce electrons. In our view, it requires more energy to form the positive value (+), which is in itself more, than it takes to form the negative value (−). A muon, if it is composed of no more than its disintegration products (an electron, neutrino, and antineutrino), is an electron which in our terms has another single negative value adhering until the negative charge is released as the third negative value in the particle decays into a neutrino and antineutrino. In value count, we see a muon as $\left(-\mp-\right)$, but we believe these values are expressed as (− o −). A muon might arise as *two* degrees (°) of potential energy react to form a negative value that adheres to an electron already present. An electron might be formed as *four* degrees (°) of potential energy react to form two negative values (− −) which "command" a positive value (+). On the other hand, if one "started from scratch" to form of the "virtual energy" in space a muon and an electron, *nine* degrees (°) of potential energy would be required for a muon versus seven degrees (°) for an electron. We believe also that different kinds of stress reactions in decay processes are involved in the paradoxes that confront physicists, but these must be discussed later. Next, we would present another principle basic to our concept.

The muon as we represent it (− o −) expresses a ratio of $2(-)/1(o)$. But in single value count it expresses a ratio of $3(-)/1(+)$. The ratio of $2(-)/1(o)$ gives it a 50 per cent redundancy of negative value. The ratio of $3(-)/1(+)$, however, gives it *more* than a 50 per cent redundancy of negative value. The muon is not a "lone" double negative in space that would command a positive value, i.e., a positive value is associated; it represents a quasi-situation that can and cannot exist: it is unstable. In our view, the two ratios of any particle, value versus value, and value versus neutral potential, play a determining role in the stability of the aggregate. A particle expressing *more* than a 50 per cent redundancy of any aspect of energy (positive, negative, or neutral) in terms of either of its ratios is unstable and/or it commands a reaction of some sort that serves to correct the situation. Thus, the muon decays.

Seen as (− o −), the muon would be strongly attracted to a positive charge (+ − +) because it is minus the *expressed* positive value in the electron (− + −) that would be repelled by the positive values in the positive charge. An electron is an "either, or" particle, which may express in terms of negative charge (− + −) or in terms of a slightly negative mass potential (− o): i.e., the difference between a muon and an electron is compounded.

In our view, a change in the ratio of energy values, positive versus negative, greatly alters the properties of a bundle of energy. A ratio of $2(-)/1(+)$ differs greatly from a ratio of $3(-)/1(+)$, but it differs more from a ratio of $1(-)/1(+)$, for this ratio would not, in our view, exist of itself alone as a particle. When no redundancy of any sort is present, nothing in terms of mass or charge would be *communicated*. The least bundle of energy communicable as *a particle with mass* or potential energy (o) is the electron $(- + -)$ or $(- \text{ o})$. In our view, the union of a single negative value $(-)$ and a single positive value $(+)$, represented by (o), or *one measure* of potential energy, would dissolve into its neutrino potential because the neutrino is the *one* measure, the *single* union, of positive and negative energy, the only indissoluble union of neutral energy that exists as a stable particle. Or, we might say, *at the minimum*, matter may be viewed in terms of positive-being $(+)$ and antimatter in terms of negative-being $(-)$, and when matter and antimatter come together, annihilation into neutrino-value ensues.

A ratio of $2(+)/1(-)$ would differ from a single positive value $(+)$ as much as a unit of positive electrical *charge* differs from a photon. In value count, the photon $(+)$ is much less than a unit of positive electrical charge $(+ - +)$, but the spin of a photon (every photon spins like a top) is twice as great as the spin of a proton or an electron. Because the photon is a moving particle it has momentum, so that it can give any particle that it hits a push. We believe that it takes a degree (°) of potential energy for a particle to possess momentum or to push another degree (°) of potential energy, be it the degree (°) of potential mass in the positive value $(+)$ of the electron, or the electron's measure of mass, seen as (o), or an atom's mass, which must be seen as macroscopic in comparison to the "submicroscopic" mass of the photon.

This brings us to another concept basic to our hypothesis. We believe that every atom in ground state is *redundant* only in terms of *neutral value*. Thus, in ground state it *communicates itself as a neutral mass*. However, in terms of its *being* or value count, it possesses *one more positive value than negative value*; and it is the small repelling force of this positive value versus the positive value of another atom that allows each atom to express itself as a discrete entity. We believe that it is the force of a single positive value $(+)$ repelling a single positive value $(+)$ that causes matter to reflect, emit, or repel light and allows photons to maintain themselves as discrete entities. (Light absorption will be discussed in a later section.)

We say that when all the opposite values are counted, any atom will have one only *net* positive value (+), which allows it to be "one of a kind," gives it *positive-being* and a measure of constant or unifying expression.

Because an atom can possess but one net positive value (+) in its normal state, in any transaction involving the *fusion of two atoms* to give rise to an isotope of higher atomic number, a positive value, or photon (+), will be emitted as gamma ray. But in any transaction where two different elements result, a net positive value (+) is not emitted because each resulting atom must have a net positive value (+) in order to be identified as "one of a kind." To use the carbon cycle, for example, carbon $_6C^{12}$ reacts with hydrogen $_1H^1$ to produce nitrogen $_7N^{13}$ and in the process a gamma ray is emitted. But at the end of the cycle when nitrogen $_7N^{15}$ reacts with hydrogen $_1H^1$ to produce carbon $_6C^{12}$ and helium $_2He^4$, the positive value (+) or gamma ray is not emitted: each atom winds up with its identifying one net positive value (+).

Today, much is said of antimatter. We believe that if an atom were constructed entirely of antiparticles, the one net positive value (+), which we see to be at the heart of the atom, would remain itself in being because it is its own antiparticle. Thus, antiatoms would repel each other sufficiently to maintain their identity. But atom and antiatom would destroy each other, because the greater attraction of opposites posed by the remaining particles in atom and antiatom would overcome the repelling force of the net positive value (+) in the atom versus the net positive value (+) in the antiatom.

We believe that *within* the atom a particle can go into antiparticle reaction in response to stress, and that the atom's behavior under certain circumstances is attributable to such inner antiparticle expression. We also believe that when stress ceases, the antiexpression ceases and the particles return to normal expression. In our view, positive action prompts positive response, and then negative reaction as stress levels are reached. Negative action prompts negative response, and then positive reaction as stress levels are reached. Both reactions, and those that follow, tend to "neutralize" and/or "equate" the situation by means of changes in expression and/or arrangement. How a particle or value reacts depends on how it is situated, as well as on the type, degree, and duration of stress, and on the minimum reaction it can make to form one or more *stable* particles and/or isotopes.

In our view, energy is *self-conserving*. Unstable particles are aggregates of energy values that arise only in response to stress as they form temporary "holdings," which have or develop quasi-redundancies, and thus they decay. We believe that in the decay process, "queer" particles are formed when in response to stress a positive value disappears by "turning negative," thereby changing the ratio and redundancy of an aggregrate of values: i.e., to become its antiparticle, a photon as such must disappear. Such "anti" expression occurs at a "submicroscopic" level. We explain by saying that a photon in space may simply disappear as it cascades into three degrees (°) of potential energy; but a positive value *bound in a mass* may have its enfolded degree (°) of potential energy "knocked out" of the positive arrangement. As this happens, we see the formation of a "queer" particle, which exists only as a process in the decay of stress-particles: i.e., the degree (°) of potential energy "knocked out" of the positive value (+) forms of this value an "anti" expression of energy that is slightly *more negative* than a single negative value, because all the neutrino-value of a positive value expresses momentarily along "horizontal" or negative lines. We symbolize this "queer" particle as: ($-\circ$), and call it q-1.

We believe that single negative values also react by going into "anti" expression. Because a single negative value can act either as a positive force or as a negative force, in order to act *oppositely* and/or to go into "anti" expression by acting as neither, a negative value must disintegrate into its neutrino value. Or, two negative values, one acting positively, may *fuse* to destroy themselves as negative energy, which in our view gives rise to another "queer" particle that we believe exists also only as a process in the decay of stress-particles. We call this "queer" particle q-2, and symbolize it as: ($\underline{|}$), to distinguish between this reaction and the ability of two negative values to act as opposites to each other in expression, one assuming the vertical stance, which we symbolize as: ($-|$).

The q-1 particle is equivalent to three degrees (°) of potential energy; q-2 is equivalent to four degrees (°) of potential energy; together, the particles are equivalent to the neutrino value of an electron ($- + -$). A positive value in a positive charge ($+ - +$) reacting to form a q-1 particle would give rise to still another "queer" particle in the lepton class: ($-\circ + -$). We do not believe the "queer" particles can be "discovered," because alone they cannot exist as such; the "anti" expression that gives rise to them takes place *within* an aggregate of energy.

When we say that a single positive value and/or a positive value in a positive charge reacts to stress to produce a "queer" particle in the lepton class, we do not intend to imply that a *proton* can thereby disintegrate into leptons. As said before, the positive charge is associated with a proton, but is not itself the proton. In our view, "queer" particles form only within unstable stress-particles and are a part of their decay process. The proton is a stable particle. Proton reactions, and the meaning of conservation of baryons, will be discussed in Section III.

In still another aspect of the formation of unstable particles, we believe they arise as the neutral energy values, i.e., $(+ -)$ combinations, react to stress by going into what we call "secondary formation" to become stronger "holding forces" that bind abnormal aggregates of particles and/or values into temporary holdings; or, in order to become their *opposite* in expression, measures of neutral energy give rise to negative or to positive force as the single negative values in the combinations act either to enhance the negative aspect of their positive partners, which we symbolize as: $\left(\overline{+}\right)$, or as the negative values act to enhance the positive aspect of a positive value, which we symbolize as: $(+ \mid)$, or as the negative values in a large group do both. The antiparticle of a stress-particle wherein aggregates of neutral values are acting to express negative and positive force, even as their equal number allows the particle as a whole to express itself as neutral, would be an opposite arrangement of it, or the switch right-to-left of a left-to-right arrangement, as though one mirror reflected the following arrangement of values:

$$\left(\overline{+} + \mid \overline{+} + \mid\right), \left(\mid + \overline{+} \mid + \overline{+}\right).$$

Because we see the single negative value $(-)$ as capable of enhancing the negative energy in the positive value, we believe a proton can act as its opposite in expression when its positive charge goes into anti-positive-charge reaction, which we symbolize as $\left(+\overline{}+\right)$. And because a single negative value $(-)$ can enhance the positive energy in a positive value, we believe an electron can act as its opposite in expression, so that we symbolize the positron as: $(\mid + \mid)$, a positive *expression* of energy.

In summary, we would say that expression of charge, or the translation from $(o +)$ to $(+ - +)$ and from $(- o)$ to $(- + -)$, as well as translation to antiparticle expression are stress reactions that tend to cease as stress ceases. Extreme stress produces unstable particles, because positive energy responds by turning negative; negative energy responds by turning neutral; neutral energy responds by turning first negative and then positive, or vice versa, and/or neutral energy goes into "secondary formation"; and in one way or another the ratio and redundancies of the particles are altered to give rise to quasi-redundancies wherein in being the aggregate expresses too much negative and/or neutral energy to allow it to be stable. The "queer" particles form and since these cannot exist in terms of mass, they disintegrate, causing the particles to disintegrate.

All the values involved in an atom may be used to form stress-particles; and many combinations or formations are possible. The same number of positive and negative values may form particles that express themselves differently and disintegrate into different particles. For example, a group of two single positive and two single negative values would communicate neutrality as negative values go into secondary formation: $(\mp \mid +)$, and the aggregate could disintegrate into two photons as the negative values formed a q-2 particle which would lapse into the field and there disintegrate into four degrees (°) of "virtual energy." The same number of values might express as a positively charged particle if one single negative value acted to enhance the positive value of the group: $(+ \mid - +)$. This arrangement might disintegrate into a positive muon and a neutrino as one of the positive values "turns negative" to form a q-1 particle $(-\circ)$, which gives the aggregate the "makings" of a positive muon when the neutrino (*) is emitted. In a larger aggregate of energy, such as we believe a neutron to be, still other stress reactions, to be discussed in a later section, would occur.

Here, we would say that we believe stress-particles lose mass in the decay processes, because they lose positive value in the formation of "queer" particles as positive value "turns negative," and they lose negative value as it "turns neutral" and disintegrates into "virtual energy," i.e., the hypothetical particles (°). The stress-particles decay because quasi-redundancies arise as the "queer" particles arise. In complex situations, more than one decay process may be required, but energy tends to disintegrate as quickly and easily as possible into stable particles, the last and least of these being the neutrinos in which are established the three basic patterns in nature.

Since matter has its being in space and operates upon or within field forces, we cannot discuss further the structure of elementary particles and the nucleus of the atom until we have presented our concept of space and the field forces within it, i.e., our "supramacroscopic" view. But first, we would summarize by saying that we believe the *one* energy is self-limiting in self-division or possible division, the neutrinos being inpenetrable and indivisible; energy operates within the limit of a law, to be discussed in more detail later, which, when transgressed, effects a change in arrangement and in what is communicated; and the creative potential is now vested in the least of it, the lapsed neutrinos (°), which react in asymmetrical fashion to produce positive and negative value when certain conditions are met.

II

The *one* energy that *was*, acted upon itself. Why and how is beyond comprehension. But we attempt to "read the result" in terms of the opposites we see around us and the asymmetry versus symmetry in the universe and its working. Our concept does not rest upon any particular cosmological theory; it could be related to any of the current concepts; but our view would alter, at least in part, the "outlook" for the future that any of the theories offer. We do not attempt to present a complete hypothesis of the creation and evolution of the universe; but since we are concerned with the behavior of matter in space, we must present our concept of the constitution of space and what it enfolds.

We believe that the division of the whole energy that *was*, which we symbolize as zero (0), *whole*, and which we see to have been twice divided, symbolized as (0/0/0), was accomplished in a manner that prohibits a return to the erstwhile whole, or evolution into meaningless being.‡

In our view, the division of the *one* energy gave rise to space, and to Prime Negative and Prime Positive energy, which, in its division, gives rise to asymmetrical measures or ratios of each type energy. We see the division of the whole in asymmetrical terms, and thus the product of (0/0/0) is symbolized as: (⊕/—o/+∘), to indicate that three different structures of energy now constitute the universe. The first of these is the more: it is space itself in its *indestructible* and therefore *positive being*. The second structure constitutes the matrix of space-energy that gives rise to the fields and field forces: i.e., to energy that is unapparent until it reveals itself when matter acts upon it or reacts with it; thus, it is *negative* in its *unapparent being*; and there is more of this Prime Negative energy than there is of the third type. We see the third structure as matter, positive in its being because each atom of it possesses one net positive value (+), and neutrinos are a "bit" positive.

We say there is infinitely more space than space-energy; infinitely more space-energy than matter; infinitely more matter in creation than man can comprehend. For, in our view, infinite means, simply: more than can be measured or used through the course of any event, or through the course of all events, either physically or mathematically, which is to say, by Homo sapiens' consciousness.

‡ Please note that the symbol for zero (0) is used to designate a whole measure of primordial energy, which is not to be confused with a measure or unit of expressed neutral energy that is designated by the smaller symbol (o). [Ed.]

Although the three structures of energy are different in their constitution, they are constituted of the same "stuff," and each of them is asymmetrical in its constitution, in that it has more of the positive, less of the negative, or vice versa. But the difference is only one measure, so that each structure is *predominantly neutral* and *communicates neutrality*. The one measure differentiating between them is reconciled as the one structure operates against the other.

We consider first Prime Negative energy, which may be thought of as original minus-one: -1. In our view, the negative sign represents a *prime* measure of negative value, which we designate as $q(-)$ to differentiate between it and the single values arising from its fission, or self-division, to produce a negatively charged particle: i.e., the prime negative value produces an equal $(-)$ and opposite $(+)$ value, even as it *conserves itself* $(-)$ *in diminished being*. Thus, $q(-)$ reacts to produce: $(-+-)$, or three single values. This charge must exist in relationship to, or with, a *prime* measure of the *whole*, or *one*, neutral and natural. Thus, the one-energy associated with the prime negative value $q(-)$ may be symbolized as: (0). In our view, this whole measure (0) is equivalent to more than a negative and a positive charge: as it undergoes self-division to produce the opposite charges that give rise to neutral expression, it must also *conserve itself* in diminished being. Thus, it produces values *equivalent to* a positive charge $(+-+)$, a negative charge $(-+-)$, and *one neutral measure* $(+-)$, to provide an aggregate of four single positive values and four single negative values. We see the whole energy (0) to be the measure of parent energy necessary to produce a neutron. Prime Negative energy thus contains a prime negative value, $q(-)$, and a neutron-equivalence, (0), and may be written $[q(-)(0)]$. We call the Prime Negative bundle: Q. In fission, the Q bundle may be seen as: $[(-+-)(+-+-+-+-)]$. It may also be seen as: $[(-\ 0)(+\ 0)(0)(-\ 0)]$, or a ratio of: $4(0)/2(-)/1(+)$, giving it a 50 per cent redundancy of neutral value, which it communicates, although in single value count it possesses a net single negative value. Any number of Q bundles might adhere through the attraction of opposite values, but this would not pose a double negative in space: for example, two measures of Q energy would constitute only a doubling of the ratio, and *the neutral redundancy which determines the situation* would persist.

We turn now to the ratio of values in a bundle of Prime Positive energy, which may be thought of as original plus-one: $+1$. In our view, the positive sign may be seen as a *prime* measure of positive energy, which we designate as $p(+)$. Following the pattern of self-conservation and the production of an equal and an opposite value, in fission p(+) produces two single positive values and one single negative value to give rise to positive charge: (+ — +). In our view, the prime measure of positive energy also exists in association with a prime measure of neutral energy (0), i.e., a neutron-equivalence, and thus Prime Positive energy may be written: [p(+) (0)]. We call this Prime Positive bundle: P. In fission, it may be seen as: [(+ — +) (— + — + — + — +)], or it may be seen as: [(+ o) (— o) (o) (+ o)], giving it a ratio of: 4(o)/2(+)/1(—), which constitutes a 50 per cent redundancy of neutral value, which it communicates, although in single value count it possesses a net positive value. Any number of P bundles adhering through the attraction of their opposite values would do no more than increase the ratio, the neutral redundancy remaining.

We discuss next the structure of space. Because there is more Q energy than P energy in expression, we see the type energy "spent" to create space to be a P SUM, made forever *inactive* or *unavailable* in order to create the "being" in which Q energy and the remaining P energy might be made available, manifest, and operable. This "spent" P SUM must be seen as *positive energy minus the possibility of exhibiting the properties associated with any type energy*: it is not manifest, nor is it observable as a field force. It neither acts nor reacts to the expression of Q or P energy, but is a quality unto itself only, a *transparent and unapparent* effect. It is energy so diminished through self-division that it is now beyond destruction, because there is nothing "small" enough to penetrate its "tissue" and nothing "large" enough to disturb its infinite being, which both penetrates and enfolds all things. Its quality is beyond comprehension, its quantity beyond measure, so that its net positive value (+) constitutes *positive being* and nothing else: space exists.

We believe that all the energy associated with the P SUM reduced itself to single values, and all the single values reduced themselves to their neutrino value; and then, in a once-only act in the "history of creation," the neutrinos underwent "five-point" fission, which we symbolize as: $\left(\cdot \vdots \cdot \right)$, to produce the "fabric" of space. We see this "tissue" as *plus value minus force*, a transparency that cannot be experienced, a "mesh" that cannot be "undone," but through and upon which manifest energy (matter) and unapparent energy (field force) act and react, giving rise to change and changing arrangements within it.

Because a measure of P energy constitutes a neutral redundancy, albeit each measure possesses a net single positive value (+), space *communi-*

cates itself in neutral terms; but its energy is so diminished that it does not act as a neutral force, posing the attraction of a neutral force. Because, in *being*, a measure of P energy possesses a net single positive value (+), in supramacroscopic terms, or as a *whole*, and in submicroscopic terms, or in one full measure of it, we see space as positive, its net positive value as the only *force constant*: i.e., space is unchanging. Thus, we symbolize one full measure of space as: [F+].

We see Q energy as a force that is constantly active, but not as a force constant, because Q energy acts and reacts in response to matter's changing arrangement and/or expression; whereas space is a force constant because it neither acts upon nor reacts to that which happens within it. Prime Negative energy communicates neutrality because it is constituted of a redundancy of neutral value, albeit the Q bundle has a net single negative value (−). We believe this energy expresses itself in neutral terms and is not self-repelling, because any two negative values in an aggregate of energy expressing a neutral redundancy may "adhere" as one acts positively and the other negatively; or, we might say, negative energy tends to "turn neutral" in response to stress. Thus, we believe that as Prime Negative energy moves through space it forms a "line of force" neutral in expression, which shares a negative effect associated with straight-line motion: it cannot complete its action. But we believe that a *positive redundancy* gives rise to a break in the flow of Q energy as its net negative value responds to the attraction of redundant positive value, causing the entire measure of Q energy to react with the positive ion. This reaction will be discussed in a later section.

We do not see Prime Positive energy in terms of matter as we know matter today. We see it as the Primordial Positive energy from which matter was created, so that Prime Positive energy as such no longer exists: matter exists in its stead. Thus, when we speak of matter we speak of P energy, and vice versa. In a later section we discuss the conversion of P energy to hydrogen. Here, we would say that in our view whereas Prime Positive energy as such no longer exists, Prime Negative energy still exists as a Prime force at large and as fields and field forces in space.

If the *one* energy had divided itself equally into positive and negative energy and divided its positive energy asymmetrically to express of it space for the most part, matter for the rest, there would be more Q energy than space. Therefore, we see the original division as asymmetrical: more positive than negative energy "created" in the beginning. In our view, the universe had its beginning in a chain reaction as the *one* energy acted upon itself to create space, Prime Negative energy, and

Prime Positive energy. This entailed the complete and everlasting disorganization of that which was; chaos reigned as reorganization, or an operation we sense as *time*, began to take place; the principles involved in the reorganization have been the same since its "beginning."

In this "beginning," we believe that clouds of P energy were left in the deeps of space and infinitely more Q energy was left throughout space. In that "instant" the system was set in motion by the reaction of Q energy attracted to the concentration of positive value that P energy posed in space, and by the reaction of the masses of P energy to each other. To explain the reaction of P energy to P energy we must return to our concept of forces operative in the universe.

Just as the singular force of light (+) becomes a complex force, or *charge*, when a positive redundancy is expressed, and the magnetic force of negative values (−) changes to *charge* when a negative redundancy is expressed, so when a *neutral redundancy* is involved (as is the case with an atom), it gives rise to a complex force: i.e., the force of gravity.

Because an atom is a neutral redundancy, bodies of matter operate under the law of gravity, and from what might be called the outward point of view, this is the predominating force. Only from a supramacroscopic point of view, when the universe as a whole is considered, and from a submicroscopic view, when the internal working of a particle is considered, does the singular force come into play. From a supramacroscopic view, bodies of matter are *sums* of positive and neutral energy that are both attracted to each other because they are subject to the law of gravity, and are repelled by each other because they are subject to the singular law arising from their net positive being, the positive repelling the positive.

Thus, in the beginning, clouds of P energy both drew together and moved apart, everywhere repelled by the positive nature of space, and thus, paradoxically, supported by it, even as the repelling force of space allowed the force of gravity (or the attraction of opposite values that constitute neutral energy) to come into play: i.e., matter communicates its neutral redundancy until upon immediate contact its positive being asserts itself. Thus, in the chaotic beginning of universal reorganization, masses of P energy that were "too close together" in relation to the sums of P energy they express "flew apart," even as masses of P energy "widely separated" drew together, the force of gravity coming into play.

And even as this was happening, Q energy was drawn to masses of P energy; and Q energy is attracted to bodies in space today, because the sum of net positive being poses a force of positive attraction. At "immediate range," the net positive value of one atom, versus its neutral energy, which serves to bind the mass, acts against the net positive value of another atom sufficiently only to allow the two atoms to maintain themselves as discrete entities unless some force of attraction bonds them; and so it is with celestial bodies: i.e., the force of gravity predominates until the bodies move within what might be called "immediate range" and the force of matter's positive being asserts itself. (Collisions of masses in space will be discussed in Section IV.) But the sum of the atoms that make up a body in space pose a singular sum of positive attraction for Q energy, even as they pose a singular sum of repulsion in relation to each other. Or, we might say, in relation to Q energy, the singular positive being of the atom takes precedence over the communication of its neutral redundancy; whereas in relation to another body, communication of neutrality takes precedence over the force of its net positive being. Or, we might say, Q energy is supramacroscopic in its relation to P energy, and thus, the singular force of net positive value predominates, whereas no one body of matter is other than macroscopic or microscopic in relation to another body in their outward relationship, so that classical law or complex forces predominate in the relationship between mass and mass.

Thus, in the beginning, Q energy was attracted to P energy. Neither space nor P energy (or matter) poses any resistance to Q energy in terms of what each communicates or in terms of being, for both space and matter are neutral and positive; but space is a repelling force insofar as matter is concerned. Therefore, Q energy flows through space toward matter, rather than vice versa.

We would say here that just as quantum action is basic and intrinsic, operating in conjunction with classical law, not invalidating it, so we believe the operation of the Q-force is basic and pervasive, operating in conjunction with classical law. Thus, the concept of momentum, for example, is not invalidated by the concept of the Q-force moving upon bodies in space and influencing their motion. This is to say, just as one may play billiards or swing a ball on a string, this motion and the input of energy giving rise to it occurring within the "larger" motion of the earth's revolving and traveling its orbit, so classical concepts describe the phenomena that occur within the phenomenon of the Q-force in action.

We believe that in the beginning of the reorganization of the universe, in order for Q energy to move toward the clusters of P energy, the Q-force must react to form its own ground, field, or path. That is, we believe neither P nor Q energy can act directly upon the gossamer "tissue" of space: both must operate upon a field, and matter is also involved with field forces. We cannot do more than touch upon the interpenetrating fields of space, and field forces, for we limit ourselves to "spelling out" our concept in terms of positive and negative value, attempting to describe a complexity so differentiated and yet so meshed that all geometries are insufficient to describe it; so that in terms of what might be called "plane geometry of value" we can give but a superficial view of what exists in depth. Thus, we will speak only of the field of space and the field forces in general terms.

We liken a measure of the general field to the simple division of a Q bundle into single negative and positive values, equivalent to its negative charge and the values in its prime neutral energy, symbolizing one measure of the general field of space as: $[F+(- + -)$ $(+ - + - + - + -)]$. The general field is thus neutral in value count and in expression. For every measure of Q energy that moved as a Prime Negative force at large, a measure of Q energy moved before it and acted to neutralize the being of a measure of space. This field remained, so that the unoccupied Q energy was attracted in the instant the space was neutralized to the next measure of space and to the nearest aggregate of P type energy.

As the Q energy reached the masses of P type energy, it reacted to form fields and field forces that penetrated, surrounded, and "trapped" the mass, determining its boundary. The Q and P bundles might adhere through the attraction of their opposite values, but this attraction would not be sufficient to produce fusion, which did not occur until the masses of P energy, penetrated by Q energy, were compressed by the more preponderant Q-force at large, causing both Prime bundles to react, giving rise to what we call Q/P fission-fusion to produce the hydrogen molecule. This reaction continued until ALL the P bundles were reduced to hydrogen.

As clouds of hydrogen were compressed by the Q energy into primitive stars, the hydrogen began to radiate its energy, and nuclear reactions gave rise to the formation of helium and a number of other elements. Then began the evolution of the stars, and of the elements created in and by second- and third-generation stars, as well as the evolution of the planets and other celestial bodies, so that the universe as we behold it began to take shape. Planetary, solar, and galactic systems evolved in which the masses maintain identity and discreteness even as they move according to their attraction and repulsion for each other; each body was set to revolving and is carried along in its orbit (i.e., its momentum is sustained) by the force of the flow of the mainstream of Q energy; the system as a whole is harmonious, the bodies within it symbiotic, many bodies influencing the course of any one body.

In stellar explosions, we believe as much matter as is in evidence, or more, was reduced to neutrinos which came to rest (°) in the general field. We do not believe they disperse in the vast expanses of empty space because the "trace" more of positive value they enfold causes space to be a repelling force insofar as they are concerned, and thus they move in the neutral general field; so that all matter is involved with or entrusted to the more preponderant Q-type energy, which moves upon its own path, acting upon celestial masses in diverse ways, which are determined by the body itself: i.e., how it is constituted, and its properties, such as density, composition of its atmosphere, surface and interior temperature, size, etc.

As Q energy comes upon a body, having been drawn to it because the mass is attractive in long-range terms, the situation becomes paradoxical: although the *being* of an atom, for example, is net positive in value, and as a whole it communicates neutrality because it is a neutral redundancy, in its *immediate expression* the atom is negative, for matter cloaks its positive being in its electron cloud. In order to act on the mass, Q energy must first act to neutralize the electron cloud by "reversing" a negative value in a measure of the Q-force: i.e., the net negative value in a Q measure reacts to express in positive terms so that this measure becomes neutral in relation to the electron; but it also "immediately" becomes opposite to, or "positive," in relation to the net negative value of the next measure of Q energy, causing the two measures to form a field or force that is neutral in expression; so that the Q energy is then neither repelled by the electron cloud nor attracted to the atom's net positive value. Nor is the atom attracted to the Q energy, the attractive force of neutral energy becoming a force of repulsion in "immediate terms.‡ Thus, Q energy neutralizes itself; it does not neutralize matter, which remains positive in relation to space, and to other positive bodies, and to the Q-force at large. Thus, the negative nature of Q energy is virtually obscured, becoming evident only in certain transactions with matter, to be discussed later; and matter acts as a catalyst that causes Prime Negative energy to react to form the fields and forces in space that "trap" and define the mass even as they brake or diversify the effect of the Q-force moving upon it.

Each body in space constitutes a sum of positive value that determines

‡ See p. 313 for an explanation of the attractive force of neutral energy becoming a force of repulsion in "immediate" terms. [Ed.]

the force of attraction it poses for Q energy. As the Q-force comes upon this planet, for example, it is coming upon a body enveloped in a magnetic field, formed by Q energy, within which the atmosphere is "trapped," so that the mass and its atmosphere are as a body of varying density. As the Q-force envelops the body, it acts as a force to keep it revolving, even as the oncoming flow acts as a force to move the body along its orbit and/or to allow it to sustain its momentum. Although the Q energy penetrates the enveloping field, for the most part the Q energy flows around the mass. By the same token, the *real* force of Q energy at large is never experienced by any one body in space: i.e., the *mainstream* of Q energy flows around the galaxy, acting on it as though it were one body. Thus, the "actual speed" of the Q flow cannot be determined. Its speed in relation to any one body is the speed at which that body travels through space; its speed is sustained but not *initiated* by the Q-force.

The Q-force flowing upon the general field possesses "substance" only indirectly. For example, the stream of plasma from the sun that impinges upon the magnetosphere of the earth travels the Q-path; the plasma itself is effectively neutral, any macroscopic volume of it having an equal number of positive and negative charges; thus, the Q-force and the plasma are neutral in relation each to the other, the only reaction arising from the intermingling of the P and Q energy being the creation of a "small" magnetic field.

The action of the Q-force with regard to bodies such as the sun will be discussed later. Here, we say only that within the universe the Q-force acts upon each iota of matter in one way or another, even as each iota of matter acts upon the other, and space affects both energy and mass. The "thousand million" changing calculations of force versus force, of immediate versus long-term attraction and repulsion, of action in individual terms versus motion as a whole, of being versus expression, produce a comprehensive answer, which may be determined in any one of its many aspects by the mathematics and laws of physics and astronomy.

If one might view the whole scene today, we think the universe would appear to center around an unoccupied area of space, the *sum* of its positive value posing constant attraction to the Prime Negative force, even as the positive value in this space acts as a force of repulsion in relation to the galaxies of matter, which the Q-force shepherds in their orbits. Wherever in space that matter is, a concentration of positive value exists, so that the Q-force is "first" drawn in this direction, and in this sense its action is always a "digression" that prevents its return to the "central point" it seeks. We experience the unmitigated flow of the Prime Negative force as indirectly as we sense the motion of the earth, "feeling" its passing only in the sense of time's inexorable passing.

We believe the universe is still in the process of "becoming," because the reorganization is not as yet complete. What reorganization means, and universal "progress" in this direction, will be discussed later. Here, we would say that the concept of a "beginning" requires the introduction of time.

Time, the incomprehensible *event of itself,* is "something" of the working of that *one* energy which was *all,* self-conserved and penetrating every event. We relate certain aspects of time's working to the flow of the Prime Negative force at large; and we believe other aspects of its operation must be allowed for in terms of utilizing some measure of the *one* energy. Time's function as a whole and its meaning reaches into infinity: i.e., is beyond the grasp of consciousness, but we believe it is concerned in part with the dispersal of positive and negative energy into the creative potential, into neutrinos ($°$).

We represent time's toll of energy as the working of one negative value versus one positive value that gives rise to energy, which cannot exist of itself alone as a particle, i.e., $(- + = 0)$, and (0) disintegrates into five degrees ($°$) of potential energy. We see this working as opposite in being and action from the force of space: space is constantly inactive, time is constantly active; space cannot be "undone" or "redone"; time, in the sense of its being $(- + = 0)$, is constantly "undone" as the energy is dispersed into neutrino value, and it is constantly "redone" as the "event" of positive and negative energy occurs in space.

We see time's action as negative force regulating positive force, which we symbolize as minus-time working against plus-time and vice versa. Minus-time takes "three steps left" and "two steps right" to give rise to a "step left," or *now.* Plus-time takes "three steps right" and "two steps left" to give rise to a "step right," or *here.* Together, minus-time and plus-time gives rise to time-in-action *here now.* Time's *action* of expansion and contraction forever produces one more negative-*now,* one more positive-*here,* or one more event: $(- + = 0)$, wherein energy is dispersed into the equilibrium of indestructible degrees ($°$) of potential energy as the negative value $(-)$ acts on the positive value $(+)$ and both are reduced to their neutrino value.

In time, therefore, source heat disappears. That is, in our view, positive action gives rise to light and heat as positive values react to stress and/or the constant force of positive space $[F+]$. And negative action equating, counteracting, or dispersing positive action gives rise to cold. Thus, as a negative value stills, equates, or disperses a positive value, temperature decreases, and in *time* there is a flow from heat to cold to equilibrium. We believe time's working takes its tithe of every complete expression of energy, and that energy moves from positive to negative to neutral expression. But in the time-reaction that gives rise to the dispersal of positive and negative value into the five degrees (°) of potential energy, the creative potential in space is increased.

In our view, the indestructible neutrino (°) constitutes the "last division of energy." It is of the *past*, which cannot be "undone." The photon, or light, which can be "undone," is of the *future*, "always happening," and yet always "undone," because in the act of happening the future flows into the past. The neutrino, or past, and the photon, or future, both *act* at the unique speed of light, which will not "mix" with other speeds. They set the pace and keep the pace of *time*. As the photon "melts" into its neutrino potential, the future "melts" into the past; energy is "disorganized" and made unavailable at the time. But as three degrees (°) of potential energy react to form a photon, the past enters into the future; energy is reorganized, and source heat in what might be called microscopic terms is made available.

We believe that in time positive value is returned, and that stress counteracts this action by turning positive value negative in giving rise to what might be called "antitime" arrangement within a mass as the q-1 particle (— ∘) is formed when a positive value "turns negative," causing negative energy to arise within the mass. Or stress gives rise to the opposite of positive expression when a photon lapses into three degrees (°) of potential energy. In either case, as positive energy disappears, within the whole of the universe the ratio of negative to positive value increases. As negative value "turns neutral" in the formation of the q-2 particle (|) which disintegrates into the equilibrium of "virtual energy" (°), the ratio of negative to positive energy is lessened, but the ratio of energy in a state of equilibrium versus energy organized as matter is increased. Thus, time's arrow points always toward the disorganization of source-heat into equilibrium.

But in our view, time also gives rise to the stress that reorganizes the energy in equilibrium, i.e., the hypothetical particles (°), into negative and positive values, although in the vastness of the universe the point of overall "saturation" in terms of degrees (°) of potential energy cannot be computed. Every time "crowding" of the neutrinos (°) gives rise to the formation of negative values and a double negative (— —) arises, commanding a positive value, Q energy is restored and/or increased: i.e., an electron is formed.

In our view, *two* negative values arising to form a double negative within a Q bundle would give rise to pair-formation: i.e., as the double negative (— —) commands a positive value, the q-measure thus formed would act against the q-measure in the bundle, the one or the other going into positron reaction. We believe that if *one* negative value arose within a Q bundle, neither the q-2 particle nor a muon would form, because we see these as stress-particles that form only *within masses* reacting to stress. As one negative value arises in a measure of Q energy, this negative value in conjunction with the net negative value of the Q bundle poses a double negative, which commands a positive value that "takes place" *before* a muon or the q-2 particle could form. This reaction changes the Q ratio to $4(o)/3(—)/2(+)$; the force of the magnetic field might thereby be enhanced, and we believe the force of this field may also be enhanced as the values in a Q bundle go into "secondary formation."

Because reorganization of positive value takes place in response to the force of the double negative (— —) situation, giving rise to an electron and/or enhancing Q-type energy, the return of source heat is unapparent, incalculable, or uncommunicable in terms of P type energy or positive value. Q-type energy is reorganized, so that time's arrow is not reversed. We believe, however, that Q energy "organized" matter in the beginning, and that Q energy continues to organize it today. But before presenting our concept of the return of source energy in what might be called macroscopic terms, we must discuss the event of matter as we know matter today.

First, however, we would say: *purely singular forces* are "unlimited" as compared to complex forces. As opposed to the complex force of gravity, which arises from a *redundancy* of neutral energy, *one measure* of neutral energy, such as is involved in a positive charge $(+ — +)$, for example, is a "singular" force, although the one measure of neutral energy is not singular in being. The only purely singular *neutral* force is that of the neutrinos. The only purely singular *positive* force is that of the photon $(+)$. In our view, there is no purely singular *negative* force. Magnetic force arises from a complex arrangement of positive and negative values, and it expresses in dual terms, giving rise to opposite poles in the magnetic field. A singular negative force $(—)$ is to be identified with "minus-time," which gives rise to the time-factor *now*, and "minus-time" precedes "plus-time" in action; but the "plus-time" force itself must be seen as negative action "turned positive" to equate negative action and/or to neutralize it and/or to offset it. Thus, time can be understood only in terms of the duality possible in negative action whereby a negative value can act both as a negative and a positive force, which in time's action is seen as past and future, and/or a *dual* operation. Time may be seen as the "unlimited" or purely singular negative force only as one views it in terms of single negative value acting first one way and then the other.

III

We believe that the transactions we describe in this section take place, for the most part, virtually simultaneously. Just as no one can say *why* the proton takes the form it does, so we cannot say why the patterns of behavior and the forms we describe arose in nature; but we believe they exist and can be related to principles we have touched upon in the previous sections.

First, we would say that in reality we see the hydrogen atom as nothing but interpenetrating fields and forces. The positive force of the nucleus operates within a nuclear field and force that is formed by Q energy, or the unapparent energy in space; the nuclear field and the forces within it normally interact with and operate within a surrounding field and force in which the negative force is operative, and this component of the atom is also formed by Q energy. In order to describe in our symbols these elusive fields and forces that are "as nothing," we must present them as something in the way of value count, describing them in homely terms, which we attempt to make meaningful but not misleading.

Thus, we begin by saying that in our view, the original Q/P fission-fusion giving rise to the hydrogen molecule involved five Q bundles versus one P bundle. But not all of this energy was expressed as mass. Part was used to form what we see to be essential to the atom: first, one *full* measure of space, which must be seen as a measure of force constant, $[F+]$, to form a space chamber to house the atom, and energy to support or delineate within the general field the space chamber as such; secondly, a field force outside the space chamber upon which the balancing negative charge can act, and within which it can be "defined" as a part of the property that constitutes the atom.

We do not believe that either the space chamber and its supporting energy or the energy that forms the field force upon which the electron acts, can be weighed or measured in terms of a *particle*: i.e., one cannot treat with space and space-energy as one treats with matter. The particles within the "property" may be said to "weigh upon it," or to be calculable as mass. Thus, the measures of prime neutral energy that are used to "construct" the space chamber and the field of the atom must be seen as a "holding force" that allows for action of the masses within the property.

We believe also that the atom must have a basis for action within itself. In our view, action arises when, at the minimum, the atom's one net positive value (+), enclosed within the neutralized space chamber, reacts to the constant positive force of space at large by going into action. Because this net positive value has no negative value to equate it, it gives to the atom a degree of temperature: i.e., it prevents any atom from reaching "absolute zero" temperature. What might be called "absolute heat" cannot be achieved because the positive value of the atom's space chamber neither acts nor reacts: i.e., [F+] is force constant.

In order to neutralize the atom's space chamber [F+], we believe a q(−) measure must be bound within it; this measure (− + −) is also necessary to attract and "hold" the space. The reacted q-measure (− + −), together with the positive charge (+ − +) associated with each nucleus, and the net positive value (+), constitute what we call the *Core force* of the atom. In the field, there is an electron to balance the positive charge of the Core force, and it operates upon a field force of its own.

We see the original formation of matter as a process wherein one P bundle is "divided" *equally* to create two protons, which are lodged in two nuclear structures as described above. The nuclear structures are provided by two Q bundles. Each proton is provided with an electron and a field force by the reaction of two more Q bundles. The fifth Q bundle emits its neutron as its q(−) measure reacts (− + −) to "bond" the pair. We describe the operation as follows:

Two Q bundles react to become: [(− + −)(+ − + − + − + −)]. The q(−) measure draws from the "deeps" of space below the general field a measure of space, securing and neutralizing it:

$$[F+]$$
$$(- + -)$$

We call this particle (− + −) the Core q-measure. The remaining neutral values, equivalent to a neutron, form a "line" or "thread of energy" to enwrap or delineate the nuclear chamber within the general field upon which it rests. We call this neutral energy the space-binding-force, and symbolize it as: (sbf). (Here, we would say again that when we speak of "binding energy" we are not speaking in the technical sense: i.e., of the amount of energy that must be supplied to pull apart all the nucleons in a nucleus. We are speaking of the ability of opposite values to adhere, via attraction.)

Meanwhile, the P bundle $[(+ - +) (- + - + - + - +)]$ is reduced to a "plasma" consisting of two positive charges, two single positive values, and three single negative values $[(+ - +)(-)(+)(-)$ $(+)(-)(+ - +)]$. In our view, the three negative values are reduced to their neutrino potential: i.e., six degrees (°) of potential energy, and they are *tithed*, three in the space chamber of each incipient atom, to provide in time the *equivalence to* the two single positive values expressed in the hydrogen molecule as matter in being. Into the nuclear structure:

$$[F+(sbf)]$$
$$(- + -)$$

three degrees (°) of "virtual energy," a single positive value $(+)$, and a positive charge $(+ - +)$ are deposited. In our view, this constitutes a proton, nucleus of the hydrogen atom:

Fig. 1—Proton, nucleus of $_1H^1$

$$[F+(sbf)°°°] \qquad\qquad [F+(sbf)°°°]$$
$$(- + -) \qquad\qquad\qquad (- o)$$
$$(+) \qquad (or) \qquad (+)$$
$$(+ - +) \qquad\qquad\qquad (+ o)$$

The values within the proton that are calculable as mass are those that lie below the line of: $[F+(sbf)°°°]$. When these particles are seen in relation to their potential energy, i.e., as $[(+ o) (+)(- o)]$, the aggregate constitutes a ratio of: $2(o)/2(+)/1(-)$. Both a neutral and a positive redundancy are present. Therefore, the positive redundancy is *communicated*, so that the proton communicates itself as a positively *charged* mass. We see the Core's q-measure as a particle, but not as a negative charge acting as such: i.e., its function is to "hold" the space, which it neutralizes even as within the space chamber the net positive value $(+)$ neutralizes it, leaving the positive charge free to express itself or to communicate the nucleus of protium as a positive mass. We call this nucleus a Prime Core, seeing it as atomic number Z 1.

As the two Prime Cores are formed, the proton pair, each posing a positive redundancy, causes the remaining three bundles of Q energy to react. We see the reaction as virtually simultaneous: two of the three remaining Q bundles form a neutral line of force around the protons, which then have trapped between them one Q bundle. This Q bundle emits its neutral energy in the form of a neutron (as will be explained later), its q(−) measure acting to bond the *space chambers* of the protons. The protons, however, continue to express themselves as positive ions, causing the surrounding Q bundles to react to provide an electron for each proton, and a neutral path or field around the Core upon which the electron operates. Each Q bundle becomes: $(- + -)$ and $(+ - + - + - + -)$. We see the electron's field-force $(+ - + - + - + -)$, which we symbolize as: (ff), to be a measure of prime neutral energy as loosely bound and expressing in terms as "elastic" as is possible to this measure. Whereas, we see the nuclear space-binding-force (sbf) as a measure of prime neutral energy as "tightly constricted" as is possible to this measure before it fuses into a mass.

Each hydrogen atom is an aggregate of energy that is *net* one positive value in being when the space chamber [F+] is counted; but each atom is also a neutral redundancy and communicates neutrality. In our symbols, the hydrogen molecule would appear:

Fig. 2—Hydrogen molecule, H_2

$$[F+(sbf)^{\circ\,\circ\,\circ}] \ (- + -) \ [F+(sbf)^{\circ\,\circ\,\circ}]$$
$$(- + -) \qquad\qquad (- + -)$$
$$(+) \qquad\qquad\quad (+)$$
$$(+ - +) \qquad\qquad (+ - +)$$
$$(- + -) \ (ff) \qquad (ff) \ (- + -)$$

In our view, the q-bond that bonds the space chambers of the atoms is a field property of the molecule, acting to bind the atoms so that they occupy a joint measure of the general field of space; this allows the molecule to share the electrons equally. Because of the q-bond, the attraction of the two positive protons for the two negative electrons "exceeds" the repulsion between the two protons plus the repulsion between the two electrons. The q-bond adds to the bond energy of H_2 (i.e., the amount of energy required to break the Avogadro number of H_2 molecules into individual atoms). Because this q-bond is not involved in molecules containing only one atom of hydrogen, hydrogen does not contribute exactly half of its calculated bond energy as determined in pulling apart the hydrogen molecule. In such cases, other bonding factors come into play. We would say here that we do not see every molecule occurring in nature to possess the q-bond that we believe H_2 possesses; unequal sharing of electrons and other considerations are involved. We are concerned here, however, with a description of the hydrogen molecule as we believe it arises in nature, and as it arose in the beginning, so that we return now to our discussion of the organization of matter in the universe.

Not every atom of higher atomic number and weight is a simple multiple of hydrogen. And in the decay of unstable isotopes, several processes are observed. We believe these phenomena arise because not every additional Core measure that gives rise to an increase in atomic number is an exact multiple of the Prime Core of hydrogen. We believe three types of Cores are involved: a Prime Core, a Beta Core, and an Alpha Core. But before we can discuss these different cores and the decay processes, the proton and electron must be examined further, and our concept of the neutron must be presented.

The neutron is believed to be a constituent particle of all nuclei of mass number greater than 1. It is unstable with respect to beta decay. In a sample of neutrons, any given one is most likely to decay after a thousand seconds. The decay products of the neutron are: a beta particle (or electron), an antineutrino, and a proton. The neutron interacts with matter predominantly by collisions and, to a lesser extent, magnetically. In our view, a neutron is a "parent" particle, equivalent to the measure of prime neutral energy in a Q bundle, or to the field-force upon which an electron operates, or to the space-binding-force of a proton; and in certain reactions and under certain conditions, this energy may be expressed as mass.

First, we believe that a "trapped" Q bundle reacts to a certain kind of stress by releasing its electron and producing a neutron. For example, the Q bundle that reacts to bond the two protons arising in Q/P fission-fusion is "trapped" between the two positive ions, each attracted to it, and the stress of their pressure upon it causes it to contract, and then the continuing pressure overcomes what may be seen as the minimum expression of repelling force: i.e., the "horizontal" force repelling the "horizontal" force. The contracted Q bundle may be symbolized: $(-+-+-+-+-+-)$. Stress causes the Q energy to react to form an electron and neutron.

When at large in space, Q energy is not subjected to "pressure," and an electron may arise without also giving rise to a neutron; the "loosely spread" neutral energy in the Q bundle remains in the field. When a proton loses its electron, its field-force does not express as a neutron, but also remains in the field. The atom's electron and its field-force are too "free" in space to be subjected to the type stress required to produce a neutron, for this Q measure can revert to the Q-force at large.

The space-binding-force of a proton, however, is a "tightly constricted thread" of prime neutral energy, and we believe it reacts to express as a neutron when stress causes positive value in the proton to "turn negative," thereby *dissolving* the Core force because the energy has become a Q-type aggregate, which must express in *unapparent* ways, or as space-energy rather than mass. Thus, the proton "disappears" and its space-binding-force appears as a neutron; for when the space chamber and energy within it revert to the general field, the space-binding-force contracts and "collapses" into a mass. Or, we might say, that the "thread" of energy may expand, but it may not contract without converting to mass.

For example, when a proton and antiproton have a "near miss," they do not destroy each other; the particles turn into a neutron and an antineutron.[139] In our view, stress causes the disintegration of the net positive values in each particle into q-1, ($-$ ∘), thereby changing the Core force in each particle to a Q-type expression in value count: i.e., from $4(+)/3(-)$ to $3(+)/4(-)$. When the proton's net positive value $(+)$ is gone, *the proton as such is destroyed.* Q-type energy in the space chambers causes the space, together with the energy it houses, to revert to the general field: i.e., to express in terms of Q energy, *unapparent,* leaving each particle's space-binding-force, which has contracted and fused into a mass. Thus, this energy *becomes* a neutron and an antineutron. Only these particles remain to be expressed in terms of mass.

When we say that the neutron forms as the space chamber and its energy revert to the general field, we do not intend to imply that the neutron does not occupy space. We say that it does not involve *one full measure* of space with its force constant: $[F+]$; it occupies a three-dimensional neutral measure of the general field. This is to say, we believe that the proton possesses a spatial property that the neutron does not possess: the proton enfolds free or independent space at the point of its nucleus which gives it a measure of force constant $[F+]$ *within its being.* We symbolize the concept that a particle may occupy three-dimensional space without involving the measure of space that would constitute its *full* potential, i.e., a measure of force constant $[F+]$, as follows: if a full measure of P energy is written in terms of single values, and the full measure of single values that make up a neutron equivalence or the full measure of single values that make up a proton are posed against the P bundle's energy values, neither particle would "fully occupy" the values in a measure of Prime Positive energy; the arrangement of the neutron's values versus the proton's makes the difference. One might say that the neutron occupies as much space as it can, whereas the proton *involves* or encompasses the measure of space its values do not occupy; or that it takes one measure of three-dimensional space "plus space" to constitute one full measure of it.

As another example of neutron formation: in an antineutrino trap, antineutrinos have combined with protons to form neutrons and positrons.[140] In our view, the antineutrino (*) contracts (∘) as it is "stopped" by a proton housing three degrees (°) of potential energy. The four degrees

(°) then present in the space chamber form two negative values that make of the proton's net positive value (+) another negative charge (− + −), thereby changing the value count of the Core force from 4(+)/3(−) to 4(+)/5(−), or to a Q-type expression of energy. The proton as such is destroyed. As the Q-type energy and space chamber revert to the general field, the one negative charge "prepares" to destroy the other by going into positron reaction; but in the act it is repelled by the greater force of the positive charge, not greater in terms of electrical charge, but in terms of two positive values acting in the positive charge to repel the one positive value in the positron. Thus, the positron is emitted *before* it can destroy the Core's q-measure, and *as* the space chamber and energy within it revert to the general field, leaving the space-binding-force, which has contracted and fused to *become* a neutron.

In both of the transactions described above, energy "turns" from positive to negative to neutral: i.e., a neutron is formed.

The proton is a stable particle; it does not decay spontaneously. But it can be subjected to stress, such as electromagnetic radiation of certain wave length, and it will react (i.e., this reaction could be written: a gamma ray plus a proton reacts to produce a neutron plus a positive meson). And in proton-proton collisions, the particles break up into mesons and baryons. A proton and antiproton can annihilate into only mesons and leptons. We believe the protons tend to react according to three general patterns, one or more of which may be involved, depending on the type stress. First, the net positive value may "turn negative," or neutrino reactions may give rise to negative energy, turning the Core force into a Q-type expression of energy, which disappears into the general field, dissolving the space chamber and the Core force, leaving the neutron which "takes place" as the space-binding-force fuses. In the second type reaction, the positive charge may go into "anti" expression, thereby causing the net positive value to fuse with it, forming a stress-particle that poses sufficient attraction to cause the Core's q-measure to fuse with it, thereby forming another stress particle, which decays into mesons and leptons as positive value continues to turn negative; and as the stress-particle decays, the empty space chamber together with the space-binding-force reverts to the general field. In the third type reaction, the space-binding-force and the Core force fuse to form a hyperon, which destroys the space chamber as such; and this stress-particle decays as positive value in the mass "turns negative."

The values in a P or Q bundle that we call a neutron-equivalence may be seen as: [(+ − +) (o) (− + −)]. This represents a neutral or uncharged core around which the positive and negative charges whirl, the one whirling in one way, the other in the other way, creating an overall magnetic field.

When free in space, we see the neutron to be a "self-magnetized" mass, its binding energy enhanced as some of its values go into "secondary formation" in response to the stress that gives rise to the particle, which we symbolize as: $(o \mp o + |)$. It expresses only in terms of a neutral redundancy, communicating itself as a neutral mass. Although it may be seen as an aggregate of energy expressing only a 50 per cent redundancy of neutral value, it is equivalent to a positive charge, a negative charge, and a neutral measure, so that in one way it may be seen as: $(o +) (o) (-o)$, or a ratio of $3(o)/1(+)/1(-)$, which expresses *more* than 50 per cent redundancy of neutral value. Thus, it is an unstable particle. In terms of potential energy, the neutron can express as *more* than the proton. Thus, no *one* measure of the Core force can support it until it has been reduced to no more than a 50 per cent redundancy of neutral value.

When a hydrogen atom, $_1H^1$, absorbs a neutron and emits a gamma ray, a photon $(+)$ in our symbols, the proton becomes a deuteron, $_1H^2$. When the neutron is absorbed, we believe it reacts by "turning positive" as a single negative value $(-)$ translates into two degrees $(°)$ of potential energy, which are tithed in the space chamber of the atom, giving it five degrees $(°)$ of "virtual energy." The "odd" positive value $(+)$ then left in the "neutron plasma" is repelled by the atom's net positive value $(+)$ and is emitted. The remaining values in the neutron constitute a *nucleon*, equivalent to fused opposite charges. We symbolize the nucleon as: $(o + - o)$. This particle expresses a ratio of $2(o)/1(+)/1(-)$, or the same potential energy possible to a proton. Only a neutral redundancy is present, so that it communicates neutrality. Thus, in our view, a neutron outside the nucleus constitutes more in value than a nucleon in a nucleus. The deuteron resulting from this transaction has a nucleon and five degrees $(°)$ of "virtual energy" in its space chamber, together with the balance of the Core force. This nucleus constitutes what we call a *Beta Core*: i.e., $Z_1 + 0$. In our symbols, it would appear:

Fig. 3—Nucleus of a deuteron, $_1H^2$

$$[F+(sbf)° ° ° ° °] \qquad\qquad [F+(sbf)° ° ° ° °]$$
$$(- + -) (o + - o) \qquad (or) \qquad (- o) (o + - o)$$
$$(+) \qquad\qquad\qquad\qquad (+)$$
$$(+ - +) \qquad\qquad\qquad\qquad (+ o)$$

As may be observed above, in our view a nucleon cannot be seen as (ooo). It must be seen as $(o + - o)$, because at least one single negative value and one single positive value must express as such to bind the particle. As the nucleon is added to the proton, the ratio changes from $2(o)/2(+)/1(-)$ to $4(o)/3(+)/2(-)$, so that the one measure of space does not contain more than a 50 per cent redundancy of potential energy.

A proton's *calculable mass* expresses a 50 per cent redundancy of neutral value and of positive value in relation to negative value; but when the positive value of the space chamber is added, the proton expresses $2(o)/3(+)/1(-)$, or more than a 50 per cent redundancy of positive value in relation to the negative value and less than a 50 per cent redundancy of positive value in relation to neutral value. In single value count, however, including the positive value of the space chamber, the proton has a ratio of $5(+)/3(-)$, or less than 50 per cent redundancy of positive value. Thus, it is a stable particle in terms of being; but it commands a reaction from Q energy which is drawn to it and acts to provide an electron that equates the positive charge: i.e., the Q energy reacts to the more than 50 per cent redundancy of positive value versus negative value that the proton in one of its aspects expresses.

Insofar as the hydrogen atom itself is concerned, the single negative value in the Core's q-measure that acts to "hold" and neutralize the space $[F+]$ must be calculated in relation to the space: i.e., this pair of values must be seen in terms of neutral *expression* (not as neutral mass), so that the ratio of the hydrogen atom may be written: $[F+-]/3(o)/2(+)/1(-)$, giving the atom 50 per cent redundancy of neutral value and/or expression, and thus it communicates neutrality and is a stable particle.

It may be noted that the hydrogen atom in one of its aspects also expresses a positive redundancy, i.e., $2(+)/1(-)$. But this "inner" redundancy, which gives the atom its net positive value, is obscured by the greater redundancy of neutral to positive value. The "inner" positive redundancy is "silenced" by the ratio of neutral to positive value, i.e., by *four* neutral measures and/or expressions versus *two* positive values, giving the atom a 50 per cent redundancy of neutral value, which "outweighs" the "inner" positive redundancy. If, as in the case of the proton, the neutral redundancy and the positive redundancy were *equal*, i.e., $2(o)/2(+)/1(-)$, then the positive redundancy would communicate itself, obscuring thereby the neutral redundancy.

Tritium, $_1H^3$, is not a stable isotope. Adding a nucleon to a deuteron would alter the ratio, but would not increase the neutral redundancy to more than 50 per cent. We believe the isotope decays because of neutrino reactions, as will be explained later.

In the formation of neutrons by "stripping" deuterons, a high energy deuteron strikes a target nucleus in such a way as to graze the edge of it, and the proton in the deuteron is stripped off, while the neutron continues to travel in a straight line. In this transaction, we believe that stress causes the nucleon to "turn negative," i.e., (o + — o) becomes (+ $\overline{+}$ — + —), giving rise to a reaction of the five degrees (°) of "virtual energy" in the space chamber. The nucleon's double negative expression commands a positive value, and three degrees (°) of the potential energy react *before* the nucleon "splits." As the nucleon becomes equivalent to a proton, the two remaining degrees (°) of potential energy left in the space chamber react to produce a negative value, which is also drawn into the positive nucleon, thereby restoring it to neutron value. The heavy mass is thrown out of the nucleus, leaving a proton, which has then lost the three degrees (°) of potential energy its space chamber once housed. In our symbols it would appear:

Fig. 4—Proton resulting as a deuteron is stripped, $_1H^1$
[F+(sbf)]
(— + —)
(+)
(+ — +)

In our view, when neutrons are knocked out of elements of high atomic number, stress has caused "virtual energy" in the space chamber to react with a nucleon "turned negative," thereby forming a neutron.

When a neutron is absorbed by an element of sufficiently high atomic number, a positive value (+) may not be emitted: a single negative value in the neutron may act upon a single positive value, reducing the pair of values to five degrees (°) of potential energy, which are housed in a Core measure that has been "stripped" of its "virtual energy" by losing a neutron, or in some other transaction. The point we would make is that if the neutron is absorbed, in one way or another it is diminished so that the energy expresses no more than 50 per cent redundancy of potential energy (o).

We believe that as time and/or stress takes its toll of matter, the neutral energy contributed by a neutron is reduced further: i.e., in time, the nucleon (o + — o) will be reduced as one negative value disintegrates into two degrees (°) of potential energy, which are stored in a Prime Core measure housing three degrees (°) to raise its "virtual energy" to five degrees (°), and the "odd" positive value left in the nucleon is emitted as a gamma ray. Or the nucleon will be reduced as one of its negative values acts upon a positive value to disperse it into five degrees (°) of potential energy, which are housed in a Core measure that has been emptied of its "virtual energy." As the nucleon is thus reduced to two negative and two positive values, it may be seen as (+ − + −) or as (+ o −), and the decrease may be said to be "barely perceptible" and/or unmeasurable. As the next toll of the nucleon is taken, in effect it disappears, because only one measure of binding energy (+ −) is left to act with a positive charge; and in time this measure disintegrates into "virtual energy" also. Thus, what might be called "imperceptible decay" gives rise to the many isotopes of the various elements that are found in nature. As the isotope reaches the point where it has too few nucleons, it must react. As isotopes absorb neutrons they may reach the point of having too many nucleons and/or they cannot sustain more "virtual energy" arising as the neutron disintegrates; "saturation" in terms of degrees (°) of potential energy spread throughout the different levels of the nucleus causes the isotope to be prone to neutrino reactions, which give rise to radioactive decay.

We believe that a free neutron decays by first "turning negative" and then "turning positive": i.e., the positive charge and the neutral measure go into "anti" expression, their negative values acting to enhance the negative aspect of the positive values in the groupings. We symbolize this: $\left[(+ \overline{} +)\ (\overline{\mp})\ (- + -)\right]$. Too much negative expression causes the neutron to emit its negative charge as a beta particle. The antipositive charge then reverts to positive expression as the negative value in the measure of neutral energy "turns neutral" by disintegrating into its neutrino value, the antineutrino (*) being emitted, the neutrino lapsing into a degree (°) of potential energy, which is tithed in the space chamber of the incipient proton. For there is then left to the aggregate a positive charge (+ − +) and a net positive value (+), or *more* than 50 per cent redundancy of positive value:

$$\left[\begin{matrix} (+) \\ (+ - +) \end{matrix} \right]$$

and this quasi-redundancy that expresses a ratio of 3(+)/1(−) or 2(+)/1(o), immediately commands a Q measure which, in turn, commands and "binds" a space chamber into which the one degree (°) of potential energy, the positive charge (+ − +), and the single positive value (+) are deposited. In our symbols, the proton thus formed would appear:

311

Fig. 5—Proton formed in neutron disintegration

$$[F+(sbf)°]$$
$$(- + -)$$
$$(+)$$
$$(+ - +)$$

Thus, a proton forms as the neutron emits a beta particle and an anti-neutrino.

Before discussing other neutron reactions, we must examine further the nucleon (o + — o), which we will refer to as such, referring to a proton as a proton to distinguish between the two nuclear particles. And we must also examine further the proton itself.

In our view, neither a proton nor a positive charge decays into a positron and a photon, because the proton has too much more in value count than these two particles, and the positive charge itself has less in value count. We do not believe the positive charge (+ — +) exists as a "free" particle in nature. We see the proton to represent it or to be a "grounded" positive charge. To simplify our symbols in the following discussion, we will use only the positive charge (+ — +) to *represent* the proton.

A proton may support two electrons, as is the case with the negative hydrogen ion. In our view, it has sufficient positive value to allow for this in terms of "binding energy" posed by attraction of opposite values. Viewing electron arrangement in terms of electrons being "packed" into K-shell, we symbolize this by posing one positive charge versus two negative charges: $\left[\begin{array}{c} (+ - +) \\ (- + -) \ (- + -) \end{array} \right]$. In the field, the electrons repel each other and they have "room" to keep their distance; the two negative charges that may be supported by one proton are not actually in closest contact with each other and/or with the proton. The distance they keep, as well as the positive nucleus shared between them, prevents what we call a double negative situation from arising that would command of the "virtual energy" in space a positive value.

An electron in an atom's electron cloud does not spiral down and fuse with the positive charge, because in closest association or if one charge actually rested upon the other, there would be equal and opposite attraction, which would serve to paralyze further action, which we symbolize as: $\left[\begin{array}{c} (- + -) \\ (+ - +) \end{array} \right]$. The electron would not fuse with its positive charge partner, because each value in the electron is as attracted to the opposite value within its own arrangement as it is attracted to the opposite value in the arrangement of the positive charge. There is no lower level of energy possible to the electron; it may "rest in equilibrium" in this situation, or one might say that in this situation both charges are paralyzed until or unless some force overcomes the "stymie" of equal and opposite forces posed against each other. Thus, in very close or "immediate" contact, the neutral energy within each particle serves *to bind it into entity, preventing fusion*; and thus the neutral energy in a particle *becomes a force of repulsion in relation to any other particle.* But stress can overcome this force: i.e., fusion can occur.

Again, we would say, our symbolical representations are not mechanical models. We believe that an electron associated with a nucleus operates upon a neutral field-force (ff), which serves to reinforce the measure of the general field of space upon which the atom has its being. Thus, there is a distribution of neutral energy throughout the atom's field as each electron is added, and this serves to provide binding energy via attraction of opposite values, so that as distance increases between the nucleus and outer electrons, the positive charge on the nucleus is not the sole factor at work to bind the electrons.

Although we believe electrons possess a measure of neutral energy, two electrons do not *adhere*, save as a prelude to annihilation in electron-positron reactions. This is to say, the double-negative situation commands positive action and/or a positive value. In the atom's field the electrons repel each other and keep their distance; the arrangement of the field force, together with other factors, determines what their activity can be.

Within a nucleus, the situation is different. In any one Core measure of an atom there would not be sufficient space for two q-measures to keep their distance, and thus a reaction must occur, as will be discussed later when decay processes are considered.

We have pointed out that the neutral energy in a positive charge and in an electron acts at closest range as a force of repulsion: i.e., this energy binds each particle into an entity, preventing its fusion with another particle. Although electrons have a measure of neutral energy that might act as a binding force between two negative charges, electrons do not adhere because like charges repel each other, and in the field they can keep their distance. Or, we might say, the singular force of the net negative value (−) in each electron repelling the net negative value (−) in the other is greater than the force of attraction the complex units of neutral energy (+ −) pose for each other. We would point out also that the electron both is and is not a Q ratio: i.e., the electron possesses net negative value, but not a neutral redundancy, which takes precedence in the Q bundle because the neutral energy is preponderant and neutrality is communicated, allowing two Q bundles to adhere. The positive charge $(+ - +)$ also has a measure of neutral energy, but this is insufficient to bind charges in the nucleus *and* to allow for their expression as rest mass: $(o +) (+ o)$ would repel. *Protons* may combine to form a new nucleus because they possess energy that is independent of the electrical charge: i.e., they represent a neutral *and* a positive redundancy. The question becomes, why are positive charges bound in a mass to form protons and negative charges are not bound in a mass to form a balancing particle with equal and opposite properties?

We answer by saying that the entire situation of positive energy in space is opposite to that of negative energy, and thus the opposite charges behave in opposite ways. Two electrons pose a double negative that destroys itself as such in commanding positive action as one electron goes into positron reaction, giving rise to photons. Electron-positron reactions will be discussed later. (See page 325). A double negative $(- -)$ arising in space destroys itself as such by commanding a positive value of the "virtual energy" in space to form an electron. Whereas when a positive redundancy arises (as we believe to be the case in neutron disintegration) it commands negative action and/or a negative value, which is always available in the Q energy that surrounds matter, so that a Q bundle immediately reacts to "ground" the charge in a space chamber, and still another Q bundle reacts in time to neutralize the proton by forming an electron to balance the positive charge. This is to say, positive charges are never "free" in space to act to repel each other, and the ever-present Q-force acts to neutralize all "doubly positive" situations. (For example, trapped alpha particles pick up electrons from their surroundings.) We believe that in the beginning, positive charges $(+ - +)$ reacted with Q energy to *become protons,* which are now formed in the disintegration processes of neutral energy, so that positive charges as such do not exist as particles, *not even momentarily as part of the decay process.* In our view, this is the "reality" that underlies the conservation of baryon number: i.e., protons cannot release their positive charge, and if their positive charge as such disappears in the formation of a "queer" particle, a neutron "enfolding" another positive charge appears, the neutron disintegrating into a proton. Thus, the positive charge is never actually lost, and never actually set free in space.

A double positive $(+ +)$ does not arise in space, because "crowding" of "virtual energy" $(°)$ gives rise *first* to two degrees $(°)$ reacting to form a negative value, creating in space a situation we see as equivalent to the mathematical operation wherein a negative number divided by a negative number produces a positive number: $(-/- = +)$. Mathematically, a positive number divided by a positive number also produces a positive number: $(+/+ = +)$. We would point out that because a positive redundancy, or a "double positive," commands a reaction of negative energy which gives rise to a proton and then to a balancing negative charge to form the equivalence of a hydrogen atom, net positive in being, the reaction that positive energy commands in space conforms to the mathematical operation $(+/+ = +)$.

Within an atom, the Core's q-measure is not free. This q-measure cannot be seen precisely in terms of a negative charge; nor can it be seen as negative binding energy in the nucleus beyond serving to "anchor" the space chamber and the net positive value $(+)$ in it. But a nucleon added to the Core force contributes negative energy and allows for what might be called a "tighter crocheting" of positive value. Using the positive charge symbol to represent the proton, we picture a proton-proton pair

as: $\begin{bmatrix} (+ - +) \\ (+ - +) \end{bmatrix}$, and a proton-nucleon pair as: $\begin{bmatrix} (o + - o) \\ (+ - +) \end{bmatrix}$, and

a nucleon-nucleon pair as: $\begin{bmatrix} (o + - o) \\ (o - + o) \end{bmatrix}$. All three pairs have the

same binding energy: i.e., two positive values adhering to two negative values represents the maximum binding energy between any of the pairs. Binding energy via attraction of opposite values would drop in strength as the particles are separated.

Except for certain decay reactions to be discussed later, we see the nucleons in the nucleus expressed in terms of "flexible" potential energy, which we symbolize by shifting the arrangement of their values, for example, $(- o + o)$, or $(+ o - o)$. We believe the positive charge is expressed as $(o +)$, or in terms of potential energy, until it goes into charge reaction $(+ - +)$. Thus a positive charge $(o +)$ in association with a nucleon $(o + - o)$ may be seen simply as a larger body expressing a positive redundancy: $[(o +) (o - o +)]$, or a $2(+)/1(-)$ ratio to balance the electron's ratio of $2(-)/1(+)$.

In our view, as protons are packed into the nucleus in large numbers, the positive charges must "contract" to express as $(o +)$, and nucleons, binding energy, become a critical necessity because two such measures $(o +) (+ o)$ would repel each other. This is to say, a positive charge cannot at one and the same time express as potential energy $(o +)$ and as charge $(+ - +)$. The way in which the Core force of atoms of high atomic number is *arranged* becomes the factor that determines the amount of binding energy, or the number of nucleons necessary to give it stability. We symbolize this by saying that if two nucleons were binding two positive charges (o +), a "double" measure of binding energy would be

acting, for this relationship, which may be seen as:
$$\begin{bmatrix} (o +) \\ (o - + o) \\ (o + - o) \\ (+ o) \end{bmatrix}, \text{ pre-}$$

sents the binding energy between positive charges when it is viewed "vertically," and when viewed "horizontally" presents the binding energy seen between a pair of nucleons. The energy is "fully compacted" and the particles are expressing at the "lowest" energy level, but in the *arrangement*, two positive charges in "charge expression" are "in force," so that there remains a double charge on the nucleus. An aggregate of two protons and two nucleons combined into one nucleus brings to the discussion the subject of the Alpha Core.

Before discussing our concept of the formation of helium $_2He^4$, or its nucleus, the alpha particle, we would say that we believe something in the nature of space itself and/or the "shape" it takes as the space-binding-force "ties off" one measure of it in independent being, determines the pattern of a proton and what the space chamber can support, establishing this pattern as a recurring one in nature. When fusion of nuclei gives rise to an isotope of higher atomic number, we believe that a joining of the space chambers and the Core force has occurred, so that the isotope has two "levels" or measures of space as well as an increased Core force; but the net positive value (+) in one of the joining nuclei must be emitted or it must disintegrate into its neutrino value because each isotope can have but one net positive value (+). When fusion of nuclei gives rise to an isotope of the same atomic number but higher atomic weight, as would be the case when two protons fuse to produce a deuteron, we believe that only the Core force of the joining proton has been absorbed, thereby causing the empty nuclear structure with its space-binding-force and "virtual energy" to revert to the general field; in this reaction, the Core force of the destroyed proton reacts to form a nucleon as energy is emitted.

Before describing the above transactions, we would say that helium arose from the first generation of the hydrogen molecules, which would have been subjected to many types of stress and to neutrons set free in space as the molecules were formed. A "second generation" of protons would have arisen as neutrons disintegrated to form them in beta decay, and in other nuclear reactions (such as in neutron absorption) these protons were emitted. The "virtual energy" in the space chamber of such a "second generation" proton would consist of only one degree (°). Protons might also have arisen as deuterons were stripped of their neutrons. Thus, in our view, the space chamber of a proton might possess no neutrino values (°), or it might possess one or three degrees (°) of potential energy. Normally, the proton will possess or will have absorbed three degrees (°) of "virtual energy," thereby conforming to its "original" or "standard" pattern. But a Prime Core can become a Beta Core, which supports five degrees (°) of "virtual energy" and a nucleon. Thus, five degrees (°) of potential energy could be housed in a Prime Core and/or in any one measure of space.

In multiple nuclear reactions, if two Prime Cores, or protons, house three degrees (°) of "virtual energy," one degree (°) will be emitted as a neutrino value (*), because crowding of the space chamber with six degrees (°) gives rise to the reaction we describe as: $3(°)=(+)$. If each proton houses one degree (°) of "virtual energy," a neutrino value (*) will also be emitted because only two degrees (°) of "virtual energy" tend to give rise to the formation of one negative value: i.e., $2(°)=(-)$, in order to offset the net positive value $(+)$ of the atom. If one proton houses three degrees (°) of "virtual energy" and another proton houses one degree (°), in the fusion of the protons a neutrino value (*) will also be emitted because four degrees (°) of "virtual energy" tend to give rise to the formation of two negative values to offset the positive value of the positive charge. Another way of describing this would be to say that even numbers of degrees (°) of lapsed energy in any one space chamber and/or on any one level in the nucleus give rise to the formation of strange or stress-particles in the Core force of the atom.

In the above paragraph we attempt to present a *principle* involved in complex nuclear reactions, which we do not attempt to explain or symbolize in detail in this presentation of our hypothesis. The reaction we describe as: $3(°) = (+)$ could take place either as two degrees (°) of the six degrees (°) in the space chamber form a negative value $(-)$ which, in conjunction with the Core's q-measure, would give rise to the double negative situation commanding three degrees (°) to react to form a positive value $(+)$; or the six degrees (°) might react, three by three, as the stress of too much "virtual energy" caused the Core force of the atom to express momentarily in negative or "anti" terms. Just as an isotope reacts to the stress of too few neutrons and/or too many neutrons, so we believe it reacts to the stress of too little or too much "virtual energy." Since "virtual energy" is neutral energy, it reacts to stress by turning negative or positive; in the case of two degrees (°) of potential energy, only a negative reaction could take place; in the case of four degrees (°), a complete reaction would produce two negative values.

To present our concept of the formation of the alpha particle in the beginning, we must start with the first generation of hydrogen: i.e., the bonded molecule as presented in Figure 2, page 304. Just as there are different ways to form different isotopes, we believe there are different ways to form the alpha particle; but we present only the reaction known as the proton-proton chain, illustrating the series of transactions in our symbols.

We believe that in nature the fusion of two protons to form a deuteron occurs as the Core forces of the protons merge; this happens after stress has given rise to the ionization of the associated hydrogen atoms, leaving the nuclei trapped in the joint field. The bonded protons would appear:

$$[F+(sbf)^{\circ\,\circ\,\circ}] \quad (- + -) \quad [F+(sbf)^{\circ\,\circ\,\circ}]$$
$$(- + -) \qquad\qquad\qquad (- + -)$$
$$(+) \qquad\qquad\qquad\quad (+)$$
$$(+ - +) \qquad\qquad\quad (+ - +)$$

As stress is prolonged and/or increased, the q-bond acts to equate or "slow" the action of the two net positive values (+) in the protons. This is to say, the q-bond ceases to be a field factor and becomes a nuclear factor as it acts to join the Core forces of the nuclei, thereby creating a "thread" of energy that is drawn into one nuclear structure. The other structure then reverts to the general field. The Core force of the ensuing isotope possesses two net positive values (+), one of which reacts to the stress by translating into a q-1 particle (− ∘). The neutrino value (*) is emitted as the q-1 particle reacts with one of the Core q-measures to form a muon. The muon poses sufficient attraction to cause one of the positive charges to fuse with it, and as this happens a single negative value in the muon disintegrates into two degrees (°) of potential energy, which are stored in the space chamber; thus, a nucleon is formed and the five degrees (°) of "virtual energy" necessary to complete a deuteron (see Fig. 3, page 308) are provided. But the transaction is not complete, for the q-bond that joined the two Core forces remains in the space chamber of the new isotope. The presence of the isotope's net positive value (+) prevents the double negative situation, i.e., a negative redundancy is not expressed in the ratio of negative to positive values present; but the stress of two negative charges operating in one space chamber causes the q-bond to go into positron reaction to equate the q-measure. The positron is repelled "instantly" by the greater force of the positive charge with its two positive values acting versus the positron's one positive value, and by the net positive value (+) in the Core force, so that the positron is emitted before it can destroy the Core's q-measure. A deuteron remains. Thus, $_1H^1 + {}_1H^1$ reacts to produce $_1H^2$ plus a positron and a neutrino.

We believe that a deuteron and a proton would not be bonded: i.e., the q-bond could not equate an unequal pair, although it could equate a pair of deuterons, giving rise to D_2. Thus, if $_1H^2$ and $_1H^1$ fuse, it would be because the lighter nucleus penetrated the other, the two nuclear structures combining as the net positive value (+) of one nucleus is emitted, giving rise to helium, $_2He^3$, which we see to have a Core force composed of a Beta measure, Z $1 + 0$, and a Prime measure, Z 1. We represent this nucleus as:

Fig. 6—Nucleus of helium, $_2He^3$

$$2[F+(sbf)^{\circ \; \circ \; \circ \; \circ \; \circ}_{\; \circ \; \circ \; \circ}]$$
$$(- + -) \; (+ \; o)$$
$$(+) \; (- \; o + o)$$
$$(- + -) \; (+ \; o)$$

In the above representation, $2[F+(sbf)^{\circ \; \circ \; \circ \; \circ \; \circ}_{\; \circ \; \circ \; \circ}]$ symbolizes two measures or levels of space in the nucleus, one containing five degrees (°) of potential energy, the other containing three degrees (°). In the transaction giving rise to this nucleus, $_1H^2 + {}_1H^1$ reacts to produce $_2He^3$ + photon (or gamma ray).

If two helium $_2He^3$ nuclei should react to give rise to helium $_2He^4$ and to two hydrogen nuclei $_1H^1$, in our view the helium $_2He^3$ nuclei would "split" each other and what we call a "fission-fusion" would occur. As one nucleus hits the other, splitting both, its nucleon travels on, lodging in the receiving nucleus to form an Alpha Core, or alpha particle, of one nucleus. In our symbols, the alpha particle would appear:

Fig. 7—Nucleus of helium $_2He^4$, the alpha particle

$$2[F+(sbf)^{\circ \; \circ \; \circ \; \circ \; \circ}_{\; \circ \; \circ \; \circ}]$$
$$(- + -) \; (o \; +)$$
$$(+) \; (o - + o)$$
$$(- + -) \; (o + - o)$$
$$(+ \; o)$$

The other helium $_2He^3$ nucleus, suddenly stripped of its nucleon, is subjected to the stress of its positive charges (o +) (+ o) repelling each other, and this reduces the net positive value (+) that is "torn" between them to three degrees (°) of "virtual energy," which then "crowd" one level of the space chamber with six degrees (°), causing the "virtual energy" to react to form two positive values (+), which "split" the nucleus as they repel each other, one positive value (+) going to one proton which will have five degrees (°) of "virtual energy" in its space chamber, the other positive value (+) going to the other proton which will have no "virtual energy" in its space chamber. Thus, $_2\text{He}^3 + {}_2\text{He}^3$ reacts to produce $_2\text{He}^4 + 2(_1\text{H}^1)$. In our view, this transaction represents "marking time," which is to say, a *net* transaction has occurred.

We have followed the proton-proton chain, using our symbols, to represent the fusion of the nuclei of the hydrogen molecule to produce a deuteron, and the fusion of a deuteron and a proton to produce $_2\text{He}^3$, and the reaction of the nuclei of two light helium isotopes $_2\text{He}^3$ to produce one alpha particle $_2\text{He}^4$ and two hydrogen $_1\text{H}^1$ nuclei. Two reactions of the first kind and two of the second are needed before one $_2\text{He}^4$ nucleus can be formed. Therefore, a cycle of five fusions would be involved. Energy is released in the form of gamma-photons, but most of it in the form of kinetic energy of the product particles. In this cycle, as described in our symbols, the same release of particles has been represented as occurs in the proton-proton chain described by physicists. But we have employed a q-bond, which we believe exists in nature to form the hydrogen molecule, although as long as this energy functions as a q-bond, or space property, it does not communicate itself as mass. When the proton is considered as a separate entity, the q-bond is not there to be accounted for; in the case of bonded protons, it is a field property, not inside the space chamber of either nucleus, and therefore it does not "weigh upon" either, so that it is not a calculable mass.

In nature many isotopes arise, and there are different ways to form the same isotope. Too many ways to "construct" the various elements present themselves for us to pursue further the buildup of atoms. We have tried to make clear the principles we see to be involved, and that the hidden neutrino transactions play a vital role.

In our view, every increase in atomic number represents the addition of a Z 1, or a Z 1 + 0, or a Z 2 measure. The Z 2 measure may be equivalent to the nucleus of $_2\text{He}^3$, which may be seen as Z 2 + 0, or it may be equivalent to the nucleus of $_2\text{He}^4$, which may be seen as Z 2 + 00. Thus, there are four types of Cores if the light helium nucleus is counted. The *sum* of these measures constitutes the atomic number of the atom. For example, there are no Z 3, Z 4, Z 5, etc. Core measures as such; higher atomic numbers are constituted of some *combination* of the above listed types of Cores. How an element decays depends on the arrangement of its different type Core measures and which type houses the isotope's net positive value ($+$), as well as which type is, or becomes, the first and the last or outermost measure. In our view, within an isotope of sufficiently high atomic number, a Z 1 measure decays via capture of K-shell electron; a Z $1 + 0$ measure decays via beta particle emission; a Z $2 + 0$ measure equivalent to the nucleus of $_2He^3$ decays via positron emission; and a Z $2 + 00$ measure equivalent to the nucleus of $_2He^4$ decays via alpha particle emission.

Whether gamma radiation (in our symbols a single positive value ($+$), and one or more may be involved) accompanies decay and/or interaction of nuclei to form new isotopes depends in part on the number of neutrino values ($°$) in the space chambers involved and in those adjoining, and whether the double negative situation occurs as a part of the process thereby commanding positive value ($+$) from the "virtual energy" in the isotope. Within any one Core measure two negative particles versus the one positive charge pose sufficient negative attraction to command a reaction of the "virtual energy" within the measure and/or within adjacent measures to form positive value ($+$). The photon is emitted in due course as the isotope's net positive value repels it.

But there are other reactions that also give rise to gamma radiation, as will be explained following. We say here only that we believe a nucleus may react to stress or rid itself of excess "virtual energy" by emission of a gamma ray as the Core force in a Prime measure housing three degrees ($°$) of potential energy expresses momentarily in negative terms, causing the "virtual energy" to form a positive value ($+$), which is emitted. And prior stress may have caused a measure of the nucleus to be emptied of its "virtual energy," so that gamma radiation is to some degree variable.

The Core measures in the nucleus of atoms of various elements vary, and so does the arrangement of them. What might be too few nucleons in one arrangement becomes too many for the element the isotope decays into, and vice versa. The most prevalent isotope of each element represents the "ideal" arrangement and quantity of nucleons for that element. When an isotope has too high a nucleon-to-proton ratio, beta decay corrects the situation. We discuss this process first, spelling out the transactions in terms of our symbols.

Beta decay. Example: carbon $_6C^{14}$ emits a beta particle to produce nitrogen $_7N^{14}$. Atomic number increases, atomic weight remains the same.

In our view, when too many nucleons are present, the nucleon in the central Beta Core measure is "crowded," and stress causes it to "turn negative," so that it commands the reaction of the five degrees (°) of "virtual energy" in the space chamber that restores it to a neutron (see page 310). The neutron decays, in the process forming a proton, and thus the Z 1 + 0 Core measure converts to Z 1 + Z 1 and atomic number increases. But proton formation in neutron decay brings to the atom another positive value (+), and it can have but one net positive value (+), so that a photon (+) or gamma ray is emitted; or the net positive value (+) of the isotope disintegrates into its neutrino value, the three degrees (°) of potential energy being deposited in the space chamber of the Prime Core, Z 1, resulting when the Beta Core is stripped of its "virtual energy" as the neutron forms. (See pages 308, 310, and 311 for modes of neutron decay.)

K-capture. Example: Argon $_{18}A^{37}$ captures an electron to produce chlorine $_{17}Cl^{37}$. When an isotope has too high a proton-to-nucleon ratio, capture of an electron, usually one from K-shell, corrects the situation. In our view, Core measures equivalent to a Beta Core plus a Prime Core with one degree (°) of "virtual energy" in it, outermost in the nucleus, are involved. The Prime Core measure that decays does not hold the net positive value (+) of the isotope. The positive charge (+ o) of the Prime Core and the nucleon (+ o − o) in the Beta Core measure below it react to express their positive values, becoming (+ − +) and (o + − + |), thereby posing sufficient positive attraction to capture an electron, causing it to fuse with the positive charge, creating a nucleon and reducing the charge on the nucleus. The nucleon drops to the lower level, its nucleon dropping into a still lower level to form a Z 1 + 0 measure of another Prime Core that houses five degrees (°) of "virtual energy," so that, in effect, another neutron-equivalence is established in the nucleus of the isotope. The now empty Prime Core measure in which the electron was captured, together with its Core q-measure, one neutrino-value (°), and space-binding-force revert to the general field. Atomic number decreases by one, as atomic weight remains the same. As an outer shell electron drops into the K-shell to fill the vacancy, in the act emitting its photon as X-ray, it creates a double negative (− −) which commands a positive value (+) from the "virtual energy" in the field and the electron is restored.

Positron emission. If an atom with too high a proton-to-nucleon ratio is sufficiently energetic, it may correct the situation by emission of a positron. As example: nitrogen $_7N^{13}$ emits a positron and a neutrino to produce carbon $_6C^{13}$. We believe a Z 2 measure equivalent to the nucleus of

$_2$He^3 (see Fig. 6, page 319) is involved. In our view, a positive charge associated with the Z 2 measure reacts to the stress of too little binding energy by forming a "queer" particle: i.e., (+ — +) becomes (—∘ + —), thus posing *more* negative attraction than an electron, i.e., sufficient negative attraction to cause the other positive charge to fuse with it, forming a nucleon as the neutrino (*) is emitted. This leaves two q-measures in the dual space chamber, constituting thereby the double negative situation that commands a reaction of the eight degrees (°) of "virtual energy" in the dual space chamber. This energy forms two positive values and one negative value, or a positive charge (+ — +), which takes the place of the two erstwhile positive charges, thereby reducing the charge on the nucleus as atomic weight remains the same. But two q-measures remain in the space chamber, creating a 50 per cent redundancy of negative charge in this area of the nucleus, and this negative redundancy gives rise to the formation of positive values from the "virtual energy" in adjoining levels of the Core or nucleus. Thus, gamma radiation occurs as the positive values are repelled by the isotope's net positive value. As the stress of two q-measures versus one positive charge in the Core force persists, one q-measure goes into positron reaction; but in the act of going into antiparticle expression, it is repelled by the stronger force of the positive charge with its two positive values acting versus the positron's one positive value, so that the positron is emitted. When the nuclear pattern adjusts to utilize the newly formed nucleon and to form the arrangement typical of the resulting element, a measure of space with its space-binding-force reverts to the general field, for one measure or level of the original Z 2 Core will be without the q-measure necessary to secure it. Thus the Z 2 measure is reduced to a Z 1 measure. We would add that although a positron, an electron, and gamma radiation have been involved, the reaction within the nucleus differs from positronium (a positron and electron bound) decay, as will be discussed later (see pp. 325-326).

Alpha decay. Example: Polonium $_{84}$Po^{212} emits an alpha particle to produce lead $_{82}$Pb^{208} and helium $_2$He^4. We believe that such decay results from neutrino reaction giving rise to positive value (+), and that a Z 2 measure housing the isotope's net positive value (+) is involved. The isotope might "stop" a photon that disintegrates into its neutrino potential, giving an adjacent Z 1 measure six degrees (°) of potential energy, three of which react to form a positive value that arises with a spin twice as great as the spin of a proton; thus it "kicks out" of the nucleus the whole alpha particle with its two tightly bound protons, and the arising positive value (+) remains to provide a net positive value (+) for the ensuing isotope. (If all six degrees (°) of "virtual energy" react to form two photons, a gamma ray (+) will be emitted.) Emission of one alpha particle corrects the situation. But in atoms of very high density a neutrino might react with the "virtual energy" in an Alpha Core measure, "triggering" the creation of a number of values that combine with nucleons to form stress-particles, and in the decay of these particles a series of steps involving alpha and beta particle emission may be commanded, decay continuing until a stable isotope is formed.

Alpha decay could also occur as the nucleus of an atom reacts to the stress of too much "virtual energy" by expressing itself in negative or "anti" terms, causing a reaction of its own degrees (°) of potential energy so that positive value arises within the isotope. We believe such reactions are a common cause of alpha decay.

The point we would make is that the higher the ratio of nucleons to protons, the more apt the nucleus is to be "saturated" with "virtual energy" so that one more degree (°) would cause a reaction. Thus, in our view, hydrogen cannot support a two-to-one ratio of nucleons to protons, because as a deuteron absorbs a neutron to become tritium, $_1H^3$, and the neutron reacts to reduce itself to a 50 per cent redundancy of neutral value, the degrees (°) of potential energy that the neutron must deposit in the space chamber, already housing the maximum five degrees (°), cause a reaction of the "virtual energy."

Neutron absorption gives rise to the formation of new isotopes. Example: nitrogen $_7N^{14}$ absorbs a neutron and reacts to emit hydrogen $_1H^1$ and carbon $_6C^{14}$. In time, the heavy carbon emits a beta particle and translates into nitrogen $_7N^{14}$. In our view, the neutron splits the nucleus of the nitrogen, releasing its Prime Core measure, equivalent to the nucleus of $_1H^1$, which takes the isotope's net positive value (+) as the hydrogen is emitted. The neutron, left in the resulting carbon isotope, reacts in the following manner: a single negative value converts to two degrees (°) of potential energy, which are stored in a Prime Core measure, giving this measure five degrees (°) of "virtual energy"; but the "odd" positive value (+) left in the neutron is not emitted because it serves to provide the new carbon isotope with a net positive value (+); a nucleon is formed from the remaining values of the neutron, converting the Prime Core measure into a Beta Core measure. But the *arrangement* of the heavy carbon isotope is not standard for this element. In time, the carbon isotope undergoes beta decay to produce $_7N^{14}$, and in this decay reaction, the nuclear pattern of the original isotope that lost a Prime Core measure is restored.

Gamma radiation: In our view, a nucleus may react to stress or rid itself of excess "virtual energy" by emission of a photon as the Core force in a Prime Core housing three degrees (°) of potential energy expresses in negative terms, causing the "virtual energy" to form a photon, which is emitted.

In *induced radioactivity*, stable nuclei are bombarded by protons that have been accelerated to high energies in a cyclotron, and new nuclei are formed which, if unstable, undergo decay. For example: carbon $_6C^{12}$ absorbs a proton $_1H^1$ and reacts to form nitrogen $_7N^{13}$, releasing energy which, in our view, is the net positive value (+) in the proton that must be emitted. But in this fusion of hydrogen and carbon the standard pattern for nitrogen is not produced. Therefore, the nitrogen isotope decays by emitting a positron (in the decay reaction previously described) thereby restoring the carbon pattern: i.e., $_7N^{13}$ emits a positron to produce $_6C^{13}$.

The positive nuclei that are formed in the decay processes soon pick up from their surroundings or, in our view, from the Q-force at large, electrons to balance their positive charge.

Atoms lose electrons and they also capture electrons. Loss of an electron would give rise to a positive ion of the element. Gain of an electron would give rise to a negative ion of the element, but in our view although the immediate or surface communication of such an ion is negative, in terms of *being* or value count, we believe the atom is neutralized in the sense that its net positive value (+) is offset by the extra negative value in the electron cloud, so that in universal or long-range terms it would be neutral.

Positrons emitted in the decay process are soon bound to encounter electrons and combine with them to form photons. A slow positron (| + |) may interact with an electron (− + −). The two particles with a total energy equivalence of $1.6 \times 10^{-13}j$ disappear by giving rise to annihilation radiation of two photons, each having $0.8 \times 10^{-13}j$ of energy. In our view, as the negative values in the positron and electron come together they form two of the hypothetical particles we call q-2 (|) and the energy is given over to the positive values (+). The q-2 particles cannot exist in terms of mass, or "real" particles; thus, they disappear into the general field, where they disintegrate into four degrees (°) of "virtual energy." The formation of the q-2 particles prevents a double negative from arising, which would serve to reconstitute electrons after their positive values spin off.

In response to a different kind of stress, we believe that positron-electron annihilation may take place as the pair form a stress-particle within which a negative value acts upon a positive value, and the two values are reduced to five degrees (°) of "virtual energy" which lapse into the general field, leaving one photon and *three* single negative values; "antinegative" energy then arises in terms of positive value replacing negative value as the three remaining single negative values disintegrate into six degrees of potential energy, which react to produce two single positive values, so that the positron-electron "stress holding" disintegrates into three photons.

Electrons "left in the field" in decay processes revert, together with their field-forces (ff), to the Q-force at large: i.e., they "leak" out of the pile. When a beta particle is emitted, in time it may be captured by an atom; or it may react with a positron; or it may "disappear" as it contracts to a q(−) measure and remains in the general field, becoming unmanifested, but we believe that sooner or later such a q(−) measure will react with a free neutron, thereby reconstituting a Q bundle in space.

In our view, when the atom is in ground state, the electron expresses as "nearly neutral," (− o), and "rests" upon its field, but stress causes it to go into charge reaction (− + −). If a photon hitting a metal surface has sufficient energy to give rise to the photoelectric effect, in our terms it has sufficient energy to activate the electron, causing it to translate from (− o) to (− + −), and/or to cause a q(−) value in the surrounding field or Q-force to react to become (− + −), whereupon the photon lapses into three degrees (°) of potential energy and disappears in space. An electron "dropping" to a lower energy level (as, for example, an electron drops to fill the vacancy caused by capture of a K-shell electron) may be likened to the electron in rest state (− o) suddenly being drawn to the positive nucleus, the electron becoming activated as it swings into action and its mass potential (o) "hits" a positive value (+) in its "reinforced" field; whereupon the electron's positive value (+) is "knocked out" of the arrangement and another positive value (+) "takes place." The electron's photon might also be "knocked out" as the electron is accelerated.

An electron in rest state (− o) may be likened to a tiny magnet. Our concept of this particle (− o) and/or of q(−) reacting to become an electron (− + −), or an electrical force, parallels in our terms Faraday's discovery of the production of electric currents by changes in magnetic force; and the contraction of an electron (− + −) into (− o) and/or q(−) represents in our terms Faraday's discovery that changes in the electric force will produce a magnetic force. Both reactions are "submicroscopic" in character.

We associate Q energy and/or *negative expression* with liquid or wave

326

action, and with an "unapparent force" arising in response to P energy and its motion, which we associate with light, heat, and matter. We believe negative action makes it possible for a body to move through space, and explain as follows.

Our concept of particles composed of opposite values, operating upon a neutral field composed of opposite values, allows us to explain *motion* in terms of its being a *series of rests*. (The modern theory of infinite sets, which makes possible a correspondence between positions and instants of time, the positions and the instants each forming an infinite set, poses the concept that motion is a series of rests: i.e., at each instant of the interval during which an object is in "motion" it occupies a definite position and thus may be said to be at rest.) We see motion in terms of its being a "mixture" of action and rest. In "submicroscopic" terms, we say that a mass moves as its negative values "grasp and adhere" to the positive values in the field or substance in which it is immersed, while the positive values, dragging at the heels of the negative values, remain secured to negative values in the field or substance, moving forward only after the negative values are secured, so that at no time is the mass "altogether moving" or "altogether still." Because it is both moving and stationary, it must be viewed in terms of velocity or of position, for when in progress it is both "here now" and "there now" until it has completed its move, whereupon a new position has been established. Thus, its motion is a "divided effort" in order to secure it in space at all times, and motion itself is a series of rests; the *absolute* speed of the mass at the limit, or at "zero hour," cannot be calculated, because at no time are the sum of its forces in action.

We summarize the principles presented in this and the foregoing sections as follows. That part of an atom expressed as potential energy (o) causes it to be subject to classical law. That part of an atom expressed as single negative and single positive values causes it to be subject to quantum law, which combines the properties of waves (negative action) and of particles (positive action), giving rise to electromagnetic radiation. But the atom's "virtual energy," ($^\circ$), operates according to a law which can be understood only in terms of the unending creative potential vested in the digits *zero* and *one*, or in the mathematical principle we symbolize as ($-/- = +$) and ($+/+ = +$), which gives rise to a "perpetually positive balance sheet." We call this law the "One law."

We believe "One law" controls the absorption of light to allow it to produce an effect on living systems; the effect is produced as light is reduced to provide "virtual energy," which is used by the organism to fulfill its needs. In our view, light can be absorbed only as the net positive value ($+$) of an atom is obscured and/or offset by negative value and/or negative expression. This gives rise to what might be called "indirect" positive value: i.e., a supply of the "very-stuff" of the universe is obtained as the light is reduced to provide neutrino value ($°$).

The elusive neutrinos do not act directly upon or with matter except in rare instances. In our view, this is because all in existence is so submerged in and involved with energy expressed as neutrinos that chaos would ensue if the operation of the neutrino were not limited and controlled by the law of light, its pace restricted to light's pace, its absorption effected for the most part as light is absorbed and its energy is transferred in one way or another.

In this presentation of our concept, we are concerned with nuclear physics, with the inorganic realm. But at some point, this realm merges into the organic: i.e., inanimate "stuff" is transformed into animate "stuff." We will touch but briefly on this transformation, describing in our symbols only one particle, which we believe gives rise to a new class of "elementary particles," the organic "stuff." We explain it by saying that we see a measure of inorganic potential energy as a simple union of positive and negative values (o), which cannot exist as a particle of itself alone, because the values annihilate, the negative value acting upon the positive. We see a measure of organic potential energy as *the union of two positive values*, which takes place as light is absorbed and reduced to the q-1 particle, giving rise to a particle we call p-1 and symbolize as: ($-°+$) or ($-*+$). We do not call the p-1 particle "queer" because we see it as a stable measure, which can exist of itself alone because the degree ($°$) of "virtual energy" stands between the negative and positive values to prevent the one from acting upon the other. The degree ($°$) of neutral energy acts as a binding force between the opposite values even as it separates them; it expresses the "least" of binding energy, but it is a singular force that gives rise to a singular particle, which enfolds all three of the singular aspects of being: negative ($-$), positive ($+$), and neutral ($°$).

The p-1 particle can pose a stronger negative attraction than a simple measure of inorganic neutral energy operating in conjunction with other values. We symbolize this as ($°\overline{+}$) versus ($\overline{+}$), or as an arrangement wherein the negative value enhances the negative force of the positive value, and the degree ($°$) of potential energy also enhances the negative force of the positive value, since it is posed on the horizontal line. In our view, once a p-1 particle is formed, it can absorb an entering photon, which is reduced to its neutrino value, and these degrees (°) of potential energy may be used to form other p-type particles. We see p-1 as a transitional particle and as the coefficient or "joint agent" that gives rise to organic material. We believe it to be a "transparent" measure of matter that bridges the organic and inorganic realms; but the p-1 particle cannot communicate itself as such because it involves no redundancy.

Returning now to the inorganic realm, we would say that because we see the neutrino values as capable of expressing binding energy, we must conclude that the "virtual energy" in the space chamber of a nucleus brings to bear on the binding energy of the isotope (i.e., it is a Core measure empty or emptied of "virtual energy" that splits off to form of one isotope two different ones), although the "virtual energy" cannot be calculated in terms of mass, or positive or negative charge.

We summarize by saying that a 50 per cent redundancy of some value, together with a measure of neutral energy (o), is needed for an aggregate of energy to communicate itself as mass, or charge. Not all of the energy in a mass can be active, or communicated, or expressed as potential energy (o), because some must be expressed as a "silent" holding force. A 50 per cent redundancy of neutral energy and no other redundancy communicates nothing but potential energy and/or neutrality, so that a neutral redundancy may hide the fact that in value count the aggregate is *net* a positive or a negative value. If a 50 per cent redundancy of positive or of negative value exists together with a 50 per cent redundancy of neutral energy, the mass will communicate itself as positive or negative as the case may be. Any aggregate that is *net a negative value* communicates itself in negative or *unapparent* ways; any aggregate that is *net a positive value* communicates itself in positive or *apparent* ways. A change in value count and/or expression of values gives rise to a change in *what* is communicated by the mass and to changes of state such as liquefying, burning, boiling, translating to gaseous state, freezing, crystallizing, etc., which we believe are due to shifting expression of the value-groupings from positive to negative to neutral or vice versa, and to binding energy going into and out of "secondary reaction" in response to stress. A 50 per cent redundancy of any value: positive, negative, or neutral, or less than a 50 per cent redundancy of any value represents a stable situation (with the one exception of a single measure of neutral energy (— +), which is not actually expressed of itself alone, the two values disintegrating into five degrees (°) of potential energy). But *more* than a 50 per cent redundancy of any value gives rise to a situation that is in some way unstable: i.e., the particle will decay, or it will command a reaction that corrects the situation.

A number of the principles we have discussed, and particularly those in the paragraph above, have been drawn from a formula we call the "Law of Communication," and its author must be acknowledged. In James Moffatt's translation of the Bible, Matt. 5:18 reads:

> ... till heaven and earth pass away, not an iota, not a comma, will pass from the law until it is all in force.

In the discourse following, Jesus states the formula of His law of communication:

Yea, yea; Nay, nay

When every "iota" of this formula is counted, we see that it consists of eight factors: (Yea)(,)(yea)(,)($\cdot$)(Nay)(,)(nay). The words bespeak the power and penetration of neutral energy and represent the expression of its force, giving the leading role to arrangement of the energy and revealing the efficiency of a 50 per cent redundancy in expression to convey and communicate an effect. Jesus' insistence that every iota be considered indicates that only part of the energy involved in any expression is communicable; some must be utilized as a "silent" force to insure the being of the expressing values, even as some is made unavailable at the time the energy is expressed. The comma in the positive segment of the formula (Yea, yea) must represent a "silent" value that acts "as nothing," but serves as a binding force to keep the two positive values from repelling each other. The same would be true of the comma in the negative segment of the formula (Nay, nay). The semicolon must represent values that appear to be "nothing," but serve to give discreteness to the positive expression and to the negative expression, even as it demands the *pause*, or time's action, which allows for the separation of neutral energy into active positive and negative charges; the semicolon also indicates that *space* is involved in every "solid" expression of energy. We see the semicolon to represent "lost energy," or one positive and one negative value, which is made unavailable in one way or another at the time the energy is expressed, as the reaction we describe as ($-+=$ o) occurs, giving rise to a potential that disintegrates into five degrees ($\circ$) of "virtual energy," indicating this to be all that one measure of space can house. Jesus says that "whatsoever" is *more* than the formula expresses "cometh of evil." These words bespeak the attraction posed by neutral energy, and also indicate that the law reveals the maximum redundancy that a particle may express of its values in one measure of space without translating to an unstable state, and the maximum degree of "unavailable" or "virtual energy" that any one measure of space may house before a reaction occurs. The formula as quoted above, and Jesus' words that follow, may be found in the King James Authorized Version of the Bible, Matt. 5:37.

In our symbols, the law of communication would be written:

$$(o)$$
$$(+ - +)/(- + -)$$

Yea, yea; Nay, nay

The "silent" values do not communicate their negative or positive or neutral natures because they are not redundant expressions; the measure of potential energy (o) disintegrates into [° ° ° ° °].

In our view, the law represents the *expression* of a neutron in *one* measure of space that gives rise to a nucleon in the nucleus as the charges fuse to produce (+ o o −) and communicate potential energy, which is all the formula expresses. Or the formula may be seen as one prime measure of neutral energy: i.e., an aggregate of four positive and four negative values (+ − + − + − + −).

Or the formula may be seen as the expression of charge, because it conforms to the famous ice-pail experiment, which demonstrated two important principles: first, the production of a charge of one sign is always accompanied by the production of an equal charge of opposite sign; secondly, all the excess charge of a hollow conductor normally resides on the outside surface, the net charge in the interior of the conductor being zero. In the formula, opposite charges are produced; the "interior" of the formula's arrangement is neutral (yea; Nay) and the semicolon insists upon "space," or we might say that the expression itself appears to be "hollow," albeit "solid."

The formula also indicates that in the *arrangement* of potential energy or mass, positive charge or values are *grouped together* to *begin* the expression: i.e., to form the nucleus, and negative charge or values are grouped together to complete the expression and allow it to communicate as a neutral mass.

If one chooses to count the colon that follows the formula, in our view the two "jots" must be seen as two like values, which we believe represent the positive values that must be included in the atom's make-up: i.e., the positive value of space, and the net positive value of the atom. Seen in this light, the formula indicates that the nucleus immediately communicates its positive charge, but underlying it and "dealing" with the space and "hidden" energy within it is a negative charge and the dual positive value that gives to each atom its positive being. The formula may be read: (Yea, yea; Nay, nay:).

Taken at "face value," the formula indicates that energy in expression moves *from* positive *to* negative expression; *from* negative *to* neutral expression: *from* neutral *to* positive and negative expression or vice versa. But viewed as a whole, the formula would say: as energy flows into equilibrium, potential energy is created, and the flow is equated and equating.

The law also reveals that the *expressed and communicable* forces are redundant or complex in their constitution; but that there are "silent" forces, which do not communicate their natures, or themselves as mass, because they are not redundant expressions. But their natures and the reality of their being and actions can be inferred through the discipline of mathematics and from the results they produce.

Thus, there is a universe behind the dark side of the mirror, a realm that cannot be entered by the senses or perceptions they give rise to. Only as faith moves hand in hand with reason can intelligence pass through the darkness to examine the unseen and look into the future.

Jesus' words, "will not pass from the law until it is all in force," indicate that the universe is still in the process of "becoming." We turn now to present our conclusions as to what "becoming" and progress in this direction means.

IV

Stars like our sun appear to be headed toward eventual "death" as all of their internal hydrogen is used up. But in our view it is possible for such stars, which began their evolution with a supply of material other than hydrogen and which have reached the main sequence phase of development, to achieve a *steady state* and thereby to become what we call "energy reactors," or producers of the hydrogen they consume.

This is to say, we believe Q energy is drawn into the sun and there converted into hydrogen. But this does not reverse time's arrow, because the hydrogen thus produced is consumed, so that a plus-minus operation or a "marking of time" occurs. The sun appears to have "spent" roughly half of its projected lifetime, which means to us that it is now a "balanced mass," or in a steady state and will never show itself to be any "older."

Taking both a "supramacroscopic" and a "submicroscopic" view, we explain our concept as follows: Each celestial body represents a sum of positive value, which determines the measure of attraction it poses for Q energy. Each measure of empty space within a celestial body and every atom within it pose one measure of positive attraction for Q energy. Every proton poses two measures of positive attraction for Q energy, and every negative ion of hydrogen poses no attraction, because in effect it is neutral. Thus, a celestial body may have a large number of negative hydrogen ions (giving its surface a negative charge), but being neutral in *long-range* effect, they do not pose a long-range repelling force in relation to Q energy, nor do they obscure the positive attraction the body has for Q energy. Its attraction for Q energy is determined by its density and by the number of positive ions and atoms that compose it.

We suggest that our sun is a mass expressing a sum of positive value, of such size and so arranged that it strongly attracts the Q-force. The attraction is such that through Q action the sun can contain within its sphere of influence its system of planets and manufacture from the energy derived from the Q-force sufficient hydrogen to "burn" to maintain them. We do not attempt to represent in our symbols the complex make-up of the sun, but say only that because of its arrangement it maintains its temperature and draws Q energy into the interior, where it is reacted.

As Q energy comes upon the sun, the sun's enormous and tenuous atmosphere composed of highly ionized gas poses such diffused attraction that less of the Q-force "digresses" around the atmosphere to "envelop" the sun, i.e., more of the Q energy is drawn through the atmosphere toward the dense concentration of positive value in the core. But as the Q energy moves deeper and deeper into the corona, positive ions trap some of it, causing it to contract and then to react to emit its neutrons, which travel on toward the interior, as its $q(-)$ values act to bond the positive nuclei; hydrogen is reconstituted as the Q energy reacts with the bonded nuclei to form electrons and their field-forces (see page 303), and free electrons in the atmosphere react with the hydrogen to give rise to a large number of negative hydrogen ions. As the oncoming Q energy penetrates this photosphere, the negative hydrogen ions, communicating a short-range negative redundancy versus the negative being of the Q energy, repel it, diversifying its flow. Thus they act as a brake upon the Q-force, mitigating its pressure upon the sun itself. But some of the Q energy reaches the interior, and here, again, positive ions trap it, causing it to emit its neutrons, which are used to manufacture hydrogen. We believe this is accomplished in nuclear reactions not necessarily identical to but like those that produce hydrogen when nitrogen $_7N^{14}$ absorbs a neutron and emits hydrogen $_1H^1$ and carbon $_6C^{14}$, which in time emits a beta particle to produce again the nitrogen isotope $_7N^{14}$, and the transaction is repeated *ad infinitum*.

This is to say, the necessary fuel is neutrons, which we believe the Q-force brings to the sun. In one or more of several possible transactions the neutrons are reacted to produce protons, electrons, and antineutrinos, which are emitted, so that the "ingredients" of hydrogen are there. The more than 50 per cent redundancy of positive value that forms in an isotope through beta decay (see pages 311 and 321) commands a full measure of the Q energy from the incoming flow, which in turn commands from the ever-present space in the sun, the necessary measure to produce a Prime Core and/or the nucleus of hydrogen. Some of the beta particles released in beta decay are radiated as they form electron-positron pairs; others are used to bond the hydrogen nuclei. The hydrogen thus produced feeds the proton-proton chain that provides most of the energy radiated by the sun, although we believe the carbon cycle also plays a part.

From the helium and hydrogen produced by the proton-proton chain, and in the operation of the carbon cycle, all the elements necessary to the sun's operation are created anew, thus preventing an excessive buildup of helium. Part of the sun's matter is lost in each of its eruptions, and this matter must be regenerated if its balance is to be maintained. We believe that the sun is sufficiently active to disperse its surplus matter. Some of the beta particles that are trapped in the sun's atmosphere as the Q energy reacts to free its neutrons are radiated as they form electron-positron pairs. Some are dispersed in solar flares: i.e., we believe that the stress of these eruptions creates hyperons of some of the positive hydrogen ions; these decay to give rise to neutrons in which the negative charges are "grounded." As the surplus electrons are "grounded" in the neutrons, Q energy is reconstituted and the Q-force is replenished, so that the sun's operation does not constitute an unmitigated drain upon Q energy at large.

We believe that in order to reach a steady state, a star must decrease its ratio of hydrogen and increase its ratio of helium and other elements to give it a stability that hydrogen masses do not possess. But this process can continue only up to a point before degenerative processes begin. The sun has lost much of its original hydrogen. In the process, it contracted, but space was left throughout the exterior "layers" of its matter until it reached its present density and a blanket of negative hydrogen ions formed in the photosphere, cooling it and equating its dense core of positive ions, allowing the sun to maintain an interior of strongly concentrated positive value. Because it contains a limited amount of material that reacts readily with neutrons to form hydrogen, it produces only a limited amount of fuel. Because the force of the mainstream of Q energy is diminished as the energy disperses through the vast chromosphere and corona, its effect as a force moving upon a moving body to sustain its motion cannot be the same as its effect on a planet or a solid body with a comparatively shallow atmosphere.

We believe each star goes through a "critical period," during which it builds up isotopes subject to beta decay, which will produce neutron-absorbing isotopes that convert the neutrons to hydrogen. If in the beginning the star has sufficient material and/or if it produces sufficient material to sustain it so that it does not consume *more* than 50 per cent of its hydrogen before it becomes a producer, it will survive its critical period and emerge as an energy reactor. Because the sun has been "behaving steadily" for so many millions upon millions of years, and because of the known elements within it, we believe it has passed its critical period and now conforms to a pattern in nature that is recurring and stable, just as the proton is a recurring and stable pattern (as evidenced in beta decay). This is to say, once a hydrogen producer "occurs," the pattern that allows for its stability recurs as each cycle of its operation is completed. Thus, we see the sun as a "presently" active hydrogen producer, as eternal as *now* is the eternal measure of time.

Although we do not believe that all main-sequence stars (or any other type stars) are necessarily evolving toward and will reach a steady state, we believe there are other energy reactors such as the sun, and that some stars are still in process of becoming such reactors, and herein may rest the "becoming" of the universe. We believe also that each celestial body now serves and, regardless of what it evolves into, will continue to serve some function indispensable in the operation of the whole system.

Thus, the universe both *is* and is *coming to be*. ALL THAT WAS remains in being *as* space and *in* space. Upon the fields spreading to encompass the masses and the galaxies they form, the Q-force at large flows. If the universe is actually expanding, rather than merely giving the appearance of expanding through some action and reaction not as yet understood, then in our view it may be that in the reaches of intergalactic space, empty space itself is still expanding. Whereas space neither acts upon nor reacts to Q and P energy within it, except in terms of being a force constant [F+], it may still be self-reacting. This is to say, each measure of its constant positive being must repel each other measure until the force of repulsion is spent in every direction.

Because there is infinitely more space than matter, as space expands, it must form in time a perimeter or band of nothing but constant positive force that repels and turns "inward" the masses of matter within it. The Q-force will never dissipate itself in following the expansion of space because so many bodies in space constitute concentrations of positive value which, together with the centering attraction of the "central deeps" of empty space, makes of Q energy a centering or gathering force both in universal and in particular terms versus the possibly still active force of expansion of space that someday must be complete. Herein, also, may rest the "becoming" of the universe. Time, which we see to be an expansion-contraction process, may be the "regulator" of the pace of space expansion, so that when it is complete one of time's functions will be completed, and time will be sensed in terms of "eternity," or eternal creation, versus man's present sense of it as past versus future.

Or, it may be that the expansion of space, and thus the universe itself, is complete; within it, however, the force of repulsion between the galaxies of matter may not as yet be spent, so that herein rests the "becoming" of order within the universe.

Someday the reorganization of ALL THAT WAS will be complete. The Q-force will travel its path, and orbital systems will take their final forms. Entropy must then be taken with the Q sign, the minus sign, —(entropy), signifying order that allows for change and exchange of energy in a dynamic system in which the creative process will not pass away.

We see the creative process to be operative today: within the universe, the unity that is light may be anywhere decimated, but it is always resurrected as by threes, neutrinos react to become light, or as by twos, they react to form negative energy that poses the double negative in space energy, thereby "lifting" positive value (+). We believe that two or three negative values will produce light: i.e., two negative values or a double negative (— —) command a positive value by means of a neutrino reaction, and three negative values acting upon each other disintegrate into six degrees (°) of potential energy, which react to produce two photons (+).

The heavens, as Jesus beheld them and as we behold them, are passing away. So, too, the earth, as it was in His day and as it is today, is passing away. But neither heaven nor earth is passing away as men expect it. In the passing, there is always rebirth, renewal, re-creation. For example, today, as evolutionists count time, the island of Surtsey was born.

Within the larger celestial systems, smaller systems operate. Within these smaller systems it is possible for very small masses to be swept into collision with the larger mass, but we believe this happens only when the small masses are composed predominantly of negative ions, which obscure or offset the net positive being of matter in ground state, so that the repelling force of the body's net positive value in being does not prevail. The attraction of neutral energy or the force of gravity overcomes it. Or, we believe, stress has caused the small mass to express itself in terms of enhanced negative value, and/or it has liquefied, which we see to be a state in which matter is giving *expression* to its negative value; again, the repelling force of matter's net positive value is obscured, so that the liquid mass "falls" upon the larger body.

As a small celestial mass travels through an atmosphere, and as it strikes another body, it is subjected to different types of stress, which may cause changes in its constitution and/or expression. *Maximum stress* might cause a small body to express itself in terms of antimatter, and thus upon impact with another body it would take its toll of the body's matter: i.e., upon impact, itself and its equivalence would convert to energy, leaving only a scar upon the terrain. In this way, we believe that in the early and chaotic development of the universe, and of any solar system, as much matter as is in evidence was converted to neutrinos; and today stellar "explosions" still subject matter to maximum stress, and thus a "stream" of neutrinos is emitted. But we also believe that once a solar system is established, *maximum stress* cannot occur within it except in *minimum terms*: i.e., in the expression of very small bodies of antimatter, because the system as a whole is harmonious, the bodies within it symbiotic, and every move made within the system (and within the universe) diminishes the *destructive potential* inherent in the power it enfolds and expresses.

V

What lies beyond the outermost limits of space? If one could satisfactorily describe the universe and the tiniest particle in it, he would not have answered that question. Nor would he have answered the question of what attraction between opposites actually *is*. What is the force that holds the opposite aspects of the least neutral particle, the "little one," in a union that cannot be put asunder? We are trying to say, simply, that God cannot be reduced to a material creation, nor can the force that binds an "iota" of it, the neutrino, be measured in terms of physical energy.

Opposites attract, but what are opposites if all in creation is made of the same fundamental "stuff," the same *one* energy? *Asymmetry* must be the basis of opposites: there are . . . "five at issue in one house, three divided against two and two against three . . ."[141] In the "house" of the least one, the neutrino, the formula (3/2 vs 2/3) may be seen to indicate that there are three "bits" of something engaging two "bits" of something, and vice versa, that gives rise to the imperishable union of *one*. And the formula indicates that in the "house" of the largest *one*, the universe, there are two kinds of the imperishable union: i.e., a left-handed (3/2) and a right-handed (2/3) "little one." Because each type neutrino may express as its antiparticle, and because each type lapses into the same degree (°) of potential energy, thereby restoring symmetry and regaining the unity of one, there are *five* types of "little ones" in the neutrino class.

Jesus, author of this formula, follows it with words that indicate matter to have its being in and to be supported by or upon a negative matrix, even as the positive bodies repel each other, and the negative bodies repel each other. (See pp. 185, 186, 209, *The Shining Stranger*.)

Nothing in a description of matter can explain how and why an elementary particle is "knowledgeable" enough and "sentient" enough to recognize its like-sign and its opposite-sign in expression, communicating this "knowledge and feeling" in its behavior.

Nor can any description of matter and the universe account for or explain thought, because thought cannot be bound entirely within the realm of mass and/or energy: it travels faster than light to reach through space and *be* as distant as 3C-9 in the act of thinking of the quasar. Thought reaches ahead of time to bring to the present its reaction to whatever is projected to take place billions of years hence; it reaches behind time to consider what *was* before the universe came into being and cosmic dust became living matter, a "stone" enfolding this potential.[142]

We have no better word than *God* as a name for all that which cannot be accounted for, explained, or measured in the terms that account for, explain, and measure the material realm and its activity. God is expressed in the majesty of the natural realm and in the intelligence of nature; God is expressed in man as intelligence, so infinite in reach and being that he can pose the question of what lies before and beyond space, time, and consciousness. God is the force of love that enfolds the universe and bonds the tiniest particle of energy. God is that in a man which enables him to love, and to so love the *world* that he would hang upon the Cross to send into the minds of future generations the symbol of creation's positive-being, and of light's positive-being and eternal presence because it is resurrected: ". . . where two or three have gathered in my name, I am there among them."[143]

We believe that Jesus spoke not as *person*, and not as historical Messiah, but as symbol of light and as symbol of man's unique power of speech, through which his eventual enlightenment is insured:

> In the beginning was the Word, and the Word was with God, and the Word was God. . . . All things were made by him; and without him was not any thing made that was made. In him was life; and the life was the light of men. And the light shineth in darkness; and the darkness comprehended it not.[144]

SUMMARY

by Oliver L. Reiser

Cosmic Humanism in Relation to
the Theory of the Living Universe

One of the important contributions of Preston Harold's synthesis appears in the views he developed with respect to the realms of life and mind. Harold left us a statement of his ideas relative to the physical sciences—unfortunately, not as complete as one might wish. However, his theory concerning mind energy and mental phenomena is quite thorough. But there is the vast domain of the biological sciences concerning the content of which we do not have a completely integrated synthesis, that is, the manner in which his hypothesis is to be applied in the biological sciences. Today this is such an intriguing area—the scene of many recent "breakthroughs"—that it is desirable to observe how his view fits in with "organismic thinking" as this is now being done in philosophical biology.

In the main, the task here is to deal with the empirical problems in the area of biology as a natural science—the arguments for the "organismic analogy" and the objections to such "wholistic thinking." It will be said by some critics that Harold's thesis that the vast universe is itself a living system follows logically from his use of terms; whereas the natural scientist wants to examine the empirical evidence that gives content and substance to such definitions and postulates. For the natural sciences, the difficulty with the "postulational systems" approach, as it is termed, is that alternative postulate constructs (arithmetics, geometries, algebras) are possible, and the postulational structures are purely formal and do not prescribe which of the alternate systems is to be accepted as the right "fit" for any given empirical realm. This point has been well put by Albert Einstein in his essay in *Sidelights of Relativity* (1923, pp. 27-45), where he states:

> As far as the laws of mathematics refer to reality, they are not certain; and as far as they are certain, they do not refer to reality.

This is generally accepted by scientists and logicians.

Of course, if one can set up what Professors Margenau and Northrop term "epistemic correlations" between conceptual and perceptual domains, it is possible to pass from the one to the other. This, indeed, is the case in Harold's scheme wherein his incompletely developed theory of knowledge—technically this would be called an "epistemological monism"—indicates how the idea of *ONE* is basic both to nature and to thought. This is why it is possible to derive physics from the primal unity. In this way, too, Harold solves the problem posed by Einstein (above), the problem of passing from postulates (including arithmetic's) to empirical reality. This part of the story has been set forth by Harold, himself, and further explicated by Winifred Babcock, in their respective expositions in the present volume, and it is not necessary to go over that ground again.

In passing, however, one may note that—according to Dr. William Desmonde—the numbers zero (0) and (1), as employed by Harold, are not related to the utilization of the binary number system in digital computers. Offhand it seems that Harold is closer to Pythagoreanism—or even the Hegelian dialectic of the transcendence of opposites—than to the Boolean algebra. And yet a diligent search on the part of a student of mathematical logic, one who is interested in the theory of automata, might reveal that there are connections, at least by implication, between Harold's "numerology" and contemporary information theory, thus indirectly relating the "hypothesis" to computer science. This should be further explored.

But to return to the "world as a living system." This idea has a long history, going back to the ancient Greeks in Western culture; and yet it has survived to come down into modern thought. For our purposes, however, it is not necessary to recount the history of the analogy of the world to the system.

So far as the possibilities are concerned, the "world" we mentioned above can refer in its widest sense to the "Cosmos as a whole," or in a more limited way to our planet, the earth. In my own thinking I have adopted and defended both versions. I would like to believe that this is also the case with Harold's hypothesis. But for me the explanation and defense of the idea of the Cosmos as a living system would require an exposition of the structure and functioning of the eight-dimensional Cosmos, and this has already been done in the book *Cosmic Humanism*. This volume may be consulted by anyone who wants that version. I feel reasonably certain, however, that when the implications of Harold's philosophy have been extracted, it will appear that his is also a multidimensional system. For example, the careful student will discover that Harold's

344

conception of the mind energy that undergirds the universe seems to be congruent with our picture as this involves the higher dimensionalities that emergent evolution under the influence of "guiding fields" seems to require.

But that is not our present task. In this summary we confine ourselves to the more moderate thesis that our Planet Earth is a living organism, referring to the more ambitious undertaking as something that will be dealt with in my forthcoming volume, *Man's Search for Cosmic Meaning*. This, of course, limits our present field of vision to a fragmentary part of Harold's grand-scale purview. Accordingly, we shall not here deal with the kingdom of "molecular biology"; with the DNA-RNA information explosion; with Harold's communication theory as a consequence of the nature of "light"; nor even with the fascinating *Yang-Yin* duality as an expression of the male-female complementarity. These are important, to be sure; but when they enter into this survey, they will be tributary to other considerations.

Nonetheless, some aspects of Harold's total picture are essential as parts of the present context, and they must be kept in mind.

Therefore, to encapsulate Harold's leading principles, let us remind ourselves that the hypothesis asserts that there is one primordial energy from which all things flow. This primordial energy is expressed in the physical world as opposite forces, namely, positive and negative and neutral (noncharged) energy. Differences in the manifestation of this energy are seen in gravitational, magnetic, nuclear, and electric energy—indeed, space itself—each of which depends on whether more or less of each value (positive, negative, neutral) is involved.

Of special interest is Harold's postulated nexus between "physical" and "metaphysical" energy, both being expressions of one original energy. Perhaps Harold will turn out to be the one thinker whose hypothesis will succeed in bridging the time-honored chasm separating the mental and the physical realms, thus reconciling the spiritual and material duality of life.

In this world-view, mind energy—an expression of the primordial energy—flows through space with the matrix energy, which is called the Q-force by Harold, and is in fact identified with "time." Mental energy can travel faster than light, which also flows through space with matrix energy, because mental energy meets with no resistance. Moreover, unlike other energy manifestations, mental energy can operate upon the field of space itself, independent of the Q-force, so that mental energy approximates timelessness.

In this metaphysics, which in some ways is reminiscent of the views

345

of Sir James Jeans and Sir Arthur Eddington, it is clear that the foundations of physical reality are constructed out of the primal energies, which are mathematical-mental in structure. Physical reality in turn gives rise to biological and psychological realms and phenomena, and these, therefore, are expressions of the Cosmic mind-force that pervades the universe. This means that the universe is a meaningful place, which is to be comprehended in terms of the communication of energies. This leads naturally to Harold's central idea about communication, namely, that communication involves a certain redundancy of the three values (positive, negative, neutral), which is necessary before that aspect of energy can be communicated by any organization mass.

In passing, it is interesting to note how the proper interactions of these energies—as interpreted in terms of the *entropy* of physics versus the *antientropy* of living systems—give rise, on the human level, to love and empathy. This in turn quite properly leads to the conception of spiritual love and thus culminates in practical, ethical conclusions. And that brings us back to the world of organisms.

On numerous previous occasions I have proposed my own version of the characteristics of what Dr. Nicolas Rashevsky has termed "organismic set theory." As far back as my volume *Philosophy and the Concepts of Modern Science* (1935), and for whatever it was worth, the notion of society as an organism was propounded and exalted. And more recently, in the theory of Planet Earth as an organism on the way to the fabrication of a *World Sensorium*, we have referred to earth as a "giant creature." But what do the critics say about such analogical speculations?

One of the earlier of the modern thinkers to examine and reject this way of thinking was the German physiologist Du Bois-Reymond. In the last century this authority argued in his book *Über die Grenzen des Naturerkennens* that before we can allow a psychical principle in the universe, it must be shown that there must be "somewhere within it, embedded in neurine and fed with warm arterial blood under proper pressure, a convolution of ganglionic globules and nerve-tubes proportioned in size to the faculties of such a mind." The physiologist therefore asserted that since no such gigantic ganglionic globules or nerve-tubes have been discovered, we must conclude that no such "psychical principle" is attributable to the universe.

This type of criticism of the organismic theory is rather conventional. The reply in the form of counter-arguments, and a reaffirmation of the thesis, has been given by Charles M. Child, the distinguished biologist, who is anything but a romanticist. I therefore quote his reply, from his

346

important volume, *The Physiological Foundations of Behavior* (1924, p. 270) as follows:

> Objections such as those that human society is not a big animal, that it has, for example, no stomach, no muscles, etc., are just as true of many organisms as for society. It has been said that the social mind has no sensorium. But do not human individuals in relation to each other and to the environment constitute the sensorium of the social mind just as truly as cells and cell groups in relation to each other and to the external world constitute the sensorium of the individual mind?

This should have quieted the critics. But still more recently, another objection has been voiced by Francis O. Schmitt,[145] from whom I quote the following:

> There are twice as many neurons in a human cortex as there are inhabitants on this planet. If each inhabitant had a private telephone wired for communication with a substantial fraction of all other inhabitants and used it constantly, would such global intercommunication constitute an emergent global entity having properties comparable to self-awareness and consciousness in human beings?

Professor Schmitt's reply is in the negative.

What is wrong with this question is that the analogy is being distorted. The ego or highest integration of brain dynamics is the psyche, but consciousness of the highest unitive entity cannot be experienced on the level of the component parts—we humans as individuals—for the constituents of the gestalt are conscious only of themselves and their part-processes. Only a superobserver, the world mind of *Sensorium*, can play that role on the level of the "planetary encephalograms"—to use my favorite term.

Our human world at present is like a low-grade organism—it is an acephalous affair, segmented like a tapeworm, with no brain and no efficient organization of the body as a whole. If society is to "get ahead," it must become a high-level organism and acquire a planetary brain and organs for integrating its vast multiplicity of now uncoordinated activities. The time has come to take the step from social segmentation to political cephalization.

All this points to the need for the cephalization of a world psychosomatic creature, a *World Sensorium*. But a high-grade organism has not only a central nervous system, with right and left brain lobes; it also has a "mind." This world mind for the planetary democracy must be a world philosophy, and it is hoped that a "cosmic humanism" can supply the cosmology for the coming global civilization. Never in history has man

347

had more knowledge—and so little wisdom. The synthesis of wisdom must, therefore, become the magnet around which all our efforts are oriented. Integrate—or die—that is the message from the emerging world organism.

Perhaps at this point it might be expected that the next step would constitute a vast extrapolation from the concept of "society as an organism," and "Planet Earth as an organism," to the theory of the "universe as a living system" that will always be able to support life. If one accepts Harold's hypothesis of the universe as a living system, then all else follows. And if one does not accept this, much if not all of Harold's system falls to the ground. Clearly, if one agrees that in the Cosmic operation the Q energy flowing through space is as the "blood" that courses through the "vascular system of a body," bringing sustenance to the "organs" within it, one does not need to look for Du Bois-Reymond's "nerve-tubes" and the "ganglionic globules"—though, to be sure, in our own version of the world organism we have surmised that human beings (and perhaps all "intelligent beings" in any extraterrestrial systems that are on the basic DNA-RNA code and, therefore, have transposable alpha rhythm frequencies?) are in fact embryonic cells (neuroblasts) of an overarching *World Sensorium.*

So let us not try to push the "analogy" too far—at least in Harold's scheme of things. For him, the "analogy" is really an "identity." The design of creation is universal in terms of the fundamental archetypes of "cross-action." We can, therefore, conclude this summary in this manner: given Harold's own terms and hypothesis, it is possible and proper to say that his world-view passes the test. But this, in the last analysis, also involves an "act of faith." However, all scientific hypotheses, philosophies, and religions require some measure of faith, and if this affirmation yields overtones of melody and harmony, this is conducive to synthesis of all levels—a consummation devoutly to be sought!

And now a word about future plans.

The above use of the language of music—*melody, harmony,* and the like—is not accidental; it is part of the neo-Pythagoreanism that permeates the entire philosophy of Cosmic Humanism. Just how, in specific terms and details, it will be possible to relate the "music logarithmic spiral" to "spherical harmonics," and this, in turn, to a "world music" for global communication satellites for radio and television broadcasting (Project Prometheus & Krishna), is still to be explained—a job sufficient in itself. But as if this were not enough, we have also obligated ourselves to integrate this thematic enterprise with the "Helium-Psychosphere"

348

concepts, while at the same time relating this also to what Earl Hubbard describes as the "birth of Mankind into the universe of outer space." All this—be assured—will receive careful attention as we present the philosophy of history that is implicit in the "cross-action" hypothesis. A subsequent book in this series of studies will put it all together, and this will appear in the volume titled *Magnetic Moments in Human History*.

Quite obviously, there is much work still to be done. It will require the collaboration of many "avatars of synthesis"—seers, scientists, and prophets who know that the era of the "manhood of humanity" is still far ahead of us as a goal to be achieved.

Glossary

The glossary contains an explanation of terms used by Preston Harold with descriptions *according to his concepts*. In the descriptions, when terms are set in italics this indicates that the reader should refer to those terms for further explanation. All terms are in the Index listing pages where they are discussed.

ALPHA SET. The beginning set of One ($+1$ vs -1).

ANTIPARTICLES. Elementary particles that arise as a reaction to stress. See *Stress Reactions*, also *Secondary Formation*.

ATOMIC MATTER. Atoms composed of balanced charges (i.e., neutral energy), which have in addition 1 unit of positive energy ($+$) in the nucleus. See *Energy, Slightly Positive, Apparent*.

COEFFICIENT. A joint agent. See *Particle, p-1*.

COMMUNICATION, JESUS' LAW OF. "Let your communication be: Yea, yea; Nay, nay: for whatsoever is more than these springeth from evil." See *Energy, Communicable, Uncommunicable, Redundancy (50 per cent), Decay Reactions, Evil*.

CORE, ALPHA. Nucleus of helium $_2He^4$. See also *Nuclear Building Blocks*.

CORE, BETA. Nucleus of a deuteron, $_1H^2$. See also *Nuclear Building Blocks*.

CORE FORCE. Is made up of constant positive force of *Space Chamber*, represented as $[F+]$, and *q-measure* ($- + -$), and *positive charge* ($+ - +$), and one *Net Positive Unit* ($+$) of energy.

CORE, PRIME. Nucleus of hydrogen $_1H^1$. See also *Nuclear Building Blocks*.

CORE, q-MEASURE. Represented as: $q(-)$. Is an *Electron* ($- + -$) that draws a measure of *Space* from the "deeps" of the general field to secure and neutralize it to provide a *Space Chamber* for the proton, so that this negative particle remains in the nucleus or *Core Force*.

COSMON. God. The whole of the Cosmos, which is greater than the sum of its parts and cannot be divided because there is nothing to divide it. The mystery of wholeness, which cannot be shared. The Mind of God or mental pattern that enfolds what was, is, and is to be.

DARKNESS. Biblical term for *Unapparent Energy* or *Matrix Energy*.

DECAY REACTIONS. Decay reactions occur when more than a *50 per cent Redundancy* of some type of energy is present, causing a spontaneous reaction as energy "springs" from matter (*Evil*). See *Communication, Jesus' Law of*. Either the loss or the gain of energy can alter the arrangement and the redundancies involved in a mass. The *Space Chamber* of a nucleus can tolerate only so much *Neutrino Energy* in *Rest State* before "crowding," or the tension created by too little energy can provoke a reaction. Therefore, one *Degree* (°) of *Energy* absorbed by the nucleus can prompt a decay reaction.

DEVOLUTION. The complete disorganization of the *Original Energy* into *Neutrinos, Space,* and *Psychons*. Occurs prior to reorganization of energy through evolution.

ELECTRON. Represented as: (− + −). Negative electrical charge. A ratio of: 2 *Units of Negative Energy* versus 1 *Unit of Positive Energy*. A ratio of: (2:1 vs 1:2), or *Communicable* expression of negative *Energy*. See also *Negative Tension*.

ENERGY, APPARENT. *Positive Energy. Light* and *Atomic Matter*.

ENERGY, BITS OF. *Original Energy* that constitutes a *Neutrino*. Originally all energy was expressed to reflect sameness. Rearranged to express otherness, *Positive Energy* that is composed of more of the original energy, and *Negative Energy* that is composed of less of the original energy, arose. A neutrino is composed of three bits of energy (positive) and two bits of energy (negative). The one bit more that makes up the positive is what differentiates the positive from the negative at this basic level.

ENERGY, COMMUNICABLE. Energy that is 50 per cent redundant in expression. A ratio of: (2:1 vs 1:2). There must be a 50 per cent redundancy of positive energy for positive electrical charge to be communicated. There must be a 50 per cent redundancy of negative energy for negative electrical charge to be communicated. There must be a 50 per cent redundancy of neutral energy for mass to be communicated. See *Redundancy* (50 per cent), also *Energy, Positive, Negative,* and *Neutral, Units of,* which are counted individually to ascertain the ratio or redundancy.

ENERGY, ORIGINAL. God as the Absolute, or totally organized energy, that existed prior to the *Devolution*.

ENERGY, MATRIX. See *Q Energy; Q-Force; Energy, Unapparent; Prime Negative Bundle;* and *Energy, Slightly Negative*.

ENERGY, MENTAL. Every aspect of intelligence, imagination, psychic energy, and extrasensory perception. See *Psychon, Logon, Cosmon*.

ENERGY, NEGATIVE, ONE UNIT OF. Represented as: (—). *Measure Number* two (2° = —). Can act in a "positive" or opposite to negative way by altering its direction or line of motion, represented as "assuming the vertical versus the horizontal stance." Therefore, two units of negative energy can neutralize each other and, in association with units of neutral energy, form and polarize a *Magnetic Field*. One only unit of negative energy operates as a singular *Mental Light Wave Group*, because this unit involves a *Psychon*.

ENERGY, NEUTRAL, ONE DEGREE OF. Represented as: (°). *Measure Number* (+1 vs —1). Is equivalent to a *Neutrino* in *Rest State*. As degrees of neutral energy go into action, they become the building blocks of which *Units* of *Positive* and *Negative Energy* are made, and these units in turn are the building blocks of which all other expressions of energy or force or matter are made.

ENERGY, NEUTRAL, ONE UNIT OF. Represented as: (— +) or (o). *Measure Number* five (5° = o).

ENERGY, NEUTRINONIC. See *Neutrinos* and *Energy, Neutral, One Degree of*.

ENERGY, PARENT. Energy that is too refined to be measured, dealt with, or thought of in physical terms. Nevertheless, it is a part of the original substance, or *Original Energy*. See *Energy, Mental*; *Psychon, Logon, Mental Light Wave Group*.

ENERGY, POSITIVE, ONE UNIT OF. Represented as: (+). *Measure Number* three. (3° = +). Does not communicate as *Positive Charge*, electrically speaking. Is equivalent to a *Photon* or *Quantum* of energy. *Light*.

ENERGY, PSYCHONIC. See *Psychon*.

ENERGY, SLIGHTLY NEGATIVE. Energy that does not express negative electrical charge but is negative in nature because of its composition. Any aggregate of units of energy in which two or more units of neutral energy (+ — + —) are associated with one additional unit of negative energy (—), so that the minimum expression of slightly negative energy would be: (— + — + —). See *Q Energy*, and *Energy, Unapparent*.

ENERGY, SLIGHTLY POSITIVE. Energy that does not express positive electrical charge but is positive in nature because of its composition. Any aggregate of units of energy in which two or more units of neutral energy (+ — + —) are associated with one additional unit of positive energy (+), so that the minimum expression of slightly positive energy would be: (+ — + — +). *Space* and *Atomic Matter* in ground state are slightly positive expressions of energy, communicating neutrality electrically speaking, because each state of energy involves a *Redundancy* of neutral energy.

ENERGY, SON OR LOGONIC. See *Logon*.

ENERGY, TRANSPARENT. See *Space*.

ENERGY, UNAPPARENT. Field forces (magnetic, gravitational, and "general") that are composed of units of neutral energy and one additional unit of negative energy that is associated with "dark" or wave motion ("waters") versus "light" and corpuscular constitution (body). The one additional unit of negative energy is insufficient to express *Negative Charge*, but it causes the aggregate of units of energy to be slightly negative, although the aggregate communicates itself as neutral electrically speaking because it possesses a *Redundancy* of neutral energy.

ENERGY, UNCOMMUNICABLE. Units of energy that are not *50 per cent Redundant* in the arrangement. Such energy is expressed in a ratio of: (1:2) rather than (2:1). Uncommunicable energy affects the behavior or reactions of the mass or force, although its presence is not communicated.

ENERGY VALUES. An energy "value" is equivalent to one unit of positive (+), or negative (−), or neutral (0) energy, or one or more in aggregate.

ENERGY, VIRTUAL. See *Neutrinos* and *Rest State*.

ENTROPY. Always increasing measure of disorder or disorganization.

EVIL. Biblical term denoting the purely material realm, matter, and/or physical energy.

FIRMAMENT. Biblical term for *Space*, which provides for "being" and/or a three-dimensional state. See *Space* and *Space Chamber*.

FORCES OF ATTRACTION. All types of forces of attraction (gravity, magnetic, nuclear binding, molecular bonding, electrical) arise from the attraction that units of positive and negative energy pose for each other. However, *Repulsion* between like types of units of energy, as well as equal and opposite attraction deriving from the arrangement of the units of energy, gives rise to complex forces. See *Gravity* and *Self-Consistency, Attraction of*.

GRAVITATIONAL FIELD. Arises because of the attraction between the energy in the *Q-Force* and the energy in a mass.

GRAVITY. Is the sum of the attraction of opposite units of energy that compose the neutral energy in all masses; minus the repelling force between two masses communicating neutrality, because each mass is actually *Slightly Positive* in its constitution (if atomic matter is involved); plus the pressure of the *Q-Force* flowing through space.

HEAVEN. Biblical term for firmament (*Space*), and firmament within. See *Space Chamber*.

INFINITE. More than can be measured or used.

LAND. Biblical term for *Proton* or *Atomic Matter*.

LIGHT. Biblical term for *Photon*, or *Quantum* of energy, or "one atom of action." Is equivalent to one *Unit* of *Positive (Apparent) Energy* (+). (3° = +).

LIGHT WAVE GROUP. Represented as: (+ − + − +). See *Slightly Positive Energy*. Light wave group may be seen as [+(− + −)+], or as a ratio of: (3+:2−). There is insufficient *Redundancy* to communicate a *Positive Electrical Charge*. Opposite types of energy involved in the light wave group give rise to opposing wave trains of different frequencies. The group is equivalent to units of positive energy conveying an *Electron* through the general field of *Q Energy*, which is *Slightly Negative*. The *Photon* (+) involved in an electron becomes light in corpuscular expression as it is "bumped" out of the arrangement, leaving only neutral energy in the field; or another photon arises as *Negative Tension* (the two units of negative energy left of the electron) calls three *Degrees* (°) of *Neutrino* energy in *Rest State* into photon formation. Light can be absorbed by inorganic matter only as the *Net* positive *Value* of an atom is obscured and/or offset by negative value and/or negative expression. In organic material, the *p-1 Particle* attracts and absorbs light (+). See *Secondary Formation*.

LOGON. Logos (Word), or *Son, Energy*, as opposed to *Parent, Apparent, Unapparent*, and *Transparent*. Logos energy is *Mental Energy* multiplied to such point of *Redundancy* that it can communicate in words and become a "programer" of *Psychons* or *Mental Light Wave Groups*. Logonic energy is possessed only by humankind, and must be self-possessed. Each human being possesses the same measure of it, and each Logon carries the complete "code script" of creation.

MAGNETIC FIELD. Is formed as one measure of *Q Energy* neutralizes itself, when two of its *Units* of *Negative Energy* "polarize," one of them taking positive (vs negative) action. See *Energy, Slightly Negative*. Also *Energy, Unapparent* and *Q Energy*. A non-electrical (polarized) type of neutrality is expressed.

MAMMON. Biblical term for the temporal, physical universe that is subject to *Time's Action*. Matter and physical energy.

MATRIX ENERGY. See *Energy, Matrix*.

MEASURE NUMBER. The number of *Degrees of Energy* (°) required to compose a *Unit* of a particular type of energy. The *Alpha Set*

355

($+$1 vs $-$1) is the measure number of primordial neutral energy, the neutrinos, each representing one degree (°) of energy: the neutrino with left-handed spin ($+$1), the neutrino with right-handed spin ($-$1). Two is the measure number of a *Unit* of *Negative Energy* ($2° = -$). Three is the measure number of a *Unit* of *Positive Energy* ($3° = +$). Five is the measure number of one *Unit* of *Neutral Energy* ($5° = -+$) or ($5° = 0$).

MENTAL ENERGY. See *Energy, Mental.*

MENTAL LIGHT WAVE GROUP. Composed of two *Neutrinos* and a *Psychon*, which form the *Singular Unit of Negative Energy*, which may act in a positive or negative way. Travels through the field of *Neutrinos* in *Rest State.*

MOTION. A "mix" of action and rest (or "holding"), as the *Units* of *Negative Energy* ($-$) "reach ahead" and secure a holding position upon *Units* of *Positive Energy* ($+$) in the field; while the positive units in the moving mass remain secured to negative units in the field, being drawn up into line to secure a new position as some of the negative units move forward. Particle is never altogether in action or altogether at rest, or unsecured in its field. Motion is the measure of new positions secured.

MU MINUS. Represented as: ($- \overset{-}{+} -$). An elementary particle that disintegrates into an electron, neutrino, and antineutrino. Has a ratio of ($3-:1+$). Or ($3:1$ vs $1:3$). Violates the *Law of Communication*. It represents more than *50 per cent Redundancy*, and therefore "springs" apart, the superfluous *Unit* of *Negative Energy* disintegrating into the two *Neutrinos* that compose it.

NEGATIVE ELECTRICAL CHARGE. See *Electron.*

NEGATIVE TENSION. Arises as pressure causes four *Degrees* (°) of *Neutrino* energy in *Rest State* to form two *Units* of *Negative Energy* ($- -$); forms a *Redundancy* of negative energy that gives rise to the "instant" formation of a *Unit* of *Positive Energy* ($+$) as three degrees (°) of neutrino energy in rest state react. Negative tension gives rise to *Electron* ($- + -$) formation. Mathematical correspondence to this reaction is: ($-1 \times -1 = +1$) or ($- \times - = +$) or ($- + -$).

NEGENTROPY. Organization versus disorganization. *Entropy* must be taken as a signed number, negentropy being the unapparent organization that accompanies the process of disorganization (apparent).

NET VALUE. The single *Unit* of *Positive* or *Negative Energy* in an aggregate of units of energy that is "left over" when all other units are balanced to provide *Units* of *Neutral Energy.*

NEUTRINOS. Represented as (*), or as (°) when in *Rest State*. (*) represents both the neutrino with left-handed spin and the neutrino with right-handed spin. (°) represents one degree of primordial energy, of which all other units of physical versus *Mental Energy* are composed and into which such energy subsides. A *Degree* of neutrino energy in rest state (°) can go into either direction of spin. Neutrinos are "energy conveyances" and are the only *Stable* neutral *Particles* (known today). Each neutrino is composed of 3 bits of positive *Energy* and 2 bits of negative energy. (See *Energy, Bits of*.) The particle communicates itself as neutral, electrically speaking, but it is actually *Slightly Positive* because the positive energy is, in itself, "the more." Because the neutrino is a slightly positive expression of energy that communicates neutrality, it is a correspondence to *Atomic Matter* i.e., carries the "code script" for its formation.)

NEUTRON. Represented as: (− + − + − + − +). Is the "parent particle" in nature that disintegrates to give rise to a *Proton, Electron,* and antineutrino. A neutron is a component of a *Prime Negative Bundle* and of a *Prime Positive Bundle*.

NUCLEAR BINDING FORCE. The attraction of units of opposite types of energy (positive and negative) for each other. This attraction finishes at closest range into the attraction of *Self-Consistency*.

NUCLEAR BUILDING BLOCKS. There are four inorganic "building blocks" that form a correspondence to the four "building blocks" of DNA in organic matter. These inorganic "building blocks" are: the nucleus of hydrogen $_1H^1$ (Z 1), the nucleus of heavy hydrogen $_1H^2$ (Z 1 + 0), the nucleus of helium $_2He^4$ (Z 2 + 00), the nucleus of light helium $_2He^3$ (Z 2 + 0). The constitution and arrangement of these four blocks in various nuclei give rise to the four natural modes of decay. The *Core* block determines which mode of decay is involved, depending on which of the blocks (each with its own mode of decay) holds the isotope's *Net* positive *Value*, and therefore constitutes the core of the nucleus.

NUCLEONS. Neutral particles represented as: (+ − + − + −) or (+ − o + −) or (o + − o) that are the residue of *Neutrons* that are absorbed in the nuclei of atoms. Neutrons lose a *Unit* of *Neutral Energy* in the process, and therefore "weigh" less in the nucleus than neutrons outside of the nucleus. As *Time's Action* takes its toll of the units of neutral energy in the nucleons, different isotopes arise in nature. A nucleon cannot be expressed entirely in terms of potential energy or mass (o) versus kinetic energy or action (− +). Hence, a ratio of (2 0 :1 — +) or (2 — +:1 0). All the energy *Values* may express as *Nuclear Binding Force* (+ — + — + —).

OMEGA SET. Same as, or a "mirror reflection" of, the *Alpha Set* (+1 vs —1), the beginning expression of One, which is restated in the "end" or Omega set.

ONE, AS PRINCIPLE. One involves the principle of universal operation in macroscopic and microscopic terms. Signifies unity of two dynamic factors. Can be dealt with only in terms of signed number or the *Alpha Set* (—1 vs +1). This principle is expressed at the basic level of energy in the *Neutrinos*, constituted "equally" but capable of opposite action or spin.

ONE, JESUS' EQUATION OF. "Five at issue, three against two, and two against three." Represented as $(3/2 \times 2/3 = 1)$ or $\left[\dfrac{1 \,/\, 1}{1} = \dfrac{1}{1}\right]$. Indicates asymmetry converting to symmetry through cross-action: $(3/2 \times 2/3 = 6/6)$ to begin a new cycle of asymmetrical operation as $(6/6)$ reasserts One $(6/6 = 1)$ which can be stated only in terms of the *Alpha Set* (—1 vs +1). $(2/3)$ corresponds to (—1) and to the neutrino with right-handed spin. $(3/2)$ corresponds to (+1) and to the neutrino with left-handed spin. Five is given as the *Measure Number* of one whole or *Neutral Unit* of *Energy*.

PARTICLE, p-1. Represented as: (— ∘ +) or (— * +). Coefficient that allows for conversion of matter to the organic state, because it attracts light and reduces photons to neutrinos in *Rest State*, providing the "food" organic material requires to build its organization. It is a unit of neutral energy with "one iota" (i.e., a neutrino) added, which keeps it from disintegrating, because the neutrino acts as binding energy and enables the unit to enhance its negative value. See *Particle, Queer, q-1.*

PARTICLE, QUEER, q-1. Represented as: (—∘). Exists only as a process in the decay of unstable elementary particles that arise as *Stress Reactions*, when a *Unit* of *Positive Energy* (+) disintegrates. Is a momentary expression of all the neutrinos involved in a unit of positive energy posed along "horizontal" or negative lines.

PARTICLE, QUEER, q-2. Represented as (⊥). Exists only as a process in the decay of unstable elementary particles that arise as stress reactions when two *Units* of *Negative Energy* go into "anti" expression (neither taking the negative nor the positive action possible to a unit of negative energy) and fuse to destroy themselves, disintegrating into four *Neutrinos* in *Rest State*.

PARTICLE, QUEER, LEPTON CLASS. Represented as: (— ○ + —). Would arise as a *Unit* of *Positive Energy* (+) in a *Positive Charge* (+ — +) reacted to form a *q-1 Particle*.

PARTICLES, STABLE. Only four stable particles appear in the Table of Elementary Particles as given by physicists. They are: Neutrinos, Electrons, Photons, and Protons. Other elementary particles decay in microseconds.

P BUNDLE. See *Prime Positive Bundle*.

PHOTON. See *Energy, Positive, One Unit* of, and *Light*. Is a stable elementary particle.

PI ZERO. An unstable elementary particle, which disintegrates into two *Photons*. Represented as two *Units* of *Neutral Energy* (+ — + —), which form within an aggregate of *Slightly Negative Energy*, giving rise to a ratio of 3 neutral units to one negative unit (3 0: 1 —) or more than a *50 per cent Redundancy*, causing a *Decay Reaction*, which releases two photons as the *Units* of *Negative Energy* lapse into *Neutrinos* in *Rest State*.

PLASMA. See *Neutrino* energy in *Rest State*.

POSITIVE ELECTRICAL CHARGE. Represented as (+ — +). The positive electrical charge is associated with the neutral energy that makes up a *Proton* (hydrogen nucleus). The positive charge is a ratio of: two *Units* of *Positive Energy* versus one *Unit* of *Negative Energy* (2+:1—) or a *Communicable* expression of positive *Energy*. Positive electrical charge is never "free" in the field; it is expressed only in association with the energy that composes a *Proton*.

PRIME NEGATIVE BUNDLE. One measure of Prime Negative energy, each measure of which is equivalent to an *Electron* (— + —) and a *Neutron* (+ — + — + — + —), together forming [(— + —) (+ — + — + — + —)]. Also called a Q Bundle, the *Q-force*, *Matrix Energy*, and *Slightly Negative Energy* versus energy that expresses a negative electrical charge. *Unapparent* versus apparent *Energy*.

PRIME POSITIVE BUNDLE. One measure of Prime Positive energy, each measure of which is equivalent to a *Positive Electrical Charge* (+ — +) and a *Neutron* (— + — + — + — +), together forming [(+ — +) (— + — + — + — +)]. Also called a P Bundle. Type of primordial energy utilized to create *Space*.

PROTON. Nucleus of hydrogen $_1H^1$. Stable elementary particle. Arises as a *Neutron* disintegrates, releasing a *Positive Electrical Charge*, which is immediately embedded in a *Space Chamber* as Q energy reacts to the strong positive attraction, so that the positive charge is never left free in the field. The proton has a "dual" *Redundancy*: a ratio of (2+:1—) or two *Units* of *Positive Energy* to one *Unit* of *Negative Energy*, and a ratio of (2 0: 1—) or two *Units* of *Neutral Energy* to one unit of negative energy. Therefore, the proton communicates both redundancies, the positive redundancy giving rise to its positive electrical charge, and its neutral redundancy giving rise to its mass. Only an association of neutral and positive energy can give rise to *Apparent* versus *Unapparent Energy*. An association of neutral and negative energy gives rise to unapparent energy when the ratio is: (2 0: 1 —). Original hydrogen was formed by the reaction of *Prime Positive* and *Prime Negative Bundles* of energy. Protons are also formed (or released) in decay reactions. See *Steady State*.

PSYCHON. A unit of *Mental Energy*. It is *Parent* energy versus *Apparent, Unapparent,* and *Transparent States of Energy*. A psychon is a primordial unit of energy, which represented a condition of "sameness" that existed prior to the advent of "otherness" arising as positive and negative energy were formed. A psychon is not involved in any way with opposite types of energy and is therefore "neutral" in a way that no other expression of energy can be. It is a unit of energy that bifurcates but does not actually separate. This gives it a three-point property that allows it to express in the harmonious ratio of (2:1 vs 1:2). Nothing resists it; therefore, it is self-resisting. It is the only type of energy that can operate apart from *Q Energy* in *Space*. There is more of it in existence than there is of physical energy (energy involved with opposites). It so permeates what we can experience of the universe that each *Unit* of *Negative Energy* (—) encompasses a psychon as the two *Degrees* of energy (°) react to form the negative unit (—). Therefore, mental energy is incorporated throughout nature.

q-BOND. The q-bond is an *Electron* (— + —) in the field of the hydrogen molecule H_2, which attracts and bonds the two hydrogen atoms, each of which is *Slightly Positive*, having one *Unit* of *Positive Energy* (+) in addition to its balanced or neutral energy. When the molecule is "pulled apart" the q-bond ceases to be operative, which accounts for the difference in the bonding energy of a hydrogen atom in a compound and the bonding energy of hydrogen as determined by "pulling apart" the hydrogen molecule.

Q BUNDLE. See *Prime Negative Bundle*.

Q ENERGY. See *Energy, Unapparent; Prime Negative Bundle;* and *Energy, Slightly Negative*. Q energy neutralizes *Space, Slightly Positive Energy*, so that *Atomic Matter* (also slightly positive) can operate within it. As Q energy flows through space, it neutralizes it, forming the "general field." Q energy permeates all of space that we can experience. As it surrounds a mass it provides a *Magnetic Field* as it neutralizes itself through the action of its *Units* of *Negative Energy*. As it surrounds celestial bodies, it gives rise to their *Gravitational Fields*. Q energy acts to organize matter. See *Negative Tension* and *Proton*. Q energy is associated with unapparent processes, with wave motion, and cold versus heat.

Q-FORCE. See *Q Energy* that flows through space. See also *Time's Entropy Arrow*.

QUANTUM. See *Light, Photon, Energy, Positive, One Unit* of.

REDUNDANCY. More than appears to be needed.

REDUNDANCY, 50 per cent. Represents a ratio of (2:1 vs 1:2), in which 50 per cent of the total is redundant. In the sense that if one-half the original or given measure is removed, the remaining measure represents the nature of the original measure. For example: if "Yea, yea" is reduced to "Yea," the affirmative (or positive) sense remains. "Yea, yea" is a "statement" that is 50 per cent redundant of affirmative value. An increase in measure or numbers, 4:2, 6:3, 8:4, etc. represents a 50 per cent redundancy as long as a 2:1 ratio is maintained. See *Communication, Jesus' Law of*, and *Energy, Communicable, Uncommunicable*.

REPULSION, FORCE OF. Like particles repel each other. A positive particle repels a positive particle; a negative particle repels a negative particle. Neutral particles attract, but at closest range the force of attraction appears to turn into a force of repulsion (see *Nuclear Binding Force*). However, in Harold's view, attraction of neutral energy does not "turn into" a force of repulsion; it finishes itself in the attraction of *Self-Consistency*.

REST STATE. *Neutrinos* in a state of "antiaction" comparable to sleep or hibernation. They may be compared to "tops" when spinning, which come to rest and can be set to respinning. Energy in this state, sometimes called "virtual" energy or "plasma," permeates the space we can experience, and provides the "reserve" of energy from which units of negative and positive energy are reorganized.

SECONDARY FORMATION. Takes place in response to stress. As the *Units* of *Negative Energy* in an aggregate of neutral energy go into positive action, the *Units* of *Neutral Energy* express positively, represented as $(+\ |)$. Or the units of negative energy act to enhance the negative aspects of positive energy, represented as: $(\overline{+})$. This is possible because all units of energy are composed of *Degrees* of *Neutral*

Energy, which are composed of *Bits* of positive and negative energy, so that there is no "purely positive" or "purely negative" energy. A unit of negative energy expressing in a positive way is nevertheless a negative unit; therefore the positive unit in association does not repel it. Antiparticles are particles in secondary formation. For example, the antiparticle of the *Electron* is the positron, represented as $(\,|\,+\,|\,)$. The antiproton arises as the unit of negative energy in the *Positive Electrical Charge* $(+ - +)$ enhances the negative value of the positive

units, which is represented as: $(+ \; \overline{+})$. The ability of the positive charge in the nucleus to go into and out of secondary formation in microseconds, thereby obscuring the *Net* positive value in the nucleus, allows for the absorption of light by inorganic substances.

SELF-CONSISTENCY, ATTRACTION OF. At closest range the attraction neutral energy poses for other expressions of neutral energy finishes itself in equilibrium or inertia, because the units of energy within a grouping are as attracted to the opposite values within their own arrangement as they are attracted to the values in the confronting particle. Equal and opposite attraction produces a "stymie" to action. Represented as: $\qquad (- + -)$
$$(+ - +)$$

SERPENT. Biblical term for a *Unit* of *Negative Energy*.

SINGULAR UNIT OF NEGATIVE ENERGY. A *Mental Wave Group* composed of: *Neutrino*, antineutrino, and *Psychon*. "Singular" denotes: individual, separate, peculiar to itself, unique, unparalleled, something considered by itself, or "strange" in relation to other single *Units* of *Energy*. The singular unit of negative energy or mental wave group is arranged in such a way that the neutral particles that compose it are expressed in "singular group action," whereas a single *Unit* of *Negative Energy* $(-)$ is always associated with other units of energy to constitute what is considered to be "physical" versus "mental" energy: i.e., an *Electron* $(- + -)$, or a *Magnetic Field*, or *Q energy*.

SLIGHTLY NEGATIVE ENERGY. See *Energy, Slightly Negative*.

SLIGHTLY POSITIVE ENERGY. See *Energy, Slightly Positive*.

SPACE. Primordial *Degrees* of *Energy* fully exerted, spent and fixed (*Firmament*) or "stretched" to form a condition of energy that expresses dimension without body, or a "tissue" of energy in and through which all other expressions of energy take place; but space itself neither acts nor reacts. Advent of space gives rise to geometry and/or three-dimensional being of the Cosmos and in the Cosmos. Space is positive in nature because *Neutrinos* are positive in nature (see *Energy, Bits of*), and space was composed of *Prime Positive Bundles* of energy, which were composed of the neutrinos, the fundamental particles, or building blocks, of which all expressions of material energy are constituted.

Space is a constant positive force in nature. It is *Transparent Energy* as opposed to *Apparent, Unapparent,* and *Parent* Energy. There is more space than can be occupied by *Q Energy* that flows through it. Therefore, there is empty space in the universe that poses a constant positive force, beginning with the "central deeps."

SPACE-BINDING-FORCE. Represented as (sbf). Neutral energy equivalent to a *Neutron* that "enwraps" or delineates the *Space Chamber* (neutralized by the *Core q-measure*) to form the nucleus of hydrogen (the proton).

SPACE CHAMBER. Represented as [F+]. One measure of three-dimensional space with its constant positive force "tied off" from the general field by neutral energy in *Q energy* as the proton is formed, within which the energy in the nucleus is "housed." The *Space-Binding-Force,* (sbf) equivalent to a *Neutron* (+ − + − + − + −), delineates the space to give the atom a basis for "being" (body) as well as for action (energy); and this is what differentiates *Atomic Matter* from other elementary particles, which occupy but do not also "involve" space. A space chamber "tied off" by space-binding-force is represented as: [F+(sbf)].

STATES OF ENERGY. Apparent (positive). Unapparent (negative). Transparent (space). Parent (mental). Son, or Logonic (in likeness to Cosmon; redundancy of Parent Energy). Cosmon (God: the undivided whole; the mental pattern that enfolds what was, is, is to be).

STEADY STATE. State reached by a star such as our sun, which has evolved into an energy reactor that produces the hydrogen to replace the hydrogen it consumes, drawing the necessary neutrons from the *Q-force* that flows around and through it.

STRESS REACTIONS. Follow the syndrome of: alarm, resistance, adaptation; or overresistance, which produces exhaustion, as does prolonged or intolerable stress. Alarm reaction: is in positive terms associated with heat (temperature increases). Resistance: is in negative terms associated with wave motion or cooling (substance liquefies or gives expression to negative energy values). Adaptation: is in neutral terms (balanced or random motion, or full exertion of holding forces within a particle).

Exhaustion: energy values lapse into *Neutrinos* in *Rest State*. Over-resistance: the syndrome is more intensely followed and repeats the pattern of energy "translating" from positive to negative to neutral expression until it is reduced to a *Plasma*. See also *Secondary Formation*.

SYNTROPY. Reorganization, indicating progress in the reorganization of original energy. Just as *Entropy* cannot be arrested or decreased, syntropy cannot be arrested or decreased, or "undone." See *Time's Entropy Arrow*.

TIME'S ACTION. One *Unit* of *Negative Energy* ($-$) acts upon one *Unit* of *Positive Energy* ($+$) to reduce the *Unit* of *Neutral Energy* ($- +$) to five *Degrees* of *Energy* ($°$), or *Neutrinos* in *Rest State*, creating a reserve of energy in the system. See *Nucleons*. Through this action, some energy is "tithed" and "banked" in the general field in every operation.

TIME'S ENTROPY ARROW. Increase of *Entropy* indicates "future" to the physicist, because the measure of entropy cannot be decreased (hence "less entropy" means "past"). Increase of entropy is equivalent to *Time's Action*, which occurs constantly. As *Q Energy* flows through space and surrounds matter, it gives rise to the pressure that causes equal and opposite attraction to be overcome, and the attraction of *Self-Consistency* is overcome. *Units* of *Neutral Energy* in *Nucleons* are dissolved as the opposite types of energy values fuse and disintegrate into energy in *Rest State*. The flow of the *Q-Force* never ceases and moves always in the direction of "next," thereby pointing Time's Entropy Arrow toward "future." The *Slightly Positive* nature of space and matter always attracts the Q-force, which is *Slightly Negative*, and because there is more space than can be occupied by Q energy, the Q-force cannot "complete" or stop its action, which is "time's action." The action of Q energy (time) is therefore "everlasting" and leads to constant creation through the process of organizing and disorganizing energy. This action will engender *Syntropy* (progress) until the universe reaches its optimum state of reorganization; in this optimum state, the optimum number of solar systems within the Cosmic system will have reached a *Steady State*, able to support and engender life abundantly.

TRANSPARENT ENERGY. See *Space*.

WATERS. Biblical term for *Matrix Energy*, or *Q energy*, negative or wave motion.

ZERO. The whole that can be understood only as it is seen to be a correspondence to One (-1 0 $+1$). Is point of departure in reckoning;

implies "naught" because the secret of wholeness cannot actually be revealed. See *Cosmon*. Division of zero gives rise to negative (minus) value and to positive (plus) value; hence to the necessity of dealing with the product of the division only in terms of signed Ones: (-1 vs $+1$). Zero, 0, represents a whole, or primordial, measure of energy, versus a unit or measure of neutral energy symbolized as (o). When used in conjunction with an atomic number, such as $Z\ 1 + 0$, the symbol 0 indicates a *Nucleon*.

References

INTRODUCTION

[1] Freeman J. Dyson, "Innovations in Physics," *Scientific American*, September, 1955, Vol. 199, pp. 74-82.

[2] Andrew A. Cochran, "Life and the Wave Properties of Matter," *Dialectica*, Vol. 19, 1965, pp. 290-312; and "Mind, Matter, and Quanta," *Main Currents in Modern Thought*, Vol. 22, 1966, pp. 79-88, The Foundation for Integrative Education, 12 Church St., New Rochelle, N.Y. 10805.

[3] See: Babcock, *If Thine Eye Be Single* (Section IX, pp. 225-226).

BOOK ONE
THE PALESTINIAN MYSTERY PLAY
Act One: Setting the Stage for *The Shining Stranger*

[4] Preston Harold, *The Shining Stranger* (New York: Dodd, Mead & Co., distributors; Wayfarer Press, publishers, 1967).

[5] Henry Miller; see comments on the jacket cover of *The Shining Stranger*.

[6] Attributed to Oscar Wilde, source unknown.

[7] Oliver L. Reiser, *Cosmic Humanism* (Cambridge, Mass.: Schenkman Publishing Co., 1966).

[8] William Shakespeare, *Hamlet*, Act II, sc. 2, l. 632.

[9] Montague Rhodes James, translator, The Apocryphal New Testament (Oxford, England: The Clarendon Press, 1966), pp. 49, 50.

[10] Luke 2:46-47.

[11] I. Rice Pereira, *The Transcendental Formal Logic of the Infinite: The Evolution of Cultural Forms* (New York: Pereira, 1966), pp. 4, 5.

[12] James, Gospel of Thomas, The Apocryphal New Testament, p. 51.

[13] *I Ching* (*The Book of Changes*) Wilhelm-Baynes tr, (New York: Pantheon, 1950).

[14] Ernest Renan, *The Life of Jesus* (New York: Random House, Modern Library, 1927), p. 386.

[15] Attributed to Will Durant.

[16] I Cor. 6:20, 7:23.

[17] Matt. 5:13-14, 25:40; John 10:34-35, 8:32.

[18] Robert L. Heilbroner, *The Worldly Philosophers* (New York: Simon & Schuster, 1961), p. 126.

[19] Nikita Khrushchev, Associated Press Release, San Francisco, September 22, 1959.

[20] Carl G. Jung, *Man and His Symbols* (New York: Doubleday, 1964), p. 261.

[21] Luke 12:15; Matt. 4:4, 6:25.

[22] Gerald Holton, "Science and New Styles of Thought," *Thirtieth Anniversary Lecture Series* (University College, University of Florida, University College Series, No. 1, May, 1967), p. 17.

[23] Rudolf Thiel, *And There Was Light* (New York: Alfred A. Knopf, 1967), p. 336.

[24] Krishnamurti, "Conversation," *Journal* (Claremont, Calif.: The Blaisdell Institute, Vol. IV, No. 1, January, 1969), p. 23.

[25] Harold, *The Shining Stranger*, pp. 304, 305.

[26] *Ibid.*, p. 319.

[27] Lord Byron, *Childe Harold's Pilgrimage* (London, England: John Murray, 1818), Canto IV, CXXXVII, p. 71.

[28] Harold, *The Shining Stranger*, pp. 380, 383.

Act Two: *The Shining Stranger* Speaks

[29] Harold, *The Shining Stranger*, p. 22.

[30] *Ibid.*, p. 104.

[31] *Equals One* (Pondicherry, India: Auroville, 1968), "The Take-Off," p. 86.

[32] Abraham Maslow, *Psychology Today* (July, 1968).

[33] Harold, *The Shining Stranger*, pp. 300, 301.

[34] *Ibid.*, p. 298.

[35] *Ibid.*, p. 305.

[36] Micah 4:5.

[37] Harold, *The Shining Stranger*, p. 393.

[38] *Ibid.*, pp. 29, 30, 31.

[39] John 14:26.

[40] Matt. 26:64.

[41] Matt. 24:35.

[42] John 5:21, 3:1-7.

[43] John 12:48, 5:22.

[44] Harold, *The Shining Stranger*, pp. 328, 329.

[45] Matt. 24:36, 42, 44, 50.

[46] Matt. 24:4-5, 23-26.

[47] Willis W. Harman, "Old Wine in New Wineskins," in *Challenges of Humanistic Psychology*, James F. T. Bugental, ed. (New York: McGraw-Hill, 1967), Chapter 33, p. 322.

[48] Harold, *The Shining Stranger*, Chapters 11 through 15. (In the discussion of the miracles, individual references will be omitted because the large number to be given would be distracting to the reader. See Index of the book.)

[49] Dr. H. A. Puharich, 432 W. 45th St., New York, N.Y.

[50] *The Graduate*, Columbia Masterworks, Stereo OS 3180, record-jacket copy by Charles Burr.

[51] Harold, *The Shining Stranger*, pp. 316-319, 332.

[52] Cyril Greenland, "Richard Maurice Bucke, *Can. Med. Asso. Jour.*, M.D., 1837-1902," 91 (1964) 385-391, quoting Bucke's *Cosmic Consciousness*.

[53] Mark 15:34.

[54] John 19:34.

[55] Harold, *The Shining Stranger*, pp. 313, 314.

[56] *Ibid.*, pp. 314, 315, 316.

[57] *Ibid.*, p. 336.

[58] *Ibid.*, pp. 166-170.

[59] *Ibid.*, pp. 50-55.

[60] *Ibid.*, pp. 82-85.

[61] Mark 10:18.

[62] Harold, *The Shining Stranger*, p. 111.

[63] *Ibid.*, p. 136 (See also p. 112 and Chapter 6).

[64] Matt. 6:33-34.

[65] Matt. 7:1-2.

[66] John 15:13-14.

[67] Clifford P. Owens, *A Story of Jesus* (Virginia Beach, Va.: A. R. E. Press, 1963), based on the Edgar Cayce readings. Also, James E. Padgett, *True Gospel Revealed Anew by Jesus*, 3rd ed. (Washington, D.C.: Church of the New Birth, 1965).

[68] Matt. 24:5.

[69] Mark 9:41.

[70] *Wall Street Journal*, September 1969. Article headlined: "Bible Sales Fall off as Religion's Influence on Americans Dwindles."

Act Three: Truth Is the Shining Stranger Mankind Seeks

[71] Harold, *The Shining Stranger*, p. 386.

[72] *Ibid.*, Chapters 6 through 9.

[73] *Ibid.*, p. 210.

[74] Ira Progoff, *Depth Psychology and Modern Man* (New York: Julian Press, 1959), pp. 215-219.

[75] I. S. Bengelsdorf, "Man Not the Only Toolmaker, Scholar Says," *Los Angeles Times*, Feb. 23, 1969, p. C1, quoting Leakey.

[76] Harold, *The Shining Stranger*, pp. 386, 387.

[77] *Ibid.*, p. 371.

[78] *Ibid.*, p. 303.

[79] *Ibid.*, pp. 51, 52, 53, 67.

[80] *Ibid.*, p. 58.

[81] *Ibid.*, p. 379.

[82] Mark 8:36.

[83] Harold, *The Shining Stranger*, pp. 348, 369.

[84] *Ibid.*, p. 362.

[85] Stuart Palmer, *Science News* 95 (1969), 356.

[86] Harold, *The Shining Stranger*, p. 347.

[87] *Ibid.*, p. 361.

[88] *Ibid.*, p. 346.

[89] *Ibid.*, p. 370.

[90] *Ibid.*, pp. 365, 362.

[91] *Ibid.*, pp. 376-379.

[92] Willis W. Harman, "The New Copernican Revolution," *Stanford Today*, Winter, 1969, p. 8.

[93] Joel A. Snow, "Taking Thought for the Morrow" (book review), *Science*, Vol. 164, 18 April 1969, p. 285.

[94] Robert Theobald, "Alternative Methods of Predicting the Future," *The Futurist*, Vol. 111, No. 2 (Washington, D.C.: World Future Society), April, 1969. See also: "Beckwith's Reply to Robert Theobald," pp. 43-46.

[95] Luke 16:9-13.

[96] J. Blanton Belk, "Man's Gotta Go Somewhere," a *Pace Magazine* reprint (Los Angeles, Calif., 835 So. Flower St., 1969), p. 3.

[97] Harold, *The Shining Stranger*, p. 392.

[98] *Ibid.*, p. 274.

[99] *Ibid.*, pp. 382-394.

[100] Ps. 121:8.

[101] Harold, *The Shining Stranger*, p. 208.

[102] *Ibid.*, pp. 386, 387.

[103] Mike Pinder, "OM," London Records, Inc. (New York) Stereo Des 18019, 1968.

[104] Geoffrey Frost, "The Cosmos and the Mind: A dialogue with Viktor Frankl," *Pace Magazine*, Vol. V, No. 8 (August, 1969), p. 36.

[105] John Sayre, "I Have Dreamed about It All My Life: A talk with helicopter inventor, Igor Sikorsky," *Pace Magazine*, Vol. V, No. 8 (August, 1969), p. 31.

BOOK TWO
IF THINE EYE BE SINGLE

[106] Sir Arthur Eddington, *The Nature of the Physical World* (Ann Arbor: Univ. of Mich. Press, 1958), pp. 103-104.

[107] John 14:9-10.

[108] John 14:10.

[109] John 5:17.

[110] John 1:1.

[111] Holton, *Thirtieth Anniversary Lecture Series*, University of Florida, p. 19.

[112] "Quote Nuclear Bonds to Be Attacked," a report on Louis Rosen, *Winston-Salem* (N.C.) *Jour.*, Vol. 74 (Feb. 17, 1969), p. 21. News Release, Los Alamos, New Mexico, February 17, 1969.

[113] Luke 16:9-11.

[114] Matt. 5:37.

[115] For a description of h and the h rule, see: Arthur Eddington, *op. cit.*, pp. 179, 183, 223.

[116] John 1:5.

[117] Luke 12:52. See also, Harold, *The Shining Stranger*, pp. 184-191, for a description of Jesus' Equation of One.

[118] John 3:16.

[119] Luke 17:21.

[120] Herman Bondi and Raymond A. Lyttleton, "Unbalanced Universe," *Time*, June 22, 1959, pp. 40, 42. [See also: Raymond A. Lyttleton, H. Bondi, W. B. Bonnor, G. J. Whitrow.] *Rival Theories of Cosmology* (London: Oxford University Press, 1960), pp. 22, 23.

[121] F. L. Kunz, "Feeling in Plants" (*Main Currents in Modern Thought*, 12 Church St., New Rochelle, N.Y. 10805) May-June, 1969, Vol. 25, No. 5, p. 143.

[122] Harold, *The Shining Stranger*, p. 294.

[123] *Ibid.*, pp. 106, 107.

[124] *Ibid.*, pp. 181-186.

[125] Victor Cohn, "First Gravity Waves Detected," *Los Angeles Times*, June 15, 1969, pp. A1, 18.

[126] John 6:63.

[127] Andrew A. Cochran, "Mind, Matter, and Quanta" (*Main Currents in Modern Thought*, 12 Church St., New Rochelle, N.Y. 10805), Vol. 22, No. 4 (March-April, 1966), pp. 79-88. See also: *Dialectica*, International Review of Philosophy of Knowledge, Editions du Griffon La Neuveville Suisse, Vol. 19, No. 314, pp. 290-312, 15.9-15.12.1965: "Life and the Wave Properties of Matter," by Andrew A. Cochran.

[128] Matt. 18:14.

[129] Reiser, *Cosmic Humanism*, pp. 190, 191.

[130] Thiel, *And There Was Light*, Plates XXXV, XXXVI, XXXVII.

[131] José Arguëlles, "Compute and Evolve" (*Main Currents in Modern Thought*, 12 Church St., New Rochelle, N.Y. 10805) Vol. 25, No. 3, January-February, 1969, p. 66.

[132] John A. Wheeler and Seymour Tilson, *The Dynamics of Space-Time* (New York: *International Science & Technology Journal*, December, 1963), reprinted by *Artorga*, Communications 70 and 71, October and November, 1964. All quotations drawn from the reprinted article.

[133] John A. Wheeler, "Our Universe: The Known and the Unknown," *American Scientist*, Vol. 56, 1, pp. 1-20, Spring, 1968 (The Sigma Xi-Phi Beta Kappa Annual Lecture, American Association for the Advancement of Science, New York, December 29, 1967).

[134] Matt. 18:20.

[135] George Gamow, *One, Two, Three . . . Infinity* (New York: New American Library, Mentor Book, 1947), pp. 62-64. See also: Reiser, *Cosmic Humanism*, pp. 412, 493, 494.

[136] Mary Jane Sherfey, M.D., "The Evolution and Nature of Female Sexuality in Relation to Psychoanalytic Theory," *Journal of the American Psychoanalytic Association*, Vol. 14, No. 1 (January, 1966), pp. 28-128. See also: pp. 49-50.

BOOK THREE
ON THE NATURE OF UNIVERSAL
CROSS-ACTION

[137] For a discussion of quarks that the layman can understand see: Jeremy Bernstein, "Physical Sciences and Technology," *The Great Ideas Today 1965* (Chicago: William Benton, publisher, Encyclopedia Britannica, Inc., 1965), pp. 351-366.

[138] For a discussion of asymmetry and handedness of neutrinos and antineutrinos, and beta decay, see: Martin Gardner, *The Ambidextrous Universe* (New York: Basic Books, 1965), pp. 262, 263.

[139] *Ibid.*, Chapter 21, and p. 226 for a discussion of antiparticles, theories on the constitution of the neutron, and the proton-antiproton reaction.

[140] For explanation of antineutrino trap, see: Irving Adler, *Inside the Nucleus* (New York: The John Day Co., 1963), pp. 108, 109.

[141] Luke 12:52.

[142] Matt. 3:9, Gen. 2:7.

[143] Matt. 18:20.

[144] John 1:1-5.

SUMMARY

145 Francis O. Schmitt, "The Physical Basis of Life and Learning," *Science*, Vol. 149, No. 165, p. 935.

Bibliography

1. Adler, Irving. *Inside the Nucleus.* New York: The John Day Co., 1963.
2. *Apocryphal New Testament, The.* Translated by Montague Rhodes James. Oxford, England: Clarendon Press, 1966.
3. Arguëlles, José. "Compute and Evolve." *Main Currents in Modern Thought*, Vol. 25, No. 3 (January-February 1969), p. 66.
4. Babcock, Winifred. *The Palestinian Mystery Play.* New York: Dodd, Mead & Company, Inc., 1971.
5. Belk, J. Blanton. "Man's Gotta Go Somewhere." *Pace Magazine* reprint (1969), p. 3.
6. Bengelsdorf, Irving S. "Man Not the Only Toolmaker, Scholar Says." *Los Angeles Times*, Feb. 23, 1969, Part C, p. 1.
7. Bernstein, Jeremy. "Physical Sciences and Technology." *The Great Ideas Today 1965.* Chicago: *The Encyclopedia Britannica* 1965, pp. 351-366.
8. "Bible Sales Fall off as Religion's Influence on Americans Dwindles." *Wall Street Journal*, September, 1969.
9. Bondi, Herman and Lyttleton, Raymond A. "Unbalanced Universe." *Time* (June 22, 1959), pp. 40, 42.
10. Byron, Lord. *Childe Harold's Pilgrimage.* London: John Murray, 1818.
11. Cochran, Andrew A. "Life and the Wave Properties of Matter." *Dialectica*, Vol. 19, No. 2 (1965), pp. 290-312.
12. ———. "Mind, Matter, and Quanta." *Main Currents in Modern Thought*, Vol. 22, No. 4 (March-April 1966), pp. 79-88.
13. Cohn, Victor. "First Gravity Waves Detected, May Supply Vast, New Energy." (Exclusive to the *Los Angeles Times* from the *Washington Post*.) *Los Angeles Times*, LXXXVIII (June 15, 1969), Section A, pp. 1, 18.
14. Columbia Masterworks. *The Graduate.* OS 3180, record jacket copy written by Charles Burr.
15. Dyson, Freeman J. "Innovation in Physics." *Scientific American*, Vol. 193, No. 3 (September 1955), pp. 74-82.
16. Eddington, Arthur. *The Nature of the Physical World.* Ann Arbor: University of Michigan Press, 1958.
17. Frost, Geoffrey. "The Cosmos and the Mind: A dialogue with Viktor Frankl." *Pace Magazine*, Vol. 5, No. 8 (August 1969), pp. 34-39.
18. Gamow, George. *One, Two, Three . . . Infinity.* New York: New American Library, Mentor Books, 1947.
19. Gardner, Martin. *The Ambidextrous Universe.* New York: Basic Books, Inc., 1965.
20. Greenland, Cyril. "Richard Maurice Bucke, M.D., 1837-1902: A Pioneer of Scientific Psychiatry." *Canadian Medical Association Journal*, Vol. 91, No. 11 (1964), pp. 385-391.
21. Harman, Willis W. "Old Wine in New Wineskins." *Challenges of Humanistic Psychology*, edited by James F. T. Bugenthal, Ph.D., New York: McGraw-Hill, 1967.
22. ———. "The New Copernican Revolution." *Stanford Today* (Winter 1969), pp. 6-9.
23. Harold, Preston, *The Shining Stranger.* New York: Dodd, Mead, Distributors; Wayfarer Press, 1967.

24. —— and Babcock, Winifred. *The Single Reality*. New York: Dodd, Mead & Company, Inc., 1971.

25. Heilbroner, Robert L. *The Worldly Philosopher*. New York: Simon & Schuster, 1961.

26. Holton, Gerald. "Science and New Styles of Thought." *University College Lecture Series*, University of Florida, No. 1 (1967), pp. 5-24.

27. *I Ching (The Book of Changes)*. Translated by Wilhelm-Baynes. New York: Pantheon, 1969.

28. Jung, Carl G. *Man and His Symbols*. New York: Doubleday, 1964.

29. Khrushchev, Nikita. Associated Press Release, San Francisco, September 22, 1959.

30. Krishnamurti, "Conversation." Blaisdell Institute *Journal*, Vol. IV, No. 1 (January 1969), pp. 23-26.

31. Kunz, F. L. "Feeling in Plants." *Main Currents in Modern Thought*, Vol. 25, No. 5 (May-June 1969), p. 143.

32. Lyttleton, Raymond A. *Rival Theories of Cosmology*. London: Oxford University Press, 1960.

33. Maslow, Abraham. "A Theory of Metamotivation." *Psychology Today*, Vol. II, No. 2 (July 1968), pp. 38-39; 58-61.

34. "Nuclear Bonds to Be Attacked." *Winston-Salem* (N.C.) *Journal*, Vol. 74 (February 17, 1969), p. 21.

35. Ostrander, Sheila and Schroeder, Lynn. *Psychic Discoveries behind the Iron Curtain*. Englewood Cliffs, N.J.: Prentice-Hall, Inc., 1970.

36. Owens, Clifford P. *A Story of Jesus*. Virginia Beach, Va.: A.R.E. Press, 1963.

37. Padgett, James E. *True Gospel Revealed Anew by Jesus*. Washington, D.C.: Church of the New Birth. Third Edition, 1965.

38. Pereira, I. Rice. *The Transcendental Formal Logic of the Infinite: The Evolution of Cultural Forms*. New York: Pereira, 1966.

39. Pinder, Michael. "OM." New York: London Records, Stereo Des 18019, 1968.

40. Progoff, Ira. *Depth Psychology and Modern Man*. New York: Julian Press, 1959.

41. "Rat race against suicide." *Science News*, Vol. 95 (1969), p. 356.

42. Reiser, Oliver L. *Cosmic Humanism*. Cambridge, Mass.: Schenkman, 1966.

43. Renan, Ernest. *The Life of Jesus*. New York: Random House, Modern Library, 1927.

44. Sayre, John. "I Have Dreamed about It All My Life: A talk with helicopter inventor, Igor Sikorsky." *Pace Magazine*, Vol. 5, No. 8 (August 1969), pp. 30-31.

45. Schmitt, Francis O. "The Physical Basis of Life and Learning." *Science*, Vol. 149 (1965), p. 935.

46. Sherfey, Mary Jane, M.D. "The Evolution and Nature of Female Sexuality in Relation to Psychoanalytic Theory." *Journal of the American Psychoanalytic Association*, Vol. 14, No. 1 (January 1966), pp. 28, 49-50.

47. Snow, Joel A. "Taking Thought for the Morrow," a review of *The Prometheus Project*, by Gerald Feinberg. Science, Vol. 164 (1969), p. 285.

48. Theobald, Robert. "Alternative Methods of Predicting the Future." *The Futurist*, Vol. 3, No. 2 (April 1969), pp. 43-46.

49. Thiel, Rudolf. *And There Was Light*. New York: Alfred A. Knopf, 1967.

50. Wheeler, John A. "Our Universe: The Known and the Unknown." *American Scientist*, Vol. 56, No. 1 (Spring 1968), pp. 1-20.

51. Wheeler, John A. and Tilson, Seymour. "The Dynamics of Space-Time." *International Science and Technology Journal*, December, 1963, reprinted in *Artorga*, Communications 70 and 71, October and November, 1964.

Index

DATE DUE
